I0308752

Samuel Sidwell Randall

History of the Common School System of the State of New York

From its Origin in 1795 to the Present Time

Samuel Sidwell Randall

History of the Common School System of the State of New York
From its Origin in 1795 to the Present Time

ISBN/EAN: 9783742807595

Manufactured in Europe, USA, Canada, Australia, Japa

Cover: Foto ©ninafisch / pixelio.de

Manufactured and distributed by brebook publishing software
(www.brebook.com)

Samuel Sidwell Randall

History of the Common School System of the State of New York

FREDONIA NORMAL SCHOOL.

HISTORY

OF THE

COMMON SCHOOL SYSTEM

OF THE

STATE OF NEW YORK,

FROM ITS ORIGIN IN 1795, TO THE PRESENT TIME.

INCLUDING

THE VARIOUS CITY AND OTHER SPECIAL ORGANIZATIONS, AND THE RELIGIOUS CONTROVERSIES OF 1821, 1832, AND 1840.

BY S. S. RANDALL

FORMERLY GENERAL DEPUTY SUPERINTENDENT OF COMMON SCHOOLS, AND LATE SUPERINTENDENT OF THE PUBLIC SCHOOLS OF THE CITY OF NEW YORK.

1871.

IVISON, BLAKEMAN, TAYLOR & CO.,

NEW YORK AND CHICAGO.

To the Memory

OF

DE WITT CLINTON,

TO WHOSE EARLY AND PERSEVERING EFFORTS, AND TRANSCENDENT STATESMANSHIP, OUR

SYSTEM OF PUBLIC SCHOOL EDUCATION

WAS SO GREATLY INDEBTED FOR ITS ORIGIN AND PERMANENT ESTABLISHMENT,

THIS WORK IS REVERENTLY INSCRIBED.

INTRODUCTION.

Having been intimately connected with the Common School System of the State of New York, for a period of over thirty years, and having, during nearly one-half of that time, occupied an important official position in the department specially charged with its supervision and administration—thereby enjoying not only all needful facilities for obtaining an accurate knowledge of its history and constitution, but also an intimate and familiar acquaintance with many of its most distinguished executive officers, counselors, and supporters throughout all its most important stages—I have felt it an obligation specially incumbent upon me, in my retirement from public duties, to avail myself of these facilities, by the preparation of the work now submitted to the public approbation. I need not say that it has been a labor of love; associated as it has been with the fondest and most cherished recollections of half a life-time, and with the memory of those eminent men, many of whom have departed from among us, who were chiefly instrumental in laying the broad foundations, and erecting the noble superstructure of our great system of Public Instruction.

It has been my aim to trace this system from its earliest inception, through all its struggles and vicissitudes, its varying phases and steady advancement, to its present vast proportions and extended scope. In doing so, I have deemed it not only important, but interesting and attractive, to give free extracts from the official language of those from time to time connected with its administration, and from the arguments and illustrations of its prominent advocates and distinguished champions in legislative halls, in public conventions, and in the discharge of subordinate functions associated with its interests and welfare. The utterances of statesmen, philanthropists, legislators, and practical administrators, in reference to the great fundamental principles of popular education, the foundations upon which they rest, their intrinsic value and necessity, their vital relation to public and national prosperity, and even to the existence of republican government, their intimate identification with social order and private and individual happiness, their inseparable connection with religion and morality, their influence and power in promoting and extending science and art in all their various manifestations, and thereby contributing to the advancement of the highest civilization, and their invariable tendency to lessen crime and avert indigence and poverty, while, at the same time, they immeasurably increase the productive industry of the community—these expositions seemed to me of such abiding interest and value to all men, as to justify their reclamation from the neglected and forgotten repositories of official documents, and their perpetuation in a more accessible, if not more enduring form.

The progress of the system, too, from the first rude attempt to gather together a few destitute and indigent children for the simplest elementary instruction, through several successive but abortive efforts to effect an organization by means of a scanty appropriation of public funds; the great and general awakening of the public mind by the marvelous development of the LANCASTERIAN method of instruction, first practised in the schools of the Public School Society in the City of New York, and afterward widely diffused, through the enthusiastic advocacy of DE WITT CLINTON; the consequent reorganization of the system under the auspices of its first Superintendent, GIDEON HAWLEY—still lingering among us, a venerable and esteemed relic of a past age; the grand conception of the DISTRICT LIBRARY system under the supervision of Gen. JOHN A. DIX; the system of COUNTY SUPERVISION, inaugurated by JOHN C. SPENCER, with the efficient co-operation of the late lamented ALONZO POTTER; the establishment and organization of NORMAL SCHOOLS for the education and proper preparation of teachers, through the exertions of SAMUEL YOUNG, CALVIN T. HULBURD, and DR. POTTER; and the long struggle and final triumph of the FREE SCHOOL SYSTEM, through the combined influence of the leading friends of education throughout the State—all these successive landmarks in the onward march of advancement, illustrated by the wisdom, the eloquence, and the exalted statesmanship of the master-minds of each period—will be found to possess a deep interest for those who, in our own times, have entered into their labors, and are reaping the rich fruits of their prescience and moral and intellectual greatness. Nor will the agitating discussions which marked the excited periods of *Sectarian Controversy*, and definitively settled the boundaries of State and Church education, be without their attractions to those who can now regard the important questions involved, free from those asperities which unavoidably attended their original promulgation. The rise, progress, and final consolidation of the noble system of public instruction in the City of New York, will also arrest the attention and interest of those in whose midst it has so successfully culminated.

It is hoped, too, that the concluding section in which an attempt has been made to review some of the leading principles of a sound educational system, and to offer such practical suggestions as long experience and much observation have served to approve, may not be wholly without benefit at a period when, in every portion of our great Republic, institutions based upon the pervading idea of free and universal education are springing up. To an enlightened public, fully awake to the vital importance of a subject closely identified with individual, social, and general happiness and prosperity, the entire work is respectfully commended.

S. S. RANDALL.

TABLE OF CONTENTS.

DEDICATION iii
INTRODUCTION v

FIRST PERIOD.—CONSTRUCTION.

Condition of Education in the Dutch and English Colonies.—Foundation of the Common School System.—Gov. George Clinton.—Act of 1795.—Govs. Jay, Lewis and Tompkins.—The New York Free School Society.—De Witt Clinton.—Lancasterian System of Instruction.—Jedediah Peck.—Reorganization of the System 1812-1814 1-23

SECOND PERIOD.—ORGANIZATION.

SECTION I.—ADMINISTRATION OF GIDEON HAWLEY, SUPERINTENDENT OF COMMON SCHOOLS, 1813 TO 1821.

Annual Reports.—Lancasterian System of Instruction.—Revision of the School Laws.—Progress of the System.—Removal of Mr. Hawley.—His Character.—Transfer of the Duties of the Office to that of Secretary of State 24-37

SECTION II.—ADMINISTRATION OF SECRETARY JOHN VAN NESS YATES, 1821 TO 1826.

Constitutional Provision of a Permanent Common School Fund.—Progress of the System.—School Celebrations.—New York Free School Society.—Controversy with the Religious Societies.—Decision of the Common Council 38-49

Section III.—Administration of Secretary Azariah C. Flagg, 1826 to 1833.

Views and Recommendations of Governor Clinton.—Seminary for Education of Teachers.—School Visitors.—County Supervision.—Mr. Spencer's Report.—Academical Education.—Text-Books.—School Libraries.—Progress of the System.—Increase of the Fund.—Public School Society of the City of New York.—Abandonment of Lancasterian System.—Death and Character of De Witt Clinton.—Infant and Primary Schools.—Second Religious Controversy. . . 50-77

Section IV.—Administration of Secretary John A. Dix, 1833 to 1839.

Messages of Gov. Marcy.—Superintendent's Reports.—Academical Preparation of Teachers.—Text-Books.—District Libraries.—James Wadsworth of Geneseo.—Augmentation of Common School Fund.—Proposed Department of Public Instruction.—U. S. Deposit Fund.—Condition of the Schools.—Children in Manufactories.—Moral and Religious Instruction.—The Bible and New Testament.—Common School Decisions and Laws. 78-96

THIRD PERIOD.—ADVANCEMENT.

Section I.—Administration of Secretary John C. Spencer, 1839 to 1842.

Character of the Secretary.—Messages of Gov. Seward.—County Visitors.—Education of Children of Foreigners.—The Schools.—Common School Fund.—Free Schools.—District Libraries.—Academical Departments for Teachers.—County Superintendents.—District School Journal.—Schools in Cities and villages. 97-118

SECTION II.—THE RELIGIOUS CONTROVERSY IN THE CITY OF NEW YORK, 1840 TO 1842.

Application of Catholic Free Schools to the Common Council.—Remonstrance of Public School Society.—Decision of Common Council.—Application to the Legislature.—Report of Secretary Spencer.—Reply of Commissioners of School Money.—Message of Gov. Seward.—Report of Acting Superintendent.—Establishment and Organization of the Ward School System.—Sectarian Teaching.—Christian Scriptures. 119–138

SECTION III.—ADMINISTRATION OF SECRETARY SAMUEL YOUNG, 1842 TO 1846.

Character of Col. Young.—Convention of County Superintendents.—State Normal School.—Teachers' Institutes.—Academical Departments for Teachers.—Messages of Govs. Bouck and Wright.—Mr. Hulburd's Report.—County Supervision.—Superintendents' Reports.—Condition of the Schools.—Official Correspondence.—The Bible in Schools. 139–197

FOURTH PERIOD.—THE FREE SCHOOL CAMPAIGN.

SECTION I.—ADMINISTRATION OF SECRETARY NATHANIEL S. BENTON, 1845 TO 1848.

State Convention of County Superintendents at Syracuse.—The Bible in the Public Schools.—Free Schools.—Col. Young.—Rev. Dr. Alonzo Potter.—State Convention of Teachers.—Francis Dwight.—Condition of the Schools.—Superintendents' Reports.—Convention of County Superintendents at Albany.—Speech of Horace Mann.—The Free School Campaign.—State Constitutional Convention.—Abolition of office of County Superintendent.—Teachers' Institutes.—State Normal School.—Death of Principal Page.—New York Free Academy. 198–245

SECTION II.—ADMINISTRATION OF SECRETARY CHRISTOPHER MORGAN, 1848 TO 1851.

Free School Campaign.—Message of Gov. Fish.—Superintendent's Reports.—Colored Schools.—Indian Children.—District Libraries.—Act for Establishment of Free Schools.—Adoption by the People.—Petitions for Repeal.—Legislative Discussions.—Free School Convention at Syracuse.—Re-submission to the People.—Re-affirmance of the Principle.—Compromise Act of 1851.—Prominent Advocates of Free Schools.—Sectarian Schools.—City and Village Schools.—Report of Code Commissioner. 246–298

SECTION III.—ADMINISTRATION OF SECRETARY HENRY S. RANDALL, 1852 TO 1854.

Character of the Secretary.—Annual Reports.—Free Schools.—District Libraries.—Academical Departments for Teachers.—New York Free Academy.—Teachers of Common Schools.—Teachers' Institutes.—Messages of Gov. Hunt.—Religious Instruction in Common Schools.—Decision in the Quigley Case.—Election of Secretary Leavenworth.—Separation of Superintendent's Department from Secretary's Office.—Dissolution of Public School Society of New York.—Ward School System.—Public Schools of Buffalo, Rochester, Hudson, Poughkeepsie, Schenectady, Albany, Brooklyn, Oswego, Auburn, Syracuse, Utica, and Troy. 299–322

FIFTH PERIOD.—STATE TAXATION AND RATE BILLS.

SECTION I.—FIRST ADMINISTRATION OF SUPERINTENDENT VICTOR M. RICE, 1854 TO 1857.

Recommendations of the Superintendent.—Messages of Gov. Clark.—Modification of the System.—District Commissioners.—Apportionment of Public Money.—Normal Schools.—Increase of State Tax.—Rate Bills.—District Libraries.—General Condition of the Schools 523–583

SECTION II.—ADMINISTRATION OF SUPERINTENDENT HENRY H. VAN DYCK, 1857 TO 1862.

Superintendent's Reports.—State Association of Teachers.—School Fund Distribution and Apportionment.—District Libraries.—District Commissioners.—Teachers' Institutes.—Official Visitations.—Object Teaching.—Acting Superintendent Keyes.—Capital of the Common School Fund.—Controversy with the Comptroller. 584–855

SIXTH PERIOD.—FREE SCHOOL TRIUMPH.

SECTION I.—SECOND ADMINISTRATION OF SUPERINTENDENT VICTOR M. RICE, 1862 TO 1868.

Recapitulation.—District Libraries.—Condition of the Schools.—Teachers' Institutes.—Oswego Normal and Training School.—State Mill Tax.—Free Schools.—Rate Bills.—Code of Public Instruction.—School Houses and Sites.—Female Teachers.—Academical Departments.—Normal Schools.—Irregular Attendance of Pupils.—Number of Uneducated Children.—Increase of State Tax.—Abolition of Rate Bill System.—Truant Children.—FREE SCHOOL ACT of 1867.—Teachers' Associations.—Union Schools.—Cornell University.—Special Report relative to Common School Education in Europe and America. 856–903

SECTION II.—ADMINISTRATION OF SUPERINTENDENT ABRAM B. WEAVER, 1868 TO 1871.

Annual Reports.—Condition of the Schools.—District Libraries.—Normal Schools.—Academical Departments.—Teachers' Institutes.—Union Free Schools.—Indian Schools.—State Board of Education.—City and Village Schools 394–442

GENERAL SUMMARY OF THE ORGANIZATION, AND RESULTS OF THE SYSTEM 443

CONCLUDING CHAPTER.

GENERAL PRINCIPLES.—PHILOSOPHY OF EDUCATION.

Coleridge's Views.—Church and State.—Education, Physical, Intellectual, Moral and Religious 444–468

HISTORY

OF THE

COMMON SCHOOL SYSTEM

OF THE

STATE OF NEW YORK.

FIRST PERIOD.—1787 TO 1814.

CONSTRUCTION.

Condition of Education in the Dutch and English Colonies.—Foundation of the Common School System.—Governor George Clinton.—Act of 1795.—Governors Jay, Lewis, and Tompkins.—The New York Free School Society.—De Witt Clinton.—The Lancasterian System of Instruction.—Jedediah Peck.—Reorganization of the System in 1812-14.

THE Common School System of the State of New York, as it now exists, is believed to be, with perhaps the single exception of that of Massachusetts, the most perfect and comprehensive in its outlines, and the most practical in its details, of any to be found in Europe or America. It has served as the model for nearly all its successors in the several States of the Union; and, during a period of more than three-fourths of a century, has tasked the abilities of our ablest and ripest statesmen in its construction and improvement. From a humble and imperfect organization, embracing a few scattered and sparsely populated school districts, in which instruction in the simplest elementary branches of study was imperfectly provided for, chiefly by parents and neighborhoods, aided by a slight contribution from a meager State fund, it has grown to a vast and magnificent system, wholly sustained by public funds, and State, district, and municipal taxation—with a complete and thorough course of instruction, open and free to every child between the ages of four and twenty-one—embracing within its comprehensive organization more than twelve thousand public schools, diffused over every section of the State, furnished with every necessary apparatus, and with public libraries numbering a million and a half volumes—and providing all requisite facilities for the education of more than one million of pupils!

It will be the purpose of this work to trace the progress and advancement of this system from its origin, through its various stages of growth, to its present state; to sketch the characters, abilities, and labors of those eminent men who, from time to time, originated or directed its operations; to note its distinctive features, as exhibited in its application to the various localities for which it was designed, including the larger towns and cities where special details of organization and administration became requisite; and to submit such practical suggestions for its future improvement and expansion, as a long and somewhat varied experience and observation may seem to warrant.

Prior to the close of the revolutionary war and the organization of the State government, very little general attention seems to have been bestowed upon the subject of popular education. Those colonial families whose wealth or competency enabled them to bestow upon their children greater advantages for instruction than the restricted ones, which were common to all classes, were compelled either to send their children "home," as it was termed, for a thorough English training—to import from thence teachers at a heavy cost—or to avail themselves of such facilities as might be afforded in the eastern colonies, where more attention had, at an early period, been given to the subject. The early Dutch colonists had, it is true, brought with them, under the direction of the government, a few teachers of approved learning; and one, at least, of the schools established by them—that of the Reformed Protestant Dutch Church—still exists in the great metropolis which their countrymen founded—its interesting annals having been faithfully commemorated by one of its latest and most distinguished teachers.*

ADAM ROELANDSDEN, who came over, in 1633, with Governor Van Twiller, appears to have been the earliest schoolmaster proper—his predecessors having discharged the double duties of minister and teacher. These schools, of which there were three in the city of New York—and, doubtless, others in the various settlements—at the close of Governor Stuyvesant's administration, were open and free to all children who chose to attend, though the course of instruction appears to have been primitive in the extreme, including only the simplest forms of arithmetic, reading, writing, and spelling.

The founders of New York, unquestionably, brought with them from the fatherland, the earliest germs of our modern system of universal education and free schools, which had already, during the sixteenth century, taken firm root in Holland, under the advice of John of Nassau, brother of William the Silent. "You must urge upon the States-General," wrote this far-seeing patriot, "that they should establish free schools, where children of quality, as well as of poor families, for a very small sum,

* Mr. H. W. Dunshee.

could be well and Christianly educated and brought up. This would be the greatest and most useful work you could ever accomplish for God and Christianity, and for the Netherlands themselves. Soldiers and patriots thus educated with a true knowledge of God and a Christian conscience, also churches and school books and printing presses, are better than all armies, armories, alliances, and treaties that can be had or imagined in the world." *

In 1665 Governor Nichols granted permission to John Shute, to open an English school at Albany; and on the accession of William of Orange, subsequently to the English occupancy of the province, a provision in its charter specifically required the appointment, by the ministers, elders, and deacons of the church, of a schoolmaster in each parish.

In 1710, the first English school west of Albany was established at Schenectady, on the Mohawk River; and forty years later, in 1750, another was opened in Schoharie. In 1710, the school still existing in the city of New York, under the name of Trinity School, was opened by William Huddleston, under the auspices of the English Church. A free grammar school had also previously been established on the King's Farm, and a school for colored children and several private schools within the city limits. † In 1755, John Nicholas Whelp, "a genuine Dutch schoolmaster and chorister," was imported from Holland by his countrymen in New York, and served acceptably in his profession until his death in 1773; and his successor was expressly directed "not only to teach reading, writing, and arithmetic, but to instruct

* Address before the St Nicholas Society of New York city, by Hon. James W. Beekman, 1869.

† Public Education in the city of New York. By Thos. Boese, Clerk Board of Education, 1868–9.

the children in the English as well as in the Dutch language." *

Similar schools were scattered at wide intervals in the various Dutch and English settlements on Long Island, Staten Island, and the shores of the Hudson, Delaware, and Mohawk; but in the distracted condition of the colony, harassed by perpetual incursions of the savages on the one hand, and the pressure of foreign war on the other, no efforts for any systematic organization were possible: and amid the struggles of the pioneers in the pathless wildernesses of the North and West for bare subsistence, facilities of even the humblest kind for the education of their children could only rarely have been found. Kings, or Columbia College, only, in the city of New York, and private and select seminaries in the most advanced settlements and principal towns, enabled wealthy parents to supply this desirable requisite for their children. At the first meeting of the State Legislature, however, after the adoption of the Constitution of 1787, Gov. GEORGE CLINTON called the attention of that body to the subject in the following terms:

"Neglect of the education of youth is one of the evils consequent upon war. Perhaps there is scarce any thing more worthy your attention than the revival and encouragement of seminaries of learning; and nothing by which we can more satisfactorily express our gratitude to the Supreme Being for his past favors—since piety and virtue are generally the offspring of an enlightened understanding."

During this session an act was passed incorporating the Regents of the University, and placing them in general charge of the colleges and academies of the State.

* Public Education in the city of New York. By THOS. BOESE, Clerk Board of Education, 1868–9.

In 1789 an act was passed requiring the surveyor-general to set apart two lots in each township, of the public land thereafter to be surveyed, for gospel and school purposes. These lands, at that time, consisted of more than seven million acres of wild, uncultivated, and unimproved territory, situated chiefly in the northern and western sections of the State.

The Regents of the University, in their annual report for 1793, called the attention of the Legislature to the numerous advantages which, in their judgment, "would accrue to the citizens in general from the institution of schools in various parts of the State, for the purpose of instructing children in the lower branches of education, such as reading their native language with propriety, and so much of writing and arithmetic as to enable them, when they came forward into active life, to transact, with accuracy and dispatch, the business arising from their daily intercourse with each other. * * The attention which the Legislature has evinced to promote literature by the liberal provision heretofore made encourages us, with all deference, to suggest the propriety of rendering it permanent by setting apart, for that salutary purpose, some of the unappropriated lands. The value of these will be enhanced by the increase of population. The State will thus never want the means of promoting useful science; and will thereby secure the rational happiness and fix the liberty of the people on the most permanent basis—that of knowledge and virtue."

Gov. CLINTON, in his address to the Legislature of 1792, had taken occasion to refer to the flourishing condition of the higher seminaries of learning, and to recommend additional aid and encouragement to those institutions. At the opening of the session of 1795, however, he initiated the great movement for the organization of a Common School System, by the following recommendation:

"While it is evident that the general establishment and liberal endowment of academies are highly to be commended, and are attended with the most beneficial consequences, yet, it cannot be denied that they are principally confined to the children of the opulent, and that a great portion of the community is excluded from their immediate advantage. *The establishment of Common Schools throughout the State* is happily calculated to remedy this inconvenience, and will, therefore, engage your early and decided consideration."

On the 11th of January a committee of the Assembly, consisting of JONATHAN NICOLL HAVENS, of Suffolk, as chairman; DAVID BROOKS, of Dutchess; DAVID PYE, of Orange; EBENEZER PURDY, of Westchester; DANIEL GRAY, of Rensselaer; ADAM COMSTOCK, of Saratoga; and RICHARD FURMAN, of New York, was appointed to take into consideration that portion of the Governor's message relating to the establishment of Common Schools throughout the State. On the 19th of February, Mr. HAVENS, from the committee, reported a bill entitled, "An Act for the Encouragement of Schools," which passed the House on the 4th, and the Senate on the 22d of March, and received the approval of the Governor on the 9th of April. By this act, the sum of $50,000 was annually appropriated, for five years, "for the purpose of encouraging and maintaining schools in the several cities and towns in this State, in which the children of the inhabitants residing in the State shall be instructed in the English language, or be taught English grammar, arithmetic, mathematics, and such other branches of knowledge as are most useful and necessary to complete a good English education." This sum was, at first apportioned to the several counties according to their representation in the Legislature, and afterward, according to the number of electors for the lower branch; to the several towns, according to the number of taxable inhabitants in each; and to the several school districts, according to the aggregate number of days instruction given during the preceding year in each. The board of supervisors of each county were required to raise by tax, on each town, a sum equal to one-half of that apportioned by the State, to be applied in the same manner. Not less than three, nor more than seven commissioners were directed to be annually chosen by the electors of the several towns, to whom were committed the supervision and direction of the schools in each, and the apportionment of public money among the several districts. Two or more trustees were authorized to be chosen by the inhabitants and legal voters of the respective districts, who were required to confer with the commissioners concerning the qualifications of the master or masters employed, or intended to be employed, in their schools, and concerning all matters relating to the welfare of the school, or to the propriety of erecting or maintaining the same, so as to entitle it to a share of the public money, "and whether the abilities and moral character of the master or masters employed or intended to be employed therein, are such as will meet with their approbation." "And if it shall at any time appear to the said commissioners that the abilities or moral character of the master or masters of any schools are not such that they ought to be intrusted with the education of the youth, or that any of the branches of learning taught in any school are not such as are intended to receive encouragement from the moneys appropriated by this act," the commissioners were required to notify, in writing, the trustees of such disability, and to withdraw the allowance of public money from the date of such notice, unless such school should thereafter be conducted to the approbation of the said commissioners. The teachers were to be paid by the trustees on an order of the commissioners on the county treasurer, who received the apportionment of public money due to his county from the State. The inhabitants and legal voters of the respective districts were also authorized "to associate together for the purpose of procuring good and sufficient school masters, and for creating and maintaining schools." Suitable provisions were made for the preparation and transmission of annual reports to the State authorities through the medium of trustees, commissioners, county clerks, and treasurers.

On the basis of this simple organization the foundations of our present Common School System were originally laid; and for a short time seemed adequate to its future expansion and success. The official returns for the year 1798—the only year in which even partial detailed reports were forwarded—show that in sixteen out of the twenty-three counties of the State, there were 1,352 schools in successful operation, in which 59,660 children were under instruction for a longer or shorter period during the year.

The appropriation made by the act of 1795 expired with the year 1800, and although the organizations already effected were partially kept up, the schools languished for the want of their accustomed support, and the system was substantially abandoned. Gov. JAY, in his annual message of this year, directed the attention of the Legislature to the subject, but without effect. Mr. ADAM COMSTOCK, of Saratoga, on the 23th of March, procured the passage of a resolution through the House, looking to the revival of the system, and its extension through another period of five years, and a clause accordingly was inserted in the annual supply bill at the close of the session, but stricken out by the Senate, and the measure fell to the ground.

Among the leading and most prominent friends of Common School education in the Legislature at this period, and for several years succeeding, was JEDEDIAH PECK, of Otsego, who first took his seat in the lower House in January, 1799. To him, more than to any other man, was due the credit of re-establishing the Common School System upon a permanent foundation, after a long and persevering struggle in both branches of the State Legislature, for twelve years. His friend, Judge HAMMOND, who was a resident of the same county, and who appears to have been intimately acquainted with him, thus sketches his character and peculiarities in his "Political History of New York" (Vol. I., pp. 123-4): "Judge PECK, although a clear-headed, sensible man, was an uneducated emigrant from Connecticut. His appearance was diminutive, and almost disgusting. In religion he was fanatical, but in his political views he was sincere, persevering, and bold; and although meek and humble in his demeanor, he was by no means destitute of personal ambition. He was an itinerant surveyor in the county of Otsego, then a new and uncultivated part of the State. He would survey your farm in the day time, exhort and pray in your family at night, and talk on politics the rest part of the time. Perhaps on Sunday, or some evening of the week, he would preach a sermon in your school house." * * * "It is due to this plain, unlettered farmer to add, that he was intent upon making some permanent provision for these institutions [the public schools]; and that he formed the project of establishing a Common School Fund in pursuance of the example then lately furnished by Connecticut, the State from whence he emigrated; that he never lost sight of it; and that to his indefatigable and persevering efforts, aided by Mr. ADAM COMSTOCK, of Saratoga, another uneducated and plain, but clear-sighted and patriotic man, we are principally indebted for our School Fund and our Common School System. What military chieftain—what mere conqueror by brute force, has conferred so deep, so enduring an obligation upon posterity?" (p. 159.)

Through the persevering exertions of these two men, an act was passed during the ensuing session of 1801, directing the raising, by means of four successive lotteries, of the sum of one hundred thousand dollars, twelve thousand five hundred of which were directed to be paid to the Regents of the University, to be by them distributed among the academies, in such manner as they should deem most proper; and the remaining eighty-seven thousand five hundred dollars to be paid into the Treasury for the encouragement of Common Schools, as the Legislature might thereafter direct. These lotteries were known as "Literature Lotteries," and were not finally discontinued until after the adoption of the Constitution of 1821, by which all lotteries were prohibited.

The proceeds of these lotteries were subsequently directed by the Legislature to be invested by the Comptroller in real estate, to await their ultimate destination.

In 1802, the Governor (GEORGE CLINTON) again called the attention of the Legislature to the subject of Common Schools. "The system of Common Schools," he observes, "having been discontinued, and the advantages to morals, religion, liberty, and good government arising from the general diffusion of knowledge being universally admitted, permit me to recommend this object to your deliberate attention. The failure of one experiment for the attainment of an important object ought not to discourage other attempts." In the succeeding year, no action having been taken during the preceding session, he renewed his recommendation in the following energetic terms: "The establishment of Common Schools has, at different times, engaged the attention of the Legislature; but, although its importance is generally acknowledged, a diversity of sentiment respecting the best means has hitherto prevented the accomplishment of the object. The diffusion of knowledge is so essential to the promotion of virtue and the preservation of liberty, as to render arguments unnecessary to excite you to a perseverance in this laudable pursuit. Permit me only to observe that education, by correcting the morals and improving the manners, tends to prevent those evils in society which are beyond the sphere of legislation."

On the 21st of February, Mr. PECK, from the joint committee of both houses on this portion of the Governor's speech, reported a bill authorizing the several towns to re-organize their schools, and raise money for their support by taxation. This bill also failed to become a law.

In 1804, the Governor again renewed his recommendation, and Mr. PECK again reported his bill, which was again destined to be defeated.

At the extra session of the Legislature, in November of the same year, Governor MORGAN LEWIS brought the subject before that body in the following language: "I cannot conclude, gentlemen, without calling your attention to a subject which my worthy and highly respected predecessor in office had much at heart, and frequently, I believe, presented to your view—the encouragement of literature. In a government resting on public opinion, and deriving its chief support from the affections of the people, religion and morality cannot be too sedulously inculcated. To them science is an handmaid—ignorance, the worst of enemies. Literary information should, then, be placed within the reach of every description of citizens, and poverty should not be permitted to obstruct the path to the fane of knowledge. Common Schools, under the guidance of respectable teachers, should be established in every village, and the indigent be educated at the public expense. The higher seminaries, also, should receive every patronage and support within the means of enlightened legislators. Learning would thus flourish, and vice be more effectually restrained than by volumes of penal statutes."

On the 4th of February, 1805, Governor LEWIS transmitted a special message to the Legislature, in which he recommended the application of the proceeds of all the State lands for the benefit of colleges and schools; the entire fund and its management to be confided to the Regents of the University, under such regulations as the Legislature might prescribe—the Regents to appoint three trustees for each district, who should be authorized to locate sites for school houses, to erect such houses wherever necessary, employ teachers, apply the district funds, and levy taxes on the inhabitants for such further sums as might be required for the support of the schools and the education of indigent children. With the exception, however, of that portion referring to the appropriation of the public lands, none of these suggestions seem to have met with any legislative response. An act was passed on the second of

April, providing that the net proceeds of five hundred thousand acres of the vacant and unappropriated lands owned by the State, which should be first thereafter sold by the surveyor general, should be appropriated as a permanent fund for the support of Common Schools; the avails to be safely invested until the interest should amount to $50,000, when an annual distribution of that amount should be made among the several school districts of the State. This act laid the foundation of the present Common School Fund. By the act to incorporate the Merchants' Bank in the city of New York, passed during the same session, the State reserved the right to subscribe for three thousand shares of the capital stock of that institution, which, with the accruing interest and dividends, were appropriated to the support of Common Schools, in such manner as the Legislature should from time to time direct. The Comptroller was subsequently authorized to invest the money, together with the proceeds arising from the lotteries previously authorized, in the purchase of additional stock of the Merchants' Bank, and to loan the residue.

During the ensuing five years, no legislative action was had in reference to this subject. The nucleus of a permanent fund having been provided, the schools were left to their own unaided resources. The organization, provided by the act of 1795, was doubtless kept up by the voluntary actions of the several towns and districts, and elementary instruction supplied for a few months in each year by teachers employed by such of the inhabitants as required their services.

In the meantime, the foundations of an educational system, destined to act a conspicuous part and to achieve a high success in the future, had been securely laid. On the 9th of April, 1805, the act incorporating the "Society for Establishing a Free School in the city of New York, for the education of such poor children as do not belong to, or are not provided for, by any religious society" became a law. DE WITT CLINTON, then Mayor of the city, Dr. Samuel L. Mitchell, the officers and members of the common council, and several other representatives of the oldest English, Dutch, and other families, were named as corporators. An eligible school building was procured on the site of the present Tryon Row, and the school publicly opened with appropriate exercises in May, 1809. The Lancasterian system of instruction was introduced, and under the name of the "Free School Society of New York," additional schools were, from time to time, opened, and the objects of the association amply and beneficently carried out.

At the opening of the session of the Legislature of 1810, Gov. TOMPKINS thus alluded to the subject of Common School education:

"I cannot omit this occasion of inviting your attention to the means of instruction for the rising generation. To enable them to perceive and duly to estimate their rights; to inculcate correct principles and habits of morality and religion; and to render them useful citizens, a competent provision for their education is all-essential. The fund appropriated for Common Schools already produces an income of about $26,000 annually, and is daily becoming more productive. It rests with the Legislature to determine whether the resources of the State will justify a further augmentation of that appropriation, as well as to adopt such plan for its application and distribution as shall appear best calculated to promote the important object for which it was originally designed."

On the 28th of February, the Comptroller, in obedience to a resolution calling upon him for information as to the condition of the school fund, reported that the amount of receipts into the treasury, up to that period, of moneys belonging to the fund, was $151,115.60, of which $29,100 had been invested in the capital stock of the Merchants' Bank, $114,600 loaned in pursuance of law, and the residue remained in the treasury.

In 1811, Gov. TOMPKINS again called the attention of the Legislature to this subject; and an act was passed during the session, authorizing the appointment by the Governor, of five commissioners, to report a system for the establishment and organization of Common Schools. The commissioners appointed under this act were, JEDEDIAH PECK of Otsego, John Murray, Jr., of New York, Samuel Russell, Roger Skinner of Washington, and Robert Macomb.

On the 17th of February, 1812, the commissioners submitted a report, accompanied by the draft of a bill, comprising substantially, with one exception, the main features of our Common School System, as it existed up to 1840. In the act as originally passed, the electors of each town were authorized to determine, at their annual town meeting, whether they would accept their share of the money apportioned by the State, and direct the raising of the equal amount required on their taxable property. This provision was, however, as will hereafter be seen, subsequently stricken out, and the reception of the public money and the tax made imperative.

The report of the commissioners, drawn up by Judge PECK, was a very able document; and as it fully illustrates the advanced views then entertained of the importance and indispensable necessity of general education; sketches the leading outlines of the system proposed for its attainment; recapitulates in a clear manner the resources at the disposal of the State for its accomplishment; and illustrates the particular method of instruction, proposed to be adopted, and known as the Lancasterian system, it has been deemed proper to present it entire.

"IN ASSEMBLY, Feb. 17, 1812.

"The Commissioners appointed by the Governor, pursuant to the Act passed April 9th, 1811, to report a system for the organization and establishment of Common Schools, and the distribution of the interest of the School Fund among the Common Schools of this State, beg leave respectfully to submit the following

REPORT:

"Perhaps there never will be presented to the Legislature a subject of more importance than the establishment of Common Schools. Education, as the means of improving the moral and intellectual faculties, is, under all circumstances, a subject of the most imposing consideration. To rescue man from that state of degradation to which he is doomed, unless redeemed by education; to unfold his physical, intellectual, and moral powers; and to fit him for those high destinies which his Creator has prepared for him, cannot fail to excite the most ardent sensibility of the philosopher and the philanthropist. A comparison of the savage that roams through the forest, with the enlightened inhabitant of a civilized country, would be a brief but impressive representation of the momentous importance of education.

"It were an easy task for the Commissioners to show, that in proportion as every country has been enlightened by education, so has been its prosperity. When the heads and the hearts of men are generally cultivated and improved, virtue and wisdom must reign, and vice and ignorance must cease to prevail. Virtue and wisdom are the parents of private and public felicity; vice and ignorance, of private and public misery.

"If education be the cause of the advancement of other nations, it must be apparent to the most superficial observer of our peculiar political constitution, that it is essential not to our prosperity only, but to the very existence of our government. Whatever may be the effect of education on a despotic or monarchical government, it is not absolutely indispensable to the existence of either. In a despotic government the people have no agency whatever, either in the formation or the execution of the laws. They are the mere slaves of arbitrary authority, holding their lives and property at the pleasure of uncontrolled caprice. As the will of the ruler is the supreme law; fear, slavish fear, on the part of the governed, is the principle of despotism. It will be perceived readily, that ignorance on the part of the people can present no barrier to the administration of such a government;

and much less can it endanger its existence. In a monarchical government, the operation of fixed laws is intended to supersede the necessity of intelligence in the people. But in a government like ours, where the people is the sovereign power—where the will of the people is the law of the land, which will is openly and directly expressed—and where every act of the government may justly be called the act of the people—it is absolutely essential that that people be enlightened. They must possess both intelligence and virtue; intelligence to perceive what is right, and virtue to do what is right. Our Republic, therefore, may justly be said to be founded on the intelligence and virtue of the people. For this reason, it is with much propriety that the enlightened Montesquieu has said: 'In a republic the whole force of education is required.'

"The Commissioners think it unnecessary to represent in a stronger point of view the importance and absolute necessity of education, as connected either with the cause of religion and morality, or with the prosperity and existence of our political institutions. As the people must receive the advantages of education, the inquiry naturally arises how this end is to be attained. The expedient devised by the Legislature is the establishment of Common Schools, which, being spread throughout the State, and aided by its bounty, will bring improvement within the reach and power of the humblest citizen. This appears to be the best plan that can be devised to disseminate religion, morality, and learning throughout a whole country. All other methods heretofore adopted are partial in their operation and circumscribed in their effects. Academies and universities, understood in contradistinction to common schools, cannot be considered as operating impartially and indiscriminately as regards the country at large. The advantages of the first are confined to the particular districts in which they are established; and the second, from causes apparent to every one, are devoted almost exclusively to the rich. In a free government, where political equality is established, and where the road to preferment is open to all, there is a natural stimulus to education; and, accordingly, we find it generally resorted to, unless some great local impediments interfere. In populous cities, and the parts of the country thickly settled, schools are generally established by individual exertion. In these cases, the means of education are facilitated, as the expenses of schools are divided among a great many. It is in the remote and thinly populated parts of the State, where the inhabitants are scattered over a large extent, that education stands greatly in need of encouragement. The people here living far from each other, makes it difficult so to establish schools as to render them convenient or accessible to all. Every family, therefore, must either educate its own children, or the children must forego the advantages of education.

"These inconveniences can be remedied best by the establishment of Common Schools, under the direction and patronage of the State. In these schools should be taught at least those branches of education which are indispensably necessary to every person in his intercourse with the world, and to the performance of his duty as a useful citizen. Reading, writing, arithmetic, and the principles of morality, are essential to every person, however humble his situation in life. Without the first, it is impossible to receive those lessons of morality which are inculcated in the writings of the learned and pious; nor is it possible to become acquainted with our political constitutions and laws, nor to decide those great political questions which ultimately are referred to the intelligence of the people. Writing and arithmetic are indispensable in the management of one's private affairs, and to facilitate one's commerce with the world. Morality and religion are the foundation of all that is truly great and good; and are, consequently, of primary importance. A person provided with these acquisitions is enabled to pass through the world respectably and successfully. If, however, it be his intention to become acquainted with the higher branches of science, the academies and universities established in different parts of the State are open to him. In this manner education, in all its stages, is offered to the citizens generally.

"In devising a plan for the organization and establishment of Common Schools, the Commissioners have proceeded with great care and deliberation. To frame a system which shall directly affect every citizen in the State; and so to regulate it as that it shall obviate individual and local discontent, and yet be generally beneficial, is a task at once perplexing and arduous. To avoid the imputation of local partiality, and to devise a plan operating with equal mildness and advantage, has been the object of the Commissioners. To effect this end, they have consulted the experience of others, and resorted to every probable source of intelligence. From neighboring States, where Common School systems are established by law, they have derived much important information. This information is doubly valuable, as it is the result of long and actual experience. The Commissioners, by closely examining the rise and progress of those systems, have been able to obviate many imperfections, otherwise inseparable from the novelty of the establishment, and to discover the means by which they have gradually risen to their present condition.

"The outlines of the plan suggested by the Commissioners are briefly these: That the several towns of the State be divided into school districts by three commissioners, elected by the citizens qualified to vote for town officers. That three trustees be elected in each district, to whom shall be confided the care and superintendence of the school to be established therein; that the interest of the school fund be divided among the different counties and towns, according to their respective population, as ascertained by the successive census of the United States. That the proportion received by the respective towns be subdivided among the districts, into which such towns shall be divided, according to the number of children in each between the age of five and fifteen years, inclusive. That each town raise by tax, annually, as much money as it shall have received from the school fund. That the gross amount of moneys received from the State and raised by the towns be appropriated exclusively to the payment of the wages of the teachers. That the whole system be placed under the superintendence of an officer appointed by the Council of Appointment. These are the great outlines of the plan. The details will appear more fully by the sketch of a law herewith submitted to the consideration of the Legislature.

"This being the plan devised by the Commissioners, let us next inquire what means the Legislature have assigned to carry it into effect. This will be explained by a reference to the report of the Comptroller of the State, made to the Legislature the 11th of February, instant. By this it appears that the school fund is composed of the following items:—

Bonds and mortgages for part of the consideration money of lands sold by the Surveyor General..	$240,370 67
3000 shares of the capital stock of the Merchant's Bank......	130,000 00
300 " " " " Hudson Bank.........	13,000 00
Mortgages for Loans....................................	101,924 52
Bond of Horatio G. Spafford, and sureties for a Loan........	3,000 00
Bond of the Mechanics' Bank in the City of New York......	10,000 00
Arrears of interest due on the bonds and mortgages of the fund	35,831 13
Balance in the Treasury on the 31st of December, 1811, belonging to this fund....................................	2,338 37
	$536,464 69

REVENUE.

The revenue of the school fund for this year is estimated at $45,216.93, arising from the following sources:

Annual interest on bond, and mortgages.....................	$21,766 93
Dividends on bank stock........	14,850 00
Probable collection from persons refusing to do military duty.	1,600 00
Proceeds of the Clerk's office of the Supreme Court..........	7,000 00
	$45,216 93

"It farther appears by the same report, that of the 500,000 acres of land which are directed by law to be sold for the benefit of the school fund, the Surveyor General has already sold 198,597 [illegible] acres, leaving 301,402 [illegible] acres yet to be appropriated to that purpose. As soon as this fund shall have produced a revenue of $50,000, that revenue, by the act of April 2d, 1805, is to be divided among the different counties of the State.

"It will readily be perceived by the *Legislature*, that if the Common School establishment were intended to be maintained by this fund exclusively, the fund would fall far short of being adequate to the object. A brief statement will make this fact very apparent:

"Let us suppose that the school fund were arrived at that point when by law it is to be divided. There will then be $50,000 of public money to be distributed among the schools; and as, by the contemplated plan, a sum is to be raised annually by tax, equal to the interest of the school fund, the gross amount of moneys which the schools will receive will be $100,000. There are in this State 45 counties, comprising, exclusively of the cities, 449 towns.

It will be very evident, therefore, that the proportion of each town must necessarily be small. As, however, the school districts are authorized to raise, by tax, a sum sufficient to purchase a lot on which the school house is to be built, to build the school house, and to keep the same in repair; and as the school moneys are devoted exclusively to the payment of the teachers' wages, the sum, however small, which each district will be entitled to, will be from these considerations so much the more efficacious. It will, however, be evident to the Legislature that the funds appropriated by the State for the support of the Common School system will, alone, be very inadequate. And the Commissioners are of the opinion that the fund, in any stage of it, even when the residue of the unsold lands shall be converted into money bearing an interest, never will be alone adequate to the maintenance of Common Schools, as the increase of the population will probably be in as great, if not a greater, ratio than that of the fund. But it is hardly to be imagined the Legislature intended that the State should support the whole expense of so great an establishment. The object of the Legislature, as understood by the Commissioners, was to rouse the public attention to the important subject of education, and, by adopting a system of Common Schools in the expense of which the State would largely participate, to bring instruction within the reach and means of the humblest citizen. And the Commissioners have kept in view the furtherance of the object of the Legislature: for, by requiring each district to raise by tax a sum sufficient to build and repair a school house, and by allotting the school moneys solely to the payment of the teachers' wages, they have in a measure supplied two of the most important sources of expenses. Thus every inducement will be held out to the instruction of youth.

"As to the particular mode of instruction best calculated to communicate to the young mind the greatest quantity of useful knowledge in a given time, and with the least expense, the Commissioners beg leave to observe that there are a variety of new methods lately adopted, in various parts of Europe, of imparting instruction to youths, some of which methods have been partially introduced into the United States. The Lancasterian plan, as it is called, which has lately been introduced into some of the large towns of the United States, merits the serious consideration of the Legislature. As an expeditious and cheap mode of instructing a large number of scholars, it stands unrivalled, and the certificates of the Trustees of the New York Free School, together with those of divers tutors, carry with them the evidence of its vast utility and success. The Commissioners, therefore, recommend that a number of Lancaster's books, containing an account of his mode of teaching, &c., be printed by order of the Legislature, and distributed among the several towns in this State.

"The Legislature will perceive, in the system contained in the bill submitted to their consideration, that the Commissioners are deeply impressed with the importance of admitting, under the contemplated plan, such teachers only as are duly qualified. The respectability of every school must necessarily depend on the character of the master. To entitle a teacher to assume the control of a school, he should be endowed with the requisite literary qualifications not only, but with unimpeachable character. He should also be a man of patient and mild temperament. 'A preceptor,' says Rousseau, 'is invested with the rights, and takes upon himself the obligations, of both father and mother.' And Quintilian tells us that 'to the requisite literary and moral endowments he must add the benevolent disposition of a parent.'

"To enable a teacher to perform the trust reposed in him, the above qualifications are indispensable. When we consider the tender age at which children are sent to school—the length of the time they pass under the direction of the teachers; when we consider that their little minds are to be diverted from their natural propensities to the artificial acquisition of knowledge—that they are to be prepared for the reception of great moral and religious truths, to be inspired with a love of virtue and a detestation of vice; we will forcibly perceive the absolute necessity of the above qualifications in the master. As an impediment to bad men getting into the schools as teachers, it is made the duty of the town inspectors strictly to inquire into the moral and literary qualifications of those who may be candidates for the place of teacher. And it is hoped that this precaution, aided by that desire which generally prevails of employing good men only, will render it unnecessary to resort to any other measure.

"The Commissioners, at the same time that they feel impressed with the importance of employing teachers of the character described, cannot refrain from expressing their solicitude as to the introduction of proper books into the contemplated schools. This is a subject so intimately connected with a good education, that it merits the serious consideration of all who are concerned in the establishment and management of schools. Much good is to be derived from a judicious selection of books, calculated to enlighten the understanding not only, but to improve the heart. And as it is of incalculable consequence to guard the young and tender mind from receiving fallacious impressions, the Commissioners cannot omit mentioning this subject as a part of the weighty trust reposed in them. Connected with the introduction of suitable books, the Commissioners take the liberty of suggesting that some observation and advice touching the reading of the BIBLE in the schools might be salutary. In order to render the sacred volume productive of the greatest advantage, it should be held in a very different light from that of a common school book. It should be regarded as a book intended for literary improvement, not merely, but as inculcating great and indispensable moral truths also. With these impressions the Commissioners are induced to recommend the practice introduced into the New York Free Schools, of having select chapters read at the opening of the school in the morning, and the like at the close in the afternoon. This is deemed the best mode of preserving the religious regard which is due to the sacred writings.

"It will naturally occur to the Legislature, as the interest of the school fund is to be divided every year among the counties and towns, as soon as it shall amount to $50,000 annually, that this sum must be forthcoming on a fixed day, annually, to meet the contingencies for which it is appropriated.

Without a certainty in the payment of the annual appropriations, the whole system will be impeded in its operation. By a recurrence to the report of the Comptroller, it will appear that the greatest part of the revenue of the school fund arises from sources which preclude the probability of certainty in the receipt. The interest arising from moneys loaned on mortgage, the net proceeds of the offices of the clerks of the Supreme Court, &c., cannot be counted on with any certainty as to time. This inconvenience must be in some way remedied; and the most advisable method that occurs to the Commissioners, will be by the annual appropriation by the State of a sum equal to the interest of the school fund, the state having recourse to the debtors of the fund for arrears of interest for its reimbursement.

"The Commissioners have deemed it proper to recommend to the Legislature the appointment of an officer, whose duty it shall be to superintend, generally, the interests and watch the operation of the Common School system. They are induced to this measure by the consideration that the system is sufficiently important to justify the measure.

"The Commissioners cannot conclude this report without expressing, once more, their deep sense of the momentous subject committed to them. If we regard it as connected with the cause of religion and morality merely, its aspect is awfully solemn. But the other view of it, already alluded to, is sufficient to excite the keenest solicitude in the Legislative body. It is a subject, let it be repeated, intimately connected with the permanent prosperity of our political institutions. The American empire is founded on the virtue and intelligence of the people. But it were irrational to conceive that any form of government can long exist without virtue in the people. Where the largest portion of a nation is vicious, the government must cease to exist, as it loses its functions. The laws cannot be executed where every man has a personal interest in screening and protecting the profligate and abandoned. When these are unrestrained by the wholesome coercion of authority, they give way to every species of excess and crime. One enormity brings on another, until the whole community, becoming corrupt, bursts forth in some mighty change, or sinks at once into annihilation. 'Can it be,' said Washington, 'that Providence has not connected the permanent felicity of a nation with its virtue.' 'The experiment, at least, is recommended by every sentiment which ennobles human nature.'

"And the Commissioners cannot but hope that that Being who rules the universe in justice and in mercy, who rewards virtue and punishes vice, will most graciously deign to smile benignly on the humble efforts of a people in a cause purely His own; and that He will manifest His pleasure in the lasting prosperity of our country.

"JEDIDIAH PECK,
JOHN MURRAY, JR.
SAMUEL RUSSEL, } *Commissioners.*"
ROGER SKINNER,
ROBERT MACOMB,

SECOND PERIOD.—1813 TO 1839.

ORGANIZATION.

SECTION I.—ADMINISTRATION OF GIDEON HAWLEY, SUPERINTENDENT OF COMMON SCHOOLS.—1813 TO 1821.

Annual Reports.—Lancasterian System of Instruction.—Revision of the School Laws.—Progress of the System.—Removal of Mr. Hawley.—His Character.—Transfer of the Duties of the Office to that of the Secretary of State.

ON the 14th of January, 1813, GIDEON HAWLEY, Esq., of Albany, was appointed by the Governor and Council, SUPERINTENDENT OF COMMON SCHOOLS, under the act of the Legislature of the preceding year. "Mr. HAWLEY," observes Judge Hammond, in his "Political History" (Vol. I., p. 346), "was then a young lawyer, resident in Albany, of habits indefatigably industrious, modest and retiring, but possessing great benevolence of heart, vigorous intellectual powers, and high literary attainments. For the paltry salary of three hundred dollars a year, he perfected a system for the management of the School Fund; the organization of every neighborhood in this great State into school districts; for a fair and equal distribution of the bounty of the State into every district; and he devised a plan of operations by which this vast machinery could be moved and managed by a single individual. The State has never rewarded him for his labors; but posterity, it is believed, will do justice to his merits, his services, and his character."

Mr. HAWLEY, in his first annual report, under date

of February 14th, 1814, informed the Legislature that at the commencement of his official term he had, in accordance with the provisions of the act of 1812, given due notice of an intended distribution of the interest of the School Fund; that although no official returns had been received from which an estimate might be formed of the beneficial operation of the act, satisfactory evidence had been obtained, that in many cases its operation had been prevented by the refusal or neglect of towns to comply with its provisions, and by the imperfection of many of its details; but that, notwithstanding these obstacles, its influence had already proved very salutary, and that, with the aid of legislative amendment, it promised to yield all that encouragement to Common Schools which it was designed to give. "It was not to be expected," he observes, "that any system for the establishment of Common Schools could be devised which, in its first form, should be wholly free from imperfections; and accordingly it has been found that the existing law is, in some respects, defective in its provisions, and obscure and doubtful in its meaning." After specifying several imperfections in the details of the act, and their unfavorable effect in the practical administration of the system, and suggesting the requisite amendments, he invites the special attention of the Legislature to the operation of that portion of the law which left it optional to the several towns to comply with its conditions and participate in its benefits or not, as the inhabitants might, at their annual town meetings, determine. "By allowing such an option to every town," he continues, "the operation of the act, depending on the pleasure and, not unfrequently, the caprice of a few individuals, will be always partial and fluctuating; it will, moreover, be embarrassed by all the difficulties which are naturally connected with instability of system and intricacy of form. It is, therefore, submitted, whether this provision of the act may not be so amended as to make it *obligatory* on towns to comply with the act, and also on the boards of supervisors of the several counties to levy on their respective towns a sum equal to that apportioned to such towns from the public money to be distributed."

These various suggestions and recommendations were approved by the Legislature, and the act amended in accordance therewith. The returns for the ensuing year from the various towns and districts were, however, so imperfect, that the Superintendent deemed it inexpedient to transmit them to that body with his annual report.

In April, 1816, however, it appeared from the report of Mr. Hawley, that returns had been received from three hundred and thirty-eight towns in thirty-six of the forty-six counties of the State; that the whole number of districts reporting was 2,631; the number of children between the ages of five and fifteen, residing therein, 176,449; and that 140,106 had been under instruction during a portion of the year reported. He estimates the whole number of districts in the State, however, at five thousand; the number of children between five and fifteen, 250,000; and the number taught, at least 200,000. The discrepancy between the actual returns and these estimates, he attributes to the incompleteness and imperfections of the reports; their entire absence in ten counties, and partial absence in several others.

"The Superintendent has also the satisfaction to learn from other sources that the establishment of Common Schools by law has already produced many great and beneficial results. The number of schools has been increased; many school houses have been built; more able teachers employed; and much of that interest which ought to be felt in behalf of Common Schools has been generally excited. The beneficial operation of the act has also been visible in the pecuniary aid which many schools have derived from it. *A perpetual annuity of twenty dollars, which is the average sum received by each district*, under the act, ought not to be considered a trifle unworthy of any account. It has been very sensibly felt, especially in those districts where, from the inability of the inhabitants, or from any other cause, Common Schools have not been kept open for the whole year; and when the revenue of the fund shall have attained its full growth, the distributive share of each district will be so much more considerable, that the munificence of the Legislature can not fail to be more gratefully acknowledged.

"But the great benefit of the act does not lie in any pecuniary aid which it may afford. The people of this State are, in general, able to educate their children without the aid of any public gratuity; and if they fail in this respect it is owing more to their want of proper schools than of sufficient means. The public gratuity is important, as it tends to excite an interest in the affairs of Common Schools which might not otherwise be felt, and in many other respects. But the great benefit of the act consists in securing the establishment of Common Schools wherever they are necessary; in organizing them on a suitable and permanent foundation; and in guarding them against the admission of unqualified teachers. These were the great ends proposed in the establishment of Common Schools by law; and under the wise and liberal policy of the Legislature, these ends have been so far accomplished as to warrant full faith in their final complete attainment."

The official returns for the two succeeding years seem amply to have verified the judgment of the Superintendent. Additional amendments to the act were made in 1815; and in his report of 1818, Mr. Hawley suggests the propriety of a full and complete revision of the several acts, with such modifications and additions as experience in the practical administration of the system may have shown to be necessary and desirable. The residue of the report for this year is devoted to a consideration of the LANCASTERIAN system of education, the general introduction of which into the Common Schools had been strongly advocated and recommended by the Governor (DE WITT CLINTON) in his speech at the opening of the session. The peculiar excellencies of this system were dwelt upon at length by the Superintendent, and its adoption, especially in the larger city and village schools, urgently and ably enforced. Under the impetus thus afforded, this method of mutual elementary instruction was very widely adopted, chiefly, however, by the incorporation of societies, and the establishment of schools in many of the cities and larger towns for this specific purpose.

This system, which for a period of nearly twenty years enjoyed so great a share of popularity, both in England and this country, appears to have had its origin in the Mission Schools of Madras, in India, from whence it was transplanted to England about the year 1789, by Dr. Andrew Bell, a clergyman of the Church of England. From his instructions and practice, Joseph Lancaster, a member of the Society of Friends, was enabled, soon afterward, to open a school in the Borough Road, near London, for its practical illustration, which, in 1805, was visited by one of the members of the New York Free School Society. This gentleman was so strongly impressed with its advantages, that on his return he at once procured its adoption in the schools of the Society. So successful was the experiment, that the most intelligent minds of the country became speedily enlisted in its favor and interested in its general extension. De Witt Clinton, in his speech on the opening of the Free School in New York, in 1809, says, "I confess that I recognize in Lancaster, the benefactor of the human race. I consider his system as creating a new era in education—as a blessing sent down from Heaven, to redeem the poor and distressed of this world from the power and dominion of ignorance." In his message to the Legislature of 1818, he says: "Having participated in the first establishment of the Lancasterian system in this country; having carefully observed its progress and witnessed its benefits, I can confidently recommend it as an invaluable improvement, which, by wonderful combination of economy in expense, and rapidity of instruction, has created a new era in education. The system operates with the same efficacy in education as labor-saving machinery does in the useful arts." President ELIPHALET NOTT, of Union College, in his address to the students of that institution, in 1811, enthusiastically exclaims, "Where is Lancaster, who has introduced and is introducing a new era in education?" The Venerable Ex-President JOHN ADAMS, writes to a friend in Cambridge, a few years later: "I have heard friend Lancaster with pleasure; he is an excellent scholastic and academic disciplinarian. I was really delighted and enlightened by that lecture." * The Trustees of the New York Free School Society, through their President, Mr. CLINTON, having been applied to, by the Commissioners for the organization and establishment of Common Schools in 1812, for information concerning the Lancasterian system, had no hesitation in giving it as their sentiments, that it was a very great improvement in the plan of education. "Although an opinion is entertained by some," they observe, "that it is in a considerable degree calculated for large schools exclusively, and therefore peculiarly well adapted for cities and populous towns; yet, from actual experiment, having in the first stage of the New York Free School, which consisted of fifteen to thirty scholars, introduced the system, and ever since pursued it with good success, they have no doubt remaining as to its utility on a small scale, and can, with propriety, recommend it for general use and practice." In corroboration, they forward the testimony of William Smith, Principal of School No. 1, John Missing, of No. 2,

* Barnard's American Journal of Education, 1861.

and Charles C. Andrews of the African Free School, as conclusive in its favor.

Mr. SMITH, who appears to have been the first person to introduce the system in the city of New York, after six years' experience as Principal of the Free School, says:

"I feel confident in asserting that the plan, if carefully and steadily pursued, will be productive of the greatest possible advantage in the education of children, and may be introduced into any Common Schools where reading, writing, and arithmetic are taught. The consideration of the number of pupils is of no importance; twenty scholars can be so disposed as to make the system profitable, in the same proportion as a thousand." "The interest of the citizens of Philadelphia, Baltimore, Boston, and other parts of the United States, has been animated by frequent visits and examinations of this school; and the laudable example of this institution has been followed by all the free, and most of the private schools of New York; and, in the cities above-mentioned, schools have been established upon the Lancasterian plan with the most promising effect."

Mr. SAMUEL W. SETON, in his Sketch of the Rise and Progress of the Public School Society, says:

"The original peculiarities of that system were, the teaching of a great number at one time and at one place and under a single teacher, through the aid of the pupils themselves; and thus, five hundred or even a thousand children might be capable of receiving, simultaneously, instruction on the same subject—the whole mass of scholars being trained to habits of industry, order, and virtue. But as it could only be carried to a limited extent, in the form in which it was prescribed by its founders, that peculiar feature of its excellence, *mutual instruction*, while it extended vast facilities to the teachers, did not afford to the pupil all the benefits which, with proper modifications, it was capable of conferring. Alterations were, accordingly suggested and gradually introduced; and the schools were greatly advanced and improved by blending in their plans and arrangements the beautiful mechanism of instruction in LANCASTER's system with the better adapted philosophy of education existing in that of his cotemporary and rival, Dr. BELL, of Madras. Indeed, LANCASTER himself had partially availed himself of it; and on his visit to the city of New York, and inspection of the system as there in operation, admiring and commending the reform, he acknowledged the wisdom and skill with which his plans had been so vastly improved for the more general purposes of education, yet retaining so much of its original and important feature of economy of means and tact of management in all the physical operations of the school. By these modifications, the principle of 'mind acting on mind' is brought effectually into operation—time economized, industry and activity promoted, the mental powers invigorated by independent action, and the discipline of the school rendered comparatively easy. The best of order at all times prevails, sometimes amidst the most profound silence, and at others during the constant motion and busy hum of actual labor—the school presenting a well organized little community, under the direction of its leaders, doing each other good, and each partaking of the benefits produced by the united labors of all."

Mr. Missing says:

"From my own personal knowledge of that beneficial plan, I do not hesitate to give it as my opinion that it has the most decided preference to the common method of tuition. I have often been astonished to see with what facility a child, unacquainted with the letters, would learn to spell, read, and write at the same time; and also how expeditiously a child unacquainted with figures would, by that practical method of arithmetic, learn the fundamental rules, so as not to by exceeded by the first arithmeticians. The order and discipline laid down by Mr. Lancaster, and the small premiums given to promote emulation and morals among the scholars, has the tendency of accelerating their improvement far beyond any thing adopted in Common Schools. In short, it is only for a person to lay aside his prejudice, and to read Mr. Lancaster's system of education, and he must be forcibly struck with the superiority of his plan; but let the same person put it in practice, and he will be more deeply impressed with its beneficial effects. I am fully persuaded that this excellent system, if duly attended to, might be introduced into Common Schools, whether the number of scholars be few or many, to great advantage, as I am confident it will lose none of its pre-eminent qualities, because the number may be small. Thirty, or one thousand, may derive equal advantage from its practical effects. A system which has, in England, received the royal patronage—which has been sanctioned by its first literary characters—which has received the support and approbation of the whole University of Cambridge—which has, perhaps, by this time, been adopted in every city, town, and village throughout the United Kingdom of Great Britain, must be considered as having many powerful arguments in its favor, and strong claim to its being adopted in every city and town in these United States, to the great advantage of the education of our youth. It is my firm belief that future generations will revere the name of Joseph Lancaster, as the founder of a system so well calculated to improve the morals, as well as to promote the education of youth, as the present generation does the name of Sir Isaac Newton for philosophy, or Howard for philanthropy."

Mr. Andrews, of the African School, adds his decided testimony to the value and efficiency of the system.

The method of instruction appears originally to have been very simple, and to have consisted in a division of the school into classes under the general supervision of the principal, and of each class into *pairs* of two pupils, each alternately acting as tutor to the other—the entire class being supervised by a teacher and assistant teacher. Its chief feature and prominent principle, amid all its subsequent modifications, was that of *mutual instruction*, as far as practicable, *among the pupils themselves*, under the charge and by the aid of competent adult instructors.

In December, 1818, Mr. LANCASTER himself arrived in New York, where he was warmly welcomed by Gov. CLINTON and other prominent citizens; visited the public schools of the city; gave a series of public lectures; and infused new life and animation into the operations of the various educational institutions which had adopted his method of instruction. Twenty years afterward, in 1838, he again visited the city, and ineffectually endeavored to re-establish his system. The lapse of nearly an entire generation had thrown it into the shade—educational science, in its rapid progress, had superseded it by new methods and more modern ideas—his proposals were respectfully declined; and a few days subsequently a fatal street accident terminated his life. All honor to his memory! As the pioneer of elementary public instruction, he accomplished a vast amount of good in both hemispheres; obtained the confidence and regard of many of the greatest, wisest, and best statesmen and philanthropists of the age; and left the impress of his genius strongly marked upon the earliest developments of our great system of public instruction.

In 1819, as appears by the Superintendent's annual report, the number of school districts in the State had reached nearly six thousand, and the number of children taught during the preceding year nearly 250,000. He again attributes the great increase and prosperity of the schools to the wise and liberal policy adopted by the Legislature for their encouragement and support. A comparison of the returns made for different years since their establishment, showed an increase in the number of the schools in a much greater ratio than that of the population, and a rapid and substantial improvement in their condition, and in the public estimation and interest.

"If these results," he observes, "were the only evidence of a beneficial operation in the system of Common Schools provided by law, they would be sufficient to establish the public confidence in the policy of that system, and to secure it a permanent duration. But it is well known that it has produced other results, not less in magnitude or merit. It has secured our schools against the admission of unqualified teachers, by requiring them to submit to examination before a public board of inspectors, and to obtain from them a certificate of approbation before they can legally be employed. It has imparted to Common Schools a new and more respectable character, by making them a subject of legal notice, and investing them with powers to regulate their own concerns. It has corrected many evils in their discipline and government, not only by excluding unqualified teachers, but by subjecting them and their course of studies to the frequent inspection of public officers. It has founded schools in places where, by conflicting interests, or want of concert in the inhabitants, none had been before established; and it has, by its pecuniary aid, enabled many indigent children to receive the benefits of education, which would not otherwise have been within their reach."

The Superintendent renewed his recommendation of the preceding year for a revision and consolidation of the several enactments relating to Common Schools, and for such amendments and alterations as experience had shown to be required. His suggestions in these respects were carefully considered by the Legislature. A bill for that purpose was introduced, and so great was the public confidence in Mr. HAWLEY, that during its discussion in the Assembly, he was invited to take a seat within the hall, and to make such verbal explanations of the objects he had in view in their several details, as he might deem expedient, or the House might require.* His views were ably and zealously sustained in the progress of the discussion, by Gen. ROOT, one of the leading and most influential members; and on the 19th of April, having passed both branches, were embodied in the act of that date. Its publication was accompanied by a full exposition of its various provisions and forms for the several proceedings required by the Superintendent.

The returns of the ensuing year (1820) were much more full and satisfactory than any previously received. In 515 towns there were 5,763 schools, from 5,118 of which reports had been duly made, showing 271,877 children under instruction during the preceding year, out of 302,703 of the requisite age. The report for 1821—the last made by him—showed in 545 towns, 6,323 districts, from 5,489 of which returns had been received; and that of 317,633 children between the ages of five and fifteen, 304,549 had been taught during the years reported. In about one-half of the towns of the State, the number taught exceeded the number between five and fifteen; and taking the whole State together, was more than nineteen-twentieths of that number. The average length of time during the year, in which schools were kept open, had also increased in about the same ratio as the number taught, and there was reason to believe that the number of children not attending any school, or not otherwise under instruction, was very small. The public money was sufficient to defray the expenses of most of the schools for about three months in each year; and in most districts poor children were permitted to attend the school free of expense, their tuition being charged, under a provision in

* Hammond's Political History of New York, I, 491.

the law, upon the tax-paying inhabitants. "The readiness with which such permission has been generally granted, wherever it has been deserved," observes the Superintendent, "is very creditable to the public spirit and liberality of the inhabitants of school districts. From these circumstances it is considered warrantable to infer, in connection with the friendly disposition everywhere manifested in the cause of education, that of the rising generation of this State, very few individuals will arrive to maturity without the enjoyment and protection of a common education." The whole amount of public money received by the several districts during the year reported (1820) was $206,348; of which $59,930 was contributed from the State Treasury—an equal amount raised by tax upon the several towns, by the Board of Supervisors; and the residue received from the avails of local funds, specifically appropriated to Common School purposes. The amounts contributed by rate bills, from those sending to schools after the expenditure of the public moneys, do not appear from the reports at this period.

To no individual in the State are the friends of Common School Education more deeply indebted, for the impulse given to the cause in its infancy, than to GIDEON HAWLEY. At a period when every thing depended upon organization, upon supervision, upon practical acquaintance with the most minute details of the system, and upon a patient, persevering, laborious process of exposition—he united in himself all the requisites for the efficient discharge of the high functions devolved upon him by the Legislature. From a state of anarchy and confusion and complete disorganization, within a period of less than eight years, arose, chiefly through his exertions and abilities, a compact and stately fabric, based upon the most impregnable foundations, sustained by an enlightened public sentiment, fortified by the best and most enduring affections of the people, and cherished as the safeguard of the State—the true palladium of its greatness and prosperity. Within this brief period, the number of school districts had doubled, and the proportion of children annually participating in the blessings of elementary instruction increased from 140,000 to 304,000, and from four-fifths to nineteen-twentieths of the whole number of suitable age residing in the State. In view of the disadvantages under which every new and untried system must, of necessity, labor before it can be commended to general adoption, and of the immense variety of interests which were, to a greater or less extent, affected by the stringent provisions of the act of 1812 and its subsequent amendments, we can scarcely fail to be surprised at the magnitude of the results which developed themselves under the administration of Mr. HAWLEY. The foundations of a noble and permanent system of popular education were strongly and securely laid, and we are now, after the lapse of half a century, witnessing the magnificent superstructure which has been gradually upbuilt on those foundations.

His removal from office, on purely political grounds, by the last Council of Appointment, prior to the abolition of that body by the Constitution of 1821, excited the strongest indignation in the public mind, without distinction of party. Judge HAMMOND, in his Political History, thus indignantly characterizes this transaction and its consequences:

"But there is one act of this Council, which, in my judgment, admits of no reasonable apology—the removal of GIDEON HAWLEY from the office of Superintendent of Common Schools. Mr. HAWLEY had, by great skill and labor, formed our Common School system. All who know him, and he is now and was then generally known, admit not only his fitness, but his peculiar fitness, for that office. On the able and faithful discharge of his duties depended not the temporary success of this or that party, but, in a considerable degree, the weal or woe of the rising generation. The Council removed him and appointed in his place Welcome Esleeck, Esq., a mere collecting attorney, who had scarce any of the requisite qualifications of a Superintendent of Schools. So gross was this outrage that the political friends of the Council in the Legislature would not submit to it. Gen. Root, soon after the appointment of Mr. Esleeck, for, as was well understood, the mere purpose of getting rid of him, introduced a bill, or attached a clause to some bill on its passage in the Assembly, enacting that the Secretary of State, should, *ex officio*, be the Superintendent of Common Schools, which soon passed through both houses with acclamation." *

* Hammond's Political History of New York, Vol. I., 570-71.

Section II.—Administration of Secretary John Van Ness Yates—1821 to 1826.

Constitutional Provision of a Permanent Common School Fund.—Progress of the System.—School Celebrations.—The New York Free School Society.—Controversy with the Religious Societies.—Decision of the Common Council.

AT the period of the transfer, by the Legislature, of the duties imposed upon the Superintendent of Common Schools to the Secretary of State, that office was filled by JOHN VAN NESS YATES, of Albany, a gentleman of cultivated literary taste, superior talents, industrious habits, and extended popularity. He entered upon the discharge of the new duties devolved upon him contemporaneously with the organic change in the Constitution, made by the State Convention of 1821. By the provisions of that instrument, the proceeds of all lands thereafter to be sold, belonging to the State, with the exception of such as might be reserved for public use, or ceded to the United States, together with the existing school fund, were declared to constitute "A PERPETUAL FUND, the interest of which shall be INVIOLABLY APPROPRIATED AND APPLIED TO THE SUPPORT OF COMMON SCHOOLS THROUGHOUT THE STATE." This solemn consecration of the fund to its legitimate purposes alone still remains a portion of the fundamental law of the State.

In his speech at the opening of the Legislature of 1822, the Governor (DE WITT CLINTON) thus referred to the condition of the system of public instruction:

"The excellent direction which has been given to the public bounty, in appropriations for Common Schools, academies, and colleges, is very perceptible in the multiplication of our seminaries of education, in the increase of the number of students, and in the acquisition of able and skillful teachers. The Lancasterian, or monitorial, system is making its way in the community by force of its transcendent merits. Our Common Schools have flourished beyond all former example.

"I am happy to have it in my power to say that this State has always evinced a liberal spirit in the promotion of education; and I am persuaded that no considerations short of total inability will ever prevent similar demonstrations. The first duty of a State is to render its citizens virtuous, by intellectual instruction and moral discipline—by enlightening their minds, purifying their hearts, and teaching them their rights and their obligations. Those solid and enduring honors which arise from the cultivation of science, and the acquisition and diffusion of knowledge, will outlive the renown of the statesman and the glory of the warrior; and if any stimulus were wanting in a cause so worthy of all our attention and patronage, we may find it in the example before our eyes, of the author of the Declaration of Independence, who has devoted the evening of his illustrious life to the establishment of a university in his native State."

The Governor also transmitted, in this connection, the proceedings of several State Legislatures, recommending the appropriation of a portion of the National domain to the purposes of education in the old as well as new States and Territories; expressing his clear conviction of the justice and policy of such a measure, and his high appreciation of its importance and value.

From the first annual report of the Acting Superintendent (J. V. N. YATES, Secretary of State), it appeared that the whole number of school districts in the State was 6,805, from 5,882 of which reports had been received in accordance with law; that the whole number of children, between the ages of five and sixteen, residing in the State during the preceding year, was 380,000; and the total number of all ages taught during an average period of eight months during the year was 342,479.

Several amendments in the details of the system, suggested by the Superintendent, were adopted by the Legislature during its session; including a provision investing the Superintendent with appellate jurisdiction over all the controversies arising under the School laws, and declaring his decision thereon final.

The annual appropriations from the funds of the State at this period were fixed, by the Act of 1819, at $80,000. The principal of these funds consisted of the Loan of 1792, then amounting to $500,000; that of 1808, amounting to $449,000; stock in the Merchants' Bank of the city of New York of the par value of $180,000, yielding an annual dividend of nine per cent.; one-half of the quit-rents, estimated at $100,000; and about $7,000 from the fees of the Supreme Court—amounting in all to $1,236,000.

The report for the year 1822, submitted to the Legislature in February, 1823, showed:

1. That all the counties of the State, fifty-two in number, comprising 649 towns and wards, and 6,255 of the 7,051 districts, had duly forwarded returns in accordance with law; and

2. That 351,173 out of 357,000 children had been instructed during an average period of eight months during the year reported, being an excess of 18,194 over the preceding year.

The Superintendent adds: "Even in Connecticut, which possesses a larger school fund than we do, and where the school system was established, and in successful operation, long before it was here introduced, the number of children educated in Common Schools is far less in proportion to its population than it is in this State." He complains of the absence of uniformity in the course of studies pursued, and the text-books in use, and of the embarrassments to which parents are subjected in selecting suitable books from the great variety offered, by the authors and compilers, for their use; and refers the remedy to the wisdom of the Legislature.

During the ensuing year (1823), three hundred and thirty-one new districts had been formed, in which 400,500 children were instructed for an average period of eight months; exceeding by 20,000 the number instructed during the preceding year, and the whole number between five and sixteen residing in the State. The sum of $182,802.25 of public money had been expended in the payment of the wages of duly qualified teachers; to which amount had been added, according to the estimate of the Superintendent, $150,000 from the avails of local funds, and the private contributions of individuals on rate bills and otherwise; making a grand total of upward of four hundred and thirty thousand dollars. "These facts," he observes, "require no comment. They demonstrate the signal success which has attended the exertions made, from time to time, by the Legislature, to disseminate useful knowledge among every class of the community." He also recommends the establishment of schools in cities and villages exclusively for colored children; and concludes as follows:

"The funds provided and secured by the Constitution for the support of Common Schools have become only in part productive. By far the largest portion is still inactive, and must continue so until advantageous sales can be made of nearly a million acres of land appropriated for that object. It is not extravagant to predict that, when that period shall arrive, the anticipations of the patriot and philanthropist, with regard to the still more extensive operation of our school system, and its favorable effects upon the condition of society, will be fully realized. Indeed, what has education not already effected! It has given man dominion not only over the elements, but it has enlarged his capacity and faculties beyond the sphere in which he moves. It has shown him that intellectual wealth is national wealth, and that it lies at the foundation of all that is useful in the arts; that its influence extends to the narrower path of private virtue and daily duty; and that, while it strengthens the tie between parent and child, husband and wife, citizen and citizen, it secures from the rude and withering hand of oppression, and from the iron grasp of despotism, those valuable institutions of government which it is no less the pride than it is the duty of freemen to maintain pure and inviolate. Common Schools, supported by law, and open alike to the poor and to the rich, together with the higher seminaries of learning, are those monuments which render the glory of a nation imperishable. And while this State is engaged in the great works of canals, and other internal improvements, she shows the boundless extent of her resources, and the energies of her character, by supporting, at the same time, upon a basis equally broad and enduring, a plan of education unequaled in its operations and effects by that of any other country in the civilized world."

In August of the ensuing year, 1824, the Superintendent issued a circular recommending *School Celebrations* in the several towns of the State, from which the following are extracts:

"The object in view is extremely important, for it is addressed as well to the affections of the parent as the feelings and interests of the citizens. The happiness of society and the freedom of our country mainly depend upon the general diffusion of knowledge; and it is our duty to devise the best means for attaining and securing that very desirable end. In a few years the children that now sit upon our knees, or play around the room, will fill our places, and become the future legislators, magistrates, and judges of our country, while we are silently descending to the tomb. How consoling will then be the reflection that these objects of our affection are about to realize our fondest hopes, and do honor to our memories! Even now, when we hear recounted the sage deliberations of the statesman, or the gallant achievements of the warrior, or the brilliant and still more useful attainments of the scholar, or the sacred and impressive eloquence of the divine, or the profound arguments of the lawyer, or the useful inventions and experiments of the philosopher, farmer, and mechanic, do not our bosoms burn with admiration, and do not the eyes and hearts of each of us exclaim, 'Would that he were my son!' If, then, these are the delightful emotions excited in us from the mere relation of the grand effects which knowledge and virtue produce, can we refuse yielding our best exertions to realize them in the persons of our children? The means, under Providence, are fully within our power, and painful will be our reflections if we neglect them.

"The plan suggested for the improvement of our Common Schools—by instituting celebrations—promises, I am convinced, far more beneficial and important consequences than any other hitherto devised. The experiment is neither doubtful nor difficult; and its benefits are certain, and their extent beyond calculation. Indeed, when we see the flourishing condition of our colleges and academies, and know that much is attributable to their public anniversaries and commencements, why should we hesitate to believe that the same means, when used in support of our Common Schools, will produce the same end? And why, permit me to ask, should not our Common Schools be placed on a footing as respectable as any other seminaries of learning? Are they not as useful? And is not their influence more generally felt and acknowledged? When we consider, also, the high character which our Common Schools have so deservedly maintained—when we find other States and countries imitating their example and quoting their success—should we not feel the strongest desire to render them still more worthy of this distinction, and still more useful to ourselves and to posterity?"

In the city of New York, the number of schools of the Free School Society had increased to six, and were in a very flourishing condition. Under the General School Act of 1812, these schools were entitled to a distributive share of the Common School Fund, in proportion to the average number of pupils under instruction; and, by a supplementary act passed in the subsequent year, that portion of the fund received by the city was directed to be apportioned and paid to the trustees of the Free School Society, the trustees or treasurers of the Orphan Asylum Society, the Economical School Society for the children of refugees from the West Indies, the African Free School, "and of such incorporated religious societies in said city, as supported or should establish Charity Schools, who might apply for the same;" such distribution to be in proportion to the number of pupils *on register.* Under the provisions of this act, several religious bodies established schools, and participated in the funds—including the Bethel Baptist Church in Delancey street, St. Patrick's, St. Peter's, and other Roman Catholic Churches, the Roman Catholic Benevolent Society, several Methodist, Episcopal, Dutch Reformed, and Baptist Churches, the German Lutheran, and Scotch Presbyterian.

In 1822, the Bethel Baptist Church, through their pastor, the Rev. Jonathan Chase, obtained from the Legislature the passage of an act authorizing the trustees to expend any surplus of their funds, beyond the payment of teachers' wages, in the erection and maintenance of additional schools—a power previously conferred upon the Free School Society. They accordingly opened a second, and soon afterward a third, school under this authority; and other religious bodies prepared to follow their example. The Free School Society became alarmed at the prospect of a serious diminution of their proportion of the fund by this activity of the Baptist, Episcopal, and Dutch Churches; and a warm controversy ensued. On the one hand, it was alleged that the Free School Society unjustly sought a monopoly of the education of the poor children of the city, and in the public fund apportioned for that purpose, and that the different religious societies which had established and were supporting such schools were equally entitled by law to those privileges; while on the other, it was answered that if such a monopoly as was pretended actually existed, it was one in which every citizen had a legal right to participate, and that such general participation was earnestly solicited and desired; that from the limited amount of the school fund apportioned to the city, its distribution among so many societies deprived it to a great extent of its usefulness by rendering economy impossible; that the inevitable result must be a large number of poor schools and inefficient teachers; and that adequate proof existed of the consequent perversion of the funds, thus obtained by some of the religious bodies, to purposes not contemplated by the act. The trustees of the Free School Society, therefore, expressed their readiness and desire to assist in procuring the passage of a law rendering their property inalienably and sacredly pledged for the avowed objects of their institution, and placing the schools in their charge under the general supervision of the Common Council, as the direct representative of the people. The religious societies indignantly responded that buildings erected by them for school purposes were no more liable or likely to be turned to other and non-legitimate uses than were those of the Free School Society itself.

A memorial was accordingly forwarded to the Legislature, in 1823, asking a modification of the act of the preceding year, prohibiting the expenditure of any portion of the public money in the erection of additional buildings, and for such an amendment of the act relative to the distribution of the school fund in the city of New York as should prevent any religious society from receiving any portion of the public money for any other than the poor children of their respective congregations. A resolution was adopted by the Legislature, toward the close of the session, referring the memorial to the Superintendent of Common Schools, with directions to report in detail, at the ensuing session, the expenditure of the school money, and the manner of its appropriation by the various societies entitled to a participation in the fund.

The Superintendent, in his report, set forth, in substance, that some three hundred children had been induced by various means to leave Free School No. 3, in Hudson street, and attend Bethel School No. 3, in Vandam street adjacent; that the reported register of the Bethel Society Schools was 1,547, upon which the public money was drawn, in accordance with law, while the whole number present on inspection was only 686; that in one of its schools in which a register number of 450 was returned, there were possible accommodations only for 300; that teachers had been employed at the cheapest rates, although nominally at salaries equal to those paid by the Free School Society—one teacher having testified that he signed an agreement for a salary of $900, with the understanding that one-half of it was to be reimbursed to Pastor Chase—another that he received $600 under a similar agreement to refund $200, as a "donation"; that by such means Mr. Chase and the Bethel Baptist Church received some $2,500; that the Lancasterian System which was adopted in these schools was brought into ill-deserved repute by the shocking inefficiency of its management; and that by funds so accumulated a building was in process of erection, the basement of which, only, dark, gloomy and ill-ventilated, was destined for the use of the school, while the upper portion, well finished and properly lighted, was to be devoted to church purposes. The report also stated that, in consequence of the successful operations of the Baptists, other religious societies were preparing to follow their example.

The Free School Society renewed their memorial to the Legislature of 1824, setting forth in addition that having for years urged their pupils to attend Sabbath Schools for religious instruction, they were pained to find those schools now made the means and opportunity of urging children to abandon the Free Schools altogether; thus leading off large numbers of pupils, who in their turn induced others to leave; and that in this manner these sectarian schools, supported by the public money, are made a most convenient means of proselyting. As a conclusive test of the results of the moral training given by their own schools, they assert that while in the past eighteen years 20,000 children had been under instruction therein, one only had been traced to a criminal court. They alleged that "the primary object of denominational schools being not a literary, but a religious sectarian education, the consequences of such training are the inevitable sharpening of the lines dividing sects, the systematic sowing in the young mind of those germs of conscientious antagonism which had so often ripened into a harvest of blood, and the destruction of Common Schools, the only common ground on which the future citizen of the Republic could from their childhood know and respect each other. To do this at all was a grievous evil; to do it at the expense of the public, whose future harmony was thus, however remotely, imperiled, was an offense against the fundamental principles of the Republic itself."* They asked, in conclusion, "that the religious societies might be restricted to what was justly deemed the obvious intention of the act providing for their participation in the school fund," accompanying their memorial with the draft of a bill, with the unanimous sanction and approval of the City Corporation, adopted after full examination and mature deliberation.

The Legislature surprised all parties by the passage of an act transferring the local distribution of the fund to the Common Council themselves, with full powers to make such assignment as they might deem just and expedient.

The Common Council immediately referred the whole subject to a special committee, whose deliberations were protracted and public—the highest talent in the city being represented on both sides. The Rev. Drs. WAINWRIGHT, MATHEWS, MILNOR, and ONDERDONK, of the Episcopal and Dutch Church, and Pastor CHASE, of the Baptist, were in attendance on behalf of the religious societies, and the venerable Col. HENRY RUTGERS, PETER A. JAY, CADWALLADER D. COLDEN, and STEPHEN ALLEN, in behalf of the Free Schools. On the part of the latter, it was urged that the intention of the Act of 1813, granting a portion of the public funds to the

* Public Education in the city of New York.—By T. Boese, pp. 100–106.

churches, was solely to aid them in the education of their own poor children; that an extension of their schools, interfering with those of the Free School Society, could never have been contemplated; that the principles by which all legislation on this subject had heretofore been guided were palpably infringed, and a fund, designed for civil purposes exclusively, diverted to the support of religons institutions, in contravention of the spirit of the acknowledged principles of our Government, which had uniformly left religion to be sustained by voluntary contributions and the individual efforts and patronage of its own votaries. The committee, "deeming the school fund of the State purely of a civil character, designed fór civil purposes, and that the entrusting of it to religions or ecclesiastical bodies was a violation of an elementary principle in the politics of the State and country," reported adversely to the future distribution of any portion of the school fund, to the schools of religious societies, and introduced an ordinance directing such distribution thereafter to be made exclusively to the schools of the Free School Society, Mechanics' Society, Orphan Asylum, and African Schools, which was unanimously adopted. In the ensuing year, a High School for males was opened, under the charge of Dr. JOHN GRISCOM and D. H. BARNES, and in 1826 a similar institution for females was established.

The administration of the general system of public instruction, by Mr. YATES, was characterized by great ability and success. He united to eminent executive talents and popular manners a lively zeal for the promotion of education and the diffusion of knowledge among the great body of the people. His various reports exhibit an accurate practical knowledge of the workings of the Common School system in all its departments; his decisions on the numerous controversies and appeals which were brought before him were marked by a sound discrimination; and his efforts for the improvement and advancement of the schools were earnest and indefatigable. In the midst of the varied and important duties devolved upon him, as the first administrative officer of the government, the interests and welfare of public education held a prominent place in his regards; and the practical wisdom of the Legislature, under the peculiar exigency which had arisen, in transferring the supervision of the schools to the State Department, was amply vindicated by the result.

Section III.—Administration of Secretary Azariah C. Flagg—1826 to 1833.

Views and Recommendations of Governor Clinton.—Seminary for the Education of Teachers.—School Visitors.—County Supervision.—Report of Hon. John C. Spencer.—Academical Education.—Text Books.—School Libraries.—Progress of the System, and Increase of the Fund.—Public School Society of the City of New York.—Its Operations, and Condition of its Schools.—Abandonment of the Lancasterian System.—Infant and Primary Schools.—Second Religious Controversy.—Its Results.

IN his annual Message to the Legislature, at the opening of the session of 1826, the Governor (De Witt Clinton) thus eloquently adverts to the subject of Common School education, the vocation of the teacher, and the necessity of a higher standard of qualification for the profession:

"The first duty of government, and the surest evidence of good government, is the encouragement of education. A general diffusion of knowledge is the precursor and protector of republican institutions; and in it we must confide, as the conservative power that will watch over our liberties, and guard them against fraud, intrigue, corruption, and violence. In early infancy, education may be usefully administered. In some parts of Great Britain, infant schools have been successfully established, comprising children from two to six years of age, whose tempers, hearts, and minds are ameliorated, and whose indigent parents are enabled by these means to devote themselves to labor without interruption or uneasiness. Our Common Schools embrace children from five to sixteen years old, and continue to increase and prosper. The appropriation for the school fund for the last year was $80,670, and an equivalent sum is also raised by taxation in the several counties and towns, and is also applied in the same way. The capital fund is $1,333,000, which will be in a state of rapid augmentation from sales of the public lands and other sources; and it is well ascertained that more than 420,000 children have been taught in our Common Schools during the last year. The sum distributed by the State is now too small, and the general fund can well warrant an augmentation to $120,000 annually.

"Our system of instruction, with all its numerous benefits, is still, however, susceptible of improvement. Ten years of the life of a child may now be spent in a Common School. In two years, the elements of instruction may be acquired, and the remaining eight years must either be spent in repetition or in idleness, unless the teachers of Common Schools are competent to instruct in the higher branches of knowledge. The outlines of geography, algebra, mineralogy agricultural chemistry, mechanical philosophy, surveying, geometry, astronomy, political economy, and ethics might be communicated in that period of time by able preceptors, without essential interference with the calls of domestic industry. The vocation of a teacher, in its influence on the character and destiny of the rising and all future generations, has either not been fully understood or duly estimated. It is, or ought to be, ranked among the learned professions. With a full admission of the merits of several who now officiate in that capacity, still it must be conceded that the information of many of the instructors of our Common Schools does not extend beyond rudimental education; that our expanding population requires constant accessions to their numbers; and that to realize these views it is necessary that some new plan for obtaining able teachers should be devised. I therefore recommend a *seminary for the education of teachers* in the monitorial system of instruction and in those useful branches of knowledge which are proper to engraft on elementary attainments. A compliance with this recommendation will have the most benign influence on individual happiness and social prosperity. To break down the barriers which poverty has erected against the acquisition and dispensation of knowledge is to restore the just equilibrium of society, and to perform a duty of indispensable and paramount obligation; and under this impression, I also recommend that provision be made for the gratuitous education, in our superior seminaries, of indigent, talented, and meritorious youths.

"I consider the system of our Common Schools as the palladium of our freedom; for no reasonable apprehension can be entertained of its subversion as long as the great body of the people are enlightened by education. To increase the funds, to extend the benefits, and to remedy the defects of this excellent system is worthy of your most deliberate attention. The officer who now so ably presides over that department is prevented by his other official duties from visiting our schools in person, nor is he indeed clothed with this power. *A visitorial authority*, for the purpose of detecting abuses in the application of the funds, of examining into the modes and plans of instruction, and of suggesting improvements, would unquestionably be attended with the most propitious effects."

On the 4th of February, Mr. JOHN C. SPENCER, from the Literature Committee of the Senate, to which this portion of the Message of the Governor had been referred, submitted a lengthy and able report, from which the following extracts will be found interesting:

"The committee concur entirely in the sentiments expressed by the Governor in relation to the importance of the vocation of a teacher, and to the propriety of occupying the time of the young in the higher branches of knowledge. The progress of improvement in the great business of education must necessarily be slow and gradual. Our Common School system is itself but of recent origin; and during the few years in which it has been in operation, incalculable good has been effected, particularly in causing the establishment of schools where none existed before, and where none would have existed but for its provisions. We cannot expect to make it at once perfect; but must content ourselves with remedies for the most obvious and important defects as they are discovered. From the observation of the committee, and from the best information they can obtain, they are persuaded that the greatest evils now existing in the system are the want of competent teachers, and the indisposition of the trustees of districts to incur the expense of employing those who are competent when they can be obtained. It is a lamentable fact that, from a mistaken economy, the cheapest teachers, whether male or female, and generally the latter, are employed in many districts for three-fourths of the year, and a competent instructor is provided only for one quarter, and sometimes not at all, during the year. The State is thus made to contribute almost wholly to the support of teachers. This is a perversion of the public bounty; and its effect on the children, who ought to be provided with the means of instruction during the year, is most disastrous; for those above five or six years old are thus excluded from school three-fourths of their time, which must be spent in mental idleness; and thus the most precious time for education is utterly thrown away. The present arrangement of the authority to license and employ teachers contributes to this result. Teachers are licensed by town inspectors, themselves generally and necessarily incompetent to determine upon the qualifications of candidates, and willing to sanction such as the trustees feel able or disposed to employ. This is essentially wrong; and the State, which contributes so large a portion of the compensation of the teacher, has a right to direct its application in such a way as to effect the object of procuring useful instruction. The remedy must be found in the organization of some local board vested with the authority of licensing teachers and of revoking the license, and charged with a general superintendence of the schools within the prescribed limits. *The division of the State into counties affords a convenient distribution of territory for this purpose;* and if it be made a condition of receiving the public donation, that teachers thus authorized shall have been employed for a portion of the year, it is believed that the sure and inevitable consequence would be the employment of instructors much more competent than the average of the present teachers. In those counties where the population is small and scattered, the standard of competency will necessarily be low; but it will advance with the means of the districts, and with the prosperity and intelligence of the counties. In other counties, where candidates were more numerous, the qualifications would be higher. The teachers would become, emphatically, a profession; more would devote themselves to it as a means of livelihood, and would prepare themselves accordingly. Such is an outline of the first efforts, which, in the opinion of the committee, should be made to obtain able teachers.

"The next object is to provide the means of qualifying the necessary number of teachers. By the report of the Superintendent, made in January, 1825, there were then in this State 7,642 school districts. That, then, is the number of teachers now required; the best evidence that can be adduced to show that there must always be a sufficient demand for those who are qualified. It is obvious that the suggestion of the Governor in his message, respecting the establishment of an institution especially for the purpose of educating teachers, will not answer the exigencies of the case. *It is entitled to much weight, however, as a means in conjunction with others,* to effect the object. But in the view which the committee have taken, *our great reliance for nurseries of teachers must be placed in our colleges and academies.* If they do not answer this purpose they can be of very little use. That they have not hitherto been more extensively useful in that respect is owing to inherent defects in the system of studies pursued there. When the heads of our colleges are apprised of the great want of teachers, which it is so completely in their power to relieve, if not to supply, it is but reasonable to expect that they will adopt a system by which young men, whose pursuits do not require a knowledge of classics, may avail themselves of the talent and instruction in those institutions suited to their wants, without being compelled also to receive that which they do not want, and for which they have neither time nor money.

"Our *academies*, also, have failed to supply the want of teachers to the extent which was within their power; although it is acknowledged that in this respect they have been eminently useful. But instead of being incited to such efforts, they are rather restrained by the regulation adopted by the Regents of the University for the distribution of the literary fund placed at their disposal. The income of that fund is divided among the academies in proportion to the number of *classical* students in each, without reference to those who are pursuing the highest and most useful branches of an English course. * * The committee are not disposed to censure the Regents; they have merely followed the fashion of the times; and it is believed that they are themselves alive to the importance of extending the usefulness of the institutions under their care, by adapting them more to the wants of the country and the spirit of the age. But if they should not be willing to extend the benefits of the fund under their control beyond classical students, still it will be in the power of the Legislature, and within the means of the State, to appropriate a capital sum that will yield a sufficient income to compensate for this inequality, and to place the English students on the same footing with the others, and thus make it the interest of the academies to instruct them. And if this bounty be distributed in reference to the number of persons instructed at an academy, who shall have been licensed as teachers of Common Schools by the proper board, it is believed the object of obtaining able instructors will soon be accomplished.

"The committee have not been able to discover why, upon every principle of justice and of public policy, *seminaries for the education of females in the higher branches of knowledge* should not participate, equally with those for the instruction of males, in the public bounty.

"*In connection with these*, the committee admit that the establishment of a *separate institution for the sole purpose of preparing teachers* would be a most valuable auxiliary. * * * They hesitate to recommend its adoption now, chiefly because the other measures which they intend to submit, and which they conceive to be more immediately necessary, will involve as much expense as ought now to be incurred. But they fondly anticipate the time when the means of the State will be commensurate with the public spirit of its Legislature, and when such an institution will be founded on a scale equal to our wants and our resources."

It will be perceived, from these extracts, that the statesmanlike conceptions of DE WITT CLINTON, and the comprehensive and perspicacious intellect of Mr. SPENCER, had, at this early period, clearly anticipated those great measures for the advancement of the Common School system which were long afterward adopted, and, in great part, through the exertions of the latter, in his official capacity as head of the department. The system of county supervision, academical departments and normal schools for the instruction of teachers, and institutions for the higher education of female pupils, are here distinctly shadowed forth, although many years were to elapse before their practical realization.

On the 14th of February, 1826, AZARIAH C. FLAGG, of the county of Clinton, was appointed Secretary of State, and the administration of the Common School system devolved upon him, *ex officio*. Mr. FLAGG had, for several years, ably represented his county in the Legislature, where he had distinguished himself for his ability and capacity as a political leader. He was a man of genial manners, shrewd sense, and quick discernment of character; of rigid and uncompromising integrity, and well adapted, in all respects, to secure the entire confidence of the community in the clearness of his judgment, the honesty of his motives, and the rectitude of his decisions. At the close of his official term, he was promoted to the office of Comptroller, the duties of which he continued, for many years, to discharge with characteristic ability and fidelity, and from whence he was transferred to a similar department in the city of New York, where he still continues to reside, at a ripe old age, not indeed exempt from some of the severe "ills which life is heir to," but honored, respected, and beloved by all who know him. His hearty, ringing, cheerful laugh; his inexhaustible fund of anecdote and happy repartee; and his stern and inexorable rebuke of every species of public extravagance, dishonesty, or fraud, will long be remembered in the halls and corridors of the capital and the metropolis.

His first annual report, as Superintendent, was transmitted to the Legislature on the 13th of March, showing a gratifying increase in the number of school districts and of pupils. He fully concurred with the recommendations of the Governor and the Literature Committee of the Senate in reference to the necessity of providing greater facilities for the preparation and instruction of teachers, and offering additional inducements for their employment in the several districts.

In January, of this year, the title of the "Free School Society of the City of New York" was changed by the Legislature, on the application of the trustees, to that of "The Public School Society;" and permission given to receive pupils at low rates of payment, from twenty-five cents to two dollars per quarter, according to the studies pursued—tuition having previously been wholly free. The act went into operation on the 1st of May, and three new schools—Nos. 7, 8, and 9—were opened before the close of the year, and the course of study remodeled and extended to higher branches. The Lancasterian or monitorial system of instruction was strictly adhered to; and an application to the trustees for the appointment of an assistant teacher in the respective schools indignantly rejected, as "abandoning the principle of the beautiful system" so productive hitherto of beneficial results. Two additional and permanent monitors were, however, assigned to each department, with a small salary: and so unpopular was the "pay system," and so difficult of execution, from the refusal of parents to pay or to send their children to the schools—nearly one-third of the attendance having fallen off—that the trustees were compelled, at first, to reduce the rates one-half, and soon afterward, in 1832, to abandon them entirely, and declare the schools thenceforward wholly free—a character they have ever since maintained.

Gov. Clinton, at the opening of the session of 1827, again reverted to the subject of education in the following terms:

"The great bulwark of Republican Government is the cultivation of education; for the right of suffrage can not be exercised in a salutary manner without intelligence. We may safely estimate the number of our Common Schools at 8,000; the number of children taught during the last year, for an average period of eight months, at 480,000; and the sum expended in education at $200,000. It is, however, too palpable that our system is surrounded by imperfections which demand the wise consideration and improving interposition of the Legislature. In the first place, there is no provision made for the education of competent instructors. Of the eight thousand now employed in this State, too many are destitute of the requisite qualifications, and perhaps no considerable number are able to teach beyond rudimental instruction. Perhaps one-fourth of our population is annually instructed in our Common Schools; and ought the minds and the morals of the rising, and perhaps the destinies of all future, generations to be entrusted to the guardianship of incompetence? The scale of instruction must be elevated; the standard of education ought to be raised; and a central school, on the monitorial plan, ought to be established in each county, for the education of teachers, and as exemplars for other momentous purposes connected with the improvement of the human mind. *Small and suitable collections of books and maps attached to our common schools, and periodical examinations to test the proficiency of the scholars and merits of the teachers,* are worthy of attention. When it is understood that objects of this description enter into the very formation of our characters, control our destinies through life, protect the freedom and advance the glory of our country; and when it is considered that seminaries for general education are either not provided in the Old World, or but imperfectly supplied by charity and Sunday schools, and that this is the appropriate soil of liberty and education—let it be our pride, as it is our duty, to spare no exertion and to shrink from no expense in the promotion of a cause consecrated by religion and enjoined by patriotism; nor let us be regardless of ample encouragement of the higher institutions devoted to literature and science. Independently of their intrinsic merits and their diffusive and enduring benefits in reference to their appropriate objects, they have, in a special manner, a most auspicious influence on all subordinate institutions. They give to society men of improved and enlarged minds, who, feeling the importance of information in their own experience, will naturally cherish an ardent desire to extend its blessings. Science delights in expansion as well as in concentration; and, after having flourished within the precincts of academies and universities, will spread itself over the land, enlightening society and ameliorating the condition of man. The more elevated the tree of knowledge, and the more expanded its branches, the greater will be its trunk and the deeper its root."

Mr. Flagg, in his annual report, as Superintendent, for this year, suggested that "the system of inspection might be improved by the *appointment of competent persons to visit the schools of a county or a larger district,* to investigate the mode of instruction, the qualifications of teachers, and the application of the public money, and to inquire into all the operations of the school system. Such inspectors would aid the schools by their advice, and add to the stock of intelligence on the subject of education, by collecting information in relation to the condition of the schools and the manner in which they are conducted; and these inspections would be the means of more effectually ascertaining what the Common Schools now effect, and what they may be made to accomplish." He recommends also the establishment of schools in the several counties for the education of teachers, the gradual introduction throughout the schools of the State of the system of mutual instruction, the improvement of the system of female education, and the judicious selection, by State authority, of suitable text-books for the several schools. "The course of instruction in the Common Schools," he observes, "*ought to be adapted to the business of life, and to the actual duties which may devolve upon the person instructed.* In a government where every citizen has a voice in deciding the most important questions, it is not only necessary that every person should be able to read and write, but that he should be well instructed in the rights, privileges, and duties of a citizen. INSTRUCTION SHOULD BE CO-EXTENSIVE WITH UNIVERSAL SUFFRAGE.'

An additional sum of $100,000 was this year apportioned by the Superintendent among the several school districts, in accordance with an appropriation made by the Legislature of 1826.

On the 21st of February, Mr. SPENCER, from the Literature Committee of the Senate, reported a bill "to provide permanent funds for the annual appropriation to Common Schools, to increase the literature fund, and to promote the education of teachers," which, with some slight amendments, was passed into a law on the 13th of April following. This Act transferred from the general fund to the Common School Fund the balance due on the loan of 1786, together with $100,000 of the bank stock belonging to the State; and to the literature fund, from the canal fund, the sum of $150,000, the income of which, together with that of the $95,000 previously belonging to the fund, was required to be annually distributed by the Regents of the University among the incorporated academies and seminaries of the State, other than colleges, in proportion to the number of pupils instructed in each for six months during the preceding year, "who shall have pursued classical studies, *or the higher branches of English education*, or both." Accompanying the bill was an able report, from which the following extracts are taken, indicative of the views of the committee on the subject of the suitable education of teachers:

"In vain will you have established a system of instruction—in vain will you appropriate money to educate the children of the poor, if you do not provide persons competent to execute your system, and to teach the pupils collected in the schools. The message of the Governor and the report of the Superintendent concur in pressing this subject upon our attention with the most anxious solicitude; and every citizen who has paid attention to it, and become acquainted practically with the situation of our schools, knows that the incompetency of the great mass of teachers is a radical defect which impedes the whole system, frustrates the benevolent design of the Legislature and defeats the hopes and wishes of all who feel an interest in disseminating the blessings of education. There are 8,114 organized school districts in the State; and if there be added the schools in the city of New York, in Albany, Troy, and Hudson, not included in the returns, and the private schools which are established in almost every county, we shall be justified in estimating the number of teachers required to carry on the business of instruction at not far from ten thousand. From what sources can this supply of teachers be obtained? and how can the great body of this multitude be rendered competent to their stations? In a free government, resting upon the intelligence of its citizens, these questions are of vital importance.

"The Governor has recommended the establishment of central schools, upon the monitorial plan, for the instruction of teachers. From the best consideration the committee have been able to bestow upon the subject, and from all the information they can collect, *a doubt is entertained whether the monitorial plan is adapted to small schools in the country, or to the higher branches of education.* The means of instruction in the ordinary mode must be provided. The colleges and academies ought to furnish competent instructors; and, indeed, to them we are indebted, but chiefly to the academies, for the qualified instructors now employed. While academies are instituted, and by proper encouragement may supply our wants, the committee would doubt the policy of establishing central schools in their vicinity, which would necessarily divert from them much of their present support."

After referring to the location of the several academies in different sections of the State, and their consequent capability of meeting the wants of the community—few portions of the State not being adequately supplied with these institutions, provided they were properly supported and encouraged—the report proceeds to specify the proposed alteration in the distribution of the literature fund, the object being "*to promote the education of young men in those studies which will prepare them for the business of instruction*, which it is hoped may be accomplished to some extent by offering inducements to the trustees of academies to educate pupils of that description;" and concludes with the following eloquent and powerful appeal:

"These are the considerations which have guided the committee in preparing the bill now presented. They have only further to say, that if any confidence can be reposed in the official communications of those officers of the Government whose duty it is to give the Legislature information on this subject—if the concurring testimony of all who have spoken or written concerning it can be relied upon, there is a radical, deep, and extensive defect in our Common School system, which deprives it of much of its value; and that defect consists in the want of competent instructors. From six to ten years of the most valuable portion of human life—of that very period when instruction is most easily imparted, and most firmly retained—is absolutely wasted and thrown away. Every one in the least acquainted with the subject knows that a boy under proper instruction can and ought to know as much at seven or eight years old as he acquires under the present system at fourteen or sixteen. Having undertaken a system of public instruction, it is the solemn duty of the Legislature to make that system as perfect as possible. We have no right to trifle with the funds of our constituents, by applying them in a mode which fails to attain the intended object. *Competent teachers of Common Schools must be provided;* the academies of the State furnish the means of making that provision. There are funds which may be safely and properly applied to that object; and if there were none, a more just, patriotic, and, in its true sense, popular reason for taxation cannot be urged. Let us aid the efforts of meritorious citizens, who have devoted large portions of their means to the rearing of academies; let us reward them, by giving success to their efforts; let us sustain seminaries that are falling into decay; let us revive the drooping, and animate the prosperous, by the cheering rays of public beneficence; and thus let us provide nurseries for the education of our children, and for the instruction of teachers who will expand, and widen, and deepen the great stream of education, until it shall reach our remotest borders, and prepare our posterity for the maintenance of the glory and prosperity of their country!"

Governor CLINTON, in his last message, at the opening of the session of 1828—one month only preceding his death—again directs the attention of the Legislature to his favorite theme, with a perceptible tone of melancholy disappointment:

"That part of the Revised Laws relative to Common Schools is operative on this day, and presents the system in an intelligible shape, but without those improvements which are requisite to raise the standard of instruction, to enlarge its objects, and to elevate the talents and qualifications of the teachers. It is understood that Massachusetts has provided for these important cases; but whether the experiment has as yet been attended with promising results is not distinctly known. It may, however, be taken for granted that the education of the body of the people can never attain the requisite perfection without competent instructors, well acquainted with the outlines of literature and the elements of science. And after the scale of education is elevated in Common Schools, more exalted improvements ought to be engrafted into academical studies, and proceed in a correspondent and progressive ascent to our colleges.

"In the mean time, I consider it my duty to recommend a law authorizing the supervisors of each county to raise a sum not exceeding two thousand dollars, provided the same sum is subscribed by individuals, for the erection of a suitable edifice for a *Monitorial High School* in the county town. I can conceive of no reasonable objection to the adoption of a measure so well calculated to raise the character of our schoolmasters, and to double the powers of our artisans, by giving them a scientific education."

Carrying our reflections back over a period embracing nearly a quarter of a century; viewing this great and good man as the leading spirit in the organization and establishment of the now magnificent system of free public school instruction in the city of New York; tracing his deep interest in its earliest efforts and in the Lancasterian method of instruction, in the transcendent value and importance of which his powerful intellect never for a moment wavered; following him in his long executive career as Governor of the Empire State, the successful founder and executor of a vast system of internal improvements, the wonder and admiration of the civilized world, and yet finding time for the encouragement and building up, step by step, of a still greater work—that of the education of a whole people; listening to his eloquent appeals and studying his masterly addresses and messages, covering almost the entire ground of modern civilization and political statesmanship—where shall we find a nobler theme for eulogy, admiration, reverence, and high regard than the illustrious CLINTON? Truly and most emphatically may it be said of him

> "Nothing can cover his high fame but heaven;
> No pyramid set off his memories
> But the eternal substance of his greatness!"

From the annual report of the Superintendent, it appeared that the number of children under instruction in the several schools of the State during the year 1826 was 441,856, being an increase of 10,225 over the preceding year, and of upwards of 300,000 over the attendance of 1816. The aggregate amount of public money received and expended by the several districts in the payment of the wages of duly qualified teachers was $222,993.77; of which $100,000 was paid from the State treasury, $110,542.32 raised by tax upon the several towns, and $12,450.45 from the proceeds of Gospel and school lots and other local funds. The productive capital of the Common School Fund had been increased during the year by the sum of $256,121.50, by various transfers from other State funds and by the avails of the sales of State lands set apart for this purpose. The Superintendent recommended the furnishing of additional facilities for Common School instruction to children engaged in manufacturing establishments, by the annual appropriation for their benefit of a share of the public money, according to the number of children instructed therein.

During the ensuing year, over twenty-six thousand pupils were added to the Common Schools; and the report for 1830 showed a further increase of about twelve thousand. The Superintendent adverts to the "serious deficiency in the supply of competent teachers as the great obstacle which it is necessary to remove before we can reasonably expect to accomplish the great results and confer the enduring benefits which were anticipated by those who founded and those who fostered our system of Common School instruction." He alludes with characteristic practical shrewdness to the inefficiency of the remedy proposed for this pervading evil, in the absence of a proper spirit of liberality on the part of the inhabitants of the respective districts themselves. "Those who have turned their attention to the subject of giving a higher character to the Common Schools in this and other States," he observes, "have recommended the establishment of seminaries for the exclusive education of teachers. This would serve to multiply the number of those who would be qualified to teach; but after being thus qualified, at the public expense, what guaranty would there be that such persons would follow the business of teaching, unless they could be as liberally compensated in a district school as in other pursuits of life? If the inhabitants of the district were resolved to have none other than teachers of the highest grade, and would pay the highest premium for talent, our academies and high schools would be thronged by persons fitting themselves for the business of teaching; and all these institutions would practically become schools for the education of teachers. If the districts could be induced to give an adequate compensation and constant employment to first-rate instructors, then it would be eminently useful to establish seminaries for the special purpose of training persons as professional instructors. * * * *If the intelligent farmers in the districts would employ a small share of their attention and practical common sense on this subject, a revolution in the character of the schools would soon be effected.*" In regard to the multiplicity of text-books in use in the several schools, he is of opinion that the proposed designation of any particular work or series, to the exclusion of others, would be injudicious and unwise. "Great improvements," he observes, "are constantly going on in the character of school books; the greatest experience and much of the best talent of the country are enlisted in this business; and the fruits of their labors are constantly giving them new claims to the approbation of the public. The adoption of a particular book would amount to a prohibition upon all improvements and subject the inhabitants to a loss of the prohibited books on hand. *The interests of the Common Schools may be seriously injured and cannot be essentially benefited by the adoption by law of any book or set of books.*" * He adds, however, "A society has been established in England for the purpose of imparting useful information to all classes of community, particularly to such as are unable to avail themselves of experienced teachers. To effect this object, treatises on the various sciences, and books of practical utility, have been published at such moderate prices as to bring them within the reach of all classes. A small sum applied to the publication and distribu-

* See also Assembly Document for 1830, No. 401, Vol. 4. Report of Common School Committee.

tion among the several school districts, of similar works, would have the most favorable influence." The establishment of school district libraries at a subsequent period proved a more effectual realization of this idea than the plan here indicated.

A memorial was presented to the Legislature during its session of this year from a committee of the citizens of Rochester, consisting of the Rev. Dr. PENNY, and Messrs. Comstock, Brown, Ward and Norton, asking for the establishment of a State seminary for the education of teachers, and a central high school in each town, with an effective general and local supervision throughout the State. This document was a very elaborate and able exposition of the soundest theories and practical details of elementary public instruction, and exerted a powerful influence in directing the attention of the friends of education throughout the State to the whole subject, and in preparing the public mind for future reforms in the system. It clearly indicated the direction in which the current of popular opinion was setting; shadowed out the principal improvements and prominent measures which were afterward adopted; recommended the establishment of three or more State normal schools for the education and preparation of teachers; the organization of central high schools of the most approved standard of excellence, so connected with all the others in each town as to exert the most salutary and beneficial influence upon the general interests of education, and to aid in the preparation of well-qualified teachers; and the organization of such a system of county and town supervision, in relation to and connection with that of the State, as should bind together the entire system in one harmonious whole, and infuse new life, activity and energy in all its parts.* Owing to the condition of the Common School Fund, at this period, insuperable objections existed to the adoption of the comprehensive plan indicated by the memorialists; and it was reserved for a no very distant period to carry out their well-considered and timely suggestions.

Governor THROOP, in his annual message to the Legislature of 1831, briefly alluded to this great interest of the State in the following terms: "There is no one of our public institutions of more importance or which has better fulfilled public expectation than that providing for instruction in Common Schools. Its imperfections may receive some correction from legislation, yet more is to be hoped from individual exertions to carry the design of the Legislature into effect within the several districts."

The annual report of the Superintendent showed an additional increase of upwards of 10,000 in the number of pupils in the several schools over the preceding years, making the entire number under instruction in 8,630 out of 9,030 districts about 500,000, a number considerably exceeding that of all the children between the ages of five and sixteen residing in the districts. The amount of public money received and expended was $230,713, which, in addition to the sum contributed on rate-bills, $346,807, amounted to $586,520 paid for teachers' wages alone. The average annual increase in the number of pupils during the past eleven years was *twenty thousand.* The productive capital of the School Fund amounted, at this period, to $1,696,743.66. After a full review of the various plans proposed for the education of teachers, the Superintend-

* Legislative Documents, 1830, Vol. 4, No. 337.

ent recommends the conversion of the several academies, equal in number, at that time, to the counties of the State, into seminaries for that purpose. "The State has done much for these institutions," he says, "and something in aid of the cause of the Common Schools may reasonably be expected from them; and if the required information to fit a person for teaching can be obtained in them, sound policy and good economy are in favor of relying upon them for this purpose."

On the question how far the expenses of supporting and maintaining the Common Schools, and supplying them with competent teachers, may advantageously be provided from the public treasury, and to what extent they may safely and successfully be committed to the inhabitants of the several districts, Mr. FLAGG compares the operation of our system in this respect with those of Massachusetts, Connecticut, Maine, Pennsylvania, Virginia, and other States, in the two latter of which the public funds were exclusively appropriated for the benefit of indigent children, while in Connecticut they were lavished in indiscriminate profusion for the gratuitous instruction of all classes; and observes: "Our system is well calculated to awaken the attention of all the inhabitants to the concerns of the district school. The power given to district meetings to levy a tax, to a limited extent, upon the property of the district, excites a direct interest with all the taxable inhabitants to attend the district meetings, whether they have children requiring school accommodations or not. The wealthy are thus prompted to act as trustees, and to watch over the concerns of the district, in order to see that its affairs are conducted with care and economy; and much of the intelligence of the district is put in requisition by the peculiarity of our plan, which might be wholly lost, if the whole expense of the tuition was provided by a State fund. It has been urged that the amount distributed from our fund is too small, and that an increase of the fund would of itself raise the standard of the Common School; but *such an increase would be much more likely to decrease the contributions of individuals* than to elevate the standard of education." A careful comparison of the official returns at this period with those of from ten to twenty years later vindicated the judgment of the Superintendent in this respect—showing a falling off in the contributions of the inhabitants to the amount of over $250,000, less than a proportionate share of the increase.

With reference to the proposed uniformity of text-books, in the several schools, the Superintendent remarks:

"No man or set of men could make out a list of class-books for the instruction of half a million of scholars which would give general satisfaction; and there is great reason to believe that the experiment to produce uniformity would do more harm than it promises to do good. In view of all the difficulties which surround the subject, the Superintendent believes that it is best to leave the selection of class-books to the intelligence of the inhabitants of the districts and towns."

"The immense importance of elevating the standard of education in the Common Schools," the Superintendent observes in conclusion, "is strongly enforced by the fact that to every ten persons receiving instruction in the higher schools there are at least five hundred dependent upon the Common Schools for their education. In urging the importance of the latter, it is not designed to depreciate the great utility of the former. In the discussions on the subject of popular education, it has, in some cases, been urged that academies and high schools were injurious to the Common Schools by withdrawing from their aid the patronage and care of those who are able to send to the former schools. There is nothing in our experience which should enable us to look with disfavor upon the higher institutions; and the patriot and philanthropist in estimating the means which are to contribute to the perpetuity of our happy form of government *will regard all our schools and seminaries as parts of the same useful and valuable system, from the university to the infant school.*"

In his report for 1832, Mr. FLAGG again institutes a comparison between our system of public instruction and those of the Eastern States:

"The school system of New York," he observes, "has been formed by combining the advantages of the different plans of supporting Common Schools which prevail in the New England States. Connecticut has a large fund which produces nearly or quite the whole amount paid for teachers' wages, and has no local tax. Massachusetts and Maine have no public fund, and the wages of teachers are provided by a town tax. Our system happily combines the principles of a State fund and a town tax. Enough is apportioned from the State treasury to invite and encourage the co-operation of the districts and towns, and not so much as to induce the inhabitants to believe that they have nothing more to do than to hire a teacher to absorb the public money. The tax authorized upon the property of the town and district has a most salutary effect in awakening the attention of the inhabitants to the concerns of the Common Schools. The power of district meetings to raise money by tax induces the inhabitants to attend the meetings and to overlook the interests and proceedings of the district, when if the whole expense was provided by a State fund, they would allow the trustees to receive and expend the money, as if it was a matter which did not interest the great body of the inhabitants of the district. Whatever differences of opinion may exist as to the best mode of providing for the expense of giving instruction to all the children of the State, the success which has attended our system warrants the conclusion that a public fund may be made eminently useful in organizing a system of universal instruction."

In relation to the "vexed question" of text-books, the Superintendent renews the expression of his opinion, that "the adoption of a particular set of text-books could be of no advantage except to the favored authors to whom the monopoly of supplying the scholars should be given. Toward all other authors who have devoted their time and talents to the preparation of books, as well as publishers who have embarked their fortune in particular works, it would operate proscriptively and with manifest injustice."

From the last annual report of Mr. Flagg, embracing the operations of the year 1831, it appeared that the number of school districts was 9,600, and the number of children instructed 494,959. He again called the attention of the Legislature to the expediency of making some suitable provision for the education of the children in the various *manufactories* in the State. "The policy of all our laws," he observes, "is to secure a good Common School education to every child in the State; and the condition of the children who are employed in the manufactories, as to their means of instruction, ought to be carefully inquired into and provided for. The diffusion of education among all classes of our population is deemed of such vital importance to the preservation of our free institutions, that if the obligations which rest upon every good citizen in this particular are disregarded, the persons having the custody of such children ought to be visited with such disabilities as will induce them from interest, if not from principle, to cause the children to be instructed at least in reading, writing, and arithmetic. Intelligence has been regarded as the vital principle of a free government; and *every parent, guardian or master who neglects or refuses to give the children under his charge the advantages of a Common School education—particularly in cases where the instruction is offered "without money and without price"—is as much an offender against the State as the man who refuses to perform any other duty which is deemed essential to the preservation of our liberties.*" A generous and noble sentiment!—admitting of a more extended application than the one for which it was more particularly designed. I regret to have been unable to find any legislative response to this philanthropic appeal.

In reviewing the administration of the Common School system, by Mr. FLAGG, during a period of seven years, extending from 1826 to 1833, it is impossible to withhold the meed of high approbation for the eminent services rendered by him at a most critical period of its history. Under his auspices, the number of school districts had increased from 7,773 to 9,000, the number of children instructed from 423,586 to nearly 495,000—a number almost equal to the entire population of the State between the ages of five and sixteen years—and the amount of public money applicable to the payment of teachers' wages from $182,790 to $305,582.78. The external organization and internal details of the system in all its parts were carefully watched over and protected; complicated questions of law arising under the provisions of the act and growing out of its local administration promptly adjudicated upon and settled; important and varied propositions for its modification, improvement, and extension examined and discussed, with that practical candor, shrewdness, and clear common sense which so peculiarly distinguished his well-balanced mind; and those equitable and legal principles established which constituted the basis upon which his successors were enabled to build up a series of judicial decisions commensurate with the vast extent of the system in its application to the numerous and perplexing details constantly requiring explanation and settlement. While steadfastly setting his face against the establishment of State seminaries for the education of teachers, and the adoption of a uniform series of text-books, and utterly failing to grasp the conception of free schools supported by general taxation, he is nevertheless entitled to a prominent place in the list of public benefactors to the rising generation.

It now becomes necessary again to revert to the progress of the Public School system in the city of

New York. The Lancasterian or monitorial method of instruction, so universally prevailing in the elementary schools of the Public School Society, after the experience of more than a quarter of a century, was now undergoing a sensible eclipse. It will be recollected that the Literature Committee of the Senate had, in 1827, through their distinguished chairman, Mr. SPENCER, expressed their strong doubt as to the adaptation of that system to the schools of the rural districts, or to the higher branches of education; and the gradual prevalence of advanced processes in the course of instruction in the Public Schools of the city of New York had insensibly weakened the hold of the monitorial plan. At about this period, too, the rage for "Infant Schools" had been imported from London and the continent; and early in 1827, an association of ladies, under the auspices of Mrs. Joanna Bethune, was organized under the title of the "Infant School Society," for the instruction of children from two to six or seven years of age. Stimulated by the success of this experiment, the Public School Society determined to detach from the schools under their charge this class of children, and to organize them into a separate department in the basement of School No. 8, to be known as the Primary Department, and open to all children capable of admission under the age of ten years. The schools of the Ladies' Association, however, had wholly discarded the Lancasterian system of instruction, with all its books, black-boards, and "sand-classes," and substituted in its stead pleasant and attractive songs for and with their pupils, a variety of calisthenic exercises suitable for children, and the oral teaching of familiar objects. These innovations were peculiarly obnoxious to the pioneer members and originators of the Society—many of whom were of the Society of Friends, and could not readily be induced to tolerate the vain frivolities of music and calisthenics. An infant department was, however, permitted to be established in the basement of School No. 10, under the counsel and direction of the Ladies Association, with a view to test the comparative excellence of the rival systems. The report of the committee appointed by the Society to pass upon the question was strongly in favor of the superiority of the new system over the monitorial; the knell of the latter was tolled; and before the grass upon the recent great champion of Lancasterianism had grown green, its reign was over —its influence gone—its power forever departed! Female teachers were admitted into the schools; the voice of music and the exuberant prattle of joyous, riotous infancy were heard—its irrepressible curiosity aroused—its desire for knowledge stimulated and gratified—and the monitors, with their huge and cumbrous books and complicated machinery, consigned "to the tomb of the Capulets."

Let us not, however, be unjust to the merits of the long triumphant and now fallen system, or indifferent to, or forgetful of, the great work it had accomplished in the organization and success of the Common School system. More than a hundred thousand children, in the city of New York alone, had been trained up under its influence and through its processes, during a period of more than twenty-five years, to usefulness, honesty, and virtue. In all the larger cities and towns of the State, noble and stately edifices had been erected for its use, and filled with its pupils; and the noblest, grandest, loftiest intellect in the Commonwealth had been a life-long worshiper at its shrine, and had, with his dying breath, solemnly commended its perpetuation to the legislative councils of the State! Surely such a system is not to be condemned or dismissed without a fair hearing, and for substantial and imperative reasons. It was a fair and stately tree of knowledge; its branches budded, blossomed, and bore rich fruit; it overshadowed the gardens of mental cultivation—and our predecessors and ourselves have reaped the abundant harvests. Let, then, its memory be hallowed and cherished, while the bones of LANCASTER and CLINTON repose upon our soil! Its work and theirs are done—*abiunt ad plures*—but for us and for our latest posterity their memory will be ever green!

The impending restoration of the free system of instruction in the schools of the Society rendered it necessary to invoke legislative aid for the increase of the public funds applicable to their support. In 1831, the Common Council were requested to apply for the imposition of a tax upon the city amounting to three-eighteenths of one per cent. in addition to the equal sum required to be added to the State apportionment. The Council complied with this request, interposing as a condition, however, its own unrestricted power over the expenditure of the fund—a representative body of commissioners, from the several wards of the city, having been previously appointed by them for its distribution. An earnest remonstrance against this dangerous innovation, based upon its liability to partisan and sectarian abuse, was presented by the Public School Society; and, during the pendency of the controversy, the flames of discord were rekindled by the application of the Roman Catholic Benevolent Society, in behalf of the Orphan Asylum under its charge, and the Methodist Episcopal Church, in behalf of its Charity Schools, for admission to a participation in the school moneys.

The Trustees of the Public School Society promptly interposed a remonstrance against this demand, alleging that the Roman Catholic Benevolent Society was a close corporation, all of whose members were of the Catholic religion—that the education given in the asylum was strictly sectarian—that its participation in the School Fund would necessarily involve compulsory contributions from tax-payers conscientiously opposed to such instruction—that the decision of the Common Council in 1825, based as it was clearly and explicitly on the principle that the Public School Money should be exclusively consecrated to the purposes of secular education, and should on no account be diverted to sectarian uses, had been deemed on all hands a final settlement of the question—that the mere fact of orphanage constituted no distinction between the claims of the Catholic and other religious organizations, as this class of children were provided for by all, and each denomination possessed equal claims in this respect upon the public funds—that such an appropriation would lead to an extensive system of religious proselytism at variance with public policy—and that whatever claims the asylum might possess to the generous sympathy and charitable support of the community, such benevolence should be exercised by private individuals and through voluntary contributions, instead of compulsory levies upon a common fund specifically appropriated to a distinct object.

On the other hand, it was urged by the Catholic claimants that their right to participate in the advantages of the school money was, at least, in every way equal to that of the Protestant Orphan Asylum, which had been admitted, under the decision and settlement referred to, to a distributive portion of the fund, and had for many years enjoyed its benefits—that while this institution was purely and distinctively Protestant in its management, its instruction, and its usages, no complaint had been made by any portion of the community, the Catholics included, against a provision so obviously beneficent and proper—that they only claimed to be placed upon a footing of just equality with their Protestant brethren in this regard—and that while ample provision had been made for the general support, clothing, maintenance, and care, in sickness and in health, of these otherwise friendless and destitute little ones, by private and associated charity, their instruction was equally the duty of the State and city, with that of others who had been officially recognized as its beneficiaries. They, therefore, called upon the Common Council to see that these unquestionable rights were no longer withheld.

These incontrovertible views were sustained by that body, as in full accordance with the cardinal principles of the ordinance of 1825, recognizing the peculiar claims of *orphan asylums* as a justifiable and the only justifiable exception to the general principle that the Public School moneys were applicable only to secular instruction. In conformity, however, with this general principle, the petition of the Methodist Church was denied; and the claim of the Common Council to the exclusive right of distribution of the School Fund of the city abandoned in favor of the Commissioners. The Methodists immediately renewed their claim in behalf of the *orphan* children attending their Church Schools; but the Common Council, by a unanimous vote, decided that exceptions to the fundamental rule of distribution could be allowed *only in the case of those who had no other home than an orphan asylum.**

Thus terminated the second of the great religious controversies which agitated the citizens of New York city, and which laid the foundation of a re-organization of its system of public instruction at a later period, without, however, disturbing the vital principle of the inadmissibility of religious sectarian instruction, or of the exclusive consecration of the Public School Fund of the State and city to the legitimate purposes of education.

* Public Education in the City of New York, 107–110.

SECTION IV.—ADMINISTRATION OF SECRETARY JOHN A. DIX—1833 TO 1839.

Messages of Governor Marcy.—Reports of the Superintendent.—Academical Preparation of Teachers.—Text Books.—District Libraries.—James Wadsworth, of Geneseo.—Proposed Department of Public Instruction.—Augmentation of the Common School Fund.—United States Deposit Fund.—Its Appropriation.—Condition of the Schools.—Children in Manufactories.—Moral and Religious Instruction.—The Bible and New Testament in the Schools.—Common School Decisions and Laws.

AT the opening of the Legislative session of 1833, Governor MARCY, in his message, thus alluded to the subject of Common Schools:

"Of all our institutions, there is none which presents such strong claims to the patronage of the Government as our system of Common Schools; and it is gratifying to know that those claims have been recognized, and to a very considerable extent satisfied. The wisdom and providence of our legislation appears, perhaps, nowhere so conspicuously as in the measures which have been adopted and the means which have been provided for the general diffusion of primary education among the children of all classes of our citizens. An active and adventurous spirit of improvement characterizes the present age. Its best direction would be toward multiplying the facilities, and consequently abridging the time and labor, of acquiring knowledge. I indulge the hope that much may yet be done in this respect for primary education. One of the most obvious improvements in relation to Common Schools would be a plan for supplying them with competent teachers. Under present circumstances, the remedy of the evils resulting from the employment of persons not properly qualified can only be applied by the trustees and inspectors; and I am not apprised that any further direction for regulating their duties in this respect could be usefully presented to the Legislature."

On the 15th day of January, 1833, JOHN A. DIX, of Albany, was appointed Secretary of State and *ex officio*

Superintendent of Common Schools. General DIX was admirably adapted by his high character, eminent talents, and gentlemanly deportment, to the effective discharge of the responsible duties of his position. Educated at West Point, he was early in life attached to the military family of Major-General Brown—from whence he was subsequently transferred to the office of Adjutant-General of the State, a post which he occupied at the period of his election by the Legislature as Secretary.

His first annual report as Superintendent was presented to the Legislature on the 8th of January, 1834, comprehending the operations of the year 1832. There were in the State 9,690 school districts, from 9,107 of which reports had been received, in accordance with law, and in which 512,475 children had been taught during the year, out of 522,618, between five and sixteen, residing in the several districts—being an increase of 17,500 over the preceding year. In reference to the amount of the public funds provided for the support of Common Schools, he expresses the opinion that the sum distributed among the several districts was amply adequate to its object. "Experience in other States," he observes, "has proved what has been abundantly confirmed by our own, that too large a sum of public money distributed among the Common Schools has no salutary effect. Beyond a certain point, the voluntary contributions of the inhabitants decline in amount with almost uniform regularity, as the contributions from a public fund increase. Should the general fund at any future day be recruited, so as to admit of an augmentation of the capital or revenue of the Common School Fund, or both, the policy of increasing the sum annually distributed to the Common Schools beyond an amount which shall, when taken in connection with the number of children annually taught in them, exceed the present rate of apportionment, would be in the highest degree questionable."

With respect to the preparation of teachers for the Common Schools, General DIX concurred generally in the views of his predecessor: that the several academies of the State, aided by liberal appropriations for this purpose from the literature fund, would be found abundantly adequate to the accomplishment of the object in view; that the establishment of teachers' seminaries, devoted exclusively to this subject, would be impracticable without at the same time requiring the district to employ such teachers when prepared, and to provide them with an adequate compensation—neither of which measures would, for a moment, be tolerated; and that the *demand* on the part of the districts for teachers of a higher degree of qualification will be met by a corresponding *supply* from the academies, whenever sufficient inducements are held out to the latter to devote a large portion of their attention to the preparation of such teachers. An enlightened appreciation, on the part of the inhabitants of districts generally, of the functions and duties of teachers; a determination to secure the highest order of ability, and to provide a suitable compensation; and a disposition to elevate the character and advance the social rank of the teacher, by assigning him that station in the regards of the community which is due to the dignity and utility of his profession—these were regarded as indispensable pre-requisites to the success of any system which contemplates the specific preparation of teachers.

On the subject of the adoption of a uniform series of text-books for the use of schools, he also adopts the views of his predecessor, and discountenances such a measure as impracticable and unjust. In reference to the establishment of *district libraries*, he says:

"If the inhabitants of school districts were authorized to levy a tax upon their property for the purpose of purchasing libraries for the use of the district, such a power might, with proper restrictions, become a most efficient instrument for diffusing useful knowledge, and in elevating the intellectual character of the people. A vast amount of useful information might in this manner be collected, where it would be easily accessible, and its influence could hardly fail to be in the highest degree salutary, by furnishing the means of improvement as well to those who have finished their Common School education as to those who have not. The demand for books would ensure extensive editions of works containing matter judiciously selected, at prices which competition would soon reduce to the lowest rate at which they could be furnished."

By an act of the Legislature, passed at this session, a portion of the surplus income of the literature fund, estimated at $3,000 per annum, was placed at the disposal of the Regents of the University, to be by them distributed to such of the academies, subject to their visitation, as they might select, and to be devoted *exclusively* to the education of Common School teachers.

At the opening of the session of 1835, Governor MARCY commended to the special attention of the Legislature the expediency of the adoption of some suitable provision for supplying competent teachers, for improving the methods of instruction, and ensuring the faithful and economical application of the public funds to such objects and in such a manner as to effect the best results. "In regard to the Common Schools," he observes, "considering their great importance in a political and moral point of view, the efforts of the Legislature should not be intermitted, until the system shall be so improved as to *assure to the children of all classes and conditions of our population such an education as will qualify them to fulfill, in a proper manner, the duties appertaining to whatever may be their respective pursuits and conditions of life.*"

The annual report of the Superintendent showed a further increase of upward of 800 in the number of school districts, and of 18,000 in the number of children instructed during the year reported. In reference to the subject of the suitable education of teachers for the duties of their position, Gen. DIX observes:

"If the foundations of our whole system of instruction were to be laid anew, it would, perhaps, be advisable to create separate seminaries for the preparation of teachers, although from the nature of our institutions it might be deemed arbitrary, if indeed it were practicable, to compel the school districts to employ them. It would be equally difficult, without a great augmentation of the School Fund, to present to the districts a sufficient pecuniary inducement to engage the individuals thus prepared; and it may be safely assumed that nothing short of a thorough conviction in the public mind that Common School teachers are, in general, incompetent to the proper fulfillment of their trusts, and that the standard of education is extremely imperfect, would accomplish the object. If that conviction can now be created, the existing evils may be readily redressed. Our Common School system is so perfectly organized, and administered throughout with so much order and regularity, and so many academies under able management are already established, that it would seem the part of wisdom to avail ourselves of these institutions, to the extent of their capacity, for the purpose of training teachers for the Common Schools. Their endowments, their organization, the experience and skill of their instructors, and their whole intellectual power may be made subservient to the public purpose in view; and with the aid which the State can lend much may be effected. But whatever differences of opinion may prevail with regard to the foundation of this plan in sound policy, the question has been settled by the Legislature, and it remains only to carry it into execution with proper energy. Should it prove inadequate to the end proposed, a change of plan may then be insisted on, without being open to the objection of abandoning a system which has not been fairly tested.

"It may not be improper to remark, in this place, that the necessary connection which exists between our Common Schools and the literary institutions of the State, including those of the highest grade, has been too frequently overlooked. *The academies have already been, in effect, without receiving from the State any direct pecuniary aid for the purpose, nurseries for Common School teachers.* The great body of those who have, either temporarily or permanently, devoted themselves to teaching, have been prepared at the academies with a view to that occupation, or to some professional employment. *The instructors of the academies have, in their turn, been educated in the colleges;* and but for the latter, or some other system of classical and scientific education, the academies would obviously be destitute of the necessary supply of tutors. Thus all our incorporate literary institutions minister to the improvement of the Common School system, on which the great body of the people are dependent for their education."

After briefly adverting to the defective state of the system of instruction in Common Schools, the Superintendent proceeds, at considerable length, to combat the idea that the education which an individual receives should be necessarily exclusively designed to fit him for the particular employment he may be destined to pursue in after life. "The attention of the great body of the people," he remarks, "should be directed to objects *beyond* the sphere of the employments on which they depend for their support. Knowledge carries with it influence over the minds of others, and this influence is power—in free governments, what is of more vital concern, it is political power." And he proceeds to illustrate those views by a reference to the range and importance of the duties devolving upon every American citizen, rendering a comprehensive education indispensable to the proper appreciation and intelligent performance of those duties, without special regard to the restricted field of labor he may himself be called permanently to occupy.

On the 8th of January, 1835, General DIX, as chairman of a committee of the Regents of the University, appointed to prepare and report a plan for the better education of teachers of Common Schools, submitted an elaborate and able report recommending the establishment and organization of a *teachers' department*, to be connected with one academy, to be designated by the Regents, in each of the eight senatorial districts of the State, indicating the course of study to be pursued in such departments, and appropriating to each the annual sum of $400 from that portion of the literature fund applicable to this object. The report was agreed to by the Regents, and ERASMUS HALL Academy, Kings County; MONTGOMERY Academy, in Orange; KINDERHOOK Academy, in Columbia; ST. LAWRENCE Academy; FAIRFIELD Academy, in Herkimer; OXFORD Academy, in Chenango; CANANDAIGUA Academy, in Ontario; and MIDDLEBURY Academy, in Wyoming, were designated for the establishment of these departments.

On the 6th of May, General PROSPER M. WETMORE, of New York, chairman of the Assembly Committee on colleges, academies, and Common Schools, submitted a very able report, concluding with a bill for the establishment of a separate "DEPARTMENT OF PUBLIC INSTRUCTION," under the superintendence of an officer to be designated as "Secretary of Public Instruction," to be appointed triennially by the Legislature, in the same manner as other State officers, who should possess the powers and discharge the duties of Superintendent of Common Schools, and be *ex officio* Chancellor of the University. The several colleges and academies were to be subject to his visitation and inspection, and especially the several departments for the education of teachers. No definite action was, however, had by the Legislature on the bill during the session, and it was not again renewed in any shape for many years.

The foundations of the SCHOOL DISTRICT LIBRARY were laid on the 13th of April of this year, by the passage of an act, in accordance with the recommendation of General DIX, authorizing the taxable inhabitants of the several school districts to impose a tax, not exceeding twenty dollars for the first and ten dollars for each succeeding year, "for the purchase of a district library, consisting of such books as they shall in their district meeting direct." The bill was ably advocated in the Senate by Colonel YOUNG, of Saratoga, and LEVI BEARDSLEY, of Otsego; and its friends were indebted for its success, in great part, to the untiring exertions and extensive influence of the venerable JAMES WADSWORTH, of Geneseo, Livingston county, an eminent philanthropist, who lost no opportunity to aid, by his ample wealth and comprehensive benevolence, every enterprise by which the mental and moral advancement of the rising generation might be promoted.

Governor MARCY, in his message at the opening of the session of 1836, thus again adverts to this great interest:

"In a government like ours, which emanates from the people—where the entire administration, in all its various branches, is conducted for their benefit, and subject to their constant supervision and control—and where the safety and perpetuity of all its political institutions depend upon their virtue and intelligence—no other subject can be equal in importance to that of public instruction, and none should so earnestly engage the attention of the Legislature. Ignorance, with all the moral evils of which it is the prolific source, brings with it also numerous political evils, dangerous to the welfare of the State. It should be the anxious care of the Legislature to eradicate these evils, by removing the causes of them. This can be done effectually only by diffusing instruction generally among the people. Although much remains here to be done in this respect, the past efforts of legislation upon the subject merit high commendation. Much has been already accomplished for the cause of popular education. A large fund has been dedicated to this object, and our Common School system is established on right principles.

"But this is one of those subjects for which all cannot be done that is required, without a powerful co-operation on the part of the people, in their individual capacity. The providing of funds for education is an indispensable means for attaining the end, but it is not education. The wisest system that can be devised cannot be executed without human agency. The difficulty in the case arises, I fear, from the fact that the benefits of general education can only be fully appreciated by those who are educated themselves. Those parents who are so unfortunate as not to be properly educated, and those whose condition requires them to employ their time and their efforts to gain the means of subsistence, do not, in many instances, sufficiently value the importance of education. Yet it is for their children, in common with all others, that the Common School system is designed; and until its blessings are made to reach them, it will not be what it ought to be.

"If parents generally were sensible of the inestimable advantages they were procuring for their children by educating them, I am sure the efforts and contributions which are required to give full efficiency to our present system would not be withheld. If I have rightly apprehended the indications of public opinion on this subject, a more auspicious season is approaching. At this time, a much larger number of individuals than heretofore are exerting their energies and contributing their means to impress the public mind with the importance of making our system of popular instruction effective in diffusing its benefits to all the children of the State. I anticipate much good from the prevalence of the sentiment that the efforts of individuals must co-operate with the public authorities to insure success to any system of general education."

At this period, the number of school districts in the State exceeded 10,000, and the number of children instructed during an average period of eight months in each year, by duly qualified teachers, was 541,400; exceeding by more than 2,000 the number between the ages of five and sixteen residing in the State, and by 10,000, the number taught during the preceding year. The Superintendent, in his annual report, repeats the expression of his conviction, "that *a school fund so large as to admit of a distribution of money to the Common Schools in any degree approaching the amount expended for their support would be likely to be injurious rather than beneficial.*" "It is, from the nature of the subject, impossible," he observes, "to fix the exact limit below which a reduction of the sum distributed—including the amount raised by taxation in the several towns—would cease to operate as an inducement to the inhabitants to assume the residue of the expenses of maintaining the schools, or beyond which its increase would render their burdens so light as to create inattention to the concerns of the districts. It may, however, be safely assumed, that *at any point between forty and fifty cents per scholar*, it is not probable that either of these evils would be felt; and that its augmentation above the maximum on the one hand, or its reduction, on the other, below the minimum above named, ought to be avoided, if practicable."

The experience of the past thirty years has shown that, however sound the views of General DIX undoubtedly were, so far as the contributions of a permanent *State fund*, not directly dependent upon the popular aid, were concerned, the reliance upon a fund made up of such contributions and the general and equal taxation of the entire community for the free education of all its future members, has fully vindicated its superior efficiency in advancing the interests of public instruction. So long as dependence upon merely *local* taxation in aid of the public funds was relied upon, the augmentation of the latter sensibly tended to diminish the proportionate contributions of the former.

At the opening of the session of 1837, Governor MARCY again brought the subject before the Legislature, in connection with the act of Congress of the preceding year, authorizing the deposit of the share belonging to the States respectively, of the surplus revenue of the United States, with such States for safe keeping until required by the General Government. He recommended the appropriation from the annual income of this fund, of an amount equal to the sum annually distributed to the Common Schools, to be applied to the same purpose as at present—the payment of the wages of duly qualified teachers—increasing the annual distribution for this purpose from $110,000 to $220,000; a liberal appropriation to the academies, having in view principally the design of rendering them more efficient as seminaries for educating Common School teachers; and the addition of the residue of such income to the capital of the Common School Fund. He also recommended the transfer of the general supervision and visitation of the several academies of the State from the Regents of the University to the Secretary of State, in his official capacity as Superintendent of Common Schools—disapproving of the proposed erection of a separate department of public instruction, and suggesting the appointment of an additional deputy to aid the Secretary in the performance of that portion of his official duties pertaining to educational supervision. He commends the efforts in progress for the promotion of popular instruction by the diffusion of education through all ranks of the people, and the devotion of talents and wealth to this great cause, and expresses his conviction that, aided by the powerful co-operation of the Legislature, its advancement may confidently be anticipated.

No definite appropriation of the proceeds of the United States Deposit Fund was made at this session; and the subject went over to the ensuing year.

From the annual report of the Superintendent, it appeared that the appropriation from the revenue of the Common School Fund had now reached the annual sum of $110,000: but that the attendance on the several schools had fallen short of that of the preceding year by nearly 10,000 pupils. This extraordinary and unprecedented diminution the Superintendent attributed, doubtless correctly, "to the prevalence of an absorbing attention in a considerable portion of the community to their pecuniary interests, rather than to the interests of education." It will be recollected that at this period over-speculation and pecuniary extravagance of every kind were more than usually rife—followed, as was inevitable, by a sudden re-action which plunged the business community into severe and protracted embarrassment. "Strong excitements in the community," observes General Dix, "especially when continued for a length of time, are, in their nature, unfriendly to the cause of education; and of such excitements none is, perhaps, so much so, as that which is characteristic of periods when fortunes are amassed without effort and by the mere chances of speculation. In the year 1834, the Common Schools were in better condition, in all respects, than they had been at any previous time; and, as is well known, that year was distinguished by a serious depression in the business affairs of the country. The interests of education seem never to be better secured than in seasons when individuals are compelled to husband their resources, and when the highest as well as the most certain rewards are those which are the fruits of patient industry. *No period seems less propitious to the promotion of those interests than that season of delusive prosperity in which multitudes are tempted, by a few instances of wealth suddenly acquired, to lay aside their accustomed avocations and embark in the precarious pursuits of fortune.*" Words of soberness and wisdom—and applicable in all time!

In his message at the opening of the session of 1838, Gov. Marcy repeats his recommendations of the preceding year, in reference to the disposition of the revenue of the United States Deposit Fund, with the additional suggestion that a portion of this fund be devoted to the purchase of School District Libraries in such districts as should raise by taxation an equal amount to that apportioned for this purpose. He expresses the opinion that the several departments in the academies designated by the Regents of the University for the preparation of teachers for the Common Schools, however ably conducted, must prove inadequate to the supply required, and recommends the establishment of county normal schools, and a contemporaneous increase in the number of academical departments for the education of teachers, the additional expense to be defrayed from the revenue of the deposit fund.

The report of the Superintendent showed a still further decrease of nearly 8,000 in the attendance of pupils during the preceding year.

The Legislature, in substantial accordance with the recommendations of the Governor, passed an act adding the sum of $160,000 from the revenue of the United States Deposit Fund, to the amount to be annually apportioned among the several districts; making the entire sum $275,000 — one-fifth of which, or $55,000, to be annually appropriated to the purchase of suitable books for the several district libraries, and the remainder to the payment of duly qualified teachers. An equal amount was required to be raised upon the taxable property of the several counties and towns, and applied to the same purposes and in the same proportion. The residue of the income from the deposit fund, after deducting certain appropriations to the colleges and academies—the latter to be applied to the benefit of the teachers' departments in the institutions designated by the Regents—was added to the principal of the Common School Fund.

On the 7th of March, the Honorable DANIEL D. BARNARD, from the Assembly Committee on Colleges,

Academies, and Common Schools, submitted a masterly and eloquent report upon the general subject of public instruction, presenting many important and valuable suggestions for the extension and greater efficiency of our systems of popular education. No specific legislative action in accordance with the recommendations of the report was had.

It is due to the memory of Governor MARCY, who, after ably filling the several high positions of United States Senator, Secretary of War, and Secretary of State, under the administrations of Presidents Polk and Pierce, suddenly expired at Saratoga, July 4, 1857, to say that none of his predecessors in the Executive chair manifested a more enlightened appreciation of the interests of Common School education and public instruction generally. His comprehensive mind readily grasped all the details of the system, and his abilities as a statesman, his patriotism as a citizen, and his heart as a man, were warmly enlisted in its support.

His successor in office, Governor SEWARD, at the opening of the session of 1839, availed himself of the earliest opportunity to impress upon the attention of the Legislature the interests of elementary public instruction; expressing his conviction of the paramount necessity of elevating the standard of education; recommending legislative co-operation in the furtherance of efforts to engraft the system of normal school instruction upon our educational institutions through the agency of the academies; strongly commending the establishment and extension of district libraries; and urging the indispensable necessity of a more thorough and efficient visitation and inspection of our Common Schools.

From the annual report of the Superintendent, it

appeared that the number of organized school districts in the State was 10,583, and the number of children under instruction, 529,000. He observes:

"Although the proper objects of public instruction are better understood than they have been at any previous time, the importance of the reform now in progress, through the establishment of district libraries and other agencies, is not perhaps so generally appreciated as it deserves to be. It is but a few years since Common School instruction was ordinarily limited to a knowledge of reading, writing, and arithmetic. The acquisitions which are now regarded as the means of education were then regarded as its objects and ends. *No plan of education can now be considered as complete which does not embrace a full development of the intellectual faculties, a systematic and careful discipline of the moral feelings, and a preparation of the pupil for the social and political relations which he is destined to sustain in manhood.* It must be conceded that the standard of Common School education in this State falls far short of the attainment of these objects; but the aim of its friends is to introduce into the established system such improvements as shall ultimately secure their accomplishment. Is this a visionary hope? Those who are most familiar with the practical workings of the system believe that it is not. *The whole reform will be accomplished by furnishing each school district with a competent teacher.* The application of the remedy is certainly surrounded with difficulties. It must be accomplished by the gradual progress and influence of opinion." * * * "There is reason to hope and believe that opinion will gradually accomplish what it seems difficult, if not impossible, to secure by compulsory measures. No people are more quick-sighted as to their true interests than the inhabitants of this State. They cannot fail to see that the education of their children will be best secured by employing competent teachers, and that the avenues to wealth and distinction, though open to all, are beset with difficulties for those who enter them without the mental preparation which is necessary to enable them to contend successfully against more favored competitors."

On the subject of DISTRICT LIBRARIES, the Superintendent remarks:

"Common School libraries are, in the strictest sense, institutions for the benefit of the people. They are, like the Common Schools, among the most effectual means of correcting, as far as human regulations can correct them, those inequalities of condition which arise from superior advantages of fortune. The intellectual endowments of men are various, and it is therefore in the order of nature that individuals shall not enter on equal terms into competition with each other for the acquisition of wealth, honor, and political distinctions. But it is in the power of human government to guard, to a certain extent, against greater inequalities, by providing proper means of intellectual improvement for all. Under any circumstances, however, those whose pecuniary means exempt them from the necessity of devoting any portion of their time to manual or intellectual exertion have an advantage over those who are compelled to gain a subsistence by their own industry. The time which may be devoted by the latter to intellectual cultivation is often extremely limited; and they will labor under still greater disabilities, if the facilities for improvement within their reach are scanty and imperfect. By raising the standard of Common School education to the greatest possible elevation, the duty of the Government will be fully discharged, so far as the foundations of moral and intellectual character are concerned, and it can do nothing further but to place within the reach of all the means of improving themselves by reading. The children of men of wealth will always be supplied with books from their own resources; but the children of those who are unable to purchase libraries must, at the termination of their Common School course, be deprived in a great degree of the means of improvement, unless public libraries are established and placed within their reach. Common School libraries are therefore particularly calculated to benefit persons of limited means, and they should comprise works on all subjects of practical usefulness, as well as books designed to excite a taste for reading. The mechanic and the farmer should be enabled to draw from them the knowledge which is necessary to enable them to make the most beneficial application of their own powers, by teaching them how to render the laws of nature subservient to their use. * * * * * *

"However great may be the advantages to result to individuals from an extensive diffusion of books, these are considerations of far less importance than the public benefit which it promises. An intellectual and reading community is far more secure against the prevalence of vice and a taste for the grosser gratifications, than an unenlightened people. The standard of moral character will advance to a certain extent as knowledge is diffused; for, whatever effort may be made to distinguish intellectual from moral culture, by those who contend that the former is not of itself a safeguard against depravity and crime, the cultivation of the mental faculties is so intimately related to the improvement of the moral sentiment that it is hardly possible the connection should be wholly dissolved."

The Superintendent also makes a strong appeal to the Legislature for the passage of a law upon the basis of that of Massachusetts, securing by compulsory enactment the instruction of children employed in manufacturing establishments.

It appears also from the report that the sum of $2,241,200 had been invested, throughout the several school districts of the State, in the building of school houses and the purchase of sites; that the annual expense of supplying such buildings with fuel, at $10 each, was $102,060; and the annual expense of supplying the several schools with text-books, at fifty cents for each pupil, was $264,456.50. The amount raised by rate-bill for the payment of teachers' wages, over and above the public money received from the State and raised by county and town taxation in accordance with law, was $477,875.27, making the whole sum, including the public money, expended for the support of Common Schools upward of $1,000,000.

In referring to the subject of *moral and religious instruction* in the schools, Gen. DIX has the following sensible, pertinent, and judicious remarks:

"However desirable it may be to lay the foundation of Common School education in religious instruction, the multiplicity of sects in this State would render the accomplishment of such an object a work of great difficulty. In Massachusetts it is provided by law that no school-book shall be used in any of the schools 'calculated to favor any religious sect.' In this State no such legal provision has been made: but the natural desire of every class of Christians to exclude from the schools instruction in the tenets of other classes has led to the disuse, by common consent, of religious books of almost every description, excepting the BIBLE and NEW TESTAMENT, which are used in more than one hundred towns as reading books.

"The spirit of jealousy by which the schools are surrounded, regarded as they are as most efficient instruments in the formation of opinions, will probably render this state of things perpetual; and it is of the greater importance, therefore, that *moral instruction and training should constitute a principal branch of the system of education.* No teacher can receive a certificate of qualification from the inspectors unless they are satisfied as to his moral character. In this respect the inspectors cannot be too rigid in their scrutiny. A teacher whose moral sentiments are loose, or whose habits of life are irregular, is an unfit instructor for the young, whatever may be his intellectual acquirements, or his skill in communicating knowledge. The lessons of moral truth which are taught at the domestic fireside, and the examples of moral rectitude which are there displayed, will be in danger of losing all their benefits, if the school-room does not reinforce them by its sanctions. If neither the atmosphere of the family circle nor of the school is free from impurity, to what other source can the young resort for those principles of morality which shall render their intellectual improvement subservient to useful purposes, and without which it might become an instrument to be wielded for the annoyance of their fellows and for their own destruction? Though moral principles may have their origin in the heart, it is not to be expected that their proper development can be effected amid the perpetual counteraction of hostile influences.

"Moral cultivation should, therefore, be one of the first objects of Common School instruction. The great doctrines of ethics, so far as they concern the practical rules of human conduct, receive the intuitive assent of all; and with them may be combined instruction in those principles of natural religion which are drawn from the observation of the works of nature, which address themselves with the same certainty to the conviction, and which carry to the minds of all observers irresistible evidence of the wisdom, the beneficence, and the power of their Divine Author. *Beyond this it is questionable whether instruction in matters of religious obligation can be carried—excepting so far as the school districts may make the* BIBLE *and* NEW TESTAMENT *class-books; and there can be no ground to apprehend that the schools will be used for the purpose of favoring any particular sect or tenet, if these sacred writings, which are their own safest interpreters, are read without any other comment than such as may be necessary to explain and enforce, by familiar illustration, the lessons of duty which they teach.*

"In connection with this subject, it is highly gratifying to consider that the religious institutions of the country, reaching, as they do, the most sequestered neighborhoods, and the Sabbath schools, which are almost as widely diffused, afford ample means of instruction in the principles and practice of the Christian faith. In countries where ecclesiastical affairs are the subject of political regulation, there is no difficulty in making religious instruction the foundation of education by arrangements independent of the action of those whom it immediately concerns. But the policy of our law is to leave the subject where it may most properly be left—with the officers and inhabitants of the school districts."

On the 4th of February, the Hon. JOHN C. SPENCER, of Ontario, was appointed Secretary of State and Superintendent of Common Schools. In passing from the administration of Gen. DIX to that of his successor, it is scarcely necessary to observe that the exertions of the former, during the six years in which the interests of the Common Schools were committed to his charge, in the elevation and expansion of the system of popular education, were unsurpassed by any of his predecessors. The impress of his clear, discriminating, and cultivated mind was stamped upon every feature of that system;

and the order, arrangement, and harmony which pervaded all its parts, were due not less to the ceaseless vigilance of his supervision than to the symmetry and beauty of the system itself. In 1837, under the authority of the Legislature, he collected together and published a volume of the decisions of his predecessor and himself, embracing a full exposition of nearly every provision of the School Act; establishing upon a permanent basis the principles of future interpretation, and exerting a highly beneficial influence upon the councils and proceedings of the officers and inhabitants of the several districts, in repressing litigation, and in defining the powers, privileges, and responsibilities of those called to the performance of any duty in relation to the Common Schools. The system of District School Libraries was also organized and put into successful operation under his immediate supervision; and to his clear and convincing exposition of the principles upon which that useful and beneficent institution was based, the ends it was designed to subserve, and the objects it was capable of accomplishing, a large share of the success which has attended its establishment is unquestionably due.

Since the close of his official term as Secretary of State and Superintendent of Common Schools, Gen. Dix has served with distinction and ability as a Senator of the United States, Secretary of the Navy under the administration of President Buchanan, a Major-General in command of an important military department in the war of the Rebellion, and Minister Plenipotentiary to the court of St. Cloud at Paris. He is now an honored and universally respected resident of the city of New York.

THIRD PERIOD.—1839 TO 1845.

ADVANCEMENT.

SECTION I.—ADMINISTRATION OF SECRETARY JOHN C. SPENCER—1839 TO 1842.

Character of John C. Spencer.—Messages of Governor Seward.—County Visitors of Common Schools.—Their Report.—Education of the Children of Foreigners.—Condition of the Schools.—Capital of the Common School Fund—Appropriation and Expenditure of.—Free Schools.—District Libraries.—Teachers' Departments in Academies.—County Superintendents.—District School Journal.—Graded Schools in Cities and Villages.

WE now enter upon a most important period in the history of the Common School system—important not only as the initiation of the great policy of county supervision, and the almost entire reconstruction of the system, through the energies of a master mind, but as the definitive adjustment and settlement of the disturbing element of religious sectarian controversy, and the establishment of an organization from which sprung into vigorous existence the present magnificent system of public school instruction in the city of New York.

JOHN C. SPENCER, to whose hands this great interest of the State had now been committed by the Legislature, was in every respect a most remarkable man. Possessed of transcendent intellectual endowments and unimpeachable moral worth, and having faithfully availed himself of the amplest facilities for extensive scholarship and professional celebrity, he united to those elements of success and future distinction an indefatigable industry, untiring perseverance, and an intense love of intellectual labor, which, in combination with a peculiar and extraordinary faculty for the comprehension and mastery of the most intricate *details* of every subject to which he directed his mind, enabled him to grasp, as with hooks of steel, all its essential features, and with unerring precision and accuracy to reach his conclusions. However complicated and involved the problem to be solved, and whatever expenditure of time and labor might be required for its complete evolution,

> "The Gordian knot of it he could unloose,
> Familiar as his garter."

Possessed of a mind "gigantic in its comprehension and microscopic in its accuracy," from the revision and codification of the entire body of the laws of the State, extending over a period of more than half a century, to the minutest architectural details of a country school-house, with its out-buildings and appendages, and from an exhausting judicial investigation of the tangled and mysterious labyrinths of a great crime, involving the character of an ancient and wide-spread institution, to the most obscure recesses of the pigeon-holes of the State Department under his charge—no enterprise was too vast—no detail too humble—for his capacious energies. Often remaining at his desk—heaped with a chaotic accumulation of papers which, under no circumstances, would he permit any one to disturb in the minutest manner, and from which no one but himself could lay hands upon any particular document required—until two or three o'clock in the morning, his rapid step and explosive closing of the doors of his official sanctum uniformly announced his presence long before noon of the ensuing day; and woe to any rash or inconsiderate trifler who should venture, without adequate and weighty reasons, to intrude upon his labors. So rigid was his discipline, and so well known were his habits in this respect, that on one occasion the worthy and venerable Deputy Secretary, Mr. CAMPBELL, in ignorance of the quality of his distinguished guest, ignominiously ejected no less a personage than WASHINGTON IRVING, who had innocently entered the inner sanctuary with a view of turning over some of the ancient Dutch records for the illustration of his immortal works. The speedy arrival of the Secretary, however, in company with the Governor (Seward), led to a full explanation, recognition, and apology; but the sensitive author of the "Sketch Book" could not be persuaded again to enter the forbidden precincts, and remained for several days in the prosecution of his labors in the clerks' department.

Mr. SPENCER was a son of Chief Justice AMBROSE SPENCER, who was a brother-in-law of DE WITT CLINTON; and, through the influence of these distinguished men and his own superior abilities, assumed at an early period a prominent political position. In 1817, he represented the Ontario District in Congress, and in the following year became an unsuccessful candidate for the position of United States Senator; in 1820, he was elected Speaker of the Assembly; in 1825, Senator from the Eighth District, in which body, as chairman of the Literature Committee, he rendered, by his able reports, as has been previously seen, most important aid in the development and advancement of the Common School system; in 1827, he was appointed one of the Revisers of the Laws of the State; in 1829, by Governor VAN BUREN, special counsel for the prosecution of the perpetrators of the Morgan outrage—a position which he soon after abandoned in disgust on the allegation that his exertions for the elucidation of the mystery and the exposure of its guilty accomplices were paralyzed by the complicity of the Executive Department, in the hands of Governor THROOP, with the leading members of the Masonic fraternity, in their efforts to suppress investigation; and in 1831 and 1833, he was again returned from the county of Ontario to the Assembly, in the deliberations and discussions of which he took a conspicuous part. His duties as one of the Revisers of the State Laws occupied him in the intervals of his other professional, legislative, and executive associations, for a period of more than twenty years, growing out of continued changes in the laws, judicial interpretations, and the frequently recurring necessity of republication. Previous to the expiration of his official term in October, 1841, he was appointed Secretary of War in the cabinet of President TYLER, from whence he was subsequently transferred to the head of the Treasury Department; and died a few years since at his residence in Albany. His passions were strong and impetuous—chastened and sobered, however, by time, domestic sorrows, and a life-long adherence to the Christian faith. He was essentially a great and good man, and of him, it may truly and pertinently be said

"Take him for all in all,
We ne'er shall look upon his like again."

Deeply impressed with the necessity of a more thorough and efficient supervision and inspection of the several schools, Mr. SPENCER, immediately upon entering upon his official duties as Superintendent, with characteristic energy and decision, procured the passage of a law authorizing the appointment by him of a

County Board of Visitors, whose duty it should be gratuitously to visit the Common Schools within their jurisdiction, and to report to the Superintendent the results of their examination, with such suggestions for the improvement of these institutions as they might deem expedient. These visitors were selected from the most intelligent citizens of the several counties, without distinction of party, and entered with promptitude and efficiency upon the discharge of their duties under specific and detailed instructions from the department.

Among their number was the Rev. Dr. ALONZO POTTER, then of Union College, Schenectady; the Rev. Drs. WHITEHOUSE and DEWEY, of Rochester; the Hon. JABEZ D. HAMMOND and D. H. LITTLE, Esq., of Otsego; JAMES WADSWORTH, of Geneseo; FRANCIS DWIGHT, Esq., of Geneva; JAMES W. BEEKMAN, of New York; THOMAS LEGGETT, Jr., of Queens; ANDREW W. LEGGETT, of Westchester; SALEM TOWN, of Cayuga, and others of equal ability and talent. Most of the Common Schools of the State were visited by them, and a mass of valuable information respecting their condition and prospects, accompanied by important suggestions for their improvement, obtained and communicated to the Legislature. With great unanimity, they recommended the plan of an efficient and systematic County supervision, under the general direction of the Department, as a substitute for the existing inefficient method of town inspection.

In his message at the opening of the session of 1840, Governor SEWARD thus adverts to the subject of elementary education:

"Although our system of public education is well endowed, and has been eminently successful, there is yet occasion for the benevolent and enlightened action of the Legislature. The advantages of education ought to be secured to many, especially in our larger cities, whom orphanage, the depravity of parents, or some form of accident or misfortune, seems to have doomed to hopeless poverty and ignorance. Their intellects are as susceptible of expansion, of improvement, of refinement, of elevation, and of direction, as those minds which, through the favor of Providence, are permitted to develop themselves under the influence of better fortunes. They inherit the common lot, to struggle against temptations, necessities, and vices; they are to assume the same domestic, social, and political relations; and they are born to the same ultimate destiny.

"The children of foreigners, found in great numbers in our populous cities and towns, and in the vicinity of our public works, are too often deprived of the advantages of our system of public education, in consequence of prejudices arising from difference of language or religion. It ought never to be forgotten that the public welfare is as deeply concerned in their education as in that of our own children. *I do not hesitate, therefore, to recommend the establishment of schools in which they may be instructed by teachers speaking the same language with themselves, and professing the same faith.* There would be no inequality in such a measure, since it happens, from force of circumstances if not from choice, that the responsibilities of education are in most instances confided by us to native citizens, and occasions seldom offer for a trial of our magnanimity by committing that trust to persons differing from ourselves in language or religion. Since we have opened our country and all its fullness, to the oppressed of every nation, we shall evince wisdom equal to such generosity by qualifying their children for the high responsibilities of citizenship."

From the annual report of the Superintendent, it appeared that the whole number of school districts in the State, on the 1st of January, 1839, the date of the reports, was 10,127; the number of children under instruction, 537,229—or an increase of 28,316 over the preceding year; the average number attending each school, 55; the average term of instruction during the year, eight months; the aggregate amount of public money expended, including the sum raised by the several boards of supervisors, in conformity with law and under special statutes, in the cities of New York, Albany, Brooklyn, and Buffalo, by voluntary taxation in towns, and from permanent local funds, was $374,411.61, which, together with the sum of $521,477.49, paid by parents on rate-bills, amounting in all to $895,889.10, was applied to the payment of the wages of duly qualified teachers—being an excess of $82,130.91 over the amount so expended in 1837. Adding the interest on the money invested in the several school-houses, the expense of fuel, books, slates, and stationery, repairs, collectors' fees, and compensation to commissioners and inspectors, amounting in all to $886,124.81, the entire estimated expense for the support of the schools during the year 1838 was $1,782,013.91, or an average cost of instruction for each child of $3.20. The average compensation of male teachers, assuming female teachers as employed for half the time at $5.50 per month, was estimated at $16.60 per month—the average compensation of such teachers in 1831 having been only $11.85, and in 1837 about $14.

The productive capital of the Common School fund, ...	$1,988,009.63
Added to that portion of the principal of the United States deposit fund which furnishes the income of $165,000 provided by law, viz.	2,750,000.00
Shows the actual productive capital to be, in 1840, ...	$4,738,009.63

"The Superintendent doubts whether this capital needs any further provision for its enlargement. While public beneficence is bestowed in such a degree as to stimulate individual enterprise, it performs its proper office. When it exceeds that limit, it tempts to reliance upon its aid, and necessarily relaxes the exertions of those who receive it. The spirit of our institutions is hostile to such dependence; it requires that the citizens should exercise a constant vigilance over their own institutions, as the surest means of preserving them. A direct pecuniary contribution to the maintenance of schools identifies them with the feelings of the people, and secures their faithful and economical management." * * * "In the State of Connecticut, the large endowment of the public schools produced lassitude and neglect, and in many instances the funds were perverted to other purposes, to such an extent that an entire change in the system became necessary.

"Free schools partake so much of the nature of charitable institutions that those who can possibly afford to educate their children at select schools will do so, in preference to sending them to the district schools for gratuitous instruction, and thus a practical distinction would be created between the children of the republic, hostile to the spirit of our Government, and inimical to those just feelings of equality among our citizens which constitute genuine republicanism. In cities, where there are large numbers who would not be instructed at all if free schools were not provided, the evil must be encountered, as being less in degree than that of total ignorance. But in the country districts such destitution rarely exists, and when it does, provision is made by law for gratuitous instruction in each particular case."

It will be perceived from this extract that Mr. SPENCER participated in the fears of his predecessors, that any considerable change in the proportions subsisting between the public fund derived directly from the State, and the contributions of individuals by local taxation and rate-bills, would necessarily prove detrimental to the true interests of Common School education. "*Nous avons changé tout cela!*" Fully assenting to the proposition that no increase of the fund drawn *directly from the State treasury*, from the avails of the sale of public lands, and other sources *independent of taxation*, would be desirable, and conceding that such additional endowment might probably have a tendency to relax the exertions and diminish the interest of individuals, we have, upon full and mature consideration and discussion, established the principle, and from experience ascertained the fact, that a system of *general taxation* on the valuation of the real and personal property of the inhabitants of the State, properly assessed, and distributed throughout its various counties and towns upon an equitable standard, *equal to the supply of whatever deficiency* may remain after the application of the public funds provided as above mentioned, so far from producing any tendency to relaxation or indifference in the public interest to the welfare and improvement of the schools, will and does, under proper supervision, immeasurably increase such interest, elevate the standard of education, and more generally and universally diffuse its blessings.

Departments for the instruction of Common School teachers having been established by the Regents of the University, under the act of 1838, in seven additional academies, reports had been received by the Superintendent from those previously designated, and from the following institutions designated under the act, viz.: Amenia Seminary, Dutchess county; Albany Female Academy; Troy Female Seminary; Genesee Wesleyan Seminary, Livingston county; Cortland Academy; Rochester Collegiate Institute, Monroe county; and Ithaca Academy, Tompkins county. These reports indicate, in the judgment of the Superintendent, the exertion of a favorable influence upon the character and qualification of teachers. The standard had been raised, the demand for competent teachers increased, and the supply augmented. He recommends a still further increase of these departments, and an increase in the allowance to them from the public funds.

Several thousand district libraries had been procured during the year reported, from the avails of the fund provided for that object, and regulations prescribed by the Superintendent for their use.

On the 13th of April, the Superintendent transmitted to the Legislature the reports of the several Visitors of Common Schools, accompanied by a condensed abstract of their views and suggestions, together with a full exposition of his own, in reference to the various proposed improvements and modifications of the system. "It has already been shown to the Legislature," he observes, "from the official returns, that at least one-half of all the schools in the State are not visited at all by the Inspectors. The reports of the Visitors show that the examinations of the Inspectors are slight and superficial, and that no benefit is derived from them. Many of the Boards unhesitatingly recommend the abolition of the office. The Superintendent is constrained to express his concurrence in these opinions." He recommends the appointment of DEPUTY SUPERINTENDENTS of Common Schools for each county, and expatiates upon the signal advantages to be secured to the interests of the Common Schools by the adoption of a system of visitation at once so comprehensive and efficient. He dissents from the views of the Visitors as to the expediency of establishing normal schools in each county for the instruction and preparation of teachers, being of the opinion that the existing system of academical departments for this purpose was preferable, and he accordingly concurs in the recommendation of his predecessor for their increase. He strongly urges the establishment, under the patronage of the State, of a *District School Journal*, to be exclusively devoted to the promotion of education; the attainment, if practicable, through the organization of some general society, of a uniformity of text-books for the use of schools; some adequate provision for the *vaccination* of children attending the Common Schools; the introduction of *vocal music*, as a branch of elementary instruction and practice; the extension of the official terms of commissioners and trustees, and the annual election of one of their number; the voluntary organization of county boards of education, and of town, county, and State associations for the improvement of Common School education; the establishment in the cities and larger towns of *graded schools*, under the charge of a local superintendent; and several minor reforms in the details of the existing system.

On the 15th of April, the Honorable JOHN A. KING, from the Committee on Colleges, Academies, and Common Schools of the Assembly, submitted an elaborate report, accompanied by a bill embracing substantially the improvements and modification of the system recommended by the Superintendent. This bill passed the Assembly on the 12th of May subsequently; but no definite action was had upon it in the Senate for want of time.

Gov. SEWARD again called the attention of the Legislature to the subject of public education, in his message of 1841, in the following terms:

"The number of children attending the Common Schools is about 570,000, and the whole number of children between five and sixteen years of age, as nearly as can be ascertained, is about 600,000. There are about eleven thousand Common School districts in the State, in all of which schools are maintained during an average period of eight months in the year. Of these school districts there are very few which have not complied with the act providing for the establishment of school district libraries. Although an injudicious choice of books is sometimes made, these libraries generally include history and biography, voyages and travels, works on natural history and the physical sciences, treatises upon agriculture, commerce, manufactures, and the arts, and judicious selections from modern literature.

"Henceforth, no citizen who shall have improved the advantages offered by our Common Schools and the district libraries will be without some scientific knowledge of the earth, its physical condition and its phenomena, the animals that inhabit it, the vegetables that clothe it with verdure, and the minerals under its surface; the physiology and the intellectual powers of man; the laws of mechanics, and their practical uses; those of chemistry, and their application to the arts; the principles of moral and political economy; the history of nations, and especially that of our own country; the progress and triumph of the democratic principle in the governments on this continent, and the prospect of its ascendency throughout the world; the trials and faith, valor and constancy of our ancestors; with all the inspiring examples of benevolence, virtue, and patriotism exhibited in the lives of the benefactors of mankind. The fruits of this enlightened and beneficent enterprise are chiefly to be gathered by our successors. But the present generation will not be altogether unrewarded. Although many of our citizens may pass the district library, heedless of the treasures it contains, the unpretending volumes will find their way to the fireside, diffusing knowledge, increasing domestic happiness, and promoting public virtue.

"When the census of 1850 shall be taken, I trust it will show that within the borders of the State of New York there is no child of sufficient years who is unable to read and write. I am sure it will then be acknowledged that when, ten years before, there were thirty thousand children growing up in ignorance and vice, a suggestion to seek them, wherever found, and win them to the ways of knowledge and virtue by persuasion, sympathy, and kindness, was prompted by a sincere desire for the common good. I have no pride of opinion concerning the manner in which the education of those whom I have brought to your notice shall be secured; although I might derive satisfaction from the reflection that, amid abundant misrepresentations of the method suggested, no one has contended that it would be ineffectual, nor has any other plan been proposed. I observe, on the contrary, with deep regret, that the evil remains as before; and the question recurs, not merely how, or by whom, shall instruction be given, but whether it shall be given at all, or be altogether withheld. Others may be content with a system that erects free schools and offers gratuitous instruction; but I trust I shall be allowed to entertain the opinion that *no system is perfect that does not accomplish what it proposes; that our system is therefore deficient in comprehensiveness in the exact proportion of the children that it leaves uneducated; that knowledge, however acquired, is better than ignorance; and that neither error, accident, nor prejudice ought to be permitted to deprive the State of the education of her citizens.*

"Cherishing such opinions, I could not enjoy the consciousness of having discharged my duty if any effort had been omitted which was calculated *to bring within the schools all who are destined to exercise the rights of citizenship; nor shall I feel that the system is perfect, nor liberty safe until that object be accomplished.* Not personally concerned about such misrepresentations as have arisen, but desirous to remove every obstacle to the accomplishment of so important an object, I very freely declare that I seek the education of those whom I have brought before you, not to perpetuate any prejudices or distinctions which deprive them of instruction, but in disregard of all such distinctions and prejudices. I solicit their education, less from sympathy, than because the welfare of the State demands it, and cannot dispense with it. As native citizens they are born to the right of suffrage. I ask that they may, at least, be taught to read and write; and in asking this, I require no more for them than I have diligently endeavored to secure to the inmates of our penitentiaries, who forfeited that inestimable franchise by crime, and also to an unfortunate race which, having been plunged by us into degradation and ignorance, has been excluded from the franchise by an arbitrary property qualification incongruous with all our institutions. *I have not recommended, nor do I seek, the education of any class in foreign languages, or in particular creeds of faith;* but fully believing, with the author of the Declaration of Independence, that even error may be safely tolerated where reason is left free to combat it, and therefore indulging no apprehension from the influence of any language or creed among an enlightened people, *I desire the education of the rising generation in all the elements of knowledge we possess, and in the tongue which is the universal language of our countrymen.*

"TO ME THE MOST INTERESTING OF ALL OUR REPUBLICAN INSTITUTIONS IS THE COMMON SCHOOL. I seek not to disturb, in any manner, its peaceful and assiduous exercises, *and least of all with contentions about faith or forms. I desire the education of all the children in the commonwealth in morality and virtue, leaving matters of conscience where, according to the principles of civil and religious liberty established by our constitution and laws, they rightfully belong.*"

It is eminently due to this great statesman, whose long and patriotic services in the national councils, since his retirement from the executive chair of his native State, have endeared him to the Republic as one of its most honored and cherished sons, to say, in this connection, that none of his distinguished predecessors in the Executive Department manifested greater interest or a more enlightened appreciation of our system of public instruction than himself. During a period of more than ordinary political excitement, his views were, to a considerable extent, misinterpreted and misunderstood; but the lapse of time, and a more impartial and dispassionate judgment, have abundantly vindicated the soundness of his principles and the purity and elevation of his motives. He is still among us—a veteran voyager, in the decline of a long and useful life, over the vast continents of the new and old world—a welcome visitor alike in the remotest territories of the United States, in Mexico, and in China; and long may he survive to enjoy a fame and a respect unrestricted by geographical limits, and confined to no nationalities in the circuit of the civilized world!

The annual report of the Superintendent presented the following condition of the financial affairs of the system:

Amount of public money apportioned by the State from the avails of the Common School and U. S. Deposit Funds..	$275,000 00
An equal amount raised by the Board of Supervisors of the respective counties.......	275,000 00
Amount raised by voluntary tax in towns....................	5,896 22
Received from the proceeds of local funds..................	20,531 65
Balance of unexpended funds of preceding year.............	1,674 91
Amount raised under special statutes in New York, Brooklyn, Albany, and Buffalo..........................	86,192 19
Total amount of public money...................	$664,294 97

The falling off during the year reported, in the amount raised by voluntary taxation in the several towns, was upward of $30,000, owing, unquestionably, to the great increase of the public fund.

The expenditures for the year reported (1839) were as follows:

From the public money apportioned and paid....	$535,429 79
From parents on rate-bills	476,443 27
Total amount expended for teachers' wages.......	$1,011,873 06

The contributions of the inhabitants of districts on rate-bills were also less by more than $49,000 than that of the preceding year.

Adding to the total amount thus expended for teachers' wages, the interest on school buildings, expense of repairs, fuel, stationery, text-books, collectors' fees, and compensation of commissioners and inspectors...... ...	913,458 00
And the total amount expended for all purposes in the support of schools for the year 1839 was....... ....,.	$1,924,331 06

The average wages of male teachers had risen to $18, and of females to $6, per month, which the Superintendent regards as "very gratifying."

With the view of ascertaining the practical operation of the academical departments for the instruction of teachers, the Superintendent had delegated the Rev. Dr. POTTER, of Union College, and D. H. LITTLE, Esq., of Otsego, personally to examine these departments and report as to their condition and efficiency for the purposes of their establishment. Both gentlemen submitted favorable reports as to the value and fidelity of the duties performed and the results obtained in these institutions. Professor POTTER, however, suggested that valuable as were, undoubtedly, the benefits thus secured, other and still more efficient agencies might be devised "for training a class of teachers with more especial reference to country Common Schools and to primary schools in villages and cities—teachers whose attainments should not extend much beyond the common English branches, but whose minds should be awakened by proper influences—who should be made familiar by practice with the best modes of teaching—and who should come under strong obligations to teach for at least two or three years. In Prussia and France, normal schools are supported at the public expense; most of the pupils receive both board and tuition gratuitously, but at the close of the course they give bonds to refund the whole amount received unless they teach under the direction of the government for a certain number of years. That such schools, devoted exclusively to the preparation of teachers, have some advantages over every other method, is sufficiently apparent from the experience of other nations; and it has occurred to me that, *as a supplementary to our present system, the establishment of one in this State might be eminently useful. If placed under proper auspices, and located near the Capitol, where it could enjoy the supervision of the Superintendent of Common Schools, and be visited by the members of the Legislature,* it might contribute in many ways to raise the tone of instruction throughout the State."

The Superintendent expressed his conviction that these academical departments ought not to be abandoned, but should be sustained and encouraged, and their number increased. He observes:

"The standard of instruction in their vicinity has been raised, the desire for competent instructors has increased, their wages have advanced, the demand for them has augmented, and a general influence in favor of primary education, of the most salutary character, has been diffused."

"Normal schools," he continues, "which are so strongly urged by some, must, after all, be essentially like those departments and the academies in which they are established. There must be a board of managers or trustees, teachers, a building, books, and apparatus. These are already furnished by the existing academies; and there can be no intrinsic defect in them which should prevent their being made as useful as any normal school. The change of name will not change the real nature of the institution. The sum of money which would be requisite to purchase ground, erect buildings for one normal school, and fit them for the purpose, would enable at least ten academies to maintain similar schools in buildings already prepared, and under managers already organized. The Superintendent does not mean to underrate those schools, nor to depreciate the benevolent motives of those who recommend them. He acknowledges, and, indeed, earnestly urges, the inestimable value and absolute necessity of institutions in which our youth may be prepared for the business of teaching. But he would use the means we already have on hand for the purpose, without incurring, what seems to him, the needless expense of providing others of a similar character. He would respectfully recommend the extension of the public patronage *to all the academies in the State*, to enable them to establish teachers' departments; and *in those counties where there are no academies, the establishment of normal schools*."

The number of volumes in the several district libraries was 422,459, and the amount of library money expended for this purpose during the year 1840—the first year after its distribution—was $94,098.56. The selections of books—chiefly from the series published by the Messrs. HARPER & BROTHERS—were in all respects admirable and satisfactory to the Superintendent, to whose judgment the works were submitted. The Superintendent observes:

"It is impossible to contemplate the fruits already realized from this part of our system of public instruction, without the highest gratification. The circulation of half a million of valuable books among our fellow citizens, without charge and without price, is a greater benefaction to our race than would be the collection in any one place of ten times the number of volumes. And when we reflect that in five years there will be *two millions* of such books in free and constant circulation among those who most need them, and who are most unable to procure them—whose minds will thus be diverted from frivolous and injurious occupations, and employed upon the productions of the learned and wise of all ages—we shall find ourselves unable to set bounds to the mighty influences that will operate upon the moral and intellectual character of our State. No philanthropist, no friend of his country and her glorious institutions, can contemplate these results, and the incalculable consequences they must produce upon a population of nearly three millions of souls, without blessing a kind Providence for casting our lot where the cultivation and improvement of the human mind are so eminently the objects of legislative care, or without feeling that every citizen in his station is bound to forward the great work, until we are as intelligent as we are *free*."

"In reference to the improvement of the Common Schools, the Superintendent has various suggestions to make. * * * Public instruction, like every other institution of our country, depends on the voluntary action of the people. Laws may be passed and systems devised, but they will have no vitality until put in motion by those for whom and on whom they are to operate. Time is essential not only to the full comprehension of any system on such a subject, but also to accommodate ourselves to its requirements, and to form those habits which are necessary to its complete execution. And in the enterprise of voluntary public instruction by a whole community, a generation may well be required to give it efficiency. Those who are impatient for that high degree of improvement which, all hope, will ultimately crown our efforts, incur the hazard of exciting despondency, when they overlook or depreciate what has been done, and represent the labor of twenty-five years as nugatory. Justice to the subject, as well as to those who have preceded us, requires that we should examine the authentic accounts of our progress, and ascertain what it really has been.

"In 1815, returns were received from 2,631 districts, in which there were 140,706 children instructed. In 1840, 10,597 districts sent in their reports, showing that 572,995 children had attended their schools. In 1815, $46,308 were paid from the treasury toward defraying the compensation of teachers, and in 1840, $220,000 were paid from the same source for the same purpose. By a previous statement it appears that the people have contributed in taxes for the support of schools $275,000, and that they have voluntarily paid in sustaining them $913,458—making a total of $1,188,458, contributed by a population of 2,432,000, of whom, probably, not one-sixth were either taxed or in any way called on to share in those expenses. A people who have thus freely expended their money, and appropriated their private means for the education of their children, to an amount nearly double the expense of administering their government, cannot, with any truth or justice, be said to be indifferent to the subject. And when we find thirty thousand trustees of school districts gratuitously rendering their services, and making their returns with order, regularity, and promptitude, we ought not to deny their appreciation of the value of the labor in which they engage, nor their merit in performing it. It is no slight proof of the value of a system which is thus administered without compulsion. Its fruits are seen in the education of one-fourth of our entire population, and of nearly every child of a proper age for the primary schools; in the advance of the wages paid to teachers—a clear indication that a higher degree of talent is employed and appreciated; and in the interest almost universally excited among our fellow citizens of every class in the success of our efforts.

"Still, like every human institution, it is susceptible of constant improvement. This is not to be accomplished by sudden changes which derange the machinery, and which, when effected, will probably be found to require alteration; and least of all, by those schemes which are so comprehensive as to be incapable of practical execution. Amendments, when experience has indicated their necessity, may be gradually incorporated in the system without obstructing it; and the introduction of new elements to aid, invigorate, and sustain what we have, and in keeping with it, will be more likely to accomplish their purpose than if they were antagonistic to what is already established.

"The great object of our solicitude is the elevation of the standard of education. Although so many children are learning to read and write and cipher, yet, with such means as are provided, they ought to learn much more. How is this to be accomplished? In the judgment of the Superintendent, mainly by the action of public opinion, and to some, although a very limited, extent, by legislation. *The first requisite is the employment of teachers who can impart a greater amount and a higher degree of instruction.* That such are to be found in our State no one can doubt. But they must be induced to present themselves by the same considerations which influence all men in their pursuits—the respectability of the employment and the certainty of adequate remuneration. Both of these depend upon public sentiment. If the community be not awakened to a sense of the value and dignity of the vocation, and are not prepared to do it justice, no system of organization, however perfect, and no amount of public beneficence expended upon the schools, will call into action the requisite qualifications. Indeed, the bounty of government will retard, if it do not paralyze, those spontaneous efforts which spring from a conviction of their necessity. If the citizen supposes that the public treasury will provide the means of employing teachers, he will have no solicitude on the subject, and one of the great principles of human action implanted in the heart of man—that which places his affections where his treasure is—ceases to operate. He will abandon the care of the whole matter to those who have undertaken to provide for its expense."

Intelligent agitation of the public mind—"the great moving power of modern times"—is, then, in his judgment, primarily to be resorted to; and for this purpose he renews his recommendation of the establishment of a journal to be exclusively devoted to the interests of primary education, and to be sent to every district at the public expense. As the official organ of the department, for the communication of instruction to school officers of every grade, respecting the general and specific duties, and an exposition of the laws in controverted cases, and as a general medium of information to teachers, parents, and pupils, such a journal, in his opinion, would prove eminently serviceable to the inhabitants, officers, and teachers of the several districts.

"The appointment of *local superintendents*," he continues, "would also have a most beneficial effect upon public sentiment. The information they could communicate, and the views they might present in public addresses, and the associations they might form, could not fail to imbue the public mind with the importance of good schools, and with the necessity of individual effort to sustain them. The whole subject would be made familiar to the people; they would come to understand that it was one in which they were most interested, and their zeal would be as effectually excited as it has been by similar means on other topics of social interest.

"Weighty as these considerations are, in favor of local superintendents, there are others which are perhaps still more impressive. *A regular supervision is indispensable to the success of every public or private undertaking.* There is not a department of the Government which is not subject to some direct and immediate control, and no individual appoints an agent for the management of any business without reserving and exercising a superintendence over him. Conscious of the absolute necessity of such a provision in the Common School system, the framers of the law endeavored to secure it by the election of town inspectors. But the object has not been obtained. The official reports show to what extent even the duty of simple visitation has been neglected. And when the nature of these visitations is considered, it will be obvious that if they were as frequent as might be desired, they could not accomplish the great purpose in view. To be of any avail, the inspection of schools must be conducted by those who are competent to judge of the qualifications of the teacher, and of the progress of the pupils, by examinations in the different studies pursued, and to suggest such improvements and modifications as will enable the student to derive the greatest amount of benefit from the schools. And time must be devoted not only to the schools and their masters, but to the trustees and inhabitants. It is no disparagement to our fellow-citizens usually chosen inspectors, to say that generally they have not themselves acquired the knowledge of the subject which is necessary to qualify them for the discharge of these duties; and it is very certain that they have not the time to bestow in their performance. As just and proper links connecting the schools with the people, and as useful auxiliaries to a county superintendent, I am convinced, upon further reflection, that they ought to be retained.

"*All writers on public education concur in the unanimous and decided opinion, that effectual supervision and inspection are more essential to the proper management of schools, and more indispensable to their improvement, than any other agency, or all agencies combined*; and the Superintendent does not hesitate to express his conviction that, until they are provided, all efforts to improve the condition of the schools, or to extend the range and elevate the character of the instruction in them, will be utterly hopeless; and he seriously apprehends that, instead of advancing, they will retrograde, and that we shall lose much of what we now have. M. Cousin, the celebrated author on popular education, attributes the success of the schools in Holland almost entirely to the constant and unremitting inspection to which they are continually subjected; and demonstrates that wherever schools have failed in other countries to meet the public expectation in the degree and amount of instruction, it has been owing to the want of such supervision.

On the 26th of May, the Legislature, by a nearly unanimous vote in both branches, passed the act drawn up by Mr. SPENCER, and reported by the literature committees of the two houses, providing for the appointment by the Board of Supervisors of each county of the State, biennially, of a COUNTY SUPERINTENDENT of Common Schools, whose duties and powers were specifically prescribed, and who was charged with the general supervision and inspection of the schools within his jurisdiction. The number of town inspectors was reduced to two; provision made for the establishment of schools for the instruction of colored children; a subscription for as many copies of the "District School Journal," edited by FRANCIS DWIGHT, of Geneva, as would be sufficient to supply each school district; and various minor amendments in the details of the system made.

In accordance with one of the provisions of the act, S. S. RANDALL, of Albany, then a clerk in the department, was appointed, by Mr. SPENCER, General Deputy Superintendent of Common Schools, with power to discharge all the duties of the Superintendent in his absence, or in case of any vacancy in the office.

Eight additional academies were designated by the Regents of the University, in which departments for the education of teachers were to be established, viz.. Hamilton Academy, Madison county; Hobart Hall Institute, Oneida county; Rensselaer Oswego Academy, Oswego county; Franklin Academy, Steuben county; Fredonia Academy, Chautauqua county; the Grammar School of Columbia College and the University, in the city of New York; and Washington Academy, Washington county—making twenty-three in all.

In October of this year, Mr. SPENCER was transferred to a seat in the cabinet as Secretary of War, and his official duties as Superintendent temporarily devolved upon the General Deputy.

From the annual report of that officer, in January, 1842, it appeared that an increase of 30,588 pupils in the several Common Schools had taken place during the year reported (1840); that the aggregate amount expended for the support of the schools, including the public money, the sum raised by county and town taxation, special statutes in cities, local funds, contributions on rate-bills, fuel, repairs of school buildings, text-books, &c., exceeded the sum of $2,000,000, of which $90,000 were expended in the purchase of books for the several district libraries, and $463,470.54 in the payment of rate-bills; and that the number of volumes in the libraries was 630,125, upward of two thousand having been added during the past year. The entire capital of the Common School fund had now reached the sum of $5,810,947.98. County Superintendents had been appointed in each of the counties of the State, and had entered upon the discharge of their respective duties with spirit and efficiency. In the cities of Buffalo, Rochester, Brooklyn, Troy, Utica, and Hudson, the public schools had been organized under special statutes, larger and commodious school buildings erected, a specific course of instruction adopted, and city superintendents appointed by the respective boards of education or common councils, charged with the general supervision and inspection of the schools. In many of the larger villages of the State, union and high schools had been established, and were in successful operation.

Section II.—The Religious Controversy in the City of New York—1840 to 1842.

Application of Trustees of Catholic Free Schools to the Common Council.—Remonstrance of the Public School Society.—Decision of the Common Council.—Application to the Legislature.—Report of Secretary Spencer.—Reply of Commissioners of School Money.—Message of Governor Seward.—Report of the Acting Superintendent of Common Schools.—Establishment and Organization of the Ward School System.—Exclusion of Sectarian Teaching.—Recognition of the Christian Scriptures, without Note or Comment.

EARLY in 1840, application was made by the trustees of the several Roman Catholic free schools in the city of New York, in conjunction with the prominent and most influential members, clerical and lay, of that religious body, for an equal participation of their schools with those of the Public School Society in the distribution of the public funds provided by the State for educational purposes. The petitioners represented themselves as dissatisfied with the organization and management of the Public School Society, which had been hitherto allowed to monopolize the business of public instruction in the city and to control its funds, wholly independent of the interests and wishes of the tax-payers, and regardless of the conscientious scruples and religious convictions of a large proportion of the citizens; that although the Society belonged to no particular religious denomination, and did not professedly attempt to teach directly the distinctive creeds of any particular sect, still its schools were practically sectarian, and its books and general tone of instruction so strongly biased in favor of Protestantism, that nearly eight thousand children under the charge of the petitioners, and with whose secular education they desired to combine daily instruction in the principles of their own faith, were prevented, from conscientious scruples, from participating in their benefits, though the petitioners, and those entertaining similar views with themselves, were heavily taxed for their support.

To these allegations the Trustees of the Public School Society responded, that so far from constituting a monopoly, as asserted by the petitioners, their association was open, under the provisions of the law by which it was created, to every citizen contributing the small sum of ten dollars to its corporate funds; that the administration of those funds and of the system of instruction committed to their charge was placed under the most strict supervision by and responsibility to the city and State authorities, and was open to public inspection and scrutiny at all times; that after an official visitation of their schools, and a thorough examination of their discipline, conduct, and methods of instruction, by officers appointed for that special purpose by the Superintendent of Common Schools, that public functionary had himself borne the most explicit testimony to their efficiency and value; that the utmost pains had been uniformly taken to eliminate from their course of study, from their text-books, and from the instruction communicated to their pupils, every taint of sectarianism; and that, from the constitution of the religious body to which the petitioners belonged, and whose special views they represented, the distinctive tenets and peculiar faith of Roman Catholicism must unavoidably enter as a prominent element into their system of instruction, thereby contravening the entire educational policy of the State as declared in its fundamental law, and the repeated decisions of the Common Council, whenever this question had heretofore been presented for their consideration.

A full hearing of all parties interested was had before the Common Council. The great importance of the principles involved in the discussion, the respectability and powerful influence of the petitioners, the interests involved in its final decision, and the talent enlisted on both sides, gave to the controversy a character of peculiar gravity and excitement. During its progress, large public meetings were called for the discussion of its merits, the press of the city took an active interest in its determination and in the principles involved, and the pulpits of the various religious sects faithfully reflected the views and wishes of their respective congregations. The two most prominent and conspicuous champions of the conflicting parties to the controversy were the late Archbishop (then Bishop) HUGHES and HIRAM KETCHUM, Esq.

The Common Council, by a nearly unanimous vote in both branches, declined to entertain the application of the petitioners, and re-affirmed the principles established by its decision in 1824 and again in 1832, "that the school fund of the State was purely of a civil character, designed for civil purposes, and that the intrusting of it to religious or ecclesiastical bodies was a violation of an elementary principle," only to be departed from in the case of orphan asylums under the charge of such religious bodies.

Undismayed by the repulse they had thus again sustained, the applicants promptly transferred the scene of conflict from the Common Council to the State Legislature. During the session of that body in 1840, several memorials were presented from large numbers of Roman Catholic citizens of New York, setting forth that the legislative enactments on the subject of public instruction in that city required, in the judgment of the memoralists, a fundamental alteration, to bring the benefits of Common School education within the reach of all classes of the population; that the original intent of those enactments was to enable every school which should comply with the law to share in the Common School Fund; that this design has been defeated by the construction put upon the statutes by the Common Council of the city, in designating the Public School Society to receive nearly the whole amount of that fund belonging to the city; that this Society, being a corporation, had acquired the entire control of the system of public education; that the tax-payers who contribute to the fund had no voice in the selection of those who administer the system, or control over the application of the public moneys. They deprecated the influence of such a corporation as dangerous and detrimental to the public interests; and complained of injustice to those whose conscientious scruples had, as they alleged, been disregarded in the system of instruction adopted by the Society. They represented that there were other schools in the city equally entitled to participate in the bounty of the State, but which, with nearly eight thousand children, were excluded from any of its benefits under the existing system; and prayed that every school established by the taxable inhabitants of the city might be entitled to a distributive share of the public school moneys, and that the control and administration of the system itself might be placed in charge of persons chosen by the electors and taxable inhabitants of the city.

These memorials, together with the remonstrances of the trustees and members of the Public School Society and others, were referred, toward the close of the session, to the Secretary of State (Mr. SPENCER), who, for want of time, was unable to report until the ensuing year. In his annual report as Superintendent of Common Schools, however, of the same year, he had alluded to this subject in connection with the number of children in the State, not included in the official reports, as under instruction in the public schools: "There are free schools," he observes, "attached to each of the seven Roman Catholic churches, at which more than five thousand children are taught six hours in each day. Although established by a particular denomination, they are open to all children without discrimination, and are, in fact, attended by those of different denominations. These are supported by the voluntary bounty of their pious and charitable founders. They do not participate in the distribution of the school fund, and consequently are not included in any return. It is known that other denominations have large free schools supported in a similar manner and without aid from the school fund; but none of them are supposed to be so numerous as those above mentioned." After stating that upward of a hundred and forty-one thousand dollars had been raised during the preceding year in that city, by local taxation, independently of $34,172.47 of the public money apportioned to the schools, he continues: "It would seem but just that all who contribute, directly or indirectly, to this fund, and especially those who paid their share of the taxes laid to obtain it, should participate in its benefits. The Common Council of New York has full power to apply the remedy and to apportion the public money among the free schools established by all the different denominations." He accordingly suggests a legislative provision, applicable to the entire State, authorizing the local authorities charged with the distribution of the public money in the several cities to apportion it among the free schools and orphan asylums, according to the number of children instructed in each for the period of four months in each year. "Independent of considerations of humanity," he observes, "independent of the obligations which rest on us as Christians, we have all a deep stake, as members of the same civil community, in the instruction of the destitute, who are destined either to become useful members of society, or to fill its prisons."

At the ensuing session of 1841, the memorials and remonstrances of the respective parties to the controversy were renewed—the message of Gov. SEWARD, as well as that of the preceding year, having, as will already have been seen, taken strong ground in behalf of the general claim set forth by the petitioners to an equal participation in the bounty of the State. These petitions and remonstrances were again referred by the Senate to Secretary SPENCER, who, on the 26th of April, made an elaborate report, from which, notwithstanding the space they occupy, it has been deemed expedient, not only from the great interest of the topics discussed, and the vital importance of the principles involved, but from the signal ability displayed in the treatment of the subject, to present liberal extracts.

After setting forth the principal allegations of the memorialists, the Secretary proceeds:

"At the last session, memorials of a similar character from a large number of Roman Catholic citizens of New York were referred to the undersigned, upon which he was unable, during that session, to report. Although these petitioners have the same equal and common rights with all other citizens to submit their grievances to the Legislature, and ask for redress, yet the circumstance of presenting themselves in the character of a religious denomination is, in itself, unfavorable to that impartial consideration of the subject which its importance demands. The hazard is incurred of giving to a question broad as the whole territory of our State, and comprehending all its inhabitants, an aspect of peculiarity, as if it concerned only those who preferred their complaints. But great injustice would be done to the subject by this mode of considering it. It embraces interests vital to the well-being of the whole community: it involves the destiny of thousands of the children of the Republic who are hereafter to take their share in the management of its affairs, and are to become good citizens or miserable outcasts—who are to sustain the laws, and assist in the preservation of peace and good order, or to fill our dungeons and prisons, and occupy our scaffolds. In the contemplation of such results, the *denominations* and *parties* into which society is divided, cannot be regarded, except so far as a just and well-ordered government is bound to protect, equally and impartially, the civil and political rights of all."

The Secretary proceeds to review the history of the legislation in reference to the apportionment and distribution of the public money in the city of New York, and of the organization and subsequent proceedings of the Public School Society, which we have had occasion heretofore to chronicle in detail.

"Thus," he continues, "by the joint operation of these various acts, and the ordinances of the Common Council, designating the schools of the Society as the principal recipients of these moneys, the control of the public education of the city of New York, and the disbursement of nine-tenths of the public moneys raised and apportioned for schools, were vested in this corporation. It is a perpetual corporation, and there is no power reserved by the Legislature to repeal or modify its charter. * * * *

"In the last report of the commissioners for school money in the city and county of New York, dated in July, 1840, it is stated that the number of schools subject to the visitations of the commissioners has increased to 115; of these, 98 are under the direction of the Public School Society. The same report states that the average number of scholars on the *registers* of these schools, during the year, was 22,955, and the number in average *attendance* 13,189. This great disparity is accounted for by the absences and irregular attendance of the pupils."

After stating the testimony borne by the report of the visitors appointed by him as Superintendent, under the authority of law, to the commodious school buildings, good teachers, excellent system of instruction, and efficient supervision provided by the society, he says:

"Certain it is that the trustees have exhibited the most praiseworthy zeal and devotion in the discharge of the great trust devolved on them; and many, if not all of them, have spared no exertions to bring into their schools the destitute children of the city.

"Notwithstanding these favorable results, the memorials referred to the undersigned complain of the operation of a system which, in fact, devolves upon any private corporation the discharge of one of the most important functions of the government without that responsibility to the people which is provided in all other cases. They allege that, in its administration, the conscientious opinions and feelings of large classes of citizens are disregarded; that other schools, maintained for the same objects, and accomplishing the same benevolent results, are arbitrarily excluded from all participation in a common fund collected by the joint contributions of all; and that a fearfully large portion of the indigent children are not reached, or in any way benefited, by the system of public education which now prevails. These are objections of the most weighty character, and cannot be overlooked by those whose duty and inclination alike prompt them to regard the greatest good of the greatest number. The merits of the Public School Society, the devotion and energy of its trustees, and the success of its schools, cannot and ought not to prevent an investigation to ascertain whether it is not necessarily limited in its operations—whether it accomplishes the main purpose of its organization—or whether its continuance violates essential and fundamental principles, and thus presents a perpetual source of irritation and complaint. The question to be determined is far more broad and comprehensive than the merits of any particular society. It involves the inquiry whether the intentions of the Legislature have been fulfilled, to furnish the means of education 'to all those who are destined to exercise the rights of citizenship.'

"There are numerous other schools in the city of New York, founded by voluntary associations, in which many thousands of the children of poverty and distress receive their education, imperfect and deficient as it may be in many instances. By a participation in the funds intended for the benefit of all, their means of extending the sphere of their usefulness will be augmented; and by extending to all who desire to exercise it the right of participating in the same means, new schools may be established, and temples of education be made as numerous as the nurseries of vice. It can scarcely be necessary to say that the founders of these schools, and those who wish to establish others, have absolute rights to the benefits of a common burthen; and that any system which deprives them of their just share in the application of a common and public fund must be justified, if at all, by a necessity which demands the sacrifice of individual rights for the accomplishment of a social benefit of paramount importance. It is presumed no such necessity can be urged in the present instance. On the contrary, the views which will be subsequently presented afford strong ground for the belief that the education of a much larger number than now are, or under any circumstances may be expected to be, provided for by the Public School Society, or any one society, will be secured by inviting the co-operation and stimulating the exertions of all who are disposed to engage in the enterprise.

"The complaint that in the schools of the Public School Society the conscientious opinions and feelings of our fellow-citizens are disregarded may, at first, appear unreasonable. But when it is considered that the best of men adhere, with a tenacity proportioned to the strength and sincerity of their convictions, to those principles of religious faith upon which, in their estimation, their present and eternal welfare depends, and that they regard as the most sacred of duties the inculcation of those principles in the minds of their children, we ought not to be surprised at their anxiety to exclude all that is hostile to their views from the establishments to whose care they are invited to commit the education of their offspring. With many, the transmission of their own creeds to these objects of their affection is a part, and a most essential part, of their own religious profession, and any influences which interrupted it would be deemed by such an invasion of their most sacred rights.

"Some of the memorialists complain that the tendency of the instruction received in the schools of the Public School Society is unfavorable, if not hostile, to those principles of faith which they hold dearer than life itself; and they allege that, consistently with their views of religious duty to their children, they cannot send them to such schools. On the other hand, those who oppose any change in the present system express their apprehensions that by allowing to all schools a free and equal participation in the school moneys, the public funds will be applied indirectly, if not directly, to the inculcation of religious dogmas of all descriptions; and some are peculiarly apprehensive of the possible extension of certain doctrines which they deem erroneous and injurious. Thus the question of sectarian influences is mutually raised, with its usual aggravations. This is a question from the consideration of which some may feel disposed to shrink, from a vague and indefinite terror of the consequences of its discussion. But it is believed there is a mode of considering it without participating in the feelings of any side, but viewing all as having common and equal rights, and animated by the same spirit of beneficence which will avoid conflict with every thing but prejudice, and conduct to safe and salutary conclusions.

"According to the principles of our institutions, no one has the authority to determine whether the religious doctrines and sentiments of any class of our citizens be right or wrong. The immunity of the Constitution and of an unequivocal public sentiment is thrown around the religious faith and profession of all our citizens; and whether a particular creed is professed by a humble minority or a powerful majority can make no other difference than to excite, in the first case, the generous forbearance of those who may temporarily have the physical power to oppress, and to animate them to the strictest fidelity to their obligations. The only object which our fellow-citizens can have is the education of all the children of the commonwealth in literature, morality, and virtue. 'No system is perfect, nor can liberty be safe, until all who are destined to exercise the rights of citizenship are brought within the schools.' '*Knowledge, however acquired, is better than ignorance*; and neither error, accident, nor prejudice ought to be permitted to deprive the State of the education of her citizens.' These principles, recently promulgated by the highest executive authority in our State, have received the cordial and entire approbation of our fellow-citizens. In approaching the subject in the same spirit which dictated them, and in endeavoring to reconcile prejudices, we must not ourselves commit the error of ascribing improper designs or erroneous principles to others. *If there be error, let reason be enlightened to combat it, if there be prejudice, let the humanizing and liberalizing influences of education be brought to bear upon it. Let not error and prejudice be perpetuated by being shut up and excluded from the light of science.*

"The object, then, being to procure education at all events, if not the best we could desire at first, yet to have education extended to all classes, in the assured hope of its continual improvement, we are to maintain the perfect equality of all our citizens in the enjoyment of their rights in determining the religious character of such instruction. Hence the first inquiry to be made is, whether these rights can be maintained under a system which vests in any permanent body or set of men the control of the public education of a city?

"The great object to be attained is the education of the greatest number possible. If we cannot, at once, have that education in the most perfect form, or in the highest degree, still, much is accomplished in having the good seed sown. It will not only fructify, ripen, and expand, but it will enrich the soil in which it is cast, and each successive harvest will be more rich and abundant than its predecessor. If the alternative be presented of having a limited number of schools, in which instruction of the highest grade is imparted, but from which one-half the proper subjects of education are absent, or of having a large number of lower pretensions and less efficiency, but so organized and situated that all may attend, and affording strong grounds for the belief that nearly all will be gathered within them, it would seem that there ought to be no hesitation in the choice, and that the portals of knowledge ought to be at once thrown open as widely as possible, with the certainty that improvement will follow the very first elements of instruction.

"It is very true that the government has assumed only the intellectual education of the children of the State, and has left their moral and religious instruction to be given at the fireside, at the places of public worship, and at those institutions which the piety of individuals may establish for the purpose. *But it is believed that in a country where the great body of our fellow-citizens recognize the fundamental truths of Christianity, public sentiment would be shocked by the attempt to exclude all instruction of a religious nature from the public schools: and that any plan or scheme of education in which no reference whatever was had to moral principles founded on these truths would be abandoned by all.* In the next place, it is believed such an attempt would be wholly *impracticable. No books can be found, no reading lessons can be selected, which do not contain, more or less, some principles of religious faith, either directly avowed or indirectly assumed.* RELIGION AND LITERATURE HAVE BECOME INSEPARABLY INTERWOVEN, *and the expurgation of religious sentiments from the productions of orators, essayists, and poets, would leave them utterly barren.*

"Viewing the subject, then, practically, it may be regarded as a *settled axiom in all schemes of education intended for the youth of this country, that there must be, of necessity, a very considerable amount of religious instruction.* The trustees of the Public School Society have, probably, no more in their schools than could be well avoided. While they profess, and doubtless sincerely, their readiness to omit everything that may justly be regarded as offensive, they yet *maintain, and properly, that education is imperfect without inculcating moral and religious principles; and hence they allow the* READING OF THE SCRIPTURES, *or portions of them, and* INCULCATE THE LEADING PRINCIPLES OF CHRISTIANITY. But it is impossible to perceive how even these principles can be taught, so as to be of any value, without inculcating what is peculiar to some one or more denominations, and denied by others. * * * Even the reading of the text of our common translation of the Scriptures is objected to by many, on account of its being, as they allege, erroneous and imperfect; while others deem its perusal by children, without explanation, positively injurious. Even the moderate degree of religious instruction which the Public School Society imparts, must, therefore, be *sectarian;* that is, it must favor one set of opinions, in opposition to another or others; and it is believed that this always will be the result in any course of education that the wit of man can devise.

"If these views are sound, this dilemma is produced: that while some degree of religious instruction is indispensable, and will be had, under all circumstances, it cannot be impartial without partaking, *to some extent,* of sectarian character, and giving occasion of offense to those whose opinions are thus impugned. But, fortunately, there is a mode of escape from the difficulty. That mode will be found in a recurrence to the fundamental principles engrafted in our Constitution, by which no law can be passed, 'respecting an establishment of religion, or prohibiting the free exercise thereof,' and by which 'the free exercise and enjoyment of religious profession shall forever be allowed in this State to all mankind.' Those by whom our government have hitherto been administered have found that practical effect could be given to these principles only by scrupulously abstaining from all legislation whatever on those subjects which involved, or were in any way connected with, religious faith, profession, or instruction; and in this course of proceeding the people have found such a safeguard against oppression—such a security against the dissensions and animosities of intolerance and bigotry—and such a gauranty of peace and tranquillity—that it has been constantly, and under all vicissitudes, unanimously approved by them.

"On this principle of what may be termed *absolute non-intervention* may we rely to remove all the apparent difficulties which surround the subject under consideration. In the theory of the Common School law which governs the whole State, except the city of New York, it is fully and entirely maintained; and in the administration of that law, it is sacredly observed. No officer, among the thousands having charge of our Common Schools, thinks of interposing by any authoritative direction, respecting the nature or extent of moral or religious instruction to be given in the schools. Its whole control is left to the free and unrestricted action of the people themselves, in their several districts. The practical consequence is, that each district suits itself, by having such religious instruction in its school as is congenial to the opinions of its inhabitants; and the records of this department have been searched in vain for an instance of a complaint of any abuse of this authority in any of the schools out of the city of New York. * * * * * It is manifest that the great source of the difficulties in New York arises from a violation of this principle. * * * * *

"If there is not entire fallacy in all these views—if the experience of twenty-five years, derived from the school districts of the interior is not wholly worthless—then the remedy is plain, practical, and simple. *It is by adopting the principle of the organization that prevails in the other parts of the State*, which shall leave such parents as desire to exercise any control over the amount and description of religious instruction which shall be given to their children the opportunity of doing so. This can be effected by depriving the present system in New York of its character of universality and exclusiveness, and by opening it to the action of smaller masses, whose interests and opinions may be consulted in their schools, so that every denomination may freely enjoy its "religious profession," in the education of its youth.

"To this plan objections have been made, that it would enable different religious denominations to establish schools of a sectarian character, and that thereby religious dissensions would be aggravated, if not generated. It is believed to have been satisfactorily shown that there must be some degree of religious instruction, and that there can be none without partaking more or less of a sectarian character; and that even the Public School Society has not been able, and cannot expect to be able, to avoid the imputation. *The objection itself proceeds on a sectarian principle;* and assumes the power to control that which it is neither right nor practicable to subject to any domination. *Religious doctrines of vital interest will be inculcated, not as theological exercises, but incidentally, in the course of literary and scientific instruction;* and who will undertake to prohibit such instruction?

* * * * * * * * *

"It is believed to be an error to suppose that the absence of all religious instruction, if it were practicable, is a mode of avoiding sectarianism. *On the contrary, it would be, in itself, sectarian; because it would be consonant to the views of a particular class, and opposed to the opinions of other classes.* Those who reject creeds, and resist all efforts to infuse them into the minds of the young before they have arrived at a maturity of judgment which may enable them to form their own opinions, would be gratified by a system which so fully accomplishes their purposes. But there are those who hold contrary opinions; and who insist on guarding the young against the influence of their own passions and the contagion of vice, by implanting in their minds and hearts those elements of faith which are held by this class to be the indispensable foundations of moral principles. This description of persons regard neutrality and indifference as the most insidious forms of hostility. It is not the business of the undersigned to express any opinion on the merits of those views. His only purpose is to show *the mistake of those who suppose they may avoid sectarianism by avoiding all religious instruction.*"

The Secretary proposes that the schools and houses of the Public School Society, together with its admirable arrangement and constant supervision, should be retained, and placed on an equal footing, in all respects, with other organizations. He regards it, however, as "an anomaly wholly unknown in any other department of the public service, that a private corporation, existing independently, not amenable in any form to the laws or to the Legislature, should be charged with what those laws regard as a part of the functions of the government—the disbursement of public moneys at its own will and pleasure—the selection of teachers, of whose qualifications it is the sole judge—and the establishment and maintenance of a system of public education according to its own ideas of propriety."

"However acceptable," he observes, "the services of such a society may have been, in the first imperfect effort to establish Common Schools; however willing the people may have been to submit to an institution which promised immediate benefit; and however praiseworthy and successful may have been its efforts—yet it involves a principle so hostile to the whole spirit of our institutions, that it is impossible it should be long sustained amid the increased intelligence which its own exertions have contributed to produce; especially when other and more congenial means of attaining the same objects have been pointed out, and when, therefore, the necessity which called it into existence has ceased. The public attention is now roused to the subject; and many thousands of the citizens of New York demand the right of controlling, through responsible public agents, the education of their children, and the application of common funds to which they have contributed for a common object. We must not forget that we live under a government of the people before such a demand can be effectually resisted. Procrastination and delay will only increase its urgency, render it more exacting, and multiply the difficulties of satisfying it. * * * It must succeed, sooner or later; and it is the part of wisdom and of duty to yield to that which is just in itself, promptly, and before agitation and excitement deprive acquiescence of all merit. We are not at liberty to say that our fellow citizens who make this claim are incapable of performing the duty which they would undertake. Our constitutions admit their competency to manage all the affairs of government; and the foundations of our *whole* system must be overturned before we can deny to them the capacity to determine on the mode, manner, and extent of instruction to be given to their offspring."

"And yet in this, as in every public business, the energies of the people require a system to regulate and conduct them to the best results. Such a system, emanating from agents of their own selection, and maintained, controlled, and superintended by them, will command the confidence and invite the co-operation of their constituents. This may be accomplished by the choice of commissioners of Common Schools, in each ward of the city, who should form a board, to which some degree of permanency may be given by allowing the election of one-third each year—which board should take the entire charge of the Common Schools of the city; receiving and disbursing the public funds; establishing schools, and a system for their government and inspection; and providing the means of testing the qualifications of teachers. They might be aided by a city superintendent, with such compensation as should secure the best talent and the whole time of the incumbent; and then leave the schools to the management of trustees chosen by those who established them, and to the general laws of the State."

In reply to this able and masterly report of the Secretary, the Public School Society and its friends, through the Commissioners of school moneys for the city of New York, in their annual report to the Superintendent, of May, 1841 (probably from the pen of HIRAM KETCHUM, Esq.), entered into an elaborate vindication of the constitution and general administration of the Society—of the system of education initiated by them and thus far successfully pursued, by the distinct admission of the Secretary himself and of the board of visitors appointed by him as Superintendent; of its results as shown by the number of children annually instructed in its hundred schools; and of its entire amenability to public and rigid scrutiny and responsibility through the Common Council, as the depositary of the entire control of the distribution of the public money appropriated to its support. Its superior claims upon the public confidence and regard were also fully conceded by the proposition of the Secretary himself to include its schools and all its property as a portion of the new organization proposed. To the allegation that "in the administration of the Society, the conscientious opinions and feelings of large classes of citizens were disregarded, and that other schools maintained for the same objects and accomplishing the same benevolent results were arbitrarily excluded from a participation of a common fund collected by the joint contribution of all," the Commissioners, after deprecating the indefiniteness of general allegations of this nature, presenting no tangible point for specific examination, proceed to infer from the discussions and publications of the views of the memorialists:

"That the violence imputed against conscientious opinions and feelings is to those of a part of the Catholic communion, who alone constitute the large classes of citizens alluded to; that the schools attached to their churches, governed by trustees of their own appointment, conducted according to their precepts of religious faith, and ministering, as may well be inferred, to children only of their own denomination, are the schools said to be maintained for the same objects and accomplishing the same benevolent results as those of the Public School Society; and that the arbitrary exclusion from a participation in the common fund, collected by the joint contribution of all, which is complained of, is the refusal by the immediate representatives of the people of the city of New York to devote a portion of the public moneys toward the support of schools erected and governed by the Catholic denomination, and inculcating their distinguishing forms and creeds.

"That the objects and results of institutions," they continued, "founded and acting upon principles so widely different as those which distinguish the schools of the sect and those of the Society, cannot be very similar, is too apparent to need illustration; and if the disregard of the conscientious opinions and feelings of large classes of citizens, in the administration of the Society, consists, as is inferred, in maintaining a perfect impartiality toward the several denominations in the schools—not giving reasonable offense, nor yielding submission to any—the Society has done no more than to be faithful to the purposes for which it was created. The motive to its incorporation is stated in the charter to be the education of *all* children, *without regard to the religious sect or denomination to which their parents belong*; and it would have been a plain infraction of their duty to fashion the exercises of the schools according to the requirements of any particular church.

"The allegation remains that the sect is arbitrarily excluded from a participation of a common fund collected by the joint contribution of all.

"In adopting a system of general education at the public expense, the object of the State was to give to its youth such an education as would fit them to discharge the civil obligations of this life, leaving it to their natural and ecclesiastical guardians to prepare them, through a parental and spiritual ministry, to render their account in another world. There ought to be, and there must be, some common platform on which all the children who are destined to act as citizens of the same republic may obtain their secular education. To that general training all the children are entitled; but it is the *public* who are to determine on its particulars and conditions, and not the parents who may claim it for their offspring. That a fund has been raised by the taxation of all, for general education, creates no right in the tax-paying sectarian to demand that any portion of it be appropriated to the spread of his particular creed. The tax was imposed on him *as a citizen*, not as the *member of a church*. Its object was to provide for a civil purpose exclusively, not to prepare the path to any designated place of worship. *The erection of a church school announces a sectarian object.* It has its exclusive rules of system and government—is superintended by trustees and teachers of a particular faith—and religious conformity is indispensable to a participation in its direction, which is not and cannot be attained by means of a civil qualification that any citizen may acquire. *It is, in truth, a part of the church establishment;* and the sectarian of another denomination justly feels that *his privileges are equally violated, whether he be taxed for the support of its religious teachers at the school desk, or for that of its religious teachers in the pulpit.* This State has never yet asserted the power to tax its people for ecclesiastical objects; and if its sovereignty comprehends such a power, *the rights of conscience require that the religion of the tax-payer be recorded on the assessment roll, and his contribution be dealt to the encouragement of his own communion.*

"The Commissioners would suggest that any difficulties in regard to such religious education of the children as may be desirable can be removed without a violation of the principles or a departure from the objects of the school system, by an application of the rule said to prevail in Holland in regard to the schools controlled by the government. A time is there set apart when the children of the respective denominations are requested to repair to the appropriate places for their peculiar worship, where they are attended by the proper ministers to their spiritual wants. If the Sabbath and the other day in the week on which the public schools are generally closed be insufficient for this purpose, some additional portion of the week might be dedicated to it. The arrangement would, certainly, throw an additional burden on the clergy without additional pecuniary recompense; but their commendable sense of duty in their sacred office would, no doubt, disregard any consideration of that sort."

The Commissioners then proceed to controvert the allegation of the Secretary, that "a fearfully large portion of the indigent children of the city were not reached or in any way benefited" by the existing system of education. They show, from the official returns of the census of 1840, and other statistics, that the number of whites of the age of twenty and upward in the entire State, unable to read or write, was 43,705, of whom 7,778 resided in the city of New York, and the remaining 35,927 in the rest of the State—being an excess of 1,732 only, in the city, out of a population of 313,000, over its due proportion in comparison with the other counties, other circumstances being equal, and no regard being had to the immense and constant augmentation of the former from foreign immigration; and conclude their report with a searching and exhaustive criticism of the measure proposed by the Secretary.

Governor SEWARD, in his message at the opening of the session of 1842, after stating that 20,000 children in the city of New York were, under the existing system of apportionment, practically unprovided with instruction, thus indicates what he deems the appropriate remedy:

"Happily, in this as in other instances, the evil is discovered to have had its origin no deeper than a departure from the equality of general laws. In our general system of Common Schools, trustees, chosen by tax-paying citizens, levy taxes, build school-houses, pay teachers, and govern schools, which are subject to visitation by similarly elected inspectors, who certify the qualifications of teachers; and all schools thus constituted participate in just proportion in the public moneys, which are conveyed to them by commissioners also elected by the people. * * * I submit, therefore, with entire willingness to approve whatever adequate remedy you may propose, the expediency of vesting in the people of the city of New York, what I am sure the people of no other part of the State would, upon any consideration, relinquish—the education of their children. For this purpose, it is only necessary to vest the control of the Common Schools in *a board to be composed of commissioners elected by the people*, which board shall apportion the school moneys among all the schools, including those now existing, which shall be organized and conducted in conformity to its general regulations and the laws of the State, in proportion to the number of people instructed. It is not left doubtful that the restoration to the Common Schools of the city of this simple and equal feature of the Common Schools of the State would remove every complaint.

"This proposition has, sometimes, been treated as a device to appropriate the school funds to the endowment of seminaries for teaching languages and faiths—thus to perpetuate the prejudices it seeks to remove—sometimes as a scheme for dividing that precious fund among a hundred jarring sects, and thus increasing the religious animosities it strives to heal—sometimes as a plan to subvert the prevailing religion, and introduce one repugnant to the consciences of our fellow-citizens; while, in truth, it simply proposes, by enlightening equally the minds of all, to enable them to detect error wherever it may exist, and to reduce uncongenial masses into an intelligent, virtuous, harmonious, and happy people."

The acting Superintendent of Common Schools (S. S. RANDALL) transmitted to the Legislature, with his annual report, copies of the reports of Secretary SPENCER and the Commissioner of School Money of the city of New York, of the previous year, accompanied with the following remarks:

"After the able and thorough discussion which this subject has received from the highest official sources, it would be presumptuous as well as unnecessary for the undersigned, whatever may be the views which he entertains in respect to it, to interpose any opinion. It is for the wisdom of the Legislature to determine to what extent, and in what mode, an effectual remedy can be devised for the alleged disabilities of a numerous and respectable class of citizens, with reference to the education of their children; whether these disabilities spring from a radical defect in the peculiar system of public instruction prevailing in the metropolis, or from a faulty administration of that system, which may be reached and corrected by means of a vigilant and efficient supervision; and whether the numerous excellences of the plan of instruction connected with the schools of the Public School Society cannot be retained, consistently with such a modification of the present law as shall secure every practicable facility for the education of that large proportion of children now withdrawn, from conscientious or other motives, from the advantages of these schools. The intelligence and discrimination of the people and their representatives may safely be relied upon to separate the peculiar aspect which this question has recently been made to assume, and the excitement in the public mind to which it has given birth, from those high considerations of public policy which an enlightened regard to the paramount interests of universal education and the welfare of the State imperiously demand.

"Our republican institutions recognize no distinction between the professors of different religious creeds; our shores are hospitably open to the inhabitants of every clime; and our systems of education were designed to embrace within their comprehensive regard every child of the Commonwealth of an age sufficient to be benefited by their instruction. With this view, and for this purpose, all our citizens, native and adopted, are called upon to contribute to the expenses incident to the maintenance of those systems, and all have an equal right to participate in their advantages. Any exclusion, therefore, theoretical or practical, from those advantages, of any portion of our citizens, in consequence, or as the result, of peculiar modifications of religious faith, or for any other reason unrecognized by our laws, should, under no pretence, be suffered to exist. Such an exclusion has a direct and powerful tendency to promote the prevalence of ignorance, and its invariable attendants, wretchedness, vice, and crime; while, at the same time, it sanctions the introduction of a new and fatal principle of public policy, deliberately discarded by the wisdom of the framers of our Constitution."

The exciting controversy was finally settled by the passage of an act on the 11th of April, 1842, "extending the provisions of the general act in relation to Common Schools in the city of New York," in accordance with the recommendations of Mr. SPENCER, by whom this act was drawn. A Board of Education, consisting of representatives from each ward, elected by the people, was organized, upon whom was devolved the general administration of the system, comprehending the schools of the Public School Society—reserving to that body, however, the exclusive supervision and direction of the schools under its charge—and confiding the immediate administration of all others to trustees elected in each ward for that purpose. By this and subsequent enactments, the religious question was definitely set at rest by a section providing that "No school shall be entitled to or receive any portion of the school moneys, in which the religious doctrines or tenets of any particular Christian or other religious sect shall be taught, inculcated, or practiced, or in which any book or books containing compositions favorable or prejudicial to the particular doctrines or tenets of any particular Christian or other religious sect, or which shall teach the doctrines or tenets of any religious sect. * * But nothing herein contained shall authorize the Board of Education *to exclude* the HOLY SCRIPTURES, *without note or comment, or any selections therefrom*, from any of the schools provided for in this act; but it shall not be competent for the said Board of Education *to decide what version, if any*, of the Holy Scriptures, without note or comment, shall be used in any of the schools: Provided, that nothing herein contained shall be so construed as to violate the rights of conscience as secured by the Constitution of this State and of the United States." This provision still remains in full force on the statute book of the State.

Section III.—Administration of Secretary Samuel Young—1842 to 1846.

Character of Col. Young.—State Convention of County Superintendents.—State Normal School.—Teachers' Institutes.—Academical Departments for Teachers.—Messages of Governors Bouck and Wright.—Mr. Hulburd's Report.—Favorable Results of the System of County Supervision.—Annual Reports of the Superintendent.—Condition of the Common Schools.—Organization of the Normal School.—Official Correspondence.—The Bible in Schools.

ON the 7th of February, 1842, the Hon. Samuel Young, of Saratoga, was appointed Secretary of State and Superintendent of Common Schools, and entered at once on the administration of the newly reconstructed system, the outlines and principal details of which had been prepared by his distinguished predecessor. Col. Young was, in many respects, an extraordinary man. Possessed of a dignified and impressive appearance and demeanor, of statesmanlike abilities and experience, penetrating intellect, stern morality, he combined with a firm will and strong prejudices the utmost suavity, warm-heartedness, and openness to conviction. On assuming the duties of his office, he publicly avowed, in his most trenchant manner, his thorough conviction of the impolicy and inefficacy of the system of county supervision, and his fixed determination to effect its discontinuance. He was, however, with much difficulty, induced by the friends of the system to be present at the approaching Convention of Superintendents at Utica; and after the deliberations and discussions of that body, he promptly and decidedly retracted his former opinions, and became, throughout his administration and subsequent public career, one of the strongest and most enthusiastic advocates of this plan of local supervision. His social qualities were genial in the extreme—seldom, however, descending to familiarity; his heart "open as day to melting charity;" and his sympathies uniformly with the destitute, the suffering, and the down-trodden. On one occasion the author of this sketch was commissioned by him to convey a most liberal benefaction to an accomplished young lady, to whom he was personally unknown, who had forwarded to him an affecting account of her struggles for the education of herself and a younger sister, dependent upon her, and who, through a concurrence of adverse circumstances, had incurred liabilities beyond her ability to meet. Both her sister and herself became, subsequently, teachers of superior excellence; and she was the first to receive, from his own hands, the highest grade of certificate prescribed by law. On another, he fearlessly braved the penalties of the laws, both of the State and United States, in protecting from arrest, under the Fugitive Slave Act, a negro waiter at his boarding-house; and, in the presence of Chief Justice NELSON—and, it is believed, without special remonstrance from him—after having effectually secured the retreat of the frightened and trembling victim of oppression, and divested himself of his coat, he fearlessly and indignantly confronted the claimant, who shrunk abashed from the stern glance of his eye, and determined attitude of resistance, and at once abandoned all further pursuit as hopeless. It has been said he was at all times open to conviction; but if there was one subject upon which no amount of argument, persuasion, or influence could move him from an inflexible and persistent opposition, it was, unquestionably, what he deemed the improvident and ruinous extension of the popular system of internal improvement by roads and canals. On this topic he omitted no occasion, however apparently inappropriate, to express his views, and denounce those of his opponents.

Col. YOUNG's first appearance in public life was as a member of the lower branch of the Legislature from the county of Saratoga, at the session of 1814; of which body he was elected Speaker in the ensuing year. In 1816, he was appointed one of the Canal Commissioners, which position he retained until 1840. In 1824, he became the Democratic candidate for Governor, against Mr. CLINTON. In 1834, he was elected to the Senate from the Fourth District; and in 1842, appointed Secretary of State. After the close of his official term, he was again returned to the Senate, and from that body retired to his farm in Saratoga, where, amid the quiet seclusion of his "hereditary acres," he closed his long and useful life.

Several petitions were forwarded to the Legislature, during its session of this year, for the repeal of so much of the Act of 1841 as related to the establishment of the office of county superintendent—characterizing it as "uncalled-for, unnecessary, useless, and expensive;" alleging that "its duties were as well, or better, performed by town inspectors;" and that "it was not additional superintendence that was most wanted, but money to pay competent and well-qualified teachers." The Hon. WILLIAM B. MACLAY, of New York, Chairman of the Assembly Committee on Colleges, Academies, and Common Schools, to whom these petitions were referred, submitted, on the 2d of April, an able report adverse to the prayer of the petitioners, which was agreed to by the House.

In this report, after adverting to the origin of the law, in the report of the several county visitors, appointed by Mr. SPENCER, and their statement that a large amount of the public money was, under the then existing system, utterly wasted; that "from one-quarter to one-third of the school children were daily absent;" that "more than half of the school-houses were inconvenient, and unfit for the purposes of education;" and that "a wide-spread and fatal apathy chilled the hopes of reform, and clogged all efforts for improvement"—Mr. MACLAY expresses the conviction of the committee that "the withering want of our schools is not money to pay, but intelligence to appreciate, and interest to sustain, the competent teacher;" that "were our public fund increased until it afforded the means to hire a competent teacher for every district, without the public mind being simultaneously awakened to a juster estimate of the importance of education, and the means of its diffusion, our school-masters would soon sink into hirelings, and become the exponents of the prevailing indifference and faithlessness of the people. We, therefore," he observes, "regard it as one of the most benign effects of this system of supervision, that by its exposure of the defects and evils of the schools, it must compel attention to the necessity of securing competent teachers." After controverting the allegation of the petitioners of the expensiveness of the system, by contrasting it, in this respect, with the operation of its predecessors, he proceeds:

"There is another view of this subject that should be kept before those who fear the expense of supervision. No one will deny that a vigilant and intelligent supervision of the schools is as essential to their operation as to that of any branch of industry. Without careful oversight, no business can flourish, no enterprise will prosper. This principle is understood and acted on in all the common concerns of life. And if our Common Schools, instead of being nurseries where five hundred and sixty-two thousand children daily assemble to prepare themselves for usefulness and respectability, were each to be converted into a workshop or manufactory, and the fruits of the labor thus employed to constitute the revenues of the State, would not a vigilant and thorough supervision be deemed indispensable to the successful prosecution of the business? And need we urge the comparative value of an income to the State of dollars and cents and an income of virtuous, intelligent, and manly citizens, worthy of the soil they inherit, of the privileges they are to enjoy, defend, and transmit to unborn generations? What consummate folly is it, then, to appropriate million upon million for the support of our ten thousand schools—to set them in operation under teachers of doubtful qualifications and little experience—to leave them to go on as they best may, in vain reliance on some supposed inherent self-regulating principle in the system, and yet expect to receive the full benefits which the expenditure of so much money, the services of so many teachers, and the time of so many children ought to confer! The incalculable loss consequent on this vain dependence we leave to others to estimate; our arithmetic has no rules for calculating the worth of that virtue, intelligence, and happiness which the neglect or perversion of the means of education has already lost to the State. * *

"Nor is it by the wasteful application of the public money alone that the State suffers, even in an economical point of view; but infinitely more by impairing the productive energies of the citizens, through a defective and baneful education. Were it necessary, it might be shown, beyond the reach of cavil, that if the sole object of the statesman were to increase the wealth of the people, without having any reference to their intellectual and moral well-being, in no way could it be so rapidly and universally accomplished as by increasing the power intelligently to use the means of prosperity. We have before us the most remarkable statistics on this point, showing that even in those employments which would seem to require but the lowest degree of mental culture, as that of tending the looms in our factories, the operative who has enjoyed the benefits of an ordinary Common School education earns, on an average, 29 per cent. more than his ignorant associates, while he who has improved those advantages earns *forty-four per cent.* more than the same unfortunate and neglected class. And these facts are not inferred from a limited observation, but are the result of extensive investigations made by the distinguished secretary of the board of education of Massachusetts. If, therefore, as we hold is indisputable, the new system of supervision must increase the efficiency of our ten thousand schools, it is certain that instead of adding in any manner to the "expenses" of the several counties, it will largely and beneficently increase their wealth, while it also ensures the wise use and enjoyment of the rewards of intelligent industry. * * * * * * * * * *

"We should fail in duty to your honorable body, and in justice to these officers, did we not express our sincere interest in the result of their important labors. We believe that the value of the office can hardly be overrated; and that if in any county it should fail of utility, it will be chargeable *not on the law, but on an injudicious appointment* under its provisions. In such cases the remedy is in the hands of the boards of supervisors, and should be firmly and prudently applied. But, judging from the communications of these officers already made to the department, we are satisfied that not only is the system working well, but daily gaining a firmly seated popularity. The visitation of districts has been carried on in every county of the State; good methods of teaching have been diffused and bad plans corrected; the interest of parents has been awakened, the ardor of the children excited, the zeal of the teacher aroused and directed; and this has been going on, not in a few districts or a few towns, but in more than ten thousand different districts, and among more than half a million of children. Such an enterprise, so far-reaching and effective, cannot fail to produce a rich harvest of blessings; and we confidently anticipate that it will fast bring on the time when our Common Schools shall become the fit nurseries of a free and virtuous people—when the children of all classes shall be proud to meet on this common platform, there to learn the first great lesson of their common brotherhood as men, and their common destiny as citizens."

On the 4th of May subsequent, a State Convention of County Superintendents, representing forty-two out of the fifty-nine counties of the State, was held at Utica. This convention remained in session three days, and its deliberations were presided over by the Hon. JABEZ D. HAMMOND, of Otsego, the author of the "Political History of New York." In addition to the regular members of the convention, there were present during its entire session, and participating, to a greater or less extent, in its discussions, the State Superintendent, Col. YOUNG; the Hon. HORACE MANN, the distinguished Secretary of the Massachusetts Board of Education, afterward President of Antioch College, Ohio; GEORGE B. EMERSON, of Boston; the Rev. Dr. WILLIAM GALLAUDET, of Connecticut; FRANCIS DWIGHT, of Albany, editor of the District School Journal; the Rev. Dr. ALONZO POTTER, then of Union College, Schenectady; the venerable SALEM TOWN, of Cayuga; Rev. Dr. GRISCOM, of New Jersey; Dr. HORACE WEBSTER, of Geneva College; and other gentlemen of distinction from different sections of the State. The subjects involved, and the marked ability which characterized the discussions, must constitute our apology, if any were necessary, for giving a sketch of its principal features, from the full report of its proceedings in the District School Journal.

Judge HAMMOND, in his remarks on taking the chair, paid a just compliment to the character and services of the several State Superintendents who had, from time to time, presided over the interests of Common Schools, concluding with a special reference to the present incumbent, whom he had known from his entrance into public life, and who, in his judgment, possessed a fitness and capacity for usefulness in the department which he so ably filled unsurpassed by any other man in the State. "If, therefore," he observed, "the system had stood still, or retrograded, the reason for it must be sought not in any want of capacity or attention at the helm, but rather to the fact that, under the former regulations, it was next to impossible for the State Superintendent to be informed specifically of the defects in its management, and where those defects existed. The object of the existing system of county supervision was that every district in the State, however secluded or remote, should be reached, and its minutest operations looked into, to the end that defects might be ascertained and reported, and the correction, if possible, applied. Another high advantage of the system was, that any improvement in the mode of teaching or government, in any portion of the State, whether in a log school-house in the county of Cattaraugus, or in the remote part of the wilds of Hamilton, should be communicated to the State Superintendent, and by him spread all over the State, through its ten thousand neighborhoods."

Letters from Ex-Superintendents DIX and SPENCER, expressive of their continued interest in the welfare and advancement of the Common School system, and regretting their inability to be present, were read; invitations extended to Col. YOUNG and HORACE MANN to address the convention during its session, and, with the other distinguished visitors present, to participate in its discussions; and committees appointed to prepare subjects for its deliberation.

After listening to an able and eloquent address from the State Superintendent, a series of resolutions were presented by Mr. MOULTON, of Oneida, declarative, in general terms, of the duty of the county superintendents to rouse the public interest, by illustrating unceasingly in their lectures, addresses, and published communications, the relations between ignorance and poverty, vice and wretchedness, knowledge and the physical and moral well-being of man; and, in every practicable mode, through their visitations, inspections, and influence, to elevate the standard of education, and extend its blessings. The fifth resolution was as follows:

> "*Resolved*, That the best police for our cities, the lowest insurance for our houses, the firmest security for our banks, the most effective means of preventing pauperism, vice, and crime, and the only sure defence of our country, are our Common Schools; and woe to us if their means of education be not commensurate with the wants and the powers of the people."

Upon this resolution an animated and interesting discussion ensued between Dr. THEODORE F. KING, of Brooklyn; Mr. JACOB C. TOOKER, of Orange; the Rev. Dr. POTTER; HORACE MANN; Mr. A. S. CLEMENT, of Dutchess; and Mr. C. C. W. CLEAVELAND, of Greene. Dr.

KING remarked that the resolution struck upon the very subject in reference to which the convention had assembled—the improvement of Common Schools. The object was to make education common to all, that, like the blessed sun, it might diffuse its radiance throughout the land, lighting up not merely the palace of the wealthy, but the lowly cottage of the poor. When our men of wealth could be taught the important lesson that their greatest interest lay, not in endowing banks and railroads, but in working those mines of inexhaustible wealth which were to be found in every district, then, and not till then, could the responsibilities assumed by the members of the convention be said to be fully discharged. In the county of Kings there were some schools, he was proud to say, that were noble monuments of its enterprise and wealth. In the city of Brooklyn, 3,000 children were in attendance upon the Common Schools; and four of the school-houses had cost $10,000 each. Yet the feeling that should be there was wanting. They who were able to sustain these institutions regarded them with indifference, if not with positive disgust. The reason was, that Common School education had been too common in one sense, and not common enough in another. The standard must be raised. He had succeeded, by unremitting effort, by addresses to neighborhoods, inspectors, trustees, and commissioners, and other means, in arousing a spirit which would ere long manifest itself in good fruits.

Mr. TOOKER objected to the assumption in the resolution that our Common Schools were the best of Common Schools, and, therefore, the best security for safety and order. Our Common Schools were *very bad;* and he suggested the substitution of the words "well regulated Common Schools."

The Rev. Dr. POTTER remarked that the resolution embodied a great many incontestible truths—truths of immense importance just at this time. The radical vice of our Common School system, in his judgment, was not the want of a proper interest in the subject on the part of teachers. It was not the want of a general conviction of the importance of education, for no truth was more firmly riveted in the public mind. The grand difficulty was the prevalent *misapprehension as to what education meant.* The phrase "well regulated Common Schools" was vastly important. That was the great truth they had to press home upon the minds of the people. It was universally admitted that education was indispensable to a free government—to human welfare; but the truth must be as generally recognized, before any radical reform could be effected, that we *might have poor schools.* The great mission to which they were called was the regeneration of the Common Schools—the infusion into them of the elements of a newer and higher life. That was a noble mission, and never were men called to a higher work.

The Hon. HORACE MANN observed that no man could deny that the resolution under discussion contained a most important and indestructible truth. What was wanted was not the education of a few, but the *education of all;* for it was obvious, look into what department of life you would, that a few ignorant and vicious men could baffle all the efforts, and jeopard all the interests, of the great majority of conscientious, able, active men contending against them. One man could destroy, one incendiary could burn, more than a thousand could build up. One bad man, acting antagonistically to the general interests of society, could defeat the efforts of forty-nine out of every fifty in the whole community. Hence the necessity of the *universality of education*. Not education merely in populous cities and towns—not in the centers of towns; but through the remotest bounds of every community—on the borders and confines of civilization—not less than at the metropolis. There were two attributes or qualities belonging to our Common Schools which it was important to present to the consideration of intelligent minds. The first was, the universality with which they might be made to operate, covering the whole surface of society, and reaching the very motives of human action. The law took cognizance only of the outward actions of men—not the spring, the motives, of those acts. Criminal jurisdiction was also local, reaching only a portion of the criminal acts; it applied, probably, only to one in several hundreds of our population. And yet, taking into consideration the property the criminal destroys, what he appropriates to his own use, what he utterly consumes and sweeps out of existence by his incendiarism, the expenses of pursuit and arraignment, the time and money spent in his prosecution and imprisonment, he ventured to say that the sum total necessary, in any community, to vindicate the law, in those few cases where it can be vindicated at all, would exceed the sum expended for the education of the entire community concerned. The courts which administered the law laid by until temptation was presented and yielded to, and then, when the mischief was done and irreparable, they set to work in their slow, harsh, and sometimes cruel, way, to do something in the way of *vengeance—redress* being utterly out of their power. But where did the Common School begin? Not with *men* who commit crime, but with *children* before they can be supposed capable of crime. Instead of turning out bad men, they turned out valuable citizens, who add to the common wealth and common happiness of society. One good teacher could do more to relieve society of these misfortunes than all the judges of the land, because he begins earlier, and his influence reaches deeper. That great institution, the Church, reached scarcely one-half the mass of community, and, addressing itself only, or chiefly, to adults, even there, could not effectually reach the evil in its germination. The schools had the advantage over every instrumentality yet devised by the ingenuity of mankind in eradicating those evils that now diminished at least one-half the value of the life of every human being. He looked on those engaged in this work as devoted to the most sacred of causes.

Mr. Clement, of Dutchess, alluded to the conclusive evidence furnished in the last annual report of his distinguished friend, who had just taken his seat, of the fact that crime and ignorance go hand in hand. This truth had been abundantly illustrated in portions of his own county. Where Common Schools most prevailed crime was comparatively unknown, and the expenses of supporting paupers were greatly reduced.

Mr. King, from the Committee on Normal Schools, reported a resolution requesting the State Superintendent to consider the expediency of adopting measures to enable New York, as well as Massachusetts, to test the usefulness and enjoy the benefits of Normal Schools for the preparation of Common School teachers.

The resolution having been read, Mr. George B. Emerson, of Massachusetts, on the invitation of Dr. Potter, came forward and addressed the Convention. He had paid a great deal of attention to the subject of Normal Schools, and the conclusions to which he had come were that they were institutions of such importance in reference to Common Schools that no one who should examine the subject fully could fail to see that they were *absolutely essential.* Referring to the feeling which he presumed not uncommon in this State, as it had been in Massachusetts, that the office of teacher of a Common School was not the most high and respectable in which any man could engage, he stated that wherever Normal Schools should have been established long enough to produce their legitimate effects, in the creation of a class of teachers such as they should be, this feeling of depreciation would universally cease. It would be seen and realized that to teach well a Common School was one of the highest duties to which any man could be called. He knew of no school—of no kind of school—which, if properly taught, would not be enough to command all the energy and tax all the resources of any man, however highly endowed. It was hardly necessary to say to such a body of men as were here assembled that in order to teach well, a man *must be specifically qualified for the task.* This was in consonance with the observation and experience of mankind in every other calling. In every thing else—in every one of the professions—to do well, an education was required, and often a long course of instruction was necessary. To say that a teacher of a school can perform his duty without such a specific education, was to say it was a lower calling than that of the mere operator on the soil or in any other occupation—that the calling which commands and affords employment for the whole life was the only one which requires no previous training. Every one who takes charge of a Common School should be so trained. Neither the colleges nor academies could, in his judgment, be relied upon for the adequate performance of this work. Most of the inmates and graduates of these institutions, if they resorted to teaching at all, did so, not as a profession or business, but as a temporary occupation subservient to other objects and pursuits. Now the great duty of teaching could not be performed in such a way. Perfect success could only be attained by regarding it as the highest and noblest employment in which a man could be engaged. The only way, therefore, in which teachers could be perfectly qualified was in schools separately devoted to the work. To every properly organized Normal School, an experimental department is indispensable, where every principle and method of instruction and discipline taught in the former can be immediately reduced to practice. This is quite impracticable in institutions where various branches of instruction not pertaining specially to teaching are pursued.

Dr. Potter, in reply, expressed doubts of his perfect orthodoxy according to the Boston standard, as set up by his friends who might be called the fathers of these schools. On this subject of Normal Schools, he could not go so far as Mr. Emerson, though he had faith in them. He would not have them to the exclusion of the existing academical departments established for the purpose. The principle on which his friends' reasoning rested was that teaching was a specific profession, and that for that profession you must have specific training. There were many examples that might be cited in opposition to this principle. There was no training for the great business of legislation beyond what the legislator enjoyed in the discharge of that most responsible trust. There was no specific education for the discharge of some of the most important functions devolved on man in the relations of life. That most important of all offices, the discharge of the parental responsibilities, was one for which no special training was contemplated or provided in any system of education. What, then, was the true principle? It seemed to him to be this: Educate a man; educate a woman; give them well-disciplined minds; and you have then prepared them for educating themselves up to the standard and wants of any profession. There were, doubtless, exceptions—as in the case of the medical profession, and, perhaps, some others—but they were only exceptions. His friend would, perhaps, remind him that you could not train a man to make a shoe or a hat without an apprenticeship. True; but the business of making shoes and hats was the business of but a small portion of the community. The great business of moulding the youthful mind was a charge which God had devolved on every human being; and, therefore, education, if it was to be specific, should prepare a man for the enlightened discharge of that important trust. He trusted the time would come when, in all our higher seminaries of learning, the science of training the youthful mind would be considered as essential as astronomy or natural philosophy—when it would be felt that the one great duty of the educated mind was to discharge the trust of teacher—and that it was one of the highest obligations reposed in man, though not a parent, to send forth again whatever light may have visited his own mind to illumine the world. He must remind the gentleman who referred him to the mechanical trades, that the business of educating a spirit—of moulding the moral principles—was a different thing from making a shoe or a table. The mechanic can lay down precise rules for holding your tool and laying out your materials, in order to bring out a material machine, but there were no such precise rules for training up the immortal spirit. Rules, he admitted, there were—rules not generally appreciated, not generally understood—and he admitted that Normal Schools for imparting a more general knowledge of these rules were all-important, as a *temporary measure*, to train up, perhaps, one generation of teachers, and *not as a permanent system*. To undertake, in this State, to pass all teachers through the mill—*to* produce ten thousand teachers—one for each school district—would require an immense outlay of funds. The principle on which these schools should be advocated should be to plant over this State five hundred good teachers as central lights—radiant points—to the end that they might spread all around them the influence of their successful example until the entire system shall be regenerated and revivified. The best mode of training teachers was by example. A good teacher was, himself, in his course of procedure, the very best means of teaching others. He was in favor of Normal Schools, in the proper place and time, but not as indispensable for every teacher. He believed the departments for training teachers in the academies were doing good, and might do more good. He believed that there were defects about them—defects that could not be fully remedied under their present constitution. The great defect was, unquestionably, in regard to training for the mechanical part of teaching. He had suggested that, if the science, or theory and practice of teaching were introduced into our seminaries, every human being might be taught how to teach as well as how to know: for the one was but the practical application of the other. But, after all, it did require a great deal of iteration and reiteration of mechanical routine that could not be introduced into an ordinary academy. It seemed to him as a necessary incident to our present system, and with which, so far as its external constitution was concerned, that system would be almost without objection, that we should have, in addition, just one thing: That was, *a great training school for teachers, at Albany*, where some three hundred might be assembled and taught in regard to the *theory of teaching, having been already taught the several branches of Common School instruction* before they came, and then put into a model or experimental school, and set to putting in practice what they may have learned, under the eye of an able superintendent. He believed *this training should be superadded to previous study in an academy*. This would furnish all that would be required to perfect our system. But it was not necessary by one fell swoop to destroy what we had. The great object should be to develop, improve, and perfect it.

Mr. M. H. FITTS, of Niagara, said he had been faithless in regard to Normal Schools, and confessed he was not satisfied now. He had taken pains to inquire into this subject; and, if he understood it, these schools differed in no respect as to book knowledge and the development of the mental powers from other schools, except in teaching how to teach. Now, he took it for granted that a man who could not learn the details of school-room management by experience is one who could not be taught these details by precept. As soon as the inhabitants of school districts were willing to pay a proper compensation for the services of competent and experienced teachers, they would find their way among us without Normal Schools. He regarded teachers as a marketable commodity, the supply of which would always keep pace with the demand.

Mr. MANN again took the floor in behalf of the

system of Normal School instruction, with which he had made himself familiar in Massachusetts during the past three years. It seemed to him that no fact was more plain and obvious than that it was one thing to learn and another to teach. The one was the ability of *acquiring*, the other of *imparting* processes as different as could be named. For a *learner*, it was only necessary to study and understand *his own mind*—to find out in what way he himself could most thoroughly master a subject; but for a *teacher*, it was necessary to know in what way *different minds*, with different natural tendencies, and different habits of thought, could accomplish the same task. How much there was in this distinction those could readily understand who know that the teacher has all varieties and shades of mind to deal with, while the mind of the learner is but one. Most readily did he admit that teaching was unlike any mechanical pursuit—but it was unlike it in being more difficult, more profound, more important—and, therefore, should be unlike it in requiring not only less, but more, preparation—vastly more—infinitely more.

It had also been said that the Creator had made every parent a teacher. True; but did it follow that because the Creator had established no institution for teaching parents, therefore all the duties of the parental relation would be well discharged without any, or would not be better discharged with, such instruction? Let the deplorable condition of thousands and millions of children, not only in our own, but in all preceding times, answer the question. If such were the legitimate inference from the fact that the Creator had established this relation without providing any mode of teaching parents, then we must discard all our schools, academies, and seminaries of learning; for in the same sense in which God has made no provision for educating parents, he has built no school-house, academy, or college. Mr. MANN then proceeded to give a full and detailed description of the methods of instruction in the Normal Schools of Massachusetts, the requisites for admission, and the practical application of the precepts given in the experimental schools. By these means the standard of education had been advanced very materially. He concluded by saying he could wish no better fortune to New York than that she should crown all her noble efforts in the cause of education by the establishment of one or more Normal Schools.

The Convention then adjourned for the hearing of Mr. MANN's public address at the church; and, after its conclusion, re-assembled at 9 o'clock in the evening, and proceeded to discuss the following resolution, reported by Mr. HENRY, of Herkimer:

> "*Resolved*, That in general *our school-houses are ill contrived, badly built, and shamefully neglected*; defective, in most instances, in being too small, and with desks and seats utterly unsuited to the wants of children, in the general want of wood-sheds, out-buildings, and play-grounds, and in location and architectural beauty; and that every effort should be made for the supply of these requisites for the comfort, improvement, health, and decency of the children."

The resolution was discussed by Mr. HENRY, Mr. WING, of Warren; Mr. SHUMWAY, of Essex; Mr. WILLIAM WRIGHT, of Washington; Mr. PATCHIN, of Livingston; Mr. MOXON, of Allegany; and Mr. ROCHESTER, of Monroe. The latter gentleman, after conceding that the condition of school-houses, as described in the resolution, was pretty generally the same throughout the State, said he had found, wherever he had an opportunity to test the experiment in his district, that those deplorable deficiencies were not so much the result of a want of liberality on the part of the people, as of ignorance of what was necessary, and absence of effort in calling attention to the subject. Wherever this was done, repairs were promptly made, or new school-houses built, without opposition or remonstrance. The subject had, in his judgment, only to be brought home to the knowledge of the people in the different localities, to lead, sooner or later, to improvement. The resolution was adopted.

The subject of *school discipline*, involving the question of *corporal punishment*, was then taken up and discussed on a resolution submitted by Mr. DOUGLAS, of Clinton, "that a teacher who can govern himself may discipline a school without resorting to corporal punishment; and that an individual who cannot govern himself is unqualified for the sacred office of a teacher of youth."

Mr. DOUGLAS took strong ground in favor of this resolution; while Messrs. HENRY, of Herkimer; FINCH, of Steuben; EMERSON, of Massachusetts; SHUMWAY, of Essex; and Dr. GRISCOM, of New Jersey, although adverse to the use of the rod, except in extreme cases, and when no other method of discipline was, after due effort, found to be available, were yet of opinion, that the *power* to inflict corporal punishment should remain in the teacher, as a last resort; and the resolution, after being amended accordingly, was laid over for consideration on the following day, when, upon a renewed discussion, in which Messrs. DOUGLAS, ROCHESTER, WING, SHAW, of Albany; BARLOW, of Madison; EMERSON, MANN, SPRAGUE, of Fulton; SALEM TOWN, of Cayuga; GALLAUDET, of Connecticut; and GRISCOM, participated, it was modified as follows:

"*Resolved*, That while we recognize in the teacher the same authority to correct his pupils as the parent has to correct his wayward child, we, nevertheless, believe that a teacher who *can* govern himself may discipline a school without resort to corporal punishment; and that an individual who *cannot* govern himself is unqualified for the sacred office of a teacher of youth."

The discussion of the subject of normal schools was then renewed between Dr. POTTER, Mr. MANN, Mr. GALLAUDET, and Prof. WEBSTER, of Geneva; and the resolution, as originally reported, adopted with a slight modification, on motion of Mr. DWIGHT, of Albany. Resolutions were adopted, on Mr. ROCHESTER's motion, earnestly inviting the active co-operation of the clergy, and members of the legal and medical profession, throughout the State, in the efforts now in progress for the improvement and advancement of the Common Schools. The subject of text-books was also discussed at considerable length, and resolutions finally adopted recommending uniformity to the greatest practicable extent consistent with the comparative merit of the different books in use. The establishment of *Union Schools* in large towns and villages was recommended, on the motion of Mr. BURDICK, of Rensselaer. On motion of Mr. SPRAGUE, of Fulton, a resolution was adopted strongly discountenancing the purchase and introduction into the district libraries of books of an immoral or frivolous tendency. Mr. WING, of Warren, submitted a series of practical resolutions on *Methods of Teaching*, which were adopted. Mr. PATCHIN, of Livingston, offered a resolution, which was also unanimously adopted, expressing great confidence in the ability and efficiency of the several teachers' departments in the academies of the State for the supply of a competent body of well-instructed teachers in the Common Schools. The co-operation of parents in securing the punctuality and regularity of attendance of their children, and the more general employment of female teachers in the several schools, was also requested.

At the conclusion of the proceedings, Mr. MANN rose to say that he looked upon this convention as one of the most important ever held in this country. He regarded it not merely as an assemblage of some fifty or sixty individuals for the promotion of temporary public purposes, or political views; but, looking to the future, he saw that these individuals were to go back into the respective districts of this vast State, and were there to operate on the fortunes not only of contemporaries, but of posterity—that they were even more than emissaries and apostles of truth—that they would create a perception of truth; for it was immaterial how much of the divine authority of truth we might receive, if we failed to create a class of minds throughout the community able to adopt and to defend the truth. There was truth enough; but the difficulty was, there was not the mind to comprehend it, the intelligence to perceive, and the will to obey it. There was the great defect of humanity. He looked upon those assembled there as missionaries to raise up this general mind; to enable all to understand those truths by which all were surrounded. Hence it was to him a matter of great interest and pleasure to meet his friends on this occasion. The members of this convention had exhibited an amount of information, a desire for investigation, and a spirit of conciliation and harmony, which he did not expect to find among so many persons brought together, for the first time, for the consideration and discussion of a subject in regard to which there was apt to be great differences of opinion. He could only wish them Godspeed. They would be compelled to contend with some dark and stormy times before they saw the result of their labors. Such labors did not come to maturity in a single season. Like the oak, they required both the sun and the storm; but, when matured, they survived through ages of change. "Go on, then, though you should meet with obstructions, with contumely—the hour of triumph will eventually come. Though it may be your destiny long to labor without witnessing the product of your toil, yet that labor—like that of the tiny insect that builds at the bottom of the sea, going on, age after age, steadily with its work, until, by and by, it brings up the rock-built continent to the surface—will, at no very distant period, bring about as great and permanent results. In parting from you, let me say that if Napoleon, when he led down his army from the Alps into Italy, was able to excite his soldiers to frantic courage, by depicting to them the honors which awaited them from their victories and triumphs—if all this could be done by presenting to them the idea of returning home in old age, gathering their grandchildren about the fireside, and being able to say: "I, too, was of the Army of Italy"—with what strong and enduring emotions ought not these deputies to be inspired, that it may be in their power to say, as this work goes progressively on, looking upon the improved condition of this great State, its internal resources developed, its intellect resplendently diffused over the country: "I, TOO, WAS A CO-WORKER WITH GOD IN THIS GREAT LABOR!"

The eloquent tones of that immortal voice are now hushed in death; and the deep silence of the grave has long rested upon the labors of POTTER, YOUNG, DWIGHT, HAMMOND, GRISCOM, GALLAUDET, KING, TOWN, and many others of their noble associates on that day; but the work of their hands, and the labor of their lives, remain an imperishable record upon our institutions of their high ambition, comprehensive intellect, and unintermitted devotion to the great and enduring interests of universal education, knowledge, religion, and virtue!

The State Convention of County Superintendents reassembled, at Rochester, in the summer of the ensuing year; at Albany, in 1844 and 1846; and at Syracuse, in 1845; and by their consultation with each other, and with the head of the department, were enabled to accomplish a vast amount of invaluable benefit to the advancement and prosperity of the Common Schools, the results of which will more fully appear in the annual reports of the superintendents, from time to time, during their continuance in office, as well as in the concurrent testimony of the executive department.

From the first annual report of Superintendent YOUNG, in January, 1843, it appears that the whole number of districts in the State was 10,893, in which over six hundred thousand children had been taught during the year reported. The total amount of public money expended in the payment of teachers was $588,506.72; and the amount contributed by parents on rate-bills was $468,688.22—making the whole sum paid for teachers' wages upward of $1,000,000. The expenditure for district libraries was $98,290.47, with which about 200,000 volumes were added to the libraries, increasing the whole number of volumes distributed throughout the several districts of the State to over one million. "The diffusion of a million of useful books," he observes, "through all the various portions of this great community, although many of them, at present, may fall in sterile places, cannot ultimately fail to produce a richly compensating reward. Time will soon remove the obstruction of servile indifference; and the imaginative ardor of youth will find and unlock these storehouses of knowledge. And it requires no effort of fancy—it simply needs a knowledge of cause and effect—to know with moral certainty that many future great and good men, who will be the benefactors and blessings of the human race, will be able to trace to the influences of these volumes the primeval dawnings of their embryo genius—the first impulse to their glorious career.

"In the quietude of private life, the gratification of a taste for reading instructive books affords a perennial source of undying enjoyment. No means so effectual have ever been devised to promote virtue, repress vice, purify and exalt the affections, expand and strengthen the mind, and raise man above the groveling propensities of his animal nature. Can a liar, a cheat, a debauchee, or a murderer, be found among those who are devoted to self improvement, and who are fond of acquiring moral and intellectual knowledge by the study of useful books? No such instance has ever existed or ever will. Nor is there so powerful an agent of preventive police, to suppress crime and diminish expenditures in the administration of criminal justice, as the diffusion of knowledge and the consequent promotion of virtue."

In reference to the several departments for the education of teachers connected with the academies of the State, the Superintendent, after conceding that those institutions had, to a considerable extent, exercised a beneficial influence on the Common Schools, by advancing the standard of qualification of teachers, and giving increased character and efficiency to the business of instruction, says: "But it must be admitted that most of these departments have practically failed in the accomplishment of the great object for which they were instituted—*the special qualification of teachers for the Common Schools*. Little has been done which would not have been substantially effected by the ordinary exercises of the academies in which the departments have been organized; and many of the academies, not participating at all in the fund set apart for this purpose, are, in reality, at present accomplishing as much for the benefit of the Common Schools as those specially designated for this object." He recommends, accordingly, the concentration of the fund upon four of the most efficient academies of the State—the diffusion of the bounty of the State over too great a surface being, in his judgment, the cause of the failure of these departments. By such concentration, the encouragement would be sufficiently liberal to induce these institutions to direct their principal efforts to the qualification of teachers; and, under proper regulations, without any violent change, the classical branches might gradually be merged into the teachers' departments, and each be thus converted, without expense for buildings or apparatus, into an efficient Normal School.

"In addition to this endowment, a sufficient annual sum might advantageously be appropriated from the literary fund, to establish and maintain a similar school in the city of Albany, at the seat of government, where it might annually be examined by the representatives of the people during the session of the Legislature.

"Such a system, it is believed, could not fail to produce the most beneficial consequences. Whatever prejudices might, at first, be entertained against schools of this description, as innovations upon our established institutions for public instruction, there cannot be a doubt that they will here, as they have already done in Massachusetts, speedily entrench themselves in the favor and affection of the people. Their whole object and design is to benefit the great mass of mankind by preparing teachers of youth, both practically and theoretically, to communicate to children a vastly greater amount of useful elementary knowledge than can possibly be effected by the antiquated modes of instruction ordinarily in use? These institutions originated in Europe; they have multiplied and constantly increased in usefulness in various kingdoms; and have produced and are producing a wonderful revolution and improvement in the combined art and science of communicating primary instruction.

"That educational science is far behind all others is a fact recognized and conceded by all who are competent to judge. On every other science, a vast amount of skill, ingenuity, and perseverance has been expended to bring them to their present degree of perfection; whilst this, the most important of all, has been confined for centuries to a dull routine, or left to the caprice of accident. The habits and instincts of wild animals have been carefully investigated in order that they might be moulded to domestication and trained to utility. But the different propensities of children, according to the old system of training, are not to be studied or regarded. All varieties are to be treated in the same manner and *whipped into uniformity*.

"There is no function of government nor field of human exertion which involves such momentous consequences as that which pertains to the education of youth. The whole juvenile population of the State, in the plastic period of childhood, is subjected to its benign or adverse influence, and may be moulded to good or to evil, to virtue or vice. Early impressions are the most indelible; and the impulse given in the school often communicates a bright or somber coloring to the longest life. In exact proportion to the acquisition of useful knowledge, man rises in the scale of being above the savage and the brute; and the only means afforded to nine-tenths of our whole population of acquiring the rudiments of this knowledge is furnished by Common Schools. These are the nurseries in which germinate the durable elements of individual happiness or degradation, and of national glory or shame. The Common School is the great fulcrum upon which the moral and intellectual attainments of a whole people may be indefinitely raised.

"But this consummation can never be attained either by a cold and inhospitable neglect, or by a "zeal not according to knowledge." An active, intelligent, and efficient supervision affords, in the opinion of the Superintendent, the best, and, indeed, the only sure means of renovation. The want of such a supervision has heretofore, for many years, been severely felt. Its consequences to our Common Schools have been a lingering and almost hopeless state of degradation. Parents have neglected to provide suitable buildings, conveniences, apparatus, and books, and have thoughtlessly abandoned the education of their children to the cheapest teacher. Officers of towns and districts have either been incompetent or disinclined to perform with efficiency their legal functions. Each of the eleven thousand school districts of the State seems to have constituted a separate principality, isolated from all the rest, groping onward alone, ignorant of its own deficiencies, unenlightened by the advancing knowledge of the age, and wholly destitute of both the power and the will to avail itself of the improved systems of instruction which are yearly developed, both in this country and in other parts of the world.

"What will the future historian who lives in more propitious and enlightened times, in a period when the culture of the human mind is justly appreciated—when government shall be brought back from its erratic course to its legitimate functions—when its efforts shall be directed to control the mental, instead of the physical, elements—when its energies shall be applied to the accumulation of moral and intellectual riches, instead of being wasted in a blind and abortive struggle to acquire material wealth—what will the historian of these times say of the present and the past!

"For a long period of years, the people of this and many other States have permitted their rulers to plunge deeply into works of labor involving pecuniary consequences to a vast amount, under the delusive expectation that such works can be conducted beneficially to the community by the mercenary machinery of government. Under this stupid delusion, created and sustained by reckless demagogues, and fostered by sectional cupidity, more than two hundred millions of dollars have been utterly sacrificed, of which enormous sum more than one-tenth has been hopelessly dissipated by the government of this State. Such a sweeping waste of the avails of human toil, together with its consequences, ponderous debt and depopulating taxation, will, in a corresponding degree, retard the onward progress of physical advancement for many years. Nor will the moral atmosphere soon be purified from the polluted influences which have been infused into it by such vast governmental dealings in 'the root of all evil.'

"The career of ignorance has ever been characterized by a continuous and imbecile warfare against the enactments of the Almighty. A destitution of correct principles, and a lack of true knowledge, have always been the generating cause of the great mass of moral and physical evil which has scourged mankind.

"Every age has furnished its sad memorials of ignorance and folly. Our catalogue will eclipse, in number, magnitude and durability, the aggregated amount of the last five hundred years. The crumbling ruins of unseemly excavations, and dilapidated and abandoned works, deforming the face of the earth, will characterize the present period, for centuries to come. These forlorn and repulsive mementoes will be the hateful chroniclers of their own disgraceful history, and of the dominant spirit of this age. 'He that runs may read—and he that reads will run!'

"Had we, in early life, been but slightly instructed in a knowledge of the laws which God has impressed on the human mind—had we been enabled to anticipate the sure operation of cause and effect, it would have been morally impossible for the devastating and demoralizing curse of a miscalled 'internal improvement,' by which millions of human beings are crushed and thousands corrupted, to have fallen upon us. And if we are anxious to protect those who will soon occupy our places in the active theatre of life from similar infatuations; if we are desirous that their welfare shall be exempted from the deleterious influence of State quacks; and that they shall not become, as we have, the passive dupes of the interested, and the unresisting victims of demagogues, we must, as the only means of safety, bestow upon their minds, through the instrumentality of well regulated schools, the panoply of knowledge. What inheritance comparable with this can the parent provide for his children? Through all the vicissitudes of life, what other safe guides can be found than virtue and knowledge? These are the only pillars of cloud and of fire which afford protection to man in his earthly pilgrimage.

"The torpid and degraded state of our Common Schools has been the theme of frequent official communication, and my able predecessors in this department have made repeated efforts to move the lethean waters. If the cold and apathetic indifference, the stagnant tranquillity of the community, could be awakened and aroused on this subject, the whole evil would shortly vanish. There is no object within the ample range of human attainment which is not readily accomplished by the united exertions of a whole people.

"Under a law passed in 1839, special visitors of the Common Schools were appointed, who gratuitously examined and reported their condition to the Legislature. Although these visitors did not concur in regard to the proper measures for reforming existing evils and abuses, yet they were unanimous in the opinion 'that the schools did not afford the kind or degree of education essential either to the perpetuity or safety of the State.' They showed that a 'large amount of the public money was utterly wasted;' that 'from one-third to one-half of the pupils were daily absent;' that 'a large proportion of the school-houses were in a deplorable condition, and wholly unfit for places of education;' and that 'a wide-spread and fatal apathy chilled the hopes of reform, and clogged all efforts for improvement.' They, therefore, 'earnestly prayed that the law should be so amended as to secure that constant and faithful supervision which should rouse parents, teacher, and child, to a sense of their deep and urgent responsibilities.' In consequence of these disclosures, and in accordance with numerous petitions from every part of the State, the law creating the office of deputy superintendent was passed by a nearly unanimous vote in both branches of the Legislature. The prominent defects which it was the object of this law to remedy consisted in the meager, incorrect, and unsatisfactory information in regard to the condition of the Common Schools, which was furnished under the requisitions of the statutes then in force; the defective supervision of the schools by the officers specifically charged with this duty; the low standard of qualifications on the part of teachers, permitted and sanctioned by inspectors; the consequent rapid increase of cheap, unqualified, and inefficient teachers; the prevailing neglect on the part of the inhabitants of school districts to provide suitable accommodations for the education of their children, or to visit and manifest an interest in the affairs of the school; the prevalence, in many districts, of private and select schools of various grades of excellence, rendered necessary by the degradation and neglect of the district school; and a pervading stagnation of public sentiment in reference to the advancement and improvement of these elementary institutions of public instruction.

"When the law creating the office of County superintendent of Common Schools was first promulgated, having been passed in a period of the most profligate and reckless legislative expenditure, it was, in the minds of many, associated with the broad and impudent system of felonious enactment, "eating out the substance of the people," and stealing the bread, and plundering the means of education from myriads of unborn children, which has brought upon the State the terrific desolation of a debt of twenty-seven millions of dollars. He who now occupies the station of State Superintendent derived his first impressions of this law from such an association of ideas; and, on entering upon the duties of the office, felt *a decided predisposition to exercise whatever influence he might possess to save the expense by an abolition of the system.* But to have passed an irrevocable sentence of condemnation upon it, without first subjecting it to the test of a rigid scrutiny, would have been manifestly unjust. A meeting of the County superintendents of the several counties was advertised to be held in the city of Utica, in May last; and one of the prominent objects of the Superintendent in being present at that convention was to obtain, if possible, an accurate knowledge, and to form a satisfactory opinion of the intelligence, zeal, and capacity for usefulness of its members. The proceedings of that convention have been widely circulated and extensively read; and it is no unmeaning compliment to allege, that for the purpose of illustrating and improving the important principles of elementary instruction, no body of men of equal information and devotedness has ever before assembled in this State. But the practical utility of the system, its adaptation to supply the deficiencies of supervision, to point out the extent of existing evils, and to suggest the most feasible remedies, to allay the bitter feuds and animosities which often mar the peace and retard the prosperity of school districts, and to rouse and inspire parental indifference with a love for the advancement and happiness of children, by the acquisition of useful knowledge in well-regulated schools, were yet to be tested. How far these important objects have been effected will, to a considerable extent, be seen and appreciated by the Legislature, on reading the able reports of the deputy superintendents herewith transmitted.

"The nakedness and deformity of the great majority of the schools in this State; the comfortless and dilapidated buildings, destitute, in many instances, of the ordinary conveniences and decencies of life; the unhung doors, broken sashes, absent panes, stilted benches, gaping walls, yawning roofs, and muddy and moldering floors—are faithfully and fully portrayed; and many of the self-styled teachers, who lash and dogmatize in these miserable tenements of suffering humanity, are shown to be low, vulgar, obscene, intemperate, ignorant, and profane, utterly incompetent to teach any thing that is good. Such are the temples of science, and such the ministers whose 'moral character, learning, and ability to teach' are officially certified by inspectors from year to year, and under whose guidance and care susceptible childhood is to receive its earliest impressions, and its first knowledge of human society! Great God! shall man dare to charge to thy dispensations the vices and the crimes, the sickness, the sorrows, the miseries, and the brevity of human life, who sends his little children to a pest house, amply fraught with the deadly *malaria* of both moral and physical disease? Instead of impious murmurs, let him lay his hand on his mouth, and his mouth in the dust, and cry 'unclean!' To cure, if possible, the callousness which is manifested in many districts on the subject of school-houses, a law should be passed authorizing the Superintendent, after proper notice, to withhold all public moneys from any defaulting school district, until reasonable accommodations for the comfort of the pupils shall be provided. Love of money must be substituted for a lack of parental affection.

"In every county in the State where the deputy superintendent has assiduously fulfilled his mission an improvement in the condition of the schools is manifest. The frequent lectures and expostulations of these officers, at meetings of the inhabitants of districts convened by them, have done much good, by arousing the thoughtless, confirming the wavering, and exciting to more vigorous exertions all the friends of education. Many compromises of obstinate district quarrels have been effected by the friendly interference and pacific counsels of these officers. In several of those frequent contests brought up by appeal, respecting sites of school-houses and divisions and lines of districts, involving questions respecting distances and convenience of travel, the statements of which, by the conflicting parties, are often utterly irreconcilable, the County superintendent, on a requisition from this department, has repaired to the spot, and carefully collected and transmitted the naked facts, upon which a satisfactory decision might be based. The number of appeals is increasing with the multiplication of districts, and now averages nearly one for every two days in the year, requiring the examination of exceedingly voluminous, complicated, and often contradictory documents, and the adjustment of a great variety of legal principles and individual interests. The amount annually paid from the State treasury for postage on these documents constitutes a serious item in the aggregate expense of the department. In addition to these appeals, the daily correspondence of the department with the inhabitants and officers of districts requiring information and advice for their guidance occupies a very large proportion of its time, and is constantly increasing. It has occurred to the Superintendent that a great saving might be effected in time and money, as well as a greater degree of practical efficiency given to the system, by the reference of all appeals to the deputy superintendent, in the first instance, for his decision, with the right to any party aggrieved thereby to bring such decision up for review by this department. A large proportion, also, of the ordinary correspondence of the department might advantageously take this direction, suitable provisions being made to defray the charge of necessary postage. The blundering, inartificial, and contradictory statements of litigants might then be elucidated and rectified by an officer, who, if necessary, could go to the district and ascertain the real merits of each case; and the painful necessity often cast upon this department, of deciding doubtful questions on crude and conflicting testimony, would be obviated, while, at the same time, a great economy of expense would be secured.

"County superintendents properly qualified for the discharge of their functions, possessing a competent knowledge of the moral, intellectual, and physical sciences, familiar with all the modern improvements in elementary instruction, and earnestly intent on elevating the condition of our Common Schools, can do much more to accomplish this desirable result than all the other officers connected with the system. Acting on a broader theater, they can perform more efficiently all that supervision which has heretofore been so deplorably neglected, or badly executed. The system of County superintendents is capable of securing, and can be made to secure, the following objects:

"It can produce a complete and efficient supervision of all the schools of the State, in reference as well to their internal management as to their external details:

"It can be made to unite all the schools of the State into one great system; making the advancement of each the ambition of all; furnishing each with the means of attaining the highest standard of practical excellence, by communicating to it every improvement discovered or suggested in every or any of the others;

"It can do much toward dissipating the stolid indifference which paralyzes many portions of the community, and toward arousing, enlightening, and enlisting public sentiment in the great work of elementary instruction, by systematic and periodical appeals to the inhabitants of each school district, in the form of lectures, addresses, &c.:

"It can be made to dismiss from our schools all immoral and incompetent teachers, and to secure the services of such only as are qualified and efficient, thereby elevating the grade of the school-master, and infusing new vitality into the school.

"An attentive examination of the interesting reports of the deputy superintendents will clearly show that the accomplishment of several of the most important of these objects is already in a state of encouraging progression.

"In these times of commercial paralysis, monetary pressure, and impending taxation, superinduced by causes which were clearly foreseen, and might easily have been obviated, it is very far from the intention of the Superintendent to advocate any system which shall add weight to the existing burdens of the community. Instead of this, it will be manifest that the system of deputy superintendents can be made to supersede official duty heretofore badly performed, and taxation heretofore imposed, with little resulting utility, to an amount greatly exceeding the expenses of this system.

"The Legislature and the people of the State rightfully hold this department responsible, in the last resort, for the faithful application of the public moneys, and the correct movement of all the pulleys and springs and wheels in the vast and complicated machinery of our system of public instruction. And it is under the weight of this responsibility that the invocation is earnestly made for such legislative action as shall cause an efficient movement among these 'dry bones,' by infusing into their stagnant and multifarious organization much more of simplicity, economy, and energy of action.

"Heretofore the halls of legislation have resounded with the clamorous appeals of mercenary demagogues, beleaguering the law-makers for splendid appropriations to erect splendid structures, and to construct splendid works, which would necessarily result, and have already resulted, in splendid debt and splendid taxation. And these meretricious appeals have found a yielding response in the easy virtue of past legislation. But as the cup of calamity is now full to overflowing, it is devoutly to be hoped that the time has come when the desolating war against the common welfare will cease, the temple of Janus be permanently shut, and the floodgates of corruption closed forever; and that the ear of the legislator will be no longer stunned by the hoarse din of the ravening brotherhood of 'internal improvement,' but that he will find both time and inclination to attend to the mute and unobtrusive wants of the rising generation.

"If fancy could congregate around the heretofore polluted temple of legislation the six hundred thousand children of this State, with their innocent smiles, beaming with ardent hopes and high aspirations, 'hungering and thirsting' after knowledge, and 'submissively lifting up their little hands in silent supplication' for kind and competent instructors, for comfortable apartments, and for all the appliances which would enable them to discover and obey the laws of the Creator, such an array would carry a resistless appeal to all the generous sympathies of the human heart. The retiring diffidence and confiding imbecility of childhood prevent all petition, and preclude all approach to the law-giver; and it is only by an effort of the imagination that the throbbings of the youthful bosom, and the desires and wants of the opening mind, can be conceived. And now, when the delusive visions of the past are superseded by sad and sober reality—when reason, long inebriated and nodding in her seat, has begun to resume her sway—when the Legislature can truly say to State mendicants, in the language of an ancient Apostle, 'Silver and gold have I none!'—shall not that conception be entertained?

"A legislative atonement for the gross errors of the past is due both to God and to man; nor can this atonement be more effectually made than by adopting the means best calculated to imbue the minds of the rising generation with much more of knowledge, of wisdom, and of virtue, than have been manifested by their predecessors."

In conclusion, he recommends the reduction of the academical departments for the education of teachers to four, and the appropriation of a sufficient sum to establish and maintain a NORMAL SCHOOL at the seat of government, where it might be subjected to the immediate supervision as well of the department as of the representatives of the people during the sessions of the Legislature; the abolition of the offices of Commissioner and Inspector of Common Schools, and the substitution of that of TOWN SUPERINTENDENT; the extension of the official term of trustees of school districts to three years, one of their number to be annually elected; the vesting of appellate jurisdiction and powers, in the first instance, in the County superintendents, reserving the right of final adjudication, on appeal from their decisions, to the State Superintendent; the extension and perpetuation of the DISTRICT LIBRARIES, and various other incidental and minor modifications of the system; most of which recommendations and suggestions, with the exception of those relating to the establishment of a Normal School and the reduction of the academical departments for the preparation of teachers, met with the full concurrence of the Legislature; and after an able and argumentative report from the Honorable CALVIN T. HULBURD, of St. Lawrence, Chairman of the Assembly Committee on Colleges, Academies, and Common Schools, were incorporated in an act which passed both branches, and became a law on the 16th of April.

During the Summer of this year, the Superintendent devolved upon HENRY S. RANDALL, Esq., the efficient County Superintendent of Cortland, the duty of preparing a special report in reference to the suitable selection of books for the several DISTRICT LIBRARIES. The report was forwarded to the department on the 1st of November, and its conclusions and principles officially adopted as the standard in the exercise of the discretion vested in the trustees of districts in the purchase of these libraries.

The first cardinal rule laid down in the report, in the character of all books to be admitted, was that they should be works "of sound and useful instruction," as contradistinguished from works of *mere* amusement and frivolity. Juvenile books, however, for the instruction and amusement of children, such as "Parley's Magazine," or the "Rollo Series" by Jacob Abbott, were not to be regarded as coming within the excluded class, and were highly recommended.

Books of an immoral character or tendency were to be rigidly excluded, whether in the shape of classics, ancient or modern, poetry, fiction, or the drama.

In reference to sectarian works, the following general rules and principles were laid down:

"*No works written professedly to uphold or attack any sect or creed in our country, claiming to be a religious one, shall be tolerated in the school libraries.*

"The question now arises, how far this rule of exclusion shall apply to an extensive class of literary works, evidently not written with a sectarian object, but which, *incidentally*, manifest the religious preferences or antipathies of their writers. This class embraces many of the standard productions of our language. There is, probably, not a historian of England who does not betray an evident leaning against the Protestants or Catholics. Clarendon and Hume are not exceptions to this remark. In biography, these predilections are displayed almost as a matter of course, in alluding to the religious tenets of their subjects. In Pope's Essay on Man, notwithstanding the volume once written to disprove it, we feel assured that the author leans toward the skepticism of Bolingbroke. Other productions as clearly evince the sway subsequently acquired over his religious views by that giant defender of Christianity, Bishop Warburton. Gibbon, throughout his magnificent History of the Decline and Fall of the Roman Empire, clearly exhibits the earlier and worse bias which has been alluded to in Pope. The whole tenor of Milton's Paradise Lost militates against the doctrine of Universalism. These instances might be indefinitely multiplied from among the choicest productions of our language. To exclude them from the school libraries would be to perpetuate a great evil to escape a smaller one.

"It may be said that in one, at least, of the instances cited, the works are not merely "sectarian," but actually of "hostility to the Christian religion"—a class already directly prohibited by the Superintendent. But if the positions heretofore assumed are correct, works attacking other religions than the Christian—for example, those of the Jew, and that class of Unitarians who utterly deny the divine character of Christ—are equally excluded. Although it behooves us to be exceedingly cautious in tolerating any work even indirectly impugning the theory of our holy religion, and although some more strictness in enforcing the rule of exclusion in relation to such may be proper, it is in vain to say that it shall be made imperative in every possible instance coming within its letter. While we would unhesitatingly condemn and reject portions of the writings of the Shaftesburys, of Bolingbroke, of Godwin, Shelley, Wolstonecraft, Paine, Lessing, Voltaire, and others of the same class, there are those which though they incidentally betray doctrines somewhat at variance with the theory of Christianity, it is evidently expedient to tolerate. The second general rule then is:

"2. *Standard works on other topics shall not be excluded because they incidentally and indirectly betray the religious opinions of their authors.*

"There is a third class of literary productions which, though ostensibly written on literary topics, not only incidentally betray religious biases, but so far digress from the subject which they purport to treat as to abound in direct defenses of the religious views of their authors, and attacks on those of other persons; and those, whatever their theme—however dispassionately they may seem to be written—however free they may be from direct and open forms of crimination—which, nevertheless, hold up any religious body to contempt or execration, by singling out and bringing together only the darker parts of their history and character. Every English historian must speak of the martyrs who suffered during the reign of Mary; he has a perfect right to express sympathy for the sufferers, indignation against the tyrannical monarch; the intelligent Roman Catholic now, as then—in the case of the Pope's legate—will do no less. But Fox's Book of Martyrs, constantly pointing to, and commenting on, the enormities of one religious body, with its pictorial embellishments of Protestants suffering the most horrible species of torture and martyrdom, would clearly, whether the narrations contained in it are, in point of fact, true or false, come under the exclusory rule. No Protestant, assuredly, would claim that a parallel work giving a history of the Catholic, and even opposite sects of Protestant, martyrs, emboweled, beheaded, or burnt by the commands of the more able and politic, but little less sanguinary, sister of the 'bloody Mary,' and by other Protestant princes and authorities, would be a safe or suitable one to be placed in the hands of his children. The high-minded and magnanimous Protestant will feel that 'the quality of mercy is not strained—it droppeth as the gentle rain from heaven' on Catholic as well as Protestant; and that it would be intolerant as it would be unjust and unmanly to ask any immunity from laws or official regulations for himself which he would not as freely concede to Catholic, or even heretic. This brings us to the third rule:

"3. *Works, avowedly on other topics, which abound in direct and unreserved attacks on, or defenses of, the character of any religious sect; or those which hold up any religious body to contempt or execration, by singling out or bringing together only the darker parts of its history or character, shall be excluded from the school libraries.*

"Is it said that under the above rules, heresy and error are put upon the same footing with true religion—that Protestant and Catholic, orthodox and unorthodox, Universalist, Unitarian, Jew, and even Mormon, derive the same immunity? The fact is conceded; and it is averred that each is equally entitled to it in a government whose very constitution avows the principle of a full and indiscriminate religious toleration. * * * * * * * * * * *

"Books written avowedly to attack or defend *political parties* should be excluded; histories, biographies, or other works, *incidentally* betraying the political predilections of the writer, may be admitted; but works which, though even ostensibly on other topics, contain repeated and direct attacks on, or defenses of, any political party, should be excluded. * * * Works discussing what may be legitimately termed politics—that is, the science of government—and which do not assume a partisan character, are properly admissible into the libraries. The Federalist, Debates in the Virginia and New York Conventions, De Tocqueville's Democracy in America, come under this head."

Biographical and Historical works are included in the same category. *Works of Fiction*, or Novels and Romances *of the highest class*, such as the Waverley Novels, the Vicar of Wakefield, Rasselas, the Pilgrim's Progress, &c., selected with rigorous discrimination, are also approved. *Poetical works* of standard excellence are eloquently commended: Dante, Byron, Shelley, Milton, Young, Gray, Cowper, Thomson, Henry Kirke White, Burns, Wordsworth, Campbell, and Mrs. Hemans; Homer, Tasso, Camoens; Spenser and Shakspeare; Malherbe, Corneille, and Racine; Lessing, Schiller, and Goethe; Bryant, Halleck, Dana, Mrs. Sigourney, Percival, Willis, and Gould—are specially mentioned with approbation. "Who ever rose," he observes, "from the perusal of Wordsworth's Tintern Abbey, or Bryant's Thanatopsis, without feeling that he had drunk in the moral of all human philosophy? Milton's Comus, Gray's Elegy, and wild and impassioned 'Bard,' Burns' Cotter's Saturday Night, Kirke White's Ode to Genius, as well as innumerable detached passages which might be cited from all the higher poets, furnish examples, varying in intensity, of the same mystic power." He adds in a note, "And, among these *chef d'œuvres*, I hesitate not to name the 'Camp Meeting Hymn,' commencing 'O

Thou in whose presence,' the authorship of which is unknown to me. Whoever the author was, he was no stranger to the 'ample pinions which the Theban eagle bore.' Indeed, every line reminds us of the sublime fire of Pindar. He who has heard it uplifted by the voices of thousands, in the depths of an American forest, will feel that its beauties have not been exaggerated."

In conclusion, he observes, "A well-selected library for general use should embrace a wide variety of topics. Men's tastes differ almost as much as their persons. Probably every one has decided mental predispositions or biases, developed or undeveloped; and if these are properly appealed to, the best and strongest qualities of the mind are called into action. Touch the wrong cord again and again, and we obtain no response. Defoe's Essay on Projects was the spear of Ithuriel to the undisclosed energies of Franklin. The creative genius of Shakspeare, the sublime majesty of Milton, even the vast and all-embracing philosophy of Bacon, might have failed to reach these. Malebranche had devoted himself to the cloister; an accidental opening of Descartes' Treatise on Man at once revealed what perhaps was as little known to himself as to others—the germ of philosophy implanted in his mind. We have no right to aver that any work on the same topic, or any method of treating it, would have produced the same effects. The waters of the rivers of Damascus may be as healing and limpid as those of the Jordan, but the latter alone can work the miracle. And it is well that it is so. It is well that mind has a natural channel through which to pour its energies, and that it seeks that channel. A literature without individuality were like a landscape in the midst of a desert—

one vast plain, stretching as far as the eye could reach in every direction, in dull and dreary uniformity and lifelessness."

Gov. BOUCK, in his message to the Legislature of 1844, thus alluded to the condition and prospects of the Common Schools:

"No interest of the State is entitled to a more favorable regard or a greater share of attention at the hands of the Legislature than that of public instruction. The intellectual and moral culture of the six or seven hundred thousand children who are speedily to succeed to the generation now on the stage of active life, and to assume the duties and responsibilities as well of government as of society in all its departments, involves in its consequences the existence and destinies of the Republic itself, and cannot be neglected without danger to the vital interests of free institutions. * * * * * *

"The substitution of a single officer charged with the supervision of the Common Schools of each town, for the board of commissioners and inspectors formerly existing, and the supervisory and appellate powers of the several county superintendents, as defined by the law of the last session, seem to have met with the general approbation and concurrence of the people. Conventions and associations of the friends of education have, during the past year, been held in almost every section of the State, indicating a concentration of interest and a direction of effort to this great subject which cannot fail to produce the most salutary results. The standard of qualification of teachers has been materially advanced; parents and the people generally manifest an increased interest in the welfare and prosperity of these elementary institutions of learning; and there are the most abundant reasons for anticipating a steady and continued improvement in all the elements of our extended system of Common School education."

From the annual report of the Superintendent, it appeared that the number of school districts in the State had increased to 10,875, in which 657,782 children out of 671,000, between the ages of five and sixteen, had been instructed during the year reported (1842). Col. YOUNG observes:

"We may reasonably congratulate ourselves upon the accession of a *new order of things* in relation to the practical workings of our system. Through the medium of an efficient county and town supervision, we have succeeded not only in preparing the way for a corps of teachers thoroughly competent to communicate intellectual, moral, and physical instruction—themselves enlightened and capable of enlightening their pupils—but also in demolishing the numerous barriers which have hitherto prevented intercommunication between the several districts. An extended feeling of interest in the condition and progress of the several schools has been awakened; and, in addition to the periodical inspections of the county and town superintendents, the trustees and inhabitants are now, in many portions of the State, beginning frequently to visit the schools of their district, striving to ascertain their advancement, to encourage the exertions of teachers and pupils, and to remove every obstacle arising from their previous indifference. Incompetent teachers are beginning to find the avenues to the Common Schools closed against them; and the demand on the part of the districts for a higher grade of instructors is creating a supply of enlightened educators, adequate to the task of advancing the youthful mind in its incipient efforts to acquire knowledge. The impetus thus communicated to the schools of one town and county is speedily diffused among those of others. Through periodical and frequent meetings of town and county associations of teachers and friends of education, the improvements adopted in any one district are made known to all; and the experience, observations, and suggestions of each County superintendent annually communicated through their published reports to all. By these means the stream of popular education, purified at its source, and relieved from many of its former obstructions, is dispensing its invigorating waters over a very considerable portion of the State.

"The reports of the several County superintendents exhibit unequivocal evidence of efficient exertions on their part in the performance of the responsible duties assigned to them by law, and by the instructions of this department. To their efforts is to be attributed, to a very great extent, the revolution in public sentiment, by which the district school, from being the object of general aversion and reproach, begins to attract the attention and regards of all. To their enlightened labors for the elevation and advancement of these elementary institutions we owe it, in a great measure, that new and improved modes of teaching, of government, and of discipline, have succeeded in a very large proportion of the districts to those which have hitherto prevailed: that a higher grade of qualifications for teachers has been almost universally required; that parents have been induced to visit and take an interest in the schools; that private and select schools have been to a considerable extent, discountenanced, and the entire energies of the inhabitants of districts concentrated on the district school; and that the importance, the capabilities, and extended means of usefulness of these nurseries of knowledge and virtue are beginning to be adequately appreciated in nearly every section of the State. Collectively considered, these officers have well vindicated the confidence reposed in them by the Legislature and the people, and justified the anticipations of the friends of education."

These high encomiums from the Governor and Superintendent of the ability and efficiency of the great body of County superintendents originally appointed by the several boards of supervisors, and of the beneficent results produced by their exertions and influence upon the Common School system of the State, were well and most abundantly deserved. Among their number were such men as FRANCIS DWIGHT, of Albany, the accomplished editor of the *District School Journal;* JABEZ D. HAMMOND, of Otsego, author of the *Political History of the State;* WILLIAM L. STONE, long and familiarly known as the editor of the *Commercial Advertiser* and the historian of Brandt, and JOSEPH MCKEEN, of New York; HENRY S. RANDALL, of Cortland, afterward Secretary of State and Superintendent of Common Schools, and the well-known author of the *Life of Jefferson;* ALBERT and WILLIAM WRIGHT, of Washington; THEODORE F. KING, of Brooklyn; the Hon. HALSEY R. WING, of Warren; THOMAS BARLOW, and EDWARD MANCHESTER, of Madison; IRA MAYHEW, of Jefferson, afterward State Superintendent of Michigan, and the author of many standard educational works; JACOB S. DENMAN, of Tompkins, the energetic founder and promoter of teachers' institutes; DAVID G. WOODIN, afterward State Senator, and JAMES CARVER; JAMES HENRY, Jr., of Herkimer, an eccentric genius, but faithful and efficient officer; STEPHEN MOULTON, and ELON COMSTOCK, of Oneida; ALEXANDER FONDA, of Schenectady; CHARLES C. SEVERANCE, and O. G. STEELE, of Erie; NICHOLAS C. BLAUVELT, of Rockland; ALANSON EDWARDS, and CHAUNCEY GOODRICH, of Onondaga; IRA PATCHIN, of Livingston; ABRAHAM G. HARDENBURGH, of Ulster; PIERPONT POTTER, of Queens; LYSANDER H. BROWN, of Jefferson; HENRY E. ROCHESTER, of Monroe; F. B. SPRAGUE, of Fulton; JOHN B. BOWEN, of Cayuga; A. S. CLEMENT, of Dutchess; H. C. WHEELER, of Yates; DAVID NAY, of Genesee; O. W.

RANDALL, of Oswego; D. S. T. DOUGLAS, of Clinton; D. H. STEVENS, of Franklin; JOHN M. HAWES, of Cattaraugus; ROSWELL K. BOURNE, of Chenango; J. C. TOOKER, of Orange; HENRY C. WHEELER, of Yates; ZEBULON P. BURDICK, of Rensselaer; THEODORE N. BISHOP, of Seneca; ALDEN S. STEVENS, of Wyoming; E. G. STORKE, of Cayuga; R. K. FINCH, of Steuben; and others, their associates in the several counties, of equal zeal and efficiency. Through the severest storms and drifts of winter, and the sultriest days of summer, they penetrated to the most distant and obscure recesses of the territory under their supervision, visiting and inspecting the several schools, ascertaining the qualifications of the teachers, calling together the inhabitants and officers, counseling with them on all the affairs of the district, the condition of its school-house, the selection of its library, and the adjustment of its controversies, and infusing their own spirit into all the details of its administration and enlisting the interest of the people in the education of their children; gathering, once in each year, all the schools of each town, at some central place, for general review and inspection, public addresses, and other exercises; and forming county associations for the promotion of the great interests they had so deeply at heart. Never before or since has so much been accomplished, in so short a period of time, for the advancement and improvement of our Common Schools. In the long interval succeeding the abolition of this class of officers, and prior to the re-establishment of the discarded system, there was, as will hereafter be seen, a general and marked retrogradation in the character, efficiency, and general prosperity of the schools, a falling off of interest in their welfare, a carelessness and absence of energy in their local administration, and an indifference in public sentiment, which, to a very considerable extent, paralyzed the exertions of the Department, and grievously disappointed the hopes, and discouraged the efforts, of the friends of education.

The discussions in the Utica Convention on the subject of NORMAL SCHOOLS, and the decided grounds in favor of such an institution taken by the State Superintendent in his annual report of the present year, served powerfully to direct the attention of the friends of Common School education to this important measure. Mr. HULBURD, of St. Lawrence, who was again at the head of the Assembly Committee on Colleges, Academies, and Common Schools, took occasion, during the early part of the session of 1844, to visit the several Normal Schools of Massachusetts, observe their practical working, make himself thoroughly acquainted with the principles upon which they were founded, and to collect a valuable body of information in regard to the general history and specific operations of similar institutions in Europe. On the 22d of March he submitted an elaborate and eloquent report, embracing the entire subject; reviewing the previous legislation of the State in reference to the establishment of teachers' departments for this purpose in the academies, and demonstrating the utter inefficiency and incompetency of these departments to supply the demand for qualified teachers throughout the State; giving a concise history of the origin and progress of Normal Schools in Europe and America, with a detailed account of their operations in Massachusetts; and recommending the appropriation from the income of the literature fund of $9,000 for the establishment, and $10,000 annually thereafter for the support and maintenance, of a STATE NORMAL SCHOOL, to be located in the city of Albany, for the education and proper preparation of teachers of

Common Schools, of both sexes, and to be composed of pupils selected from the several counties of the State in proportion to the representation of such counties in the popular branch of the Legislature. The committee observe:

"It will appear that the principal reliance of the friends and supporters of the Common Schools for an adequate supply of teachers has, from a very early period, been upon the academies; that the inability of the latter to supply the demand induced, in 1837, an increase of $150,000 to the fund applicable to their support, for the express purpose of enabling them to accomplish this object; that the Regents of the University, the guardians of these institutions, explicitly recognized the condition on which it was granted, accepted the trust, and undertook its performance; that, to use the language of one of the Superintendents, 'the design of the law was not sustained by the measures necessary to give it the form and effect of a system;' that, to remedy this evil, one academy was specially designated in each Senate district, with an endowment of $500, to provide the necessary means and facilities of instruction, and an annual appropriation of $400 for the maintenance of a department for the education of teachers; that soon afterward the sum of $28,000 was added to the literature fund, from the avails of the United States deposit fund, and eight additional academies required to organize and maintain similar departments: that finally the number of these departments was augmented to twenty-three, and every exertion put forth to secure the great results originally contemplated in their establishment; and that, in the judgment of successive Superintendents of Common Schools, the Regents of the University, and the most eminent and practical friends of education throughout the State, these institutions, whether considered in the aggregate, or with reference to those specially delegated from time to time for the performance of this important duty of supplying the Common Schools with competent teachers, have not succeeded in the accomplishment of that object. 'Having, therefore,' to revert again to the language of the Superintendent before referred to, 'proved inadequate to the ends proposed,' may not now 'a *change of plan* be insisted on, without being open to the objection of abandoning a system which has not been fairly tested?' And have the academies any just reason to complain, if they are not longer permitted to enjoy undiminished the liberal appropriation conferred upon them by the State for a specific object, which they have not been able satisfactorily to accomplish?"

After giving a detailed history of the origin and progress of Normal Schools in Europe and Massachusetts, and of the prominent peculiarities of the system, its methods of instruction, &c., the committee proceed:

"A good teacher cannot be prepared as a merchant or manufacturer fills an order for goods. Even Adam Smith excepts education from the mercantile or economical law, that the supply will follow and equal the demand. 'In every age, even among the heathen,' says Martin Luther, 'the necessity has been felt of having good school-masters, in order to make any thing respectable of a nation. But, surely, we are not to sit still and wait until they grow up of themselves. We can neither chop them out of wood nor hew them out of stone. God will work no miracles to furnish that which we have the means to provide. We must, therefore, apply our care and money to *train up and make them*.'

"By common consent, it is necessary to serve an apprenticeship of years to know how to make a hat, a shoe, a coat, or erect a building. A common understanding seems to prevail among most Christian denominations that no one shall be recognized as rightfully having 'the cure of souls,' who has not, preparatory to the exercise of that function, spent some time with an approved divine, or at some seminary specially instituted for the education of the ministry. The State, too, has not regarded it as beneath its care to require that no man shall be recognized as competent to take charge, in its courts of justice, of the property, the reputation, or the life of his fellow-men, until he has gone through a course of seven years' study, three of which are to be spent in the office of a practicing lawyer. It has also denied hitherto, to those who assume the care of the body, the aid of its laws to collect pay for their services, unless a fixed course of study or attendance upon lectures has been rigidly pursued and properly certified. Yet, thus far, neither common consent, nor common understanding, nor statutory provision have required any apprenticeship, any special education, the spending of any fixed term of time, preparatory to entering upon an employment where is laid the very foundation of all these superstructures. Here inexperienced, unskillful hands are permitted to make *experiments* to perfect themselves; and yet the *subjects* of these experiments are *immortal beings!*

"It is the teacher's high prerogative to develop the faculties of human beings. If he mistake his calling, if he mistake the true principles of his art—to *educate*, to develop—and aim merely to *instruct*, to instill—not only the *child*, but the *man* will carry to the grave the sad effects of this ignorance and incompetency. Such a course stunts and dwarfs the whole mental and moral nature; it renders the intellect a mere passive recipient of words and signs—and words and signs only, instead of ideas it will evolve; it will be clothed with a vesture of apparent information, but the power, the originality, the expansion of the mind, are enfeebled, constrained, and circumscribed. It creates the form—it constructs the mechanism—of education, without breathing into it a living soul. It prepares the child to make use of his acquisitions just as the ancient Roman artist did, who was taught to copy with life-like precision the Grecian master-pieces—just as does the serf of the Russian noble, who is trained to execute at command difficult pieces of music, or make fac-similes of paintings of the best modern Italian or Flemish masters without the slightest advance of the operative or intellectual stature, or without one power of producing an original conception.

"How many of our ten thousand teachers have ever known that education—even a Common School education—should be directed to the due development, the symmetrical cultivation of the physical, the moral, and the intellectual faculties of every child! How many have known the constant, careful, practical use to be made of this knowledge, if possessed, in the treatment of every child; that to educate the moral powers, to the exclusion or total neglect of the intellectual, would be detrimental in the extreme—rendering their subject the victim of superstition, and the sport of passing delusion; while to educate the intellect, to the neglect of the moral nature, would be to give talent and power without principle—in other words, to educate for the penitentiary, the prison cell, the scaffold, or the grave of the suicide?

"Again, how many are ignorant of the distinction between intellect and feeling—between ideas and emotions—know not that these two classes of mental operations are called into activity by very different objects, cultivated by different processes; and that as one or the other predominates, in the mental constitution, very different results, both in conduct and character, are produced!

'Oh woe for those who trample on the mind,
That deathless thing! they know not what they do,
Nor what they deal with! Man, perchance, may bind
The flower his foot hath bruised; or light anew
The torch he quenched; or to sweet music wind
Again the lyre-string from his touch that flew:
But for the soul! oh tremble and *beware*
To lay rude hands upon God's mysteries there!'

"In addition to the true discernment of his duty as an educator, there are other requisites, without which, perhaps, no one should be permitted to have the care of the young. Time will not permit us to dwell here upon the importance of a teacher's social and moral qualifications—his mildness, his generosity, his patience, his sense of decorum, his kindness, his cheerfulness, his love of virtue, his reverence for his Maker. These constitute the most precious traits, the richest ornaments of childhood: and there is no parent so debased as not to desire, even in the depth of his debasement, that his child should grow up the possessor of all these qualities. Yet how often have the very means that should have implanted and cherished all these graces been neglected in the unsuitable selection of a teacher, the constituted delegate of the parent! How can the teacher cause his pupil to feel the truth and beauty of what has never touched or entered his own soul?

"We are, sometimes, almost tempted to believe that much of what has been written and sung about our earliest moments is but the dreaming of a beautiful fancy: and yet, who that pauses amid 'being's busy bustle,' and thinks upon childhood—all its joys and its brief tears—its soft purity and its brave gentleness—its charity that 'thinketh no evil'—its hope that 'believeth all things'—does not *feel*, as well as know, that it is the one green spot to which manhood often looks back, and sighs that but once only through it runs the thoroughfare of individual existence! How rarely, too, is the evening of any life so dark that the dimmed eye of age, sightless though it be to all things present, does not fix and fasten upon that far off auroral brightness! How easily are we thus, by observation and experience, brought to believe that

'Heaven lies about us in our infancy!'

"If thus pure and precious and permanent are the impressions of childhood, how inappreciably important the character of the agents that produce them! The parent—the *mother*—is the first natural observer of these glimpses of a higher nature. How easily we can excuse that beautiful superstition which teaches her that the smiles of her sleeping infant are 'gleams of fairy visitings' or angel ministrations! * * * Too soon, by the force of circumstances, the child is removed from maternal guidance, and placed under the care of the school-master. Shall that most sensitive plant blossom with culture, or droop by neglect? Shall it expand in part, and be blighted in part? Shall it grow up with noxious excrescences and unsightly distortions, or exhibit the graceful proportions of symmetrical beauty? Under God, these are questions that for answer depend almost wholly upon the character and the qualifications of the teacher."

In reference to the more general employment of competent and well qualified *female teachers*, and their proper preparation for the duties of the profession, the committee observe:

"It is not the result of gallantry, or of that complaisant homage which in every refined and Christian nation is the accorded due of the female sex, that has given to that sex *an unequivocal preference in teaching and controlling the young.* It is not superior science, but *superior skill in the use of that science*—it is the *manner* and the very weakness of the teacher that constitutes her strength, and assures her success. For that occupation she is endued with peculiar faculties. While man's nature is rough, stern, impatient, ambitious, hers is gentle, tender, enduring, unaspiring. One always wins; the other sometimes repels: *the one is loved; the other sometimes feared.* Kindness and quickness of apprehension, frank sympathy with the young, endear and attach; and when the scholar's confidence and attachment are once gained, he is henceforth easily taught and governed. In childhood, the intellectual faculties are but partially developed—the affections much more fully. At that early age, the affections are the key of the whole being. The female teacher readily possesses herself of that key, and thus, having access to the heart, the mind is soon reached and operated upon; while the male teacher seeks, in direct approaches to the understanding, to implant scientific truth. Hence we have the solution of the problem of the superior success of female teachers with small scholars. While, also, the habits of female teachers are better and their morals purer, they are much more apt to be content with, and continue in, the occupation of teaching. It is an employment to which they are peculiarly adapted, and wherever they have attempted they have succeeded. In Massachusetts, where females have been most employed, they have been most appreciated. At the Normal Schools in that State, where both sexes were received, and where only such were admitted as signified their intention to become teachers, the number of females over males preponderated more than three to one.

* * * * *

"It will be noticed that the committee speak of the establishment of *one* Normal School. Did our present means seem to warrant it, the committee would, with confidence, recommend the immediate establishment *of at least one in each of the eight Senatorial districts.* If one is now established, and that is properly endowed and organized, there cannot be a doubt that not only one will be called for in each of the eight Senatorial districts, but that in a brief period very many of the large counties will insist upon having one established within their limits. The establishment of *one* is but an experiment—if that can be called an experiment which, for more than a century, has been in operation without a known failure—which, if successful, will lead the way to several others. It is believed that several of the academies now in operation can and will be converted into Normal Seminaries when the proper period arrives: in this way there will be no loss of academic investment, and the great interests of the public will be as well, or better, subserved than they are at present.

"The committee believe the experiment should be tried at the Capital; if it cannot be tested in presence of all the people, it should be before all the representatives of the people. As a government measure, it is untried in this State; the result, therefore, will be of deep interest. Here, at each annual session of the Legislature, can be seen for what and how the public money is expended; here can be seen the exhibition of the pupils of the seminary and of the model school; here, if unsuccessful, no report of interested officials can cover up its failure, or prevent the abandonment of the experiment; here citizens from all parts of the State, who resort to the Capital during the session of the Legislature, the terms of the courts, &c., can have an opportunity of examining the workings of the Normal School system—of learning the best method of teaching, and all the improvements in the science and practice of the art—those who in the Spring and Autumn pass through the city to and from the great metropolis, and those who from all parts of the Union make their annual pilgrimage to the Fountain of Health, will pause here to see what the Empire State is doing to promote the education of her people."

The bill reported by the committee was ably and vigorously supported by Mr. HULBURD and the Hon. MICHAEL HOFFMAN, of Herkimer, and passed both

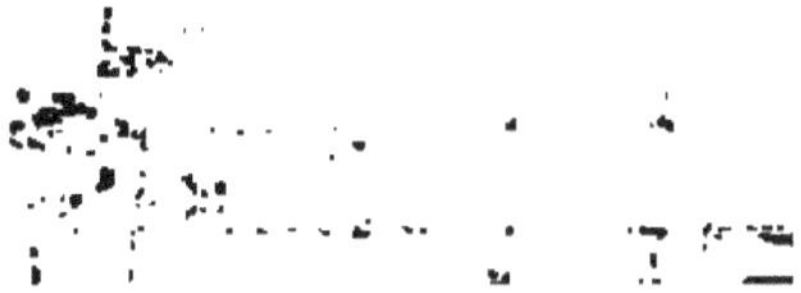

[illegible]

[illegible] of the establishment of [illegible]

[illegible] Board of Health, [illegible] the education [illegible]

committee was [illegible] and the Hon. [illegible] and passed [illegible]

ALBANY NORMAL SCHOOL.

houses on the 7th of May. The institution was, by the terms of the act, placed under the direction of the Superintendent of Common Schools and the Regents of the University, who were authorized and required, from time to time, to make all needful rules and regulations for its management and government, and to appoint an executive committee, consisting of five persons, including the Superintendent of Common Schools, to whom its immediate government and direction should be committed.

In pursuance of this act, the Regents, on the 1st of June, appointed Col. SAMUEL YOUNG, Superintendent of Common Schools; Rev. Dr. ALONZO POTTER, Rev. Dr. WILLIAM H. CAMPBELL, the Honorable GIDEON HAWLEY, and FRANCIS DWIGHT, Esq., members of the Executive Committee; who proceeded to adopt the necessary measures for the organization and establishment of the institution. DAVID P. PAGE, of Newburyport, Mass., was appointed Principal; GEORGE R. PERKINS, of Utica, Professor of Mathematics; FREDERICK I. ILSLEY, of Albany, Teacher of Music; and J. B. HOWARD, of Rensselaer, Teacher of Drawing. A suitable building was procured in an eligible location for the temporary occupancy of the school; and on the 18th of December, 1844, the institution was formally opened by a public address from the Superintendent of Common Schools. Twenty-nine pupils only were in attendance; this number speedily increased to upward of one hundred; and an *experimental* or *model* school for practice, comprising upward of a hundred children of both sexes, was, at the commencement of the second term, attached to the institution.

The introduction of TEACHERS' INSTITUTES, as a constituent portion of the Common School system, in connection with the practical preparation of teachers, was, at this time, in full and successful operation, and destined speedily to take its place as one of the most important features in the progress of educational improvement. The subject was first brought to the attention of the friends of education by a series of resolutions submitted to the Tompkins County Teachers' Association in October, 1842, by J. S. DENMAN, the efficient superintendent of that county, setting forth the necessity of united and efficient action on the part of teachers for the elevation of their profession and of the standard of Common School education generally, and recommending the establishment in that county of an institute where all the teachers might meet semi-annually in the Spring and Fall, preparatory to the commencement of the Summer and Winter terms, for the purpose of receiving instruction and listening to lectures from scientific educators, and in the discussion of plans for the improvement of the schools and the most approved methods of teaching and discipline. This proposition having been received with great favor, the first Teachers' Institute was opened at Ithaca on the fourth day of April, 1843, under the supervision of Mr. DENMAN, assisted by SALEM TOWN, of Cayuga; Prof. JAMES B. THOMSON, of Auburn, and the Rev. DAVID POWELL, as instructors and lecturers. Twenty-eight teachers were in attendance, and instruction was given daily, for a term of two weeks, in the best modes of governing and teaching, including a critical analysis and review of the various elementary and many of the higher branches of education. During the Autumn of the same year several similar institutions were opened in different sections of the State; and, in the succeeding year, their operations were greatly enlarged and extended.

At the opening of the session of the Legislature of 1845, Governor SILAS WRIGHT, in his annual message, thus eloquently alluded to the subject of Common School education:

"No public fund of the State is so unpretending, yet so all-pervading—so little seen, yet so universally felt—so mild in its exactions, yet so bountiful in its benefits—so little feared or courted, and yet so powerful—as the fund for the support of Common Schools. The other funds act upon the secular interests of society, its business, its pleasures, its pride, its passions, its vices, its misfortunes. This acts upon its mind and its morals. Education is to free institutions what bread is to human life—the staff of their existence. The office of this fund is to open and warm the soil, and sow the seed from which this element of freedom must grow and ripen into maturity; and the health or sickness of the growth will measure the extent and security of our liberties. The thankfulness we owe to those who have gone before us, for the institution of this fund, for its constitutional protection, and for its safe and prudent administration hitherto, we can best repay by imitating their example, and improving upon their work, as the increased means placed in our hands shall give us the ability.

"Few, if any, instances are upon record in which a fund of this description has been administered, and its bounties dispensed through a period of forty years, with so few suspicions, accusations, or complaints of the interference of either political or religious biases to disturb the equal balance by which its benefits should be extended to our whole population. *Our school fund is not instituted to make our children and youth either partisans in politics or sectarians in religion*, but to give them education, intelligence, sound principles, good moral habits, and a free and independent spirit—in short, to make them American freemen and American citizens, and to qualify them to judge and choose for themselves in matters of politics, religion, and government. Such an administration of the fund as shall be calculated to render this qualification the most perfect for the mature minds, with the fewest influences tending to bias the judgment or incline the choice, will be the most consonant with our duties and with the best interests of our constituents. Under such an administration, education will most flourish, and the peace and harmony of society be best preserved."

From the annual report of the Superintendent, it appeared that in 10,990 school districts the number of children taught during the year was 709,156, or more than fifty thousand greater than that of the preceding year. The amount paid for teachers' wages was $992,222, of which $447,566, or nearly one-half, was raised on rate bills; the expenditure for the several district libraries was $94,950.54; and the aggregate number of volumes in the several libraries, 1,098,396. The productive capital of the Common School fund was $1,992,916.35, from the avails of which the sum of $275,000 was apportioned for school and library purposes. An equal sum was raised upon the several counties by their respective boards of supervisors; $18,000 by voluntary vote of towns; $200,000 in the several cities under special laws; and $18,000 from the avails of local funds.

In reference to the operations of the several County superintendents during the preceding year, Col. YOUNG remarks:

"The influence exerted by this class of officers on the promotion of the interests of elementary instruction throughout the State has been, in most counties, very favorable. By a periodical and careful supervision of the several schools, by occasional lectures, frequent visitations, judicious counsels, and the communication to the inhabitants, officers, and teachers of each district and each town of the various improvements in the art and science of instruction which may from time to time have been discovered, and by composing local dissensions, they are enabled to combine the system into one harmonious and efficient whole, to concentrate public opinion in its favor, and widely to diffuse its benefits and blessings. From the results of their labors during the past year, it appears that a gradual but very perceptible improvement in the general condition of the schools is in progress; that the standard of qualifications of teachers has been advanced; that an increasing interest in the subject of education has been manifested on the part of the public generally, and especially by parents; that more enlightened and efficient modes of mental discipline are becoming prevalent, antiquated prejudices disappearing, and the paramount importance of an early and general diffusion of knowledge more widely appreciated.

"These are encouraging symptoms. There can, indeed, be little doubt that the systematic exertions of the several County and town superintendents, in conjunction with the trustees and other officers of the several districts, have mainly contributed to give that impulse to the public sentiment, in this respect, which has resulted so auspiciously. Seventy county officers, possessing the confidence of their fellow-citizens generally, distinguished for their devotion to the cause of education, and for their scientific attainments and moral worth, acting under the immediate direction and supervision of the State Superintendent, and each, within the district assigned to him, carrying into efficient operation a system of local supervision, instruction, and discipline, sanctioned by the most enlightened experience of the age, aided and sustained by nine hundred town officers, imbued with the same spirit, and participating in the same generous emulation, and operating, directly or indirectly, through the agency of the trustees, upon the teachers of nearly eleven thousand school districts, must necessarily exert a powerful influence in carrying forward the spirit of improvement, in diffusing knowledge, and in promoting the advancement of sound learning. * * * * * * * *

"In no less than seventeen of the largest counties, 'Teachers' Institutes' have been established during the past two years, in which upward of one thousand teachers have been instructed, during periods varying from two to six or eight weeks immediately preceding the commencement of their respective terms of instruction, by the most competent and experienced educators whose services could be procured, in conjunction with and under the immediate supervision of the County superintendent. * * * Among the numerous improvements which the experience of past imperfections has introduced into the practical operation of our system of Common Schools, there is none which combines greater utility and value than these local and temporary institutions; and, in the judgment of the Superintendent, they are highly deserving of legislative aid." * * * * * * *

In conclusion, the Superintendent observes:

"There is much in the prospect thus opened to us cheering and encouraging to the friends of free institutions, to the friends of education, and of civil, social, and moral progress. The great idea of education, in its most comprehensive acceptation, consists in that development, culture, and discipline of all the faculties of our nature which shall fit us for the highest sphere of usefulness, and the highest degree of enjoyment of which that nature, in the circumstances by which we are surrounded, is susceptible. On the flourishing condition of our schools repose the hopes of the present and the destinies of the future. Without a sound moral and intellectual education, the function of self-government can neither be duly appreciated nor successfully maintained. The constitutions of several of the South American republics appeared theoretically to be well calculated to secure human liberty. But paper provisions are powerless unless they are also impressed on the hearts and combined with the intelligence of the people. Without an accurate knowledge of their rights and duties, and a determination to maintain them, no community can long be free; and the melancholy truth that the South American republics have fallen into revolutionary decrepitude or degenerated into military despotisms affords us an impressive admonition. Indeed, without going beyond our own borders, premonitions of an anti-social spirit; of insubordination to law; of combinations to perpetrate violence, riot, incendiarism, and murder—are sufficiently alarming in their rapid increase during the last few years. If the same spirit pervaded a majority of the community, the existing governments would be at an end; and as human society cannot exist without a superintending power of protection, the aid of some more energetic and despotic form of government would necessarily be invoked to administer justice, to maintain order, and to shield the poor from the exactions of the rich—the weak from the aggressions of the strong.

"The great extent of the American Republic; its rapidly increasing population; the diversity of habits, pursuits, productions, and interests, some of which are regarded as hostile to others—render necessary, at all times, the cultivation of a liberal spirit of forbearance and conciliation. Without the diffusion of education, such a spirit, in sufficient strength to maintain harmony, cannot exist. It may be safely affirmed that there is now no people of equal numbers on the face of the earth, who, if placed under such institutions as ours, would maintain the government for a single year. And unless moral and intellectual culture shall, at least, keep pace with the increase of numbers, this Republic will assuredly fall. On the careful cultivation in our schools of the minds of the young the entire success or absolute failure of the great experiment of self-government is wholly dependent; and unless that culture is increased, and made more effective than it has yet been, the conviction is solemnly impressed by the signs of the times that the American Union, now the asylum of the oppressed and 'the home of the free,' will, ere long, share the melancholy fate of every former attempt at self-government. That Union is and must be sustained by the moral and intellectual power of the community; and every other power is wholly ineffectual. Physical force may generate hatred, fear, and repulsion, but never can produce union. THE ONLY SALVATION FOR THE REPUBLIC IS TO BE SOUGHT FOR IN OUR SCHOOLS. It is here that the seeds of liberty and of good government must be sown and made to germinate and grow, and produce rich fruit in abundance. Every improvement that can be given to these primary institutions affords an additional guaranty for the permanent maintenance of rational freedom.

"The duration of the life of man should be estimated, not by the years of his physical existence—which would be to degrade him to the level of the brute—but by the period of the expansion and enjoyment of his moral and intellectual faculties. Hence it has been affirmed with philosophic truth that 'he who shortens the road to knowledge lengthens life.' The cradle and the grave are in such close proximity, even when the interval is most extended, that human existence may be regarded as nearly a blank, unless the early portion of the brief space by which they are separated is sedulously devoted to the development of the mind. The undying part of our nature has been impressed by its Creator with an unconquerable desire for knowledge—not that limited acquaintance with the external forms of things which is bestowed upon the animals by instinct, but a knowledge vastly more minute and discursive, and which embraces within its scope all the properties and laws both of mind and matter. The earth itself, with all its appendages, is much too small a theater to satiate the inquisitiveness even of children; and if human powers were commensurate with human aspirations, the daring ken of man would be thrown through the abyss of heaven to the *Ultima Thule* of the works of God—to the farthest verge in fathomless space, in which the energies of creative power have not yet been consummated—to regions where the embryo *nebula* of unformed worlds are in the transition or the quiescent state, obedient to the primeval fiat of the Almighty.

"It is in the period of youth, while the mind is unincumbered by secular cares, that these aspirations, which have been bestowed for wise and holy purposes, are the most insatiate; and it is then, when the curiosity is intense, the memory retentive, and the habits plastic, that a broad foundation of moral and intellectual culture should be laid. Every advancing step in the communication of knowledge should be adapted to the capacity of the learner, so that the entire process, from its commencement, shall be a continued and gratifying intellectual exercise. The dull and repulsive routine of former times, and which is yet too much in vogue, converted the preparatory exercises in the acquisition of knowledge into a mere cold and mechanical effort of memory; and, during the first years of the pupilage of children, the little sufferers were daily subjected to the infliction of a species of mental treadmill, whose monotonous evolutions produced only *the broken fragments of words without meaning and sounds without sense.* It is the business of the accomplished educator to remove every obstruction in the paths of knowledge—to open in succession its aromatic fountains to the young aspirant—'to wake the soul by gentle strokes of art'—and to call into healthful exercise all the juvenile faculties.

"To combine in perfection the combined art and science of imparting knowledge to the young is the work of time and of effort. Success in any of the departments of human occupation can be commanded only by previous care and preparation. Without a knowledge of the nature of soils, of plants, and of domestic animals, and also of the different modes of culture, the farmer would be unsuccessful. The artisan must be acquainted with the qualities of the material subjected to his skill, and the best modes of converting it to the purposes of utility. Without study and practice, the chemist would not be able to pursue matter to its simple and elemental forms, and to ascertain its properties by analysis and synthesis. If, then, the proper management of inert matter cannot be usefully performed by unpracticed hands, who will have the temerity to commit the living and immortal minds of children to the careless and unskillful! Matter is subjected by its laws to constant mutation, BUT THE IMPRESS WHICH, IN THIS LIFE, IS AFFIXED UPON THE MIND IS ETERNAL!"

In reviewing the administration of the Common School system by Col. YOUNG, it is impossible not to perceive the vast impulse which was given to all its varied operations by the penetrative and reflective mind, and the originality, energy, and public spirit of that distinguished statesman. Bringing to the discharge of the peculiar duties of his office as Superintendent no previous experience, and imbued with strong prejudices against some of the most prominent features of the system of public instruction committed to his charge, he not only speedily rendered himself familiar with its details, but divesting himself of all those unfavorable preconceptions which had obtained possession of his mind, dispassionately surveyed the entire bearings of the system, and, having convinced himself of its value and utility, devoted his best energies and all his powerful influence to its advancement. The impress of his vigorous mind and strong understanding will long remain upon the system he so well and wisely loved, and so fondly and enthusiastically cherished.

Some of the peculiar and characteristic traits of his mind, and his happy facility of terse and strong expression, are to be found in his correspondence with the officers and inhabitants of school districts for the settlement of questions in controversy. A few only, involving important principles, can be selected for this purpose.

To an inquiry as to the propriety of the use of the New Testament as a reading-book in the Common Schools, he replies:

"I regard the New Testament as in all respects a suitable book to be daily read in our Common Schools, and I earnestly and cordially recommend its general introduction for this purpose. As a mere reading-book, intended to convey a practical knowledge of the English language in its purity and simplicity, it is one of the best text-books in use; but this, although of great utility to the pupils, is of minor importance, where the moral influences of the book are duly considered. Education consists of something more than mere instruction. It is that training and disciplining of all the faculties of the mind which shall systematically and harmoniously develop the future man for usefulness and for happiness in sustaining the various relations of life. It must be based upon knowledge and virtue; and its gradual advancement must be strictly subordinated to those cardinal principles of morality which are nowhere so clearly, and distinctly, and beautifully inculcated as in that book from whence we all derive our common faith. The highest and most finished *intellectual* cultivation, in the absence of careful and sound *moral* discipline, can never accomplish the great end and aim of education. It 'plays round the head, but comes not near the heart.' It may constitute the accomplished sceptic, the brilliant libertine, the splendid criminal—but can never bestow upon mankind the benefactors of the race, the enlightened philosopher, the practical statesman, the bold and fearless reformer. The nursery and family fireside may accomplish much; the institutions of religion may exert a pervading influence; but what is commenced in the hallowed sanctuary of the domestic circle, and periodically inculcated at the altar, must be daily and hourly recognized in the Common Schools, that it may exert an ever-present influence—enter into and form part of every act of the life—and become thoroughly incorporated with the rapidly-expanding character. There must not be one system of mental and moral discipline for the family and another for the school—one for the closet and another for the world. The same incomparable standard of moral virtue and excellence which is expounded from the pulpit and the altar, and daily held up to the imitation and admiration of the family circle, should also be reverently kept before the mind and the heart in the daily exercises of the school.

"If these views are correct, where shall we look for lessons of innocence, virtue, purity, and integrity, worthy to be compared with those which are already, we may hope, endeared to the best affections of the children, in the New Testament? Upon what more exalted standard shall we form the future characters of those whose education is committed to our charge? Parents and teachers should never forget that to them is entrusted the solemn and responsible task not only of communicating knowledge and instruction, but of forming, moulding, and directing the future character of the children entrusted to their care. The direction which the susceptible mind of the child is made to assume in the neglected district school may and does affect not merely its own happiness or misery, but the happiness or misery of thousands whom, in its diversified connections, it influences and controls. It may be fraught with consequences which, in their results, may renovate society, elevate the standard of public and private virtue, and carry forward the destinies of the race to a point hitherto deemed unattainable; and, on the other hand, may cast a withering and hopeless blight over the fairest prospects of humanity.

"But I have said enough in illustration of the paramount importance which I attach to moral and religious culture in our schools; and I trust no objections will be interposed to the general introduction and daily use of the TESTAMENT, not only in yours, *but in every other school in the State.*"

To a brief note from a Jewish resident of New York, informing him that his recent "order to introduce the

NEW TESTAMENT in the public schools of the State of New York would be the means of *driving from them all the children of Jewish parents*," he thus responds:

"What you deem an 'order' is no more than an earnest *recommendation*, submitted to the judgment, the discretion, and the conscience of those who have the selection of books for district schools.

"I claim the right of frankly expressing my opinions, and I concede the same right to all others, both Jews and Gentiles, believers and unbelievers; nor would I adopt any order, nor exercise any power, other than the power of persuasion, to change the conscientious belief of any human being, on any subject whatever. I may think that the unalloyed doctrine of pure morality; a love and reverence for the Creator; an attachment to truth, justice, and purity; an abnegation of selfishness; a forgiveness of injuries; an abstinence from revenge and cruelty; and a susceptibility to the claims of charity and the impulses of benevolence—are more effectually inculcated and more indelibly impressed upon the minds of the young by the NEW TESTAMENT than any other book whatever. I may believe that its requirements are more eminently calculated to promote 'peace on earth and good-will to men;' I may believe that the Christian religion has done much to establish the great truth of social equality that 'God of one flesh has made all the children of men,' and that it has been more efficacious in eradicating slavery and oppression; in elevating the social condition of woman; in short, in softening and civilizing mankind—than any other creed whatever. I may *and do*, after years of reading, reflection, and observation, believe all this. But I am aware that others, doubtless with equally good intentions, may entertain different notions of morality, and adopt other systems of human happiness, and, consequently, give a preference to other creeds and other books. Over their consciences I shall never attempt to exercise any control. Their whole responsibility is to a much higher tribunal."

To one of the County superintendents (O. W. RANDALL, of Oswego) he writes:

"You inform me that your opinion that *habitual profanity* would be a sufficient ground for annulling a teacher's certificate is deemed by some teachers altogether too rigid, and you ask my views on this subject.

"I cannot imagine under what construction of law or code of morality an individual addicted to *habitual profanity* could ever have *obtained* a certificate as a qualified teacher. But such a certificate having been procured, no matter by what means, I should deem it the imperative duty of any tribunal having the power, to affix upon it at the earliest moment the blot of annulment, and if possible, of oblivion.

"Good moral character is made by the statute an indispensable requisite to the qualification of a teacher. Profane cursing and swearing is a legal offense, punishable by fine, and, in default of payment, by imprisonment.

Can ebony be mistaken for topaz? Can 'good moral character' be ascribed to him who 'habitually' puts both the laws of God and man at defiance?

"Most of the crimes which afflict and disgrace society can plead that they are based upon some of the animal gratifications. It is to satisfy his real or fictitious physical wants that the thief commits larceny. The glutton, in the indulgence of his appetite, is sustained by a precedent, '*running on all fours*,' in the swine; and the gross debauchee can claim the goat and the monkey as his brothers; but profanity is a spontaneous exhibition of iniquity—a *volunteer* sin, committed without temptation and without reward—a bastard vice, destitute of parentage, and wholly disowned by nature. Phrenologists profess to find the location upon the human skull of all the animal propensities. No one, however, has yet been able to detect the 'bump' of profanity. Pandora's box is full without it; and the *amateurs* in human mischief and human misery have superadded this as a mere *gratuitous evil*.

"I can conceive of nothing more horrible and repulsive than to send innocent little children to a school where they will be taught, either by precept or example, to stammer oaths and to lisp profanity. This is to poison the whole stream of life at its very source."

To Mr. SPRAGUE, of Fulton, another superintendent, who had informed him that a few of the teachers in his county were in the practice of *attending balls*, &c., he writes:

"Having myself, when young, indulged in the practice which you name, I cannot find it in my heart to utter an official reprimand against these teachers. I should be met by that troublesome text, 'let him who is without sin,' &c. In my youth I attended balls and danced, and I confess I have never seen cause to regret it.

"I wish innocent amusements for the young could be multiplied, varied, and made so attractive as wholly to exclude all questionable or dangerous indulgences. Youth must and will have amusements and hours of relaxation; and the character of these amusements often leaves a durable impression. I wish there were twenty sports for the young, as innocent, as social, as healthful, and exhilarating as dancing. It appears to me that when properly conducted—and any thing may be perverted and abused—it is not only harmless but beneficial. It has been practiced in all ages, among all nations, savage and civilized; and has been tolerated, if not encouraged, by the great majority of sects, denominations, and creeds, of Jews, Christians, and Pagans, from the beginning of the world to the present day. *Singing* is equally universal. It is applied to devotional as well as to secular exercises; and if our minds were disencumbered of all the prepossessions of youth and the prejudices of education, it would, perhaps, be difficult for us to prove that dancing might not, with equal propriety, be applied to both purposes. I am aware that my opinion, in these respects, will not be deemed orthodox by all. Should it not meet with your approbation, you will please to reject it."

FOURTH PERIOD.—1845 TO 1851.

THE FREE SCHOOL CAMPAIGN.

SECTION I.—ADMINISTRATION OF SECRETARY NATHANIEL S. BENTON—1845 TO 1848.

State Convention of County Superintendents at Syracuse.—The Bible in the Public Schools.—Free Schools.—Col. Young.—Rev. Dr. Alonzo Potter.—State Convention of Teachers.—Francis Dwight.—Condition of the Common Schools.—Annual Reports of the Superintendent.—Convention of County Superintendents at Albany.—Speech of Horace Mann.—The Free School Controversy.—State Constitutional Convention.—Abolition of the Office of County Superintendent.—Its Causes and Results.—Teachers' Institutes.—Progress of the State Normal School.—Death of Principal Page.—Free Academy of the City of New York.

ON the 3d of February, 1845, the Hon. NATHANIEL S. BENTON, of Herkimer, was appointed Secretary of State and ex-officio Superintendent of Common Schools. Judge BENTON had previously filled, with honor and ability, a judicial position in his own county, and a seat in the Senate of the State. It is no disparagement to him to say that his abilities were inferior to those of his distinguished predecessors in the department committed to his charge; but it is due to his memory to say that, during his brief administration, he resisted, to the utmost extent of his power and influence, the retrograde movements of the Legislature, in reference to the supervision and consequent general efficiency of the schools; that he was a firm and devoted advocate of the principle of FREE SCHOOLS; and that his administration of the Common School system was characterized by an enlightened and discriminating regard to the public interests and welfare.

During the preceding year several changes had been made in the office of County Superintendent. Messrs. RALPH H. SPENCER and J. J. ROCKAFELLOW had succeeded the former incumbents in Allegany; J. TAYLOR BRODT, in Broome; WORTHY PUTNAM, in Chautauque; DAVID R. RANDALL, in Chenango; D. S. McMASTERS, in Clinton; S. J. FERGUSON, in Delaware; HENRY H. INGRAHAM, in Dutchess; E. S. ELY, in Erie; P. MONTGOMERY, in Jefferson; Hon. SAMUEL E. JOHNSON, in Kings; SIDNEY SYLVESTER, in Lewis; MARSENA TEMPLE, in Madison; ALEXANDER MANN, in Monroe; Dr. D. MEREDITH REESE, in place of Col. WILLIAM L. STONE, deceased; JOSHUA COOKE, in Niagara; WILLIAM S. WETMORE, in Oneida; ORSON BARNES, in Onondaga; AUGUSTUS T. HOPKINS, in Ontario; HORACE K. STEWART, in Orange; J. O. WILSEA, in Orleans; LEWIS R. PALMER, in Otsego; MORGAN HORTON, in Putnam; P. H. THOMAS and J. B. WILKINS, in Rensselaer; SEABURY ALLEN, in Saratoga; JOHN H. SALISBURY, in Schoharie; CHARLES SENTELL, in Seneca; CHARLES RICH and FREDERICK SPRAGUE, in St. Lawrence; SAMUEL A. SMITH, in Suffolk; JOHN D. WATKINS, in Sullivan; ELIJAH POWELL, in Tioga; SMITH ROBERTSON, in Tompkins; LEMON THOMPSON, in Warren; SAMUEL COLE, in Wayne; JOHN HOBBS, in Westchester; J. S. DENMAN, in Wyoming; THALES LINDSLEY, in Yates; JOHN OLNEY, in Greene; and NELSON WHITMAN, in Hamilton.

The meeting of the State Convention of Superintendents, in April of this year, at Syracuse, was honored by the presence of the State Superintendent, Mr. BENTON; the Rev. Dr. POTTER, of Union College; the Hon. HENRY BARNARD, State Superintendent of Rhode Island; Hon. IRA MAYHEW, State Superintendent of Michigan; GEO. B. EMERSON, of Boston; the Rev. SAMUEL

J. MAY and the Rev. Mr. CASTLETON, of Syracuse; the Rev. JOSIAH HOLBROOK and LYMAN COBB, Esq., of New York; SALEM TOWN, of Cayuga; and Mrs. EMMA WILLARD, of the Troy Female Seminary The principal topics of discussion, during its session, were the introduction and use of the BIBLE in the Public Schools, and especially in those of the city of New York, and the necessary measures to oppose the movement, then in progress, for the abolition of the system of county supervision.

The Rev. Dr. POTTER on being requested to address the Convention, in referring to the present position of the County Superintendents, regretted that they should be opposed in the discharge of their many and arduous duties, and that a portion of our fellow citizens could be still blind to the fact that a constant and regular supervision of our schools was necessary. He advised conciliation, patience, and reiterated efforts on the part of the superintendents, and their abstinence from all political or partisan discussions. He then passed to the subject of moral and religious instruction, dwelt upon its importance, and especially upon the value of the BIBLE as its chief exponent—counseling, at the same time, a scrupulous regard to the rights and prejudices of different classes of the community. He concluded by introducing the following resolution embodying these views:

"*Resolved*, That this Convention regard the introduction of the BIBLE into schools as an object earnestly to be desired; but that the time and manner in which this object is to be accomplished is a question which ought to be decided by the inhabitants of the districts; and that in all measures for the promotion of moral and religious culture in our schools, sacred regard ought to be had for the rights, and tenderness manifested toward the scruples and prejudices, of all."

This resolution called forth an animated and prolonged discussion, in which the Rev. Mr. MAY, of Syracuse; LYMAN COBB, and Dr. D. MEREDITH REESE, of New York; Mr. ELY, of Erie; Mr. MANN, of Monroe; ALBERT and WILLIAM WRIGHT, of Washington; Mr. HENRY, of Herkimer (President of the Convention); Mr. SPENCER, of Allegany; Mr. LINDSLEY, of Yates; the Rev. Mr. CASTLETON, of Syracuse, and others, participated. Mr. MAY expressed his full concurrence in the principles of the resolution. Mr. COBB dissented from the reservations implied by leaving this question to the fluctuating determination of the inhabitants of the several school districts; alluded to the impressive influence upon the children of the reading of the Bible at the opening of the public schools in the city of New York; and insisted upon the importance and indispensable necessity of its full and decided recognition as a sacred book, pre-eminently superior to all others, and from which all our moral and religious principles are to be deduced. He desired that the resolution should be so modified as to recommend the urgent influence of the County superintendents for its daily reading in every school of the State.

Dr. POTTER remarked that he had certainly intended to embody these views in his resolutions. He thought, nevertheless, that the trustees and inhabitants of the several districts, and not any authoritative body, should decide this matter. He would, however, cheerfully accept the proposed amendment; and the resolution was modified accordingly.

Mr. MANN, of Monroe, and Mr. LINDSLEY, of Yates, were of opinion that the passage of this resolution, as modified, would be in clear contravention of the principle asserted in its terms; and that, while recognizing the exclusive right of the districts to determine for themselves what measure and method of moral and religious instruction they would have, the County superintendents were directed to insist upon a particular mode.

The Rev. Mr. CASTLETON, of Syracuse, said the crisis had come—the ground had been taken, and would be maintained. The Bible must not be expelled; or if it were, its expulsion would expel Christians and believers from your enterprise. It was not the mere *neglect* of the Bible against which he desired to raise his voice, but against its entire *expulsion*. To teach science without morality was, in fact, to teach that morality was not an essential portion of education; to teach morality without religion was to affirm that the latter was wholly unconnected with the former; and to teach religion without the Bible was to deny the Bible by the allegation that it was not essential to religion. How could teachers, in enforcing the moral principles of justice, mercy, truth, and benevolence, refer to the sanctions of the Bible in confirmation of the dictates of reason and conscience, when that book was expelled from the schools as unfit and improper to be read?

Dr. D. MEREDITH REESE, of New York, gave a history of the controversy which had for some years existed, and was still to a considerable extent pending, in the city of New York, on this subject. The statute of 1842, as amended by that of 1844, under which the present system of Ward Schools, as distinguished from those of the Public School Society, grew up, contained a distinct provision, that no school organized under its authority should be entitled to receive any portion of the school money, in which "the religious doctrines or tenets of any particular Christian or other religious sect shall be *taught*, *inculcated*, or *practiced*, or in which any book or books containing compositions favorable or prejudicial" to such particular doctrines, or which should teach such doctrines—expressly prohibiting, however, the Board of Education from *excluding* from any of the schools "the HOLY SCRIPTURE, without note or comment, or any selections therefrom," or from determining *what version*, if any, of such Scriptures, without note or comment, should be used in any school—reserving the rights of conscience secured by the Constitution of the State and United States. During a period of more than thirty years, under the administration of the Public School Society, no school in the city of New York had been opened without the reading of the Holy Scriptures. Roman Catholic as well as Protestant teachers read them continually, and without objection. On his last official visitation to the schools as County superintendent, he found *thirty-three* of the schools established and organized by this act, *from which the Bible had been excluded as a sectarian book.* "I earnestly protested," continued Dr. REESE, "against this exclusion of the Word of God. I gave a public challenge to all persons to come forward, if they could, and show that any child or parent, Catholic or Protestant, had ever objected to the use of the Bible. The exclusion was, to the last degree, wanton and uncalled for. It was not the work of the people—not even the Catholic portion of the people—but a miserable contrivance of corrupt politicians." He then represented these facts to the officers of the wards, and having ascertained that they would do nothing, notified the Board of Education that such schools had forfeited their share of the public money, and obtained an explicit and strong decision from Col. YOUNG, then Superintendent of Common Schools, that the Bible could not legally be regarded as a sectarian book. The schools in question, however, succeeded, for the time being, in obtaining possession of the public money. After presenting the whole subject to the consideration of a public meeting, at which over five thousand people were present, and which strongly sanctioned the stand he had taken, Dr. REESE brought the matter before the Common Council, who by a nearly unanimous vote adopted an ordinance prohibiting the City Comptroller from paying over any portion of the public money to those schools from which the Bible had thus been illegally excluded, and none had accordingly since been paid to any in which the Bible had not been read. The use of either the Protestant or Douay version, as the majority of parents might prefer, if "without note or comment," had been authorized and sanctioned. He continued:

"Let it ever be proclaimed, that the BIBLE is a sectarian book—that it is unfit to be read in our schools, and listened to by our children—and what kind of a moral education can you confer upon the rising generation? Such an announcement alone would be fatal to all good morals and all proper education. These resolutions open the door for the exclusion of the Bible wherever prejudice is alleged to exist against it. Every State superintendent, from the period of the first organization of the system, has borne unequivocal testimony in favor of its use in our Common Schools, and the explicit language of the statute authorizing the establishment of Ward Schools in the city of New York prohibits its exclusion, while in those of the Public School Society it has uniformly been in daily use since their first organization.

"It has been observed in this debate that truth must prevail—that the Bible can be in no danger—and that, therefore, no efforts are needed in its defense. But is this the course you pursue in regard to philosophical and scientific truth? If so, then your schools are themselves superfluous. Science and philosophy can never be put down, but morals and virtue may; and though the Bible is in no danger, our liberties are in great danger. And if we tamely surrender the Bible at the clamorous bidding of those who would drive it from our schools, we shall soon see it driven from our churches also. At the present time there are but six schools in the city of New York where the Bible is excluded. But aside from all local considerations, I should deprecate the passage of the resolution. The evil to result from it would, I fear, extend to every city and town in the State. Its passage would be disastrous in the extreme."

Dr. POTTER, in reply, observed, that he advocated the introduction of the Bible into all the schools, as soon as practicable, by *persuasion*, but not by *compulsion*; that the Superintendents and others should *recommend* its introduction, but not *exact* it; that the Superintendents, as officers, were merely *advisory* ones; that no resolutions of theirs would be compulsory, but that all measures of this nature must, after all, be referred to the people, as the proper tribunal to decide upon them. The resolution, in its terms and spirit, referred to the introduction of the Bible into schools where now it is not read; and it was difficult to see how a measure designed to aid that object could tend to the exclusion of the Bible any where. In the city of New York its use was provided for by a law of the State. No such law existed in respect to the country; and, in its absence, it was almost too obvious for argument that the people—the inhabitants of the several districts—were the proper arbiters in the premises. The resolution affirmed the great desirableness of introducing the Scriptures where they were not now used, and declares the inhabitants to be the proper judges as to the time and manner of such introduction. Was not this better and wiser than coercive legislation—more in harmony with the genius of our institutions and the spirit of the Common School system? That system made the people the governors of the schools in the several districts. The State Superintendent had only an appellate jurisdiction, the County Superintendents were only advisory officers. The whole theory of the system involved the idea that the *people* were to administer it—the State, through its officers, acting the part of patron and supervisor. For a country like ours was not this better than the centralized absolutism of Prussia or Austria, where the people do little for education, and the government almost every thing? The gentleman had stated that in no instance had the people in the city of New York, either parents, teachers, or children, objected to the introduction of the Bible into their schools. This showed that it was safe to refer this question to the people. When proper prudence was used, no objection would usually be encountered; and the objections of a small portion of the inhabitants would, by no means, render it the duty of the majority to resolve upon exclusion. Wise and good men would, however, always be more anxious to subdue opposition by kindness and persuasion than to overthrow it by the mere force of majorities. They would bide their time. If they were unable to secure the introduction of the Bible peaceably, they would wait—consoled, in the mean time by the reflection that through the singing and reading books in schools, the example and precepts of the teacher, as well as through the daily discipline, they could do much for moral and religious culture, even though the Bible were not read in school hours. It was an end which they would keep steadily in view, but there was a still higher end which could still be attained—even that for which the Bible itself was given—the imparting of its influences and principles through the inculcations of living expounders of its truths. Nor should we, in discussing this subject, overlook the aid we derive, in this good and great work, from the clergy, from Sunday Schools and Bible Classes, and from parental instruction.

After some remarks from Dr. Reese, in explanation

of his views, and the adoption of a supplementary clause disclaiming any application to the city of New York, for the regulation of the schools in which, a special statute existed, the resolution of Dr. POTTER, as modified, was unanimously concurred in.

The Hon. N. S. BENTON, State Superintendent, on being introduced to the convention, remarked that he had at all times since its establishment cordially concurred in the present efficient system of public instruction; and fully appreciated the great importance of the services rendered by the County superintendents, and the magnitude and extent of the duties and powers devolved upon them. He observed:

"I learn that there are memorials from some fourteen counties in favor of abolishing the existing system of county supervision. I am apt to think that in some cases this movement has arisen from political antipathies, unfortunately but too strong among the people. Opposition of a sectarian description, I am informed, has existed in one or two cases. These causes are made to work against the system itself—most unjustly and improperly, as I firmly believe. Gentlemen who are County superintendents, of whichever political party, will at once perceive that they are marks for the opposite party in their own county to aim at. They should, therefore, redouble their prudence and circumspection. It is for us to sustain the system; and this chiefly by making it worthy, in the highest degree, of public confidence and favor.

"I desire to say to this convention, though it is, perhaps, not proper that I should be committed on this subject—yet I do not hesitate to say that it is my opinion that in the end *we shall find* FREE SCHOOLS, *in all respects, the best adapted to our wants and condition;* and I am persuaded that, *as a matter of* ECONOMY, *they are preferable to any other system.* I propose to prepare myself to show, as I hope and believe, that this system would bear less heavily upon the property of the State than the present mixed system. And I cannot but look forward with joy to the state of things when wealth which is really no distinction will cease to be regarded as such, and the children of all our citizens be placed upon a footing of happy and honorable equality."

This was touching, for the first time, in high official quarters, the key-note of the great conflict for FREE SCHOOLS, which was destined in the ensuing administration to break out, and at a still later period to become triumphant by the solemn recognition and adoption of the principle of UNIVERSAL EDUCATION IN PUBLIC SCHOOLS FREE TO ALL. An able report in favor of this great measure was also made during the session of the convention by DAVID NAY, of Genesee.

Addresses were made during the meeting by the Honorable HENRY BARNARD, of Rhode Island; Rev. Dr. ALONZO POTTER; GEORGE B. EMERSON, Esq., of Boston; the Rev. SAMUEL J. MAY, of Syracuse; and Mrs. EMMA WILLARD, of Troy, who was waited upon, at her rooms, by the members of the convention in a body, for that purpose.

A committee of the convention, of which Mr. DWIGHT was chairman, also visited the public schools of Syracuse. Mr. DWIGHT, in his report, stated that he first visited the schools of that city five years ago, at which time an itinerant lecturer took a model of the best school-house in the place, and exhibited it about the State, to show how bad a school-house could be! Since that time a magical change had been wrought: and he now felt justified in holding up the school-houses, their arrangements, the methods of instruction, their teachers, patrons, and scholars, as models of what schools *should be*. Then Syracuse was one of the lowest—now it was one of the highest in the scale of improvement. He also paid a high compliment to the schools of Camillus, Marcellus, and Skaneateles; and referred in terms of commendation to the surprising change manifest, in all these respects, throughout the State.

Mr. BARNES, of Onondaga, submitted the following resolution:

"*Resolved*, That the Hon. SAMUEL YOUNG, *for* his devotion to the cause of education; for his comprehensive and practical recommendations and suggestions: the untiring ardor with which he consecrated the energies of his great intellect to the elevation of our system of Common Schools—deserves and will receive the thanks, not only of this convention, but of all the friends of equal and universal education throughout the world."

Mr. ROCHESTER, of Monroe, rose to second the resolution. He most fully concurred in its expression of the high estimate in which Col. YOUNG was held by the members of this Convention. It had been his fortune, almost from his earliest acquaintance, to differ with him on almost all the political questions of the present day; and, perhaps, it was his duty to confess that he had imbibed a strong prejudice against him. From the official position, however, recently occupied by him, not only had all such prejudices been removed, but Col. YOUNG had been placed high in his respect and esteem; and he believed that he but expressed the opinion of the superintendents and of the intelligent friends of education every where, when he said that he had shown himself a most honest and capable public officer, and an enlightened and efficient advocate of popular education.

The Hon. HENRY BARNARD said that, disconnected as he was from all political relations and parties in this State, resolved to know or to care for no man's political faith, so he be true to the great cause of popular education and human progress, he should be happy, with the permission of the convention, to add his voice to the unanimous vote which this acknowledgment of Col. YOUNG's services will receive from all present. His manly and energetic administration of your wide-spread school system; his fearless assertion of the great principles of virtue and morality in his official papers, correspondence, and reports; and the noble manner in which he came forward and surrendered his preconceived opinions and prejudices against the system of county supervision adopted by his predecessor in office, avowed his determination to give that system a fair trial, and, when he had done so, openly and publicly, and on all occasions, acknowledged it to be a valuable improvement on the old plan—these things have won for him the highest respect of all the friends of education in other States. It has fallen to the lot of but few men to be able to do so much for the more complete and universal education of the people as he has done, by his early and continued advocacy of the school library enterprise and the establishment of Normal Schools and Teachers' Institutes. These measures will mark a new era in the history of popular education in your State, and will most materially strengthen the hands and the hearts of those who are laboring in this field in other parts of the country. Every teacher, every parent, every school officer, ought to be grateful to the late Superintendent for his agency in establishing these institutions; and sure I am that the thousands and hundreds of thousands of children, whose capacities for happiness and usefulness will be increased by the better instruction they will thus have been made to receive, will "rise up and call him blessed!"

The resolution was unanimously adopted, and the convention adjourned.

Shortly after the retirement of Col. YOUNG, he was appointed by the Regents of the University to supply the vacancy in the Executive Committee of the State Normal School, created by the transfer of the Rev. Dr. ALONZO POTTER to Pennsylvania, as Bishop of the Episcopal Church. Perhaps no man in the State had rendered more important and efficient services to the cause of Common School education than

DR. POTTER. In all the great movements which so eminently characterized the administrations of Gen. DIX, Mr. SPENCER, and Col. YOUNG, for the elevation and advancement of the system of public instruction; in the introduction of teachers' departments in the several academies; in all the measures which led to the reconstruction of the system, and the establishment of the plan of county supervision; and in the organization of the State Normal School—he was an active and energetic participator; and by his eloquent addresses, his indefatigable labors, and his able and zealous co-operation, strengthened the arms and encouraged and stimulated the exertions of the friends of education throughout the State. His mind was eminently practical and conservative in its tendencies, preferring to retain all established institutions so long as they continued to accomplish the purposes for which they were designed, rather than prematurely to hazard the untried chances of innovation; gradually to engraft the new upon the old, as the exigencies of the time appeared to require; and in all things to make due allowances for the opinions, the habits, and even the prejudices of those who were unprepared to receive and welcome the advancing doctrines, and cordially to carry out the new measures, of a progressive age. This feature of his character enabled him, at all times, to exert a much more powerful influence on public opinion than could otherwise have been attained by talents however brilliant, or abilities however superior. It rendered him also an invaluable counselor in all public bodies where the collision of opposing interests and views, and the excitement of debate, endangered that calm consideration and judicious settlement of principles which the importance of the subject required.

In July of this year, the first STATE CONVENTION OF TEACHERS assembled at Syracuse, under the presidency of JOHN W. BULKLEY, then of Albany, and subsequently, for many years, and still, the City Superintendent of Brooklyn. Addresses were delivered by C. W. ANTHONY, of Albany; Prof. CHESTER DEWEY, of Rochester; Prof. SIMEON NORTH, afterward the distinguished President of Hamilton College; and FREDERICK EMERSON, of Boston. Reports were presented on various subjects of educational interest; and resolutions adopted endorsing the system of county supervision, the reading of the BIBLE as a portion of the exercises in the several Common Schools of the State, and the establishment of a teachers' journal under the editorial supervision of EDWARD COOPER, of Westchester, to be published at Syracuse, by Mr. L. W. HALL.

The death, on the 13th of December, of FRANCIS DWIGHT, Esq., editor of the *District School Journal*, the able and efficient County Superintendent of Albany, and a member and Secretary of the Executive Committee of the State Normal School, threw a deep shade of gloom over the hearts of the friends of Common School education generally throughout the State. To talents of a high order, and the most varied scientific and literary accomplishments, Mr. DWIGHT united an enthusiastic attachment to the interests of public instruction, and an indefatigable devotion to its advancement in all its departments, which rendered him a valuable co-operator in every enterprise for its promotion. Perhaps no man in the State exerted a wider and more varied influence than himself upon the great educational movements of the period, through his connection with the official organ for communication with the several school districts, and his position as County superintendent. The *Journal*, on his death, passed into the hands of his associate and friend, the author of this history; and his place as County superintendent was ably filled by the appointment of Gen. RUFUS KING, afterwards Adjutant-General of the State.

From the annual report of Superintendent BENTON, communicated to the Legislature on the 20th of January, 1846, it appeared that in the eleven thousand districts of the State, 736,000 children had been taught during the year reported (1844), only 17,000 of whom had, however, been under instruction for a period exceeding six months, and 147,000 only for a period of four months and less than six. The increase in the whole number instructed, over those of the preceding year, was nearly 27,000. In the city of New York, 50,000 children had been under instruction in the various public schools. In the nine thousand districts personally visited by the several County superintendents during the preceding year, 7,566 school-houses were of framed wood, 567 of brick, 519 of stones, and 552 *of logs:* of which 3,783 were in good, 2,700 in ordinary, and 2,760 in *bad*, repair; 8,613 had one apartment only; 6,462 were found wholly destitute of play-grounds; and upward of *five thousand* were *wholly destitute* of privy accommodations, while two thousand of the remainder were furnished only with single privies. *Every district* in the counties of Kings, Monroe, and New York, was suitably provided for in these respects; while in Allegany, Broome, Chautauque, Chemung, Columbia, Franklin, Greene, Lewis, Putnam, Seneca, St. Lawrence, Suffolk, Tioga, and Warren, over seventy-five per cent. of the whole number of districts, in Steuben over eighty, and in Sullivan nearly ninety, were *entirely* destitute of these necessary appendages. The average wages of male teachers was about $14, and of females, $7.50. The amount of public money received and applied to the payment of teachers' wages was $629,856.94, and the amount contributed by parents on rate-bills, $458,127.78, to which if the amount of local funds belonging to towns—$20,000—be added, the total expenditure for teachers' wages during the year was $1,007,984.72. The usual appropriation for libraries, $95,000, was expended in the addition of 100,834 volumes, making the whole number 1,115,250. The Superintendent observes:

"The marked difference between the whole number of children, over five and under sixteen years of age, reported by the trustees, and the reported number under instruction for a period less than four months, shows that a very considerable portion of the children in the State do not attend school for a time required to entitle a district to its share of public money. * * * * What proportion of the whole number of children in the State are excluded from all participation in the benefits of our Common Schools, on account of the poverty of their parents, or of the refusal or neglect of the trustees to make the exemptions on this account required by law, cannot now be accurately ascertained, and probably never will be, however important these facts may be. The Superintendent believes that the number in the whole State, embracing our large cities, populous villages, and manufacturing towns, whose destitution entitles them to be placed on the list of free scholars, is much larger than has been generally supposed by accurate observers; and *the lowest probable estimate we can form of that number is over forty-six thousand.*" "Among other obstacles to be encountered is the reluctance of many parents to participate in the benefits afforded by these exemptions, owing to the manner in which this *bounty*, as they call it, is bestowed. They will not send their children to the schools to be *reproached for their poverty, and assailed with taunts that they are educated at the expense of their more fortunate neighbors.*"

In conclusion, the Superintendent remarks:

"The successful progress and practical results that have hitherto marked the steady advance of our Common School system present to the mind of the philanthropic statesman, the patriotic citizen, and the moralist, a theme for profound reflection on the prospects of the future, and for grateful recollections of the past thirty years. During this time, amidst all the asperities that have marked the conflicts of mind with mind on other topics, civil and social, the revolutions of political parties, and a material change in the fundamental law of the State, this great and invaluable institution has stood like an ocean rock, unharmed and unmoved!"

On the 12th of May, the State Convention of County Superintendents re-assembled at Albany, under the presidency of the General Deputy Superintendent, S. S. RANDALL. Judge BENTON, the State Superintendent; the Hon. HORACE MANN, of Massachusetts; the Hon. HORACE EATON, Superintendent of Common Schools, and afterward Governor of Vermont; Dr. THEODORE F. KING, late of Brooklyn, State Superintendent of New Jersey; Prof. PIERCE, of the Lexington Normal School in Massachusetts; Prof. D. P. PAGE, Principal of the New York State Normal School; Prof. J. D. THOMSON, of New York; EDWARD COOPER, of Westchester, editor of the "Teachers' Advocate;" and other distinguished gentlemen, were in attendance.

In October, 1844, WILLIAM BARNES, DAVID PARSONS, and N. P. STANTON, Jr., a committee appointed by the ONONDAGA COUNTY TEACHERS' INSTITUTE, presented the following report on the subject of FREE SCHOOLS—being the earliest official action we have been able to find on this important topic:

"The committee on Free Schools respectfully report: That they are deeply impressed with the incalculable importance of this subject to the best interests of the American people. We believe that the time has arrived when the discussion and agitation of this question is called for, and when it would be productive of good results. The committee are in favor of the Free School system for the following reasons:

"1. *We maintain that every human being has a right to intellectual and moral education; and that it is the duty of government to provide the means of such education to every child under its jurisdiction.* Man is not born with the matured mind which education produces. Unlike the brute creation, who receive by nature the knowledge necessary for their future support and happiness, men totally uneducated would die, or live in misery. The intelligence of brutes remain stationary for ages; man has the capacity of continual progression, and seems designed for a state of education and progressive improvement. If man, in a state of total helplessness, and without the natural education of the brute creation, has no right to demand the intellectual and moral culture so essential to his existence and happiness from his fellow men, then his right to 'life and liberty' is of no consequence. The right to the air we breathe is not more necessary to physical existence than culture to mental health. Who would accept the gift of life, unaccompanied with the cultivation of the intellect and moral faculties?

"The community, or government, its representative, is bound to provide the intellectual and moral culture without which the people will be miserable. The presence of uneducated persons in the body politic impairs the happiness of its other members—we feel sorrow for their degradation, and are injured by their actions and crimes. Government conceives it to be its duty to construct 'internal improvements'—how much stronger is the obligation to make improvements on the uncultivated soil of mind? If, for the common benefit, our government is bound to build jails, prisons, lunatic asylums, and canals, the duty to educate the people is as much greater as the results of it would be more beneficial than the construction of those works.

"2. As a means for the *prevention of crime*, we approve the Free School system. The cause of crime is a defective moral education. The means which government uses to reform the offender, and prevent the repetition of the offense, have but little influence to effect the objects; they do not reach the *cause* of crime—a defective moral training. Accordingly, we find that convicts often commit crimes as soon as they are at liberty, and even while witnessing the execution of criminals. * * It will be found universally true that the *minimum* of crime exists, where the *maximum* of moral education is found. The prevention of the repetition of crimes by the offender or others—the great object of human punishment—has never been, and never can be, attained by the present system. *The diseased moral nature must be cured, or the cause of crime will ever remain.* In view of these facts, does not a system of *prevention*, which strikes at the foundation of crime, become the imperative duty of government?

"3. The Free School system is in accordance with the nature of our democratic institutions. Is it not proper that persons created with equal rights, and destined to govern our nation—with whose right action our happiness is intimately connected—should receive the education so necessary to a correct discharge of their duties? Why should the child of *accident*, alone, receive that intellectual and moral culture which *ennobles* man? Let the children of our nation have equal privileges for ennobling themselves from brute existence.

"Perhaps in this neglected spot is laid
Some heart once fragrant with celestial fire;
Hands that the rod of empire might have swayed,
Or waked to ecstacy the living lyre!"

Under the Free School system, the Washingtons, the Franklins, the Henrys, the Jeffersons, who now live and die unknown, would live to benefit, to purify, and exalt the race. From the immutable laws of mind, the largest part of the great men of our country must come from the poorer classes. The children of the rich do not generally form those habits of energy or perseverance—steady, unwearied, continuous labor—without which no man can attain eminence. The Free School system would benefit the poorer classes, and develop talent which is now chilled by the Greenland winds of poverty; it would benefit the children of the rich, by the lesson, invaluable to them, that they are just such beings as the children of the pauper, and that if they would attain greatness they must work and toil with untiring energy and perseverance. FREE SCHOOLS ARE TRULY THE AMERICAN SYSTEM OF EDUCATION. They are already in successful operation in several of the cities of our State and Union. The committee indulge the hope that the State of New York will soon extend her liberality, *and either by a tax or general fund assume the entire support of our Common School system.* They report the following resolution:

"*Resolved*, That we approve of the Free School system, and recommend its adoption in this State."

On the 24th of April, 1845, DAVID NAY, Esq., County Superintendent of Genesee, during the session of the State Convention of Superintendents, at Herkimer, presented a report from the Committee on Free Schools, in which he says:

"Every consideration of duty urges the recommendation and adoption of the most speedy and efficient measures for the support of public instruction. It has been ascertained from statistical sources that more than seven-eighths of this entire community receive their education from Common Schools; hence it follows that as are our schools, so is the education of the people. If the system for their support is found defective, it becomes our duty to suggest and provide a remedy. It is not to be supposed that the system is yet perfect, or that the best measures have yet been adopted to perfect and secure an education for all the sons and daughters of our State. Although we have a fund, and an annual appropriation from the fund of $275,000, and an amount equal to that appropriation annually raised by tax, for the support of our Common Schools, yet it is matter of fact that even this amount is insufficient fully and satisfactorily to answer the object of the appropriation. There are children in the State, and, we have reason to believe, in almost every county in the State, who do not attend any school, for the very obvious reason that their parents have not the means to pay their rate-bill; and the self-respect and pride of those parents forbid that they should be exonerated from such payment by the trustees. Nor is this all. Without funds from some public source, sufficient to defray the entire expense of our schools—and that, too, in such a manner as to make them acceptable to the rich, and available to the poor—we give rise to private and select schools; thus creating a distinction in society that ought not to exist in a community of freemen, who profess to believe in, and attempt to sustain the principles of republican liberty. The question then arises, how shall this evil be averted? Your committee are of opinion that we should follow the example of many of our sister States, and of the cities of New

York, Buffalo, Rochester, and Poughkeepsie in our own State, *by adopting at once a system of school education that shall be free*, thus affording facilities for instruction to all, whether rich or poor. Will it be said that the Free School system imposes too heavy a tax on the wealthy and those who have no children to educate? As well might the same objection be urged against raising a tax for defraying the expenses of our courts of justice in the trial of criminal causes, for the support of the poor, and for levying taxes in time of war for the national defense. In the city of New York some of the most wealthy citizens petitioned the Legislature for the passage of a law to tax their property for the support of the public schools, thereby making them free for all, both rich and poor. In this they acted upon the principle that it was unsafe to live in a community where any portion of the rising generation are suffered to enter upon the stage of active life without a mental and moral education. Ask the cities and superintendents of those cities where the Free School system has been adopted, and where the experiment has been successfully and triumphantly tested, whether they are willing to abandon it? No; they cling to it with an unyielding tenacity, as the only means of affording an education to all their children, and of securing adequate protection to persons and property.

"Under all the circumstances, your committee have come to the conclusion *that it is not only a duty, but a wise policy, to adopt the Free School system, throughout the length and breadth of the entire State*, and that it should become a law. Therefore,

"*Resolved*, As the sense of this convention, that we are decidedly in favor of a Free School system; believing it better calculated to promote the interest and secure the permanency of our civil and religious institutions than any other system that can be devised."

This resolution, after considerable discussion, was withdrawn, and the following substituted in its place:

"*Resolved*, That the establishment of Free Schools, throughout this State, be respectfully commended to the consideration of all its citizens."

During the session of the convention of 1846, public addresses were delivered on the general subject of Popular Education, by Messrs. MANN, BENTON, and EATON; the Normal School was visited, and after a lecture from the Principal, Mr. PAGE, to the assembled students, appropriate remarks were made by Professor DAVIES, JACOB ABBOTT, Mr. MANN, and Mr. HENRY, of Herkimer.

On the coming up of the question of the practicability and expediency of engrafting the FREE SCHOOL SYSTEM upon our existing organization, Mr. MANN, on the call of the convention, delivered an animated and eloquent speech in its favor, explaining the grounds upon which it rested, illustrating its excellences, examining and refuting the arguments brought to bear against it, and commending its adoption on every principle of public policy and sound statesmanship. No apology can be necessary for the presentation of the most essential portion of this masterly defense in the eloquent language itself of the distinguished speaker:

"Strange as it may seem," observed Mr. MANN, "the subject of FREE SCHOOLS, and of the right of a State to maintain them, is never agitated in Massachusetts. I recollect no public document in which this question is discussed, nor have I ever been present at a meeting where it was debated. It is a thing universally taken for granted, and, probably, there is not a gentleman present who has not thought more upon the subject than I have. If there be any such thing as 'innate ideas,' we, in Massachusetts, are born with an innate idea of Free Schools; and a citizen with us would be as much surprised at having a *rate-bill* presented to him for the attendance of his children at the district school as he would, if called upon to pay for enjoying the free light of the sun or the common air of heaven. To argue this question, therefore, would seem almost like arguing a question respecting the existence of an INSTINCT: you may prove with ever so much logical force that it does not exist; but when you have finished your demonstration, there it is!

"The revolution before us contemplates the prospective establishment of a system of Free Schools for the State of New York; and I acknowledge that when any new measure is propounded, the burden of proof rests upon those who ask for a change.

"I will take up but a single point pertaining to this great subject; namely, the OBLIGATION OF A STATE, ON THE GREAT PRINCIPLES OF NATURAL LAW AND NATURAL EQUITY, TO MAINTAIN FREE SCHOOLS FOR THE UNIVERSAL EDUCATION OF ITS PEOPLE; and I thank the convention for turning my attention to this point, which was never before so distinctly presented to my mind.

"Shall the schools of a State be free? Shall they be open to all? Shall they invite and welcome all? Shall they provide that amount and quality of instruction for all which is indispensable to the welfare of the individual—to the brother, sister, father, mother—to the voter, in municipal affairs—to the juror, witness, and citizen—to every one who by law inherits a portion of the sovereignty of this great Republic? I propose to discuss the question whether, according to the great, immutable principles of natural law and equity, this shall be done; or whether, on the other hand, each child shall be dependent for the education he may obtain upon chance or charity, or parental providence; and whether, if chance does not favor, nor charity smile, nor parents provide, the child shall be left without education until he provides for himself. Sir, it appears to me, that a child born in winter may as well be left without warmth or shelter until he provides it for himself.

"Were it not that the question of Free Schools involves the question of *taxation*, I suppose that but few would feel any objections against them; and still fewer, in the face of this community, and in the increasing light and liberality of the nineteenth century, would avow their objections. He must be a pretty bold man who, at this day, in New England or New York, would resist the utmost diffusion of educational means. But Free Schools imply *taxation*: and it is a problem which no statesman has ever yet been able to solve, how to make taxes agreeable to all who pay them. Taxation has always been one of the characteristics of arbitrary power, and hence Republicans are jealous of it. Taxation was one of the main causes of Colonial resistance to the authority of Great Britain; and hence an aversion to it seems to run in our blood. I have always observed amongst our people an exaggeration of ideas on this subject—a feeling in each individual, whatever the amount of the tax may be, he will have to pay the whole of it. It is the hydrostatic paradox repeated, where the whole pressure bears upon each part. And hence it is that those who will admit that a thorough, comprehensive, and Christian education—an education of all our faculties and susceptibilities of body and mind—is the equivalent of health and long life, of individual, social, and national happiness, prosperity, and renown; nay, that education, good or bad, is the synonym of heaven and hell—I say, those who admit all this still maintain that each family must pay for its own; that come prosperity or come adversity to the individual or to the community; come honor or come infamy; come blessedness or come perdition—every man must pay for himself. The knot of this unwedgable problem lies in the word *pay*. 'Why should I, who have no children,' says one, 'pay to educate yours?' 'Why should I,' says another, 'who have reared a family of children, and educated them, now pay a second time in order to educate yours, thus bearing a second burden?' Now I am no apologist for unnecessary taxation. But it does not follow because despots make grievous exactions of their *subjects*, that *citizens* or *voters* will overtax *themselves*. The latter have the power of restriction in their own hands, and can pronounce a peremptory veto whenever they please.

"Again, taxation for judicious and worthy objects is not to be considered a burden, but only as the common condition of existence. We cannot enjoy life, nor even subsist, without expenditure. Our daily food, our shelter, our raiment, are taxes—each man being his own assessor. In a wisely administered government, taxes are the fares which we pay on railroad cars—

the price for being safely carried and well provided for through the journey of life.

"In the next place, it seems to me obvious that all objections to taxation for the support of Free Schools derive their plausibility from the fact that they are made by an individual, *in his individual character*—as an isolated, solitary being having no relations with the community around him—having no ancestors to whom he himself is indebted—and as one, also, who is to leave no posterity having any claim upon him. In the midst of a populous community, to which he is bound by innumerable ties—having had his own fortune and condition almost predetermined and foreordained by his predecessors, and being about to exert upon others as commanding an influence as has been exerted upon himself—the objector argues with us just as he would argue if there were only himself and his family on the western continent, and one other man and one other family on the eastern continent, and they and their families were the first and the last of the whole race. The arguments generally used by men against taxation for Free Schools are applicable only to such a case as this. Well, sir, if there were but one family in this hemisphere, and one other family in the other, and if the head of one of these families should call upon the other to help educate his children, I admit, except so far as good neighborhood might be concerned, there would be some soundness in such an objection; and I can conceive that the force of the appeal would be even more diminished, if a single family on a neighboring planet should make such an appeal to a single family on this planet. In self defense, or in selfishness, one might say to the other, 'What are your fortunes to me? You can neither molest nor assist me. Please to keep your own side of the oceanic or the planetary spaces that divide us.'

"But is this the relation that we sustain to each other? Has not every member of the community thousands around him, on whom he acts, and who are continually re-acting upon him? Have we not all derived advantages from our ancestors, and are we not bound, as by an oath, to transmit these advantages, even in an improved condition, to our posterity? In this age of the world, in the present condition of society, no man can sink into his individuality, and sever the relations which bind him to others. The mind and heart must be enlarged until they become co-extensive with our enlarged relations. The individual no longer exists as an individual merely, but as a citizen among citizens—as a descendant of those who have gone before—as the ancestor of those who are to follow; and hence as the recipient of great blessings from the one, and the medium and transmitter of those blessings to the other. From these new relations new duties are evolved. Society must be preserved; and in order to preserve it, we must look not only to what one family needs, but to what the *whole community needs*; not merely to what one generation needs, but to the wants of a succession of generations. To draw conclusions without considering these facts is to leave out the most important part of our premises.

"Now, what is the fundamental, the permanent, the indispensable need and necessity of every people? I say it is EDUCATION. Though deficient in every thing else—though weak, impoverished, anarchical, education will give strength, competency, and order; though abounding in every thing that heart could desire, yet take away education, and all things would rush to ruin as quickly as the solar system would return to chaos if gravitation and cohesion were destroyed. We need laws regulating all the rights of property, of persons, and of character. We need freedom of the press, freedom of speech, and freedom of conscience. For these purposes we must have wise legislators; but we never shall have wise legislators with a foolish constituency.

"If education, then, be the most important interest of society, it must be placed upon the most permanent and immovable basis that society can supply. It should not be founded upon the shifting sands of popular caprice or passion, or upon individual benevolence: but if there be a rock any where, it should be founded upon that rock. What is the most permanent basis—that which survives all changes—which retains its identity amid all vicissitudes? It is PROPERTY. I mean the great, common, universal elements, which constitute the *basis* of all property—the riches of the soil, the treasures of the sea, the light and warmth of the sun, the fertilizing clouds, and streams, and dews, the winds, the electric and vegetative agencies of nature. Individuals come and go; but these great bounties of heaven abide. Individual estates expand into opulence or shrink into poverty; but the munificence of heaven is as endless as time!

"We hear much said, not merely in courts of law, but in the marts of business, and in the common speech of men, *of the rights of property*. Would it not be refreshing to hear something of the *rights of men*? Have not men rights as well as property? Were men made for the property, or the property for men? It is of some consequence to know which is principal and which is adjunct or accessory. As I read the sacred pages, *men*—not any one man, not any one generation, but the *race*—were to have "dominion" over all other created things. Now I wish to examine, for a moment, this question—*how much*, what *quality* and *description* of ownership any one man, or any one generation, can have in the natural, substantive, enduring elements of wealth—in the soil—in metals and minerals—in precious stones, and in more precious coal, and iron, and granite—in the sun, and the winds, and the waters. Has any one man, or any one generation, I ask, such an absolute ownership in these ingredients of all wealth, that his rights are invaded when a portion of them is taken for the benefit of contemporaries and of posterity? I reply, certainly not. The earth and the fullness thereof were created for the race collectively. These were not created for Adam alone, nor for Noah alone, nor for the first discoverers or colonists who may have found or have peopled any part of the earth's ample domain. No! they were created for all; but to be possessed and enjoyed in succession. Each generation, subject to certain modifications for the encouragement of industry and frugality, has only a life lease in them. There are reasonable regulations in regard to the outgoing and incoming tenants—regulations which allow the incoming tenants to anticipate a little their full right to possession, and which also allow the outgoing generations a brief control of their property after they are called to leave it. Let me illustrate this great principle of natural law by a reference to some of the unstable elements, in regard to which the property of each individual is strongly qualified. Take the streams of water or the winds, for example. A stream, as it descends from its sources to its mouth, is successively the property of all through whose lands it passes. My neighbor, who lives above me, owned it yesterday, while it was passing through his lands; I own it to-day, while it is descending through mine; and the contiguous proprietor below will own it to-morrow, while it is flowing through his, as it passes onward to the next. But the rights of each successive owner are not absolute and unqualified. They are limited by the rights of those who are entitled to subsequent possession. While a stream of water is passing through my demesne I cannot corrupt it, so that it shall be valueless and offensive to the adjoining proprietor below. I cannot detain it in its downward course, or divert it into some other direction, so that it shall leave its channel dry. I may use it for various purposes—for agriculture or manufactures, or for other objects—but in all my uses of it, I must have regard for the rights of my neighbors lower down. So no two proprietors, nor any half dozen proprietors, by conspiring together, can deprive an owner who lives below them all, of the ultimate rights which he has to the use of the stream in its descending course. So we see here that a man has rights—rights of which he cannot be divested, without his own consent, in a stream of water before it reaches the limits of his estate, at which latter point he may, somewhat emphatically, call it his own; and in this sense a man who lives at the outlet of a river, on the margin of the ocean, has certain unqualified rights in the fountains that well up from the earth at the distance of thousands of miles. So it is with the ever-moving winds. No man has a permanent interest in the breezes that blow by him, and cool and refresh him as they blow. From whatever quarter of the compass they may come, I have a right to use them as they are sweeping by; yet I must use them in reference to those other participants and co-owners whom they are moving forward to bless. It is not lawful for me to corrupt them—to load them with noxious gases or vapors, by which they will prove valueless or detrimental to him, whoever he may be, toward whom they are moving. The light of the sun, too, is subject to the same benign and equitable laws. As this ethereal element passes by me, I have a right to bask in its beams, or to employ its quickening powers. But I have no right, even on my own land, to build up a wall, mountain high, that shall eclipse my neighbor's eyes.

"Now, all these great principles of natural law, are incorporated into, and constitute a part of, the civil law of every civilized people; and they are obvious and simple illustrations of the great proprietary laws by which individuals and generations hold their rights in the solid substance of the globe, and in the elements that move over its surface. * * * * I say, then, that no man, however he may have acquired his property, has any natural right, any more than he has a moral one, to hold it, or to dispose of it, irrespective of the needs and claims of those who, in the august procession of the generations, are to succeed him on this stage of existence. Holding his rights subject to their rights, he is bound to make provision for their highest wants.

"Generation after generation comes from the creative power of God. Each one stops for a brief period upon the earth, resting only as for a night, like migratory birds upon their passage, and then leaves it forever to others, whose existence is as transitory as his own; and the flocks of water-fowl, which annually sweep across our latitudes in their passage to another clime, have as good a right to make a perpetual appropriation to their own use of the lands over which they fly as any one generation has to arrogate perpetual dominion and sovereignty, for their own purposes, of that portion of the earth which it is their fortune to occupy during their brief temporal existence. * * * * * * * *

"But the present wealth of the world has an additional element in it to that flowing from the universal beneficence of the Creator. Much of all that is capable of being earned by man has been earned by our predecessors, and has come down to us, from them, in a consolidated and enduring form. We have not built all the houses in which we live, nor all the roads on which we travel, nor all the ships which we navigate. But even if we had, whence came all the arts and sciences, the discoveries and inventions, without which, and without a common right to which, the valuation of the property of a whole nation would scarcely equal the inventory of a single man? Whence came a knowledge of agriculture, without which we should have nothing to reap; or of astronomy, without which we could not traverse the oceans; or of chemistry and mechanical philosophy, without which the arts and trades cannot flourish? Most of these were prepared by those who have gone before us—some of them have come down from a remote antiquity. Surely all these boons and blessings belong as much to our posterity as to ourselves. They have not descended to us to be arrested and consumed here, or to be sequestrated from the ages to come.

"But now we come to another stage in our argument. In regard to the wealth formed from the great substantive ingredients which are the property of all mankind, and which belong equally to successive generations—*at what time* is it to be transferred from a preceding to a succeeding generation? Is each existing generation, and each individual of an existing generation, to hold fast to his possessions until death relaxes his grasp, or is something of the transfer to be yielded beforehand? If the incoming generation have no rights until the outgoing have retired, then is every individual that enters the world doomed to perish on the day he is born. His wants cannot be delayed until he himself can supply them. The demands of his nature must be answered before he can provide for them. The infant must be fed before he can earn his bread; he must be clothed before he can prepare garments; and it is just as clear that he must be instructed before he can engage a teacher. Here, then, the claims of the succeeding generation, not only upon the affection and care, but upon the *property* of the preceding one, attach. God having given to the second generation as full and complete a right to the incomes and profits of the world—to the soil—to the sun's light and warmth—to the rain—to the chemical and vegetative laws by which the mysterious processes of nature are carried on—as he has given to the first; and to the third as full and complete a right as to the second, and so on, while the world stands—it necessarily follows that they must come into a partial and qualified possession of these rights, by the paramount laws of nature, as soon as they are born. No human enactments can abolish or countervail this paramount and supreme law.

"Coincident, too, with this great law is the wonderful provision that the Creator has made for the care of offspring in the affection of the parents. Heaven did not rely merely upon our perceptions of duty toward our offspring, and our fidelity in its performance. A powerful, all-mastering instinct of love was therefore implanted in the parental, and especially in the maternal, breast, to anticipate the idea of duty, and to make duty a pleasure. For all those children who have been bereaved of parents, or, who—worse than bereavement—have only monster parents of intemperance or cupidity, or any other form of vice, society is bound to be a parent, and to exercise the same rational care and providence that a wise father would exercise for his own children.

"I think we are now prepared to meet the question, fully and directly, at what time, to what extent, and for what purposes, upon the great principles of natural law, the incoming generation is entitled to participate in the benefits of the world's wealth. I answer, their claim to a portion of it begins with the first breath they draw. The new-born infant must have sustenance, and shelter, and care. If the parents cannot supply these, society succeeds to the place of parents, and must supply them. If at any period previous to the age of discretion, the parents are removed, or parental ability fails, society, at that point, is bound to step in and fill the parents' place. To deny such support and succor would be equivalent to a sentence of death—a capital execution of the infant, at which every soul shudders. But to preserve a child's *life* only, and then to stop, would be, not the bestowment of a blessing or the performance of a duty, but the infliction of a curse. A child has interests far higher than those of mere physical existence. Better that the interests of the natural life should not be cared for than that the higher interests of the *character* should be neglected. If a child has claims to bread, to keep him from perishing, he has far higher claims to *knowledge*, to keep him from error and its retinue of calamities. If a child has a claim to shelter, to protect him from the destroying elements, he has a far higher claim to be rescued from *the infamy and perdition of vice and crime*. If you will not legalize infanticide, you must supply sustenance. If you will not prepare madmen or incendiaries to destroy property and life, you must enlighten the intellect. If you will not invoke moral ruin, you must train up the young in the way they should go. In a word, you must educate the mind as well as sustain the mere physical existence.

"The time when this obligation attaches corresponds with the age when the work can be most beneficially and efficaciously performed. As the right of sustenance, then, is of equal date with birth, the right to systematic intellectual and moral training begins at least as early as when children are ordinarily sent to school. At that time, then, by the great and irrepealable law of nature, *every child succeeds to so much more of the property of the community as is necessary for his education. He is to receive this, not in the form of property, but in the form of education.* Under a republican form of government, this obligation of the predecessors, and the consequent right of the successors, extends to and embraces the means of such an amount of education as will fit each individual to perform the common duties of a citizen. It may go further than this point; it certainly cannot stop short of it. The places and processes where this transfer is to be provided for, and its amount determined, are the district school meeting, the town meeting, legislative halls, and conventions for establishing or revising the fundamental laws of the State. *If it be not done there, the community is faithless to its trust.*

"I bring my argument, then, to a close; and I present a test of its validity, which, as it seems to me, defies denial or evasion.

"In obedience to the laws of God and to the laws of all civilized nations, society is bound to protect natural life; and that natural life cannot be protected without the appropriation and use of a portion of the property which society possesses. We prohibit *infanticide* under penalty of death. We practice a *refinement* in this particular. The life of an infant is inviolable even before it is born; and he who feloniously takes it is as subject to the extreme penalty of the law as though he had cut down manhood in its vigor, or taken away a mother, by violence, from the midst of her maternal cares. But why preserve the natural life of a child—why preserve unborn embryos of life, if you do not intend to watch over and protect them, and expand them into usefulness and happiness? You have no right—neither nature nor God confer any right—to inflict the curse of birth, the curse of ignorance, and vice, and poverty, and all their attendant unspeakable calamities upon any creature. You are brought, then, to this inevitable test: EITHER EXTINGUISH THE NATURAL LIFE, OR PROVIDE THE MEANS TO MAKE THAT LIFE A BLESSING. *Give us the right of infanticide*, OR GIVE US FREE EDUCATION!"

The following preamble and resolutions were then reported to the convention for its consideration and discussion:

"*Whereas*, The system of FREE SCHOOLS, as adopted by Massachusetts, and by several of the large cities and towns of this and other States, has been found, by the practical experience of years, to work well, securing a more general and punctual attendance of scholars, awakening a more widely extended and deeper interest in the minds of the great mass of the people in the success of our primary nurseries of education, thereby ensuring the elevation of the standard of Common School instruction, and more widely diffusing the inestimable blessings of a sound and generous education; therefore,

"*Resolved*, That this convention, fully impressed with the importance of the various considerations involved in this question of Free Schools, and believing that it is one that, sooner or later, will receive the approbation of all, do most respectfully commend the subject to the calm and dispassionate consideration of the sovereign people of this State, and to the favorable notice of the members of the convention about to assemble to revise the Constitution of the State.

"*Resolved*, That a certified copy of the above preamble and resolution be presented to the presiding officer of the convention referred to, with the request that the same may be laid before that honorable body for their consideration."

The resolutions were warmly supported by Messrs. WILKINS and THOMPSON, of Rensselaer; MACK, of Rochester; WILLARD, HARRINGTON, and VALENTINE, of Albany; DUBOIS, of Ulster; COOPER, of Onondaga; DENMAN, of Wyoming; HENRY, of Herkimer; and THOMSON, of Cayuga; who contended, in substance, that the time for engrafting the system of Free Schools upon our existing organization had fully come; that public sentiment in every section of the State was prepared to adopt and sustain it; and that its recognition would not only relieve trustees and other officers of school districts from the oppressive burdens under which they were now compelled to labor in the periodical assessment and collection of taxes and rate-bills, but would bring within the fostering influences of the schools thousands of indigent children, the claims of whose parents or guardians to exemption were now either overlooked or disregarded, and who, consequently, were virtually deprived of the inestimable blessing of education. The paramount duty and obligation of the State thus to afford to each of its future citizens, without distinction or discrimination, the amplest facilities for a sound and comprehensive mental and moral education were strongly insisted upon, and clearly and fully demonstrated; the superior advantages of the Free School system, wherever it had been introduced within the State, as in New York, Buffalo, Rochester, Brooklyn, Williamsburgh, Hudson, Poughkeepsie, Utica, and other places, pointed out and elucidated; and the importance of present action, in view of the pending reorganization of our frame of government, forcibly and eloquently urged. On the other hand, Messrs. WRIGHT, of Washington; ALLEN, of Saratoga; TERHUNE, of Greene; ROBERTSON, of Tompkins, and others, while conceding to its fullest extent the principle that the schools throughout the State should be free and open to all, without discrimination, restriction, or charge, and supported by the taxable property of all its citizens, in proportion to the valuation of each, doubted the expediency of a radical change in the existing organization, at the present time, and contended that, however sound in theory and valuable in practice such a change might be, the public sentiment was not yet prepared for it; that its merits had not, as yet, been generally or sufficiently discussed; and that by insisting upon its adoption, under such circumstances, the most imminent danger might accrue to the system as it now existed. At the close of the discussion the preamble and resolutions were adopted by a vote of more than two-thirds of the members of the convention.

The State Constitutional Convention assembled at Albany on the 1st of June ensuing. On the 12th, on the motion of Mr. BOWDISH, of Montgomery, a standing committee on Education, Common Schools, and their appropriate funds, was appointed by the President (Hon. JOHN TRACY, of Chenango), consisting of Mr. HENRY NICOLL, of New York, as chairman, and Messrs. BOWDISH, of Montgomery; MUNRO, of Onondaga; A. W. YOUNG, of Wyoming; TUTHILL, of Orange; WILLARD, of Albany; and HUNT, of New York; to whom were referred a resolution by Mr. BOWDISH for an inquiry into the expediency of the establishment of a system of Free Schools for the State; a resolution by Mr. ROBERT CAMPBELL, of Otsego, as to the propriety of "a constitutional provision for the security of the Common School, literature, deposit, and other trust funds, from conversion or destruction; and the establishment, by the Legislature, of such a system of Common Schools as will, by taxation, bestow the facility of acquiring a good education by every child in the State;" and the preamble and resolutions of the recent State Convention of County Superintendents in favor of the adoption of the Free School system.

On the 22d of July, Mr. NICOLL, from the committee, reported for the consideration of the convention a series of propositions for incorporation into the proposed constitution, declaring the inviolable appropriation of the capitals of the Common School, literature, and deposit funds of the State to the support of Common Schools and academies respectively; and providing "that the Legislature should, at its first session after the adoption of such constitution, and from time to time thereafter, as should be necessary, provide by law *for the free education and instruction of every child between the ages of four and sixteen years, whose parents, guardians, or employers, shall be resident in the State, in the Common Schools now established or which should thereafter be established therein;* the expense of such education and instruction, after applying the public funds as above provided, to be defrayed by taxation, at the same time and in the same manner as provided by law for the liquidation of town and county charges;" this latter proposition to be separately submitted to the people of the State for their approval or rejection.

On the first day of October, Mr. BOWDISH made a

powerful and eloquent appeal in behalf of this great measure, in which he was ably sustained by Mr. NICOLL, of New York; Mr. WORDEN, of Ontario; Mr. G. W. PATTERSON, of Livingston; Mr. RUSSELL, of St. Lawrence; and others; and on the 8th, the day preceding the adjournment, the first section reported by the committee, permanently and inviolably appropriating the Common School fund to the support of Common Schools, was, after some discussion, adopted, three members only voting in the negative. Mr. NICOLL then moved the adoption of the following section, to be separately submitted to the people for their ratification:

"THE LEGISLATURE SHALL PROVIDE FOR THE FREE EDUCATION AND INSTRUCTION OF EVERY CHILD OF THE STATE IN THE COMMON SCHOOLS NOW ESTABLISHED, OR WHICH SHALL HEREAFTER BE ESTABLISHED THEREIN."

This section was adopted by a vote of 57 to 53 on a call for the ayes and noes; and, on motion of Mr. CHARLES H. RUGGLES, of Dutchess, a provision added, directing the Legislature to provide for raising the necessary taxes in the several school districts to carry out the intention of the section. As thus modified, the entire ninth article of the proposed constitution, as reported by the committee, was agreed to by the convention, and ordered to be engrossed. A recess was then taken for dinner.

On the re-assembling of the convention in the afternoon, Mr. ARPHAXED LOOMIS, of Herkimer, offered a resolution to refer the article thus adopted *to a committee of* ONE, *with instructions to strike out all that portion relating to the establishment of Free Schools, and report the same as amended,* INSTANTER, *to the convention.* Mr. TAGGARD, of Genesee, sustained, and Mr. TOWNSEND of

New York, opposed, this motion; but, under the operation of the previous question, it prevailed by a vote of 61 to 27. Mr. LOOMIS immediately reported as instructed, and his report was agreed to by the convention. The ninth article, as finally adopted, and as it now stands, was as follows:

"The capital of the Common School fund, the capital of the Literature fund, and the capital of the United States Deposit fund, shall be respectively preserved inviolate. The revenue of the said Common School fund shall be applied to the support of Common Schools; the revenue of the said Literature fund shall be applied to the support of academies; and the sum of $25,000 of the revenues of the United States Deposit fund shall each year be appropriated to and made a part of the capital of the said Common School fund."

Thus terminated the first effort for the establishment of FREE SCHOOLS; and an interval of more than twenty years was destined to elapse before its final accomplishment. An entire generation of children were destined to pass from birth to full maturity before the exertions of its indefatigable advocates and champions throughout the whole of the intervening period should be crowned with success.

On the 1st of October, SAMUEL L. HOLMES, of Westchester, received the appointment of General Deputy Superintendent of Common Schools, in place of Mr. Randall, whose resignation and temporary retirement from the State had become necessary from failing health.

The annual report of the Superintendent for the year 1847 showed a considerable increase in the number of children under instruction, and of about 58,000 volumes to the several district libraries. Under the provisions of an act passed the preceding year, schools for the instruction of Indian children had been organized in Onondaga, Cattaraugus, Allegany, and St. Regis reservations, under circumstances eminently favorable to the intellectual and moral improvement of this class of the population.

"A successful administration of the school laws of the State," observes the Superintendent, "requires an intelligent and active local as well as general supervision; and without the former, it is believed the present organization must eventually be abandoned, and one less complex in its details and stringent in its requirements adopted in its place. * * * After struggling through a long series of years to elevate our schools, to infuse a greater zeal, and excite a higher interest in regard to them, without advancing one step in attaining these objects, actual visitation and inspection were provided as a substitute for an inefficient local supervision. The results of this change have been and are now seen and deeply felt in our own State and by our own people, and have justly excited commendation and approval wherever they are known in other States."

By an act passed in February of this year, on the recommendation of the Superintendent, the inhabitants of the several school districts were authorized to apply, in their discretion, the whole or such portions of the library money as they might deem expedient, in the purchase of either books, maps, globes, or scientific apparatus for the use of their schools respectively.

At the special session of the Legislature in November succeeding, an act was passed *abolishing the office of County Superintendent*. For this measure the friends of the system, although they had with entire unanimity resisted it for a series of years, were not altogether unprepared, aware as they had become of the great unpopularity of the office, growing out of the injudicious selection in many instances of the incumbents, by the respective boards of supervisors, whose functions, however useful and important in other respects, had no especial reference to the educational wants and interests of the community. Political qualifications were not unfrequently made the prominent tests of fitness for the discharge of the responsible duties of school supervision; and while for the greater number of these officers were eminently qualified for their position, and faithful to its high trusts, there were but too many who were justly obnoxious to the charge, not only of incapacity and want of moral character, but of a perversion of the responsible functions conferred upon them to sinister personal and political ends; and the indignation excited by these instances of disregard of duty and moral obliquity gradually extended itself to other localities where no reasonable grounds for suspicion existed. The meager compensation also attached to the office—$500 per annum, only—when taken in connection with the amount of time and labor required for the faithful performance of its duties, precluded the possibility of obtaining, except in rare instances, the services of men of the necessary qualifications and character; and the slight pecuniary burden of defraying one-half of this salary from the county treasury was magnified and dwelt upon by the interested, the narrow-minded, and the designing, until the Legislature was annually flooded by petitions for the abolition of the office, as unnecessary, oppressive, and improperly administered. Committee after committee, to whom these petitions were referred, reported against the adoption of the measure desired, and the soundest and most convincing arguments were brought to bear upon the great and manifest utility of the office. It was clearly and repeatedly shown that the abuses complained of were such as admitted of an easy and practical remedy, while the advantages secured by the retention of this class of officers could be obtained through no other agency. Public clamor, however, persisted, year after year, in demanding the repeal of the obnoxious act, and in the face of the avowed and strong opposition of the successive heads of the department, of the several committees of both houses of the Legislature charged with the supervision of the interests of public instruction, and of the great body of the most enlightened friends of education throughout the State, this most unfortunate and ill-advised measure was consummated.

The Hon. CALVIN T. HULBURD, of St. Lawrence, Chairman of the Committee on Colleges, Academies, and Common Schools, of the Assembly, in 1843, in an able report, made at that session, after enumerating the various advantages to be derived from the system, observed:

"After a full and deliberate investigation, the committee have unanimously concurred in the preservation of the County Superintendent system: believing it to be, with the additional power now conferred (that of jurisdiction on appeal), not only *the most economical and efficient*, but the *most important provision in our complex and extensive organization of public instruction.*"

Mr. L. H. BROWN, chairman of the same committee, in 1845, after a thorough and able investigation of the whole subject said:

"No benefit would be likely to accrue from abolishing the office of County Superintendent which would not be more than countervailed by the evils that would necessarily ensue. Public attention has been called to the state of the schools; the importance of giving such a character to the district school as would supersede the necessity of select schools has been made evident; a demand for an improved order of teachers, and for more uniformity in text-books, has been induced; a better style of school edifices has been substituted; and a marked improvement has taken place in the manner of the scholars, as well as in their attendance and proficiency. *These are believed to be the legitimate results of a good system of county supervision.*"—"*These officers have brought about a new era in the State; they have done more for the cause of primary education, within three years, than had been done for half a century previously.*"

The Hon. HORACE MANN, of Massachusetts, in his annual report, as Secretary of the Board of Education of that State, for the year 1845, said:

"The great State of New York, *by means of her County Superintendents*, State Normal School, and otherwise, is carrying forward the work of public education *more rapidly than any other State in the Union, or any country in the world*."

The Hon. HENRY BARNARD, late Superintendent of Common Schools of the State of Connecticut, and formerly Commissioner of Public Schools of Rhode Island, in an address delivered before a State Educational Convention, at Syracuse, in April, 1845, said:

"I have watched the progressive improvement in the organization and administration of the school system of this great State with intense interest; and I regard it, at this time, *as superior to any other of which I have any knowledge*, for its extent, its liberality, its efficiency, and the general intelligence and activity with which its wide-spread affairs are administered. Resting on the broad basis of the whole people, acting through the minute territorial subdivision of school districts, this admirable structure rises harmoniously with the political organization of the State in other respects, through towns and counties, till it finds its natural head in the State, as represented in the legislative and executive departments; and proceeding hence, its action, at once simple and direct, is spread out through your county and town superintendents to the trustees of school districts, elected directly by the people, for whom they act, and with whom they sympathize, and whose cordial and intelligent support, as parents and individuals, is the main condition of success, in every one of the eleven thousand school districts. *But the most admirable feature in your school system is the provision for County Superintendents*—the enlisting of the services of fifty or sixty intelligent men, acting under the specific requirements of the school laws, and the general direction of the head of the school department, directly upon every school, and every teacher, and every district and town school officer; and very widely upon the parents of the children, as well as the children themselves, within their corporate limits. *There is nothing to be compared with this in the school system of any other State.* Under the continued operation of this plan of supervision, the spirit of improvement must be aroused, and must pervade every town and every district in the State. I should look upon it as a calamity to the cause of school improvement in other States should this experiment of county supervision be arrested or defeated at this time. *There is nothing in all the wise legislation of your State, in regard to public instruction*, unless, perhaps, the liberal appropriation for district libraries, *which the friends of public education elsewhere are so anxious to see adopted into the school system of their respective States. Its abolition would be everywhere regarded as a long stride backwards.* It would be better to curtail the amount distributed to the schools for other purposes than to save in the compensation of this class of officers, *whose labors, at least, double the value of all your school expenditures*, by awakening and diffusing public and parental interest, and giving life, intelligence, and progress to teachers and local school officers."

But, perhaps, the most full and complete exposition of the advantages and benefits to be derived from the system of county supervision will be found in the following communication by the Hon. JOHN C. SPENCER, in reply to an inquiry relative to his views on this subject, pending the attempt for the repeal of this provision of the system:

LETTER OF THE HON. JOHN C. SPENCER.

"ALBANY, March 24, 1846.

"DEAR SIR: I cannot refuse a compliance with the request, contained in your letter of the 21st instant, to express my views in reference to the bearing which the office of County Superintendent of Common Schools has upon the interests of those schools, assuming that its duties are faithfully discharged. The subject is one of such vital importance to the welfare of the rising generation, and to the whole community, that I should deem myself recreant to the duty of a good citizen, if I should, when thus called upon, withhold the expression of an opinion, however slight may be its claims to consideration.

"The views and opinions which were communicated by me, officially, to the Legislature in 1840 and 1841, upon this subject, not only remain unchanged, but have been strengthened and confirmed by subsequent reflection and observation, and by the experience of the last four years. As I can add nothing to what was then said, I beg your indulgence for repeating some of the considerations which were then urged, in a condensed form.

"1. No public or private undertaking can possibly succeed without some supervision which can detect imperfections and errors arising from negligence or incompetency, and can promptly apply the needful remedy. It would be disrespectful to you, and to every intelligent person who may peruse these remarks, to suppose that this proposition required a single word to demonstrate its truth.

"2. To accomplish the purpose of its creation, the supervision must be conducted by those who understand their duties, who are qualified to discharge them, and who are themselves under supervision, and responsible to others.

"Apply these plain principles to our Common Schools. There are twelve thousand of them, at least, scattered over the broad surface of this State, in which some eight hundred thousand children are instructed. How is it to be known whether these schools are rendering any useful service? How are the defects in their organization, their arrangements, the system of instruction, or the capacity of their instructors, or the fidelity of their officers, to be ascertained, without the investigation and scrutiny of competent persons? And how can their deficiencies be supplied and their errors corrected without such knowledge?

"3. Every other mode of insuring this supervision, than that of local superintendence over a district of country, has utterly failed, and, from the nature of things, must fail. The records of the department show that the simple duty of visiting the schools, by the inspectors of the different towns, has always been grossly neglected. In the year 1839, 4,397 schools only, out of 10,127, were visited, *even once*, during the year. This is taken as a *specimen*, not as an average, for it is believed that the average of visits for two years preceding 1840 would *fall short of this number*. And these visits, when made, were productive of very little benefit. It is no disparagement to our fellow-citizens, who were usually chosen inspectors, to say, that generally, they had not themselves acquired the knowledge of the subject which is necessary to enable any one to discharge the duties of such an office. They were not, ordinarily, competent to judge of the qualifications of teachers, or to test the progress of the pupils, by examinations, or to detect the errors of the system of instruction, or to suggest improvements. But upon this point we have the most conclusive evidence, in the reports of the county visitors, who, in 1840, visited the schools in many counties, and communicated the results of their observations to the department, and which were submitted to the Legislature in 1841. [See No. 133 of Assembly Documents of that year.] A reference to their reports will, at once, satisfy every one of their intelligence, capacity, and fidelity. Among them will be found the names of our most distinguished citizens, and conspicuous particularly for the zeal and devotion they have uniformly exhibited for the improvement of our elementary institutions. Upon this point, of the total inefficiency of the system of inspection and supervision which then prevailed, their testimony is as decided as it is intelligent and disinterested. It is, of course, idle to expect any personal attention to the schools by the State Superintendent. He can only supervise the whole machinery, by general directions, and keep it in order by watching its general movement, and by regulating and controlling the chiefs of sections, holding them to a strict accountability, and personally acquainting himself with the manner in which they discharge their duties.

"It is evident, then, I think, that unless the present (the county) or some similar system of local inspection and supervision be maintained, there will be none whatever, and our schools will be left wholly to the management of their teachers, without any efficient responsibility, and at liberty to discharge or neglect their solemn duties, as may suit their own convenience, without aid or advice to sustain them, to point out their errors, or to suggest improvements.

"The present system (that of 1841) is a harmonious whole: the result of many years of gradual development of the necessities of the schools, and the means of supplying them. It has been matured slowly, step by step, by the wisdom and patriotism of men of all parties and denominations, until it has reached a degree of perfection that challenges the admiration of all our sister States. *And no one feature has met with such universal approbation as that now under consideration*—the arrangement and distribution of what may be termed the executive department. You and I know the estimation in which this feature is held by those distinguished friends, advocates, and laborers, in the cause of elementary instruction, HORACE MANN, of Massachusetts, and HENRY BARNARD, the Secretary of the Board of Education of the State of Connecticut. They consider this feature as placing our system altogether above those of their own States, and as furnishing, in itself, the means, equally certain and practicable, of future improvement.

"The opinions of that ardent, and active, and laborious friend of education, Dr. ALONZO POTTER, who has lately removed from us, are also well known. He had observed the operations of the system with all the anxiety of a devoted friend, and the convictions of experience corroborated and confirmed all his anticipations of the absolute necessity of such superintendence. In this connection should be noticed the testimony of our disinterested, most intelligent, and devoted friend, the lamented FRANCIS DWIGHT. You know how intensely this very subject occupied his mind during the last year of his most useful life, and with what care and labor he was collecting information, to lay before the Legislature, in order to show the inestimable importance of the existing plan of local superintendence to the success, and even to the useful existence, of our Common Schools. His minute and thorough acquaintance with the working of the system throughout the State, his disinterested and noble devotion to the cause, and the frankness with which he yielded his opinions to the force of evidence and of truth, render his testimony worthy of the most profound respect and consideration. He believed that where the duties of County Superintendents had been performed, with anything like fidelity, they had been eminently beneficial; that the schools had improved, the teachers had improved, parents were awakened to a sense of the importance of these nurseries of mind, and the general sympathy of the community, in favor of the schools, and their improvement, had been excited, invigorated, and extended. From the facts and results which he communicated to me, from time to time, for several months previous to his death, I came to the same conclusion which he had formed: *that the plan of inspection and supervision, through County Superintendents, had worked admirably in every county where it had been fairly and honestly executed, and that it was the mainspring of our whole system, which kept in life and motion and regulated its movements in a manner as perfect as could be accomplished by human contrivance.* And I heartily and entirely concurred with him, that if this *mainspring* was removed, irregularity, disorder, and confusion, would inevitably follow—the present strong feeling in favor of our schools would not only subside, but that there would be great danger of its giving place to disgust and disappointment.

"So far as I can learn, but two objections have been made to the present system. One is, that in some instances there have been unfortunate selections of persons as County Superintendents, and that these persons have neglected their duties, and perverted their stations to other than their legitimate purposes. But I cannot bring myself to believe that any intelligent man would be influenced in his judgment of a system by the negligent or improper conduct of a portion of those who are appointed to execute it. Such a test would prove all our political institutions to be equally unworthy of support; for there is not one of them that has not, at some time, been in incompetent and unfaithful hands. So long as a corrective is vested in the immediate representatives of the people, it is impossible that the evil can be extensive or permanent. The other objection referred to is the expense to the counties. This brings me back to the question whether our Common School system is of such value to posterity that *any expense* ought to be incurred in maintaining and improving it? If the plan of County Superintendents is calculated to preserve that system, to render it more capable of good, to secure competent teachers, and insure their fidelity, then a reasonable expenditure for that object is, and should be, as much a part of the whole system as the payment of teachers' wages.

"I have endeavored, in compliance with your request, to show that this plan of county superintendence is *essential* to the working of our system; that it forms an *indispensable link* in the chain of connection between the principal executive and the teacher—between the State and the pupil. Much more might have been said, but I felt the necessity of brevity—less I could not say. I confess I feel deeply and earnestly for the continuance of what I sincerely believe to be the most valuable and important feature in our system of popular instruction; and I fervently hope that this Legislature will, at least, allow it an opportunity for more full and extended experiment, in the confident expectation that it will more and more commend itself to the intelligent approbation of our fellow-citizens.

"Very respectfully, your friend,

"J. C. SPENCER."

"SAMUEL S. RANDALL, Esq."

With all these strong testimonials before them, the Legislature of 1847, nevertheless, saw fit to repeal the act creating the office of County Superintendent; and thus, in the judgment of many of our most distinguished and eminent fellow citizens, to take the first step in a career of manifest retrogradation.

Its effect upon the prosperity and advancement of the Common School system was, in many essential respects, most disastrous. During a period of nearly forty years, the progress of that system had been uninterruptedly onward and upward; and a succession of wise enactments had strengthened and consolidated its foundations and expanded its usefulness in every direction. The destruction of that feature which, perhaps, more than any other, had come to constitute its most distinctive characteristic and crowning excellence, giving to its details their peculiar symmetry and power, was the first *retrograde* step in its history. Its consequences were speedily manifested in the comparative inefficiency and inutility of the local and general supervision of the schools—in the absence of any connecting link between the department and the several town and district officers and the inhabitants of the respective districts—in the discontinuance of a local appellate tribunal where the numerous controversies constantly springing up relative to the external affairs and internal arrangements of the districts might be equitably adjusted by a disinterested officer on the spot—in the facilities afforded for a perversion or wrongful appropriation of the public funds by the absence of any responsible check—and in the utter impracticability of obtaining, with any accuracy, those statistical details, in reference to the practical operation of the system, so indispensable to the department, to the Legislature, and the public. Nine hundred town superintendents, however well qualified for the discharge of the special duties devolved upon them, within their limited jurisdiction, were wholly unable to supply the place and fulfill the functions of county officers in constant communication with the State Superintendent and with each other, whose abilities were or should have been unquestioned, whose influence was extensive, and their means of usefulness unrestricted. The dial of progress and improvement was set back for a long series of years—only to be restored and advanced by a radical and fundamental change in the entire system.

Some compensation was, however, made by the passage, during the same session, of an act for the encouragement of TEACHERS' INSTITUTES, by which the sum of sixty dollars was required to be annually appropriated, from the income of the United States Deposit fund, to the use and benefit of each of these institutions. An act was also passed authorizing the appropriation of such portion of the library money as the Superintendent, on special application for that purpose, might direct, to the payment of teachers' wages, where the number of volumes in such library exceeded one hundred, or in large districts one hundred and twenty-five, and where the district was properly supplied with maps, globes, black-boards, and scientific apparatus, for the use of the schools.

At the opening of the Legislature of 1848, the Governor (JOHN YOUNG) thus adverted to the subject of education:

"In our country, for reasons that have been so often and so well stated that I need not repeat them, the education of its children has been, and, I trust, will continue to be, matter of the deepest solicitude. Common Schools, from their universality, reaching every neighborhood, and shedding their influence upon every family and into every mind, expelling the primary causes of vice and crime, and erecting altars to patriotism and virtue, have justly been considered the peculiar objects of legislative care.

"The practical importance of the State Normal School for the education of teachers is beginning to be felt; and in the tone, strength, and vigor given to Common Schools, by distributing through the State teachers who shall have been thoroughly instructed, it is believed will be found most convincing arguments in defense of reasonable, but liberal, appropriations by the State to this object."

The annual report of the Superintendent for the ensuing year, 1848, exhibited an increase of about eight thousand children under instruction; and in the number of volumes in the district libraries of 107,847, during the preceding year, making the entire number 1,311,000. In reference to the question of *Free Schools*, the Superintendent thus eloquently and earnestly discourses:

"The extension of Free Schools in the State is progressing moderately, and laws are passed at nearly every session of the Legislature providing for their establishment in wealthy and populous villages, while the poorer and less populous districts in the same towns are left to struggle on, from year to year, in the best way they can, sustaining a school, perhaps, only four months in the year, to secure the next apportionment of the public money. Is this policy just? Is it *right* to discriminate in this manner between the school children of the State? Why should ample provision be made for the children residing in particular localities, and others be turned over to the naked bounties of the State, which, although munificent in the aggregate, are only sufficient to pay a few weeks' tuition for each child? This great and essential question turns simply on the *mode of taxation*. By changing this, and requiring the boards of supervisors to raise upon the *counties* respectively a sum equal to the amount apportioned from the treasury to each county for the support of schools, and upon the *towns* another sum equal to the apportionment of each town from the school funds—increasing the local taxation of the counties not to exceed five-tenths of a mill on the valuation in any county—our schools might be rendered nearly *free* to every child in the State. Our fellow-citizens have heretofore cheerfully acquiesced in the imposition of a tax to support the government, and sustain the credit of the State, of more than twice the amount proposed to be raised in the plan suggested. What improvement, internal or external, is more worthy of the fostering care of the Legislature, or of greater importance to the community, than the *mental improvement* of those who are soon to exercise all the privileges of citizens, and wield the destinies of the State? It would be an unjust impeachment of the patriotism and good sense of the people to suppose they would not cheerfully embrace and cordially approve any reasonable measure which will reflect so much honor on the present, and confer such benefits on the future."

Of the abolition of the office of County Superintendent he observes:

"The act abolishing the office seemed to be in accordance with the popular will, and should be cheerfully obeyed; but the wisdom and expediency of the measure must be tested by the experience of the future. The labor and expense thrown upon this office in consequence of this legislative act cannot justly, and, therefore, does not, form any ground of complaint with the undersigned. With the other official duties devolved upon the incumbent of this office, a personal supervision and inspection of the schools, however desirable, is wholly impracticable. This question is then presented to the grave consideration of the Legislature and the people of the State: Are we to dispense entirely, with all personal visitation, inspection, and supervision, except what may be performed by the local town officers? And are we not, hereafter, to have any statistical information of the condition of our school-houses, and of the condition of the winter and summer schools, from year to year; the number of schools visited, and pupils in attendance; the course and extent of the studies pursued; with the compensation paid to teachers, their time of employment, sex, and qualifications? To repeat the just encomiums bestowed upon our system in all its parts, as it recently existed, and which distinguished educators and philanthropists in other States have urged upon the consideration of their legislatures as worthy of being incorporated into their own systems, might seem disrespectful. Other plans might be suggested that would, no doubt, if adopted, greatly add to the efficiency of our local inspection and supervision, and take the place of that which has recently been abolished; but whether at this time any suggestions of this sort would be likely to meet with public favor may well be questioned."

The operations of the State Normal School, during the past three years, had greatly tended to strengthen the confidence of the people in this Institution, and to realize the expectations of the friends of education generally throughout the State. The number of pupils was about two hundred, and the semi-annual graduating classes varied from forty-five to sixty-five. The whole number of graduates up to the 1st of January, 1848, was two hundred and thirty-four; of whom two hundred and twenty-two were actually engaged in teaching in the Common Schools of the State; and out of five hundred and thirty-seven, who had been pupils of the Institution since its commencement, four hundred and twenty-one were then employed as teachers.

The Institution, at this period, however, received a severe blow, and the friends of education sustained an irreparable loss, by the death of David P. Page, its distinguished Principal, which took place on the 1st of January, 1848. Although still in the prime of life, Mr. Page had attained a reputation and standing as a teacher hitherto unsurpassed in the Union. To intellectual qualifications of the highest order, he added all those moral virtues and Christian graces which are so indispensably requisite to every instructor of youth. He was, in all respects, admirably adapted to the successful performance of the high functions which had been devolved upon him, and which he had accepted and entered upon with unfeigned diffidence in his own capacity and strength for so great an undertaking; and to the perfect order, system, and harmony which he infused into all the departments under his charge, and his luminous expositions of the duties, obligations, and responsibilities of the teachers he was training, a large share of the prosperity and success of the institution was pre-eminently due. His admirable course of lectures on the "Theory and Practice of Teaching," annually delivered to the pupils prior to graduation, embraced a comprehensive and exhaustive view of the whole subject, and were, in all respects, worthy of his genius and character as a model teacher, and of the extensive appreciation which its subsequent publication has universally received among the friends of popular education throughout his own and other States. Prof. PERKINS, who had been associated with him since the organization of the school, succeeded him as Principal; and WILLIAM F. PHELPS, one of its earliest pupils and graduates, was placed in charge of the Experimental School. DARWIN G. EATON, WILLIAM W. CLARK, and ANN MARIA OSTROM, also pupils of the institution, were promoted to professorships.

On the 12th of April an act was passed for the permanent establishment of the school, appropriating $15,000—afterward increased to $25,000—for the erection of a suitable building for its accommodation in a commodious location, in the immediate vicinity of the Capitol and State Hall, where the institution is still in successful operation. Prof. PERKINS was succeeded as Principal in the school by S. B. WOOLWORTH, of Cortland, who was succeeded by DAVID H. COCHRAN.

By an act passed May 7, 1847, the Board of Education of the city of New York was authorized, in case the act should be approved by a majority of legal voters in the city, at a special election to be held for that purpose, to establish a Free Academy, with collegiate powers, for the advanced education of the pupils of the Public Schools. Such approval having been obtained by a vote of 19,400 in favor, against 3,400 opposed, the institution was duly organized early in 1848, by the appointment of Prof. HORACE WEBSTER, of Geneva College, as President, and a full corps of professors and tutors.

Section II.—Administration of Secretary Christopher Morgan—1848 to 1851.

Progress of the Free School Controversy.—Message of Governor Fish.—Reports of the Superintendent.—Colored Schools.—Indian Children.—District Libraries.—Act for the Establishment of Free Schools.—Its Adoption by the People.—Petitions for its Repeal.—Legislative Discussions.—Mr. Kingsley's Report.—State Free School Convention at Syracuse.—Resubmission to the People.—Popular Vote.—Repeal of the Act Defeated.—Compromise Act of 1851.—Prominent Advocates of the Free School System.—Sectarian Schools.—Schools in Cities and Villages under Special Laws.—Report of the Code Commissioner.

ON the first day of January, 1848, the Hon. Christopher Morgan, of Cayuga, who, under the provisions of the Constitution of 1846, had been elected Secretary of State in November of the preceding year, entered upon the discharge of his official duties as *ex officio* Superintendent of Common Schools. Since the repeal of the system of county supervision, these duties had become so onerous, through the great increase of the number of districts, and of local officers charged with their immediate administration, that it was found almost wholly impracticable for an officer of no previous experience in this respect, and charged with the performance of a variety of other official duties of an independent nature, to devote any considerable share of his time and attention to the department of Common Schools. The daily correspondence of this department, involving the necessity of examining and answering from seventy to eighty letters of inquiry and advice from officers and inhabitants of the several districts; the investigation and decision of the numerous appeals from the proceedings of district meetings, the acts of trustees and town superintendents; the examination of reports from the various officers charged with the local administration of the system, and the preparation of the annual reports to the Legislature—demanded the entire time and energies of any one individual, and rendered it absolutely necessary to devolve the principal labors of the department upon the Deputy Superintendent. The incumbent of that office at this time was ALEXANDER G. JOHNSON, of Troy, a gentleman of superior talents, and in all respects well qualified for the duties of the position. This arrangement enabled the Superintendent, Mr. MORGAN, while exercising a general supervision over the affairs of the department, to devote all the time he could spare from his other official duties to the conduct and management of the great FREE SCHOOL CONTROVERSY, which was now in progress, and into which he at once entered with all the enthusiasm and energy of his nature.

At the opening of the session of the Legislature of 1849, Governor HAMILTON FISH, in his message, expressed his strong conviction of the necessity and desirability of the restoration of the office of County Superintendent, and spoke in the highest terms of the success of the State Normal School, which, in his judgment, was entitled to be no longer regarded as an experiment.

From the annual report of the Superintendent, it appeared that the number of school districts in the State at this period was 10,621; the number of children under instruction during the year 1847, 775,723; the total amount of money expended in the support of the schools, $1,103,682, of which $639,000 was contributed from the State Treasury, and $400,600 from rate-bills; the amount expended in the purchase of libraries and school apparatus, $61,624; and the number of volumes added to the libraries during the year, 27,862, making an aggregate of 1,338,848 volumes. In fifteen counties of the State, schools for colored children had been organized, at which nearly five thousand children were in attendance, and for the support of which the sum of $17,000 had been expended. The whole number of colored children in the State was estimated at not less than 11,000. "The colored population," observes the Superintendent, "is enumerated in the census of the State, and is a part of the basis of the distribution of the school fund. Colored children are enumerated by the trustees in their annual reports; they draw public money for the district in which they reside, and are equally entitled with white children to the benefit of it. In the rural districts of the State, they are generally admitted into the Common Schools. If unreasonable prejudice exclude them from the village schools, the trustees are empowered to establish separate schools for them. They draw the public money to which they are entitled, and the trustees can exempt those parents who are unable to pay a rate-bill, the exemptions becoming a charge upon the whole district. A special appropriation for incorporated villages only excites prejudice and parsimony. The trustees of the village will generally expend the special appropriation for the colored children, and the public money drawn by them will be shared among the white children of the other schools. There seems to be no satisfactory reason for this special appropriation. It cannot be justly urged that negroes are an especial burden to incorporated villages, any more than to cities or rural districts, and that they are therefore entitled to an extraordinary allowance of money to educate them." Schools for the instruction of Indian children had been established upon the St. Regis, the Onondaga, the Cattaraugus and Allegany, and the Shinecock reservations, in all of which about 375 pupils had been instructed.

The Superintendent informed the Legislature that applications had been made to him from the trustees and inhabitants of some four hundred districts for his official approbation to the diversion of the whole or portions of the library money to the payment of teachers' wages, under the act of 1847, and that such approbation had *in every instance been withheld*, "believing that every volume in a well selected library is a perpetual teacher to all who will go to it for instruction; that *the district libraries cannot be too large;* and that the people are in no danger of learning too much." "Selections for the district libraries," he observes, "are made from the whole range of literature and science, with the exception of controversial books, political or religious—history, biography, poetry; philosophy, mental, moral, and natural; fiction—indeed, every department of human knowledge contributes its share. The object of this great charity was not merely to furnish books for children, but to establish in all the school districts a miscellaneous library suited to the tastes and character of every age. By means of this diffusive benevolence, the light of knowledge penetrates every portion of the State, and the sons of our farmers, mechanics, merchants, and laborers have daily access to many well selected books, of which, but for this sagacious policy, a majority of them would never have heard. If knowledge is power, who can calculate the energy imparted to the people of this State by the district school and the district library?"

Teachers' Institutes had been held, under the provisions of the act of 1847, in sixteen counties, in which upward of one thousand teachers had been in attendance. An increase in the appropriation for this object was urgently recommended.

In reference to the local supervision of the schools, and the office of County Superintendent, he observes:

"It is believed that the friends of the Common School system in the State very generally desired the continuance of the office. It was, however, abolished, and without even proposing a substitute. There is now no intermediate officer between this department and the town officers. Such an office is needed as the medium of communication with the nine hundred town superintendents, and eleven thousand school districts. The territory is too large, its subdivisions too many, its relations too diverse, the local offices too numerous, and the interval between the department and them too wide, to permit that actual and minute supervision which is necessary to an efficient administration of the school laws. The undersigned would therefore recommend to the Legislature two measures, either of which, in his opinion, will be approved by the friends of the Common School system, and will supply a want daily felt in this department: 1st. A repeal of the Act of 1847, and a restoration of the office of County Superintendent—making it elective by the people; or, 2d. *The election of a superintendent in every assembly district*, except in the city of New York and the cities which now have or shall hereafter have a city superintendent, or board of education. Among the powers and duties of such district superintendent should be the following: to make the abstract of the reports of the town superintendents in his district; to recommend persons from his district as pupils of the State Normal School, and for State certificates of qualification as teachers; to visit each school in his district at least twice a year, once in the summer and once in the winter, and to make such reports of his visitation as may be required by the State Superintendent; and to hear and determine all the controversies arising in his district under the school laws, an appeal being allowed from his decision to this department."

The Superintendent then proceeds to examine the present condition of the school law in reference to its provisions for the support of schools, and to base upon it a recommendation for the adoption of the Free School System:

"The mode of supporting a school under the present system," he observes, "is as follows: The trustees employ a qualified teacher, for stipulated wages,

At the close of his term, they give him an order upon the town superintendent for such portion of the public money as may have been voted by the district for the term, or in case no vote has been taken for such portion as they think proper; but in no case can they legally draw for more money than is due the teacher at the date of the order. If the public money is not sufficient to pay his wages, the trustees proceed to make out a *rate-bill* for the residue, charging each parent or guardian according to the number of days' attendance of his children. They have power to exempt indigent persons, and the amount so exempted is a charge upon the district, and may be immediately collected by tax, or added to any tax thereafter levied. After the rate-bill is completed, thirty days' notice of its completion is given by the trustees, one of whom must be in attendance on a day and at a place appointed in said notice, once a week for two successive weeks, to receive payment; and during the whole of the thirty days any person may pay to either of the trustees, or to the teacher, the sum charged to him upon the rate-bill. At the expiration of the thirty days, if all the persons named in the rate-bill have not voluntarily paid, the trustees put it, with their warrant, into the hands of the district collector, who has the same authority to collect it, by levy and sale of goods and chattels, as a town collector. He is also authorized to collect fees, not only upon the money paid to him, *but upon that paid voluntarily to the trustees, or the teacher*, and is allowed thirty days to make his return to the trustees.

"A more troublesome or vexatious system could not well be devised. The teacher, having performed his contract, is yet obliged, unless the trustees advance the money, to wait thirty or sixty days for his pay. The first thirty days' delay under the notice is of no advantage to any one. The time of the trustees is spent uselessly; nothing is gained by the payment to the trustees or teacher. Is there any other instance upon the statute book in which legislation compels a man to wait sixty days for his wages, after he has completed his work? In the absence of any contract, the wages of the laborer are due and payable when his work is done. In the case of the teacher, the payment of his wages is postponed for sixty days after his school is closed, for payment from trustees cannot be enforced until the time fixed by law for collection has expired. Any slight error in the apportionment of the rates, or in the legal form for making it, subjects the trustees to a suit, by any one of whom a few cents may have been illegally collected; and, unfortunately, there are not wanting, in every town, persons ready to avail themselves of such errors. The trustees can, if they choose, make out a tax for the amount of exemptions, and the collector is bound to collect it for the trifling fees upon a five or ten dollar tax-list. Courts may, it is true, deny costs to a plaintiff in a suit against trustees where the latter appear to have acted in good faith, and boards of supervisors may order a tax to be assessed upon a district to refund both costs and expenses incurred in suits by or against them on account of the discharge of their official duties; but the law allows them nothing for their responsibilities and labor, either in the discharge of their duties or in the prosecution or defense of suits.

"Now a FREE SCHOOL SYSTEM may be devised that shall relieve trustees from the duty of making out rate-bills or tax-lists in any case, and from all litigation arising therefrom, and which shall secure to the teacher his pay when his work is done. It may be made applicable only to the towns, requiring the cities, however, to make their schools *free*, but leaving them to adopt such an organization as shall be suited to their peculiar wants.

"Teachers complain of the rate-bill system, not only because it improperly withholds their wages, but because the trustees find great difficulty in exercising with fidelity and at the same time satisfactorily the power of exemption. While the cupidity of the tax-payer is excited, the *pride* of men of moderate means is aroused, and their *sense of independence* revolts at being certified and put upon the record as indigent persons.

"The rate-bill system requires every person to pay in proportion to the attendance of his children. How strong, then, is the inducement of many parents to wink at absence and truancy, and how little are they inclined to second, by parental authority, the efforts of the teacher to enforce punctuality and regularity of attendance! The fact that the number of children attending school less than four months uniformly exceeds the number attending a longer time furnishes strong evidence for believing that the rate-bill system is the principal cause of the irregular attendance of scholars.

"Letters have been addressed to the Superintendent, from various parts of the State, urging him to recommend to the Legislature the Free School system, and assuring him that the people are ready to sustain such recommendation. It is urged by its opponents that those who have property are taxed to educate their own children as well as the children of the poor; and that those who are thus blessed with property, but denied children, are also obliged to contribute something for the education of the indigent. Those who have omitted their duty, or are more fortunate than their neighbors in the possession of property, have no reason to complain of the trifling burthen which good fortune imposes upon them.

"*Are* property holders wronged or injured by this system of taxation? Property is the creature of law. Its ownership is regulated by law; even the income of some kinds of property is limited by law. Human beings are property in South Carolina, and the taxes assessed upon them, and paid out of the earnings of their labor, go to the support of Free Schools, while in this State there can be no property in man. Land is property, and in civilized countries it constitutes the bulk of all property, yet it is not property in the absence of law. What idea of property in land has the Camanche Indian, or a Calmuck Tartar? To him the land is as free for his roaming as the air for his breathing, or the water for his drink. The wild Bedouin will guard as his own his tent, his camel, his wife; but his laws are the keenness of his scimetar and the fleetness of his steed. The security of property is one of the paramount objects of government; but how shall that security be obtained? By the stern restraints and crushing force of military power? The experience of the last year in Europe and America has proven that there is greater security for persons and property in the general intelligence and education of the people than in an overawing soldiery. Europe has been convulsed—cities have been the scenes of fearful and mortal strife—fields have been laid waste by the contending armies—governments have been overthrown—revolution has followed revolution—uncertainty and insecurity are stamped upon all things—political changes have been effected only by civil war and commotion. The people of the United States, on the other hand, have effected the choice of a Chief Magistrate, involving a change in the policy of the government. It was accomplished in a day, with the cheerful and peaceful acquiescence of the Union. These are the results of the intelligence and moral elevation of the American people. There is a moral and intellectual power in the universal education of the people which furnishes more abiding security for persons and property than disciplined armies. Property must be taxed to support a soldiery: why should it not, then, contribute to a system of protection which may preclude the necessity of armies? Crimes and pauperism are too often the results of ignorance. The detection and punishment of the one, and the support of the other, are mainly effected by the imposition of taxes upon property. Is it not wise, then, to establish a system of education, universal and complete, which may, in a great measure, prevent the commission of crime, and avoid the evils of pauperism?"

On the 26th of March, 1849, the "ACT ESTABLISHING FREE SCHOOLS THROUGHOUT THE STATE" was passed by the Legislature. Its prominent provisions were as follows:

Common Schools in the several school districts of the State were declared free to all persons residing in the district over five and under twenty-one years of age. It was made the duty of the boards of supervisors of each county to raise annually by tax, on their respective counties, in addition to an amount equal to that apportioned by the State, an amount upon each *town*, in such counties, equal to the sum apportioned by the State to such town, thereby requiring an assessment upon the whole county equivalent to *twice* the amount apportioned by the State. In addition to this, the trustees of each *district* were required, within thirty days preceding the time of its annual meeting, to prepare an estimate of the amount necessary to be raised in the district for the support of its school, for fuel, furniture, school apparatus, repairs, and insurance of school-house, and contingent expenses, during the ensuing year, over and above the amount thus provided by law, and received from the State, and the income of local funds, and to post the same conspicuously on the school-house door and other public places in the district. At such annual meeting the legal voters of the district were authorized and required to pass upon such estimates, item by item, and to cause to be levied on the taxable inhabitants of the district such amount as the majority of voters should approve and determine. In case of their refusal or neglect to raise such an amount as, in conjunction with the public money apportioned by the State, and raised under the preceding provisions of the act, and the local funds applicable to that purpose, would support a school, for at least four months in each year, keep the school-house in proper order, and furnish the necessary fuel, then the trustees were required to employ a teacher, repair the house, and supply it with all necessaries for that period, and levy a tax upon the district accordingly. Free and gratuitous education was required to be given in each of the Public and Common Schools in each of the cities of the State; and the electors throughout the State were required to determine by ballot, at the ensuing November election, whether the act should or should not become a law, and take immediate effect.

Very little opposition was made to the act; and at the annual State election its provisions were sanctioned and approved by a vote of 249,872 in its favor to 91,951 against—a majority of 157,921. Four counties only—Tompkins, Chenango, Cortland, and Otsego—gave majorities against it, amounting in the aggregate to 1,257, while the aggregate majorities in its favor, in the remaining fifty-four counties, was 158,181.

The official term of the Secretary having expired, Mr. MORGAN was re-elected; and on the 10th of December, S. S. RANDALL was re-appointed Deputy Superintendent, in place of A. G. JOHNSON, appointed Deputy Secretary.

By an act passed on the 30th of March, of this year, the sum of $250 was appropriated annually for three years to the trustees of such academies as the Regents of the University should designate, for the instruction of at least twenty pupils of each, for four months of each year, in the science of Common School teaching.

Notwithstanding the almost unanimous vote of the electors of the State in favor of the act for the establishment of FREE SCHOOLS, it was met at the very outset of its practical administration by the most determined and wide-spread hostility. In nearly half the counties of the State, the sessions of the board of supervisors had passed over before the official annunciation of its adoption, and consequently no provision had been made for the additional town tax required by the law. The large deficiency of funds thus occasioned was in these counties left to be supplied by the voters of the several school districts; and, in addition to this, in these and a large proportion of the remaining counties, the inequality in the taxable property of the several districts contributed, to a very great extent, to render the operation of the new law burdensome and oppressive. Many of the heaviest tax-payers had no direct interest in the schools; and wherever they constituted a majority of the legal voters in the district, or through their influence were able to control such majority, all appropriations for the support of the schools beyond the minimum term of four months required, as a condition of receiving the public money, were refused. The validity and *constitutionality* of the act were, in some influential quarters, seriously questioned, upon the ground of its conditional submission to the people; a very general disaffection toward its provisions and toward the system itself sprung up in nearly every section of the State, especially in the rural districts, where it was nearly universal; and petitions for its immediate repeal or modification were poured in upon the Legislature from all quarters.

During the session of 1850, several bills were brought forward in each house for this purpose, and for the removal of the obnoxious features of the law. Able reports were made by the Hon. JAMES W. BEEKMAN, of New York, chairman of the Literature Committee of the Senate, and by the Hon. LEWIS KINGSLEY, from a select committee raised on this subject in the Assembly, in both cases strongly and uncompromisingly adverse to the *repeal* of the act, but assenting to and proposing such legislation as should remove all reasonable grounds of complaint in its practical execution. In the House, the Hon. SILAS M. BURROUGHS, of Orleans, chairman of the Committee on Colleges, Academies, and Common Schools, reported a bill providing for the levying of a general State tax of $800,000 annually for the support of the schools, in conjunction with the revenue of the school fund, leaving whatever deficiency should remain to be supplied by rate-bill, as heretofore. The bill passed the Assembly by a vote of 70 to 30, but failed to receive the concurrence of the Senate, which body, however, passed a bill, reported by the Hon. CHARLES A. MANN, of Oneida, and concurred in, on the last day of the session, by a close vote in the House, referring the direct question of the repeal of the act of 1849 to the voters of the State, at the ensuing annual election.

The friends of FREE SCHOOLS, after the most strenuous and persevering, though ineffectual, efforts to obtain such amendments or modification of the law as might render its provisions generally acceptable, determined, under these circumstances, to make a firm and compact stand against its unconditional repeal. They united with great unanimity in the call for a STATE CONVENTION at Syracuse on the 10th of July. The report of Mr. KINGSLEY, from the select committee of the Assembly, faithfully represents the views entertained by the most intelligent and well-informed opponents of the existing law. Fully appreciating the importance and value of the universal education of the people, and aware of the progressive efforts from time to time made by the Legislature for the promotion of this great object—freely admitting that it is the unquestioned right and highest duty of the State to provide such education, *free to all*, the committee yet insist that the Schools established under its supervision, and supported by its bounty, should be so suported by such a system of taxation as should diffuse its burdens "in a fair, just, and equal proportion, *according to the different interests different persons may have in the subject, or the immediate or remote benefits they may derive from the sums* thus appropriated." "We claim not," they observe, "that the State should so bestow its means as to give every one, freely, a *collegiate* or even an *academic* education; but only that it is bound by every consideration of utility and justice to furnish the means for the *common* education of every child within its boundaries—that it should give to every one an opportunity for so improving the powers which nature's God has given him that he may be enabled to discharge the ordinary duties of life with ease, and correctly, and be also prepared to proceed farther and farther into the great ocean of science which lies before him. Else the State has not performed all its duty—it has not done all in its power to increase the virtue, safety, prosperity, and happiness of its people—and in so far is a debtor to those who made it." The committee, after reviewing the history and progress of the Common School system, from its inception to the present period, when from a productive capital of upwards of two millions of dollars the sum of $285,000 was annually appropriated from the public treasury for the support of schools and school libraries, and an army of nearly 800,000 children gathered into those institutions, and referring to the immediate impulse to the adoption of the act of 1849, growing out of the ascertained exclusion from the Common Schools of the State of *nearly fifty thousand* indigent children, whose parents either declined, from motives of pride and a spirit of independence, to claim or were refused the exemption provided by law, go on to say:

> "This law has now been in operation some four months only; and yet we are daily receiving petitions for its amendment, or its total and entire repeal. Already there have been presented over forty petitions for its amendment, and over *two hundred and fifty for its repeal.* They come from every corner of the State—from our villages, our secluded districts—from our boards of supervisors, our town meetings, our district meetings, our public officers—from public meetings—from the high and the low, the rich and the poor—those who voted for and those who voted against it—all ages, conditions, and classes are here—and respectfully ask us either to make essential and important amendments to the law, or by its repeal to place us where we were before. In this manner and for these purposes some *twenty thousand names*, of which over *seventeen thousand* are for *repeal*, have been presented to us; and we are called upon by every consideration of duty and interest to listen to these complaints, and grant such relief as may be in our power to bestow."

After canvassing the objections to the law, arising on the one hand from the unequal pressure of taxation, and on the other from the discretionary powers vested in the inhabitants of districts to limit the continuance of their schools to four months in each year, by refusing the necessary appropriations for their support for a longer period, the committee proceed:

"It is further claimed by the petitioners for repeal that it is not the duty of the government to support Common Schools by compulsory taxation; that it is a law of nature that the parent should take care of the education of his children, while the law, in effect, takes it from him and gives it to the State; that minors are taxed for their property without their consent; that old men who have by their industry accumulated property, and educated their own children in such a manner as they thought best, are now taxed for the education of the children of others; that the law, though intended for the benefit of the poor man, works against him, as it, in many instances, shuts up the school against his children during eight months of the year; that the old law afforded all needed help to the poor, and was voluntary, while the present is compulsory; that the law is unconstitutional, or, if not, is unjust and cannot be sustained; that it helps the vicious and indolent only—with a thousand other objections of a minor character, equally applicable to the old and new law, and which, if valid here, would be equally valid against any taxation for any purpose whatever."

The majority of the committee, believing that the law was susceptible of amendment, had prepared a bill for that purpose "They have thought it their duty, in view of the overwhelming majority in favor of Free Schools, at the last election, to *amend* the law rather than *repeal* it—to cure its infirmities rather than to take away its existence." With this view, they were in favor of the imposition of a direct *State tax*, for the raising of a sufficient amount to support the schools of the State, in conjunction with the funds already at its disposal; but, apprehensive of the strict constitutionality of such a tax, they proposed a similar *county tax*—apportioning its avails in an equitable manner among the several districts in the ratio of numbers and attendance of pupils—and requiring the schools to be kept open for eight months during each year.

The minority, on the other hand, represented by Mr. KINGSLEY, dissented from these views and conclusions. While they would not rashly propose to go back to the former system, if any other alternative presented itself, they felt "constrained to think that in the present crisis no other course is open before us; that no other plan will satisfy our people, or remove the deep and all-pervading feeling of hostility which exists against the present law; that, amend it as we may, it will still be the system of which they so heartily disapprove now—of which, we fear, they would as heartily disapprove hereafter."

"It is beyond a doubt," they continue, "that the people *do* disapprove of the details, at least, of the present law. Its operation has had a withering and a blasting effect. Is it not, then, reasonable to believe that although the law be amended, and its more repulsive provisions stricken out, if it still retain any of its old features, it will, notwithstanding all its amendments, be unpopular with the people. We think that it is; and, thinking so, cannot turn a deaf ear to the thousands of petitioners who have asked its *unconditional repeal*. They ask that they may return, for the present, at least, to their old and well-tried system, satisfied as they are that it is not always well to change from a good and available plan to one untried and unknown. The Free School system promised well; the name had in it a charm—it was pleasant to the ear of a poor man—it sounded musically to him as he thought of the benefits it would confer on his children around him; the man of moderate means and the man of wealth were as charmed as he; all thought not of its possible evils, but looked only at its probable benefits, and the good it had done in the crowded city; and the result was that a majority, counting by its tens and hundreds of thousands, spoke in favor of the law. A few months only and the feeling is changed; the poor man finds, as the law commences its workings, that his children are deprived of a part even of their former privileges—for the school-house door is now closed at times when it was open before—and there are stern feelings rising in the breast of the rich man against him, as one whose children he is obliged to educate by compulsion, which he is loth to do; the man of moderate wealth, the man of great wealth, and the one who has educated his own family, according to the means with which he was blessed, now find their taxes increased—their poor neighbors educating their children upon the funds the law has wrung from them—and they imbibe a stern prejudice against it in all its aspects, provisions, and features. The minority are constrained to believe that, amend that law as we may, it will be looked upon with an unfavorable eye, and regarded by all with unconquerable feelings of aversion."

After reviewing the principal features of the amendments proposed, the minority continue:

"But we base an objection upon another ground still. Admitting, as we may safely do, the abstract justice of the imposition of this additional tax, still it would be *unwise and impolitic*, from the general disapprobation with which it would be regarded. It cannot be doubted that great opposition will be made to such a tax, and that the system which requires it will be viewed with a very general disfavor and repugnance. If this be so, the law cannot have a good effect—our Common Schools cannot prosper. To flourish they must be established in the affections of our people; they must not be met with opposition or ill-will; our districts must not be the arena of personal strife and animosities—for as surely as they are, so surely will the cause of popular education languish and decay—so surely will rank grass and weeds grow around our school-house doors—so surely will our Common School system be numbered among "the things that were," wounded and killed by the lavish kindness of its friends. From such a result may we be mercifully spared!

"Other objections throng to our minds, "thick as autumnal leaves in Vallambrosa," but we forbear to mention them. Enough, it seems to us, has been said, and we, therefore, leave this part of the subject with the remark that these reasons have influenced us to think that the present law should be unconditionally repealed. To this conclusion we have come with great reluctance; but it is one from which our better convictions, our sincere desire for the prosperity of our Common Schools, will not permit us to escape. If we err, it is not from the heart.

"But we are asked, are you opposed to Free Schools? Our answer is *an emphatic negative*. OUR COMMON SCHOOLS SHOULD AND MUST BE FREE; but we are *not of opinion that the present law makes them so*, however it may be named; or rather that the *principle* of the present law is no more a free school one than was the principle of the former. Under each system no one was excluded; every one could then, as every one now, find an open door, and a teacher to educate him. The only real difference in the two is, that in the one the money was raised by a rate-bill; in the other, by a direct tax; in each instance the property of the district pays the amount, though in different proportions. Both, then, may be called Free School systems, if we correctly understand the term, and apply it to a system which provides that a certain amount shall be raised by a *tax*, and then all children shall share in its benefits.

"But we opine that the Free School system, as the people now understand it—as they understood it at the last election—means something different from this; that it means *one which is sustained directly by the State, without any individual taxation whatever*, except in a small degree, as we will presently mention. Such a system the minority are desirous of having. At the present it may be impossible; but "there's a good time coming," and we hope at a day not far distant that a system like this will be ours. For the present, however, we think there is no other course for us to adopt but to return to our old rate-bill system.

"The minority would not be understood, in any part of their argument, to take decisive grounds against the support of our Common Schools by the bounty of the State. They do think that it will never be wise to *entirely* dispense with the rate-bill system. As just mentioned, we are in favor of a Free School law by which the State shall furnish all the means, except a very small portion to be raised in a proper manner from those sending to school. But we also think it well not to pass from the rate-bill system to this with too great rapidity. It should be a gradual change, and one for which the people will all be prepared—which will not come upon them unawares, but which will be foreseen, expected, and desired. *Through such a change we are now passing.*"

The minority of the committee concurred with the majority in reporting for the consideration of the House a bill submitted by Mr. McLean, of Livingston, re-submitting the question to the people of the State for their decision; and in conclusion remark:

"Let what will be the action of the Legislature in regard to this momentous question, your committee earnestly hope that it will be for the benefit of our Common Schools; that by us their interests may be protected and nourished, their prosperity increased, and their means of usefulness enlarged and extended; that whatever system may finally be adopted will be loved of the people—a system whose roots will enter deeply into their hearts and affections, and whose kindly shade will extend over all the State its grateful protection and shelter: then will we all pray, 'Lord, ever let it flourish; Lord, ever keep its verdure green!'"

On the 10th of July, the Free School State Convention assembled at Syracuse, consisting of a large collection of delegates from every section of the State.

The Hon. Christopher Morgan, State Superintendent, was elected President. On taking the chair, he thanked the convention for the honor conferred upon him, and remarked that he came to the convention, in common with the numerous assembly present, as a friend of free and universal education, and to inform himself of the views and wishes of its advocates and supporters throughout the State. He was attached to no particular mode of carrying out the great principle; but, as a citizen of New York, he came to claim for every child that degree of instruction in science, literature, and morality that is necessary to enable the son or the daughter of the poor man to stand up as the equal of the child of the rich—so that, starting with equal advantages, the prizes of life may be won by the most meritorious and deserving. He respected the motives of the large class of his fellow-citizens opposed to the present law; yet, whatever reproach might be brought upon him, he should do all in his power to advance the education of all the children of the State at the expense of those who have the means. He was every day told by some one, "I have educated my own children, and why should I pay for the education of the children of others?" He would say to all such: "Neither, perhaps, have you a child in the poor-house or the penitentiary; and yet you are paying a large amount every year for the support of the children of others who are there, mainly because they have been deprived by your selfishness, and that of others like you, of the blessings of education."

The following resolutions were reported by the committee appointed for that purpose:

"1. That the proposition before the convention and the State was, not that our present Common School law, in all its provisions and details, is perfect; but that this law should be maintained in so far as it provides that *our Common Schools shall be free to all the children of the State.*

"2. That the principle upheld by this convention—the principle which should be fixed and established in the political economy of this State—is that THE PROPERTY OF THE STATE SHOULD EDUCATE THE CHILDREN OF THE STATE, or, in the words of the first section of the act of 1849, "COMMON SCHOOLS, in the several school districts of this State, SHALL BE FREE TO ALL PERSONS *residing in the district over five and under twenty-one years of age.*

"3. That the true welfare of a State is to be attained, not wholly by highways and canals, by asylums and penitentiaries, by a police and standing army, but by the development of the physical, intellectual, and moral energies of the people; therefore, if the former should be sustained at the public expense, much more should the thorough education of the whole people be amply provided for from the same source.

"4. That the emphatic vote of the people, at the last election, in favor of the act establishing FREE SCHOOLS throughout the State, was clearly indicative of the deliberate sanction and approval of the PRINCIPLE which dictated the enactment of that law; and that no defect in the subordinate *details* of the provision thus made for the universal education of the children of the State can warrant or justify *the abandonment of that principle*, or the total repeal of the law.

"5. That we pledge ourselves to use every proper means of influence in our power, individually and collectively, to procure the renewed sanction of the people to the great PRINCIPLE OF FREE SCHOOLS, as the only sure and effectual palladium of their freedom, happiness, and prosperity—as the best safeguard of their rights, and the surest preservative of those noble institutions handed down to us by the fathers and framers of our Republic.

"6. That we are opposed to the restoration of the old school law, because its operation had become contrary to the principles of democratic government. While it professed to be liberal, it gave the avaricious parent an excuse for keeping his children from the schools; while it should have furnished intellectual aliment free to all the children of the State, it virtually drove thousands and ten of thousands from the school-houses, by wounding their pride, and branding them as paupers, or refusing them the exemption to which, under its provisions, they were entitled. While it should have discriminated between the right of the child and that of the parent or guardian to public beneficence, it often treated unkindly and blasted the hopes of the former, on account of the improvidence or misfortune of the latter; and while it was far better than no system of public education, it did not supply the wants of the rising generation who were calling for "light, more light still."

"7. That we will most cordially unite in the recommendation to the Legislature of such an amendment of the act of 1849, establishing Free Schools, as shall make the expense of supporting such schools, over and above the revenue of the Common School fund, a charge upon the real and personal property in the State, county, or town, equitably assessed according to a just and fair valuation of such property, and such other modifications of the act as they in their wisdom shall see to be best and deem expedient and proper."

These resolutions were ably and eloquently sustained by Messrs. O. B. PIERCE, of Oneida; BLOSS, of Monroe; WALDO; the Rev. SAMUEL J. MAY, of Syracuse; STARR, of Rochester; the Rev. HENRY MANDEVILLE, of Albany; Dr. LORD, of Ohio; and WALKER, of New York. Mr. McMASTERS, of New York, then took the floor in opposition to the resolutions and the entire system of Common School education. The State, he observed, in prescribing a system of public education, and taxing the people for its support, assumed an authority which did not belong to it. It purposed, in so doing, to invade the family sanctuary, and rob the parents of their authority over their children. Each individual was entitled to use the products of his toil as he pleased, and all contributions for educational purposes should be made as a matter of charity. In reference to every species of religious instruction introduced into the public schools, the State proposed to invade the province of the church. By the exclusion of what was termed dogmatic religious teaching, true religion was wholly ignored. No religion could exist without dogmas. Mr. McMasters was replied to by Mr. Randall, of Albany, who invited all the opponents of the Free School system who might be present to present their views and objections, and thereby enable its friends to answer their arguments, and meet them fairly on their own grounds.

Mr. Bascom, of Seneca, thereupon avowed himself an opponent of both the act of 1849 and the Free School system itself; and as a challenge had been thrown out by Mr. Randall, he would accept it, and take up the gage. He had no sympathy with that sordid meanness of avarice which would withhold education from the poor. He found no one in the convention willing to swallow the law as it was, nor any one who denied the right of every child to a good education. He thought an unwise course had hitherto been pursued by the State. At an early day, the public lands of the State were pledged for the education of the people. A permanent fund, yielding a revenue of $275,000 annually, had, from this and other sources, come into the possession of the State, which should have been exclusively applied to the education of the poor. We had heard much of the school system of New England, as superior to that of the Empire State. But a Senator of this State (Mr. BEEKMAN, of New York) had shown, by incontrovertible statistics, last winter, that New York stood higher in this respect than any other State of the Union, or nation of the earth. He objected to the law and to the system, because it had not secured the good-will of the people, which was every thing in carrying out any enterprise. He referred to the bad effects of the law in diminishing the interest of the people in education, and weakening the incentives which were necessary to true improvement. He instanced, as an illustration, the peasantry of a certain district in Europe, who some years ago were industrious, virtuous, brave, and happy; but the church stepped in, and by her bounties, dispensed with too liberal hand, that peasantry had now become the *lazzaroni* of Italy. He contended that real and personal property should be placed on an equal basis for the purpose of taxation. The latter was not now half taxed, on account of the deductions allowed for debts, while those debts were not regarded as real property. Public institutions also, such as banks, railroads, and canals, should not be taxed for educational purposes in the localities where they are situated, but for the benefit of the school fund of the State generally.

Mr. GREELEY, of New York, replied to the objection of Mr. MCMASTERS, that the State had no legitimate power to educate its children. What was the State? Who constitute the commonwealth? The *people* were the State, and we, the people, could do by our majorities what might be deemed essential for the public good. All conceded to the State the power to build prisons, penitentiaries, and poor-houses; and why has it not power to build school-houses, where the necessity for prisons and poor-houses might be removed? As to religious instruction, he did not conceive dogmas essential to religion. "Pure religion and undefiled" was, as defined by the Apostle James, "to visit the widows and fatherless in their affliction, and to keep ourselves unspotted from the world." There was no danger in the great doctrines of love to God and love to men. Why should dogmas of any kind be linked to this beautiful principle? We do not propose to banish this kind of religion from any of our schools. The contest, he said, into which we were about entering, was between universal education, on the one hand, and popular ignorance, on the other. He spoke of the increased prosperity of our schools under the new law. The number of these institutions had greatly increased, and who would oppose a system that gathers our children in the eleven thousand school-houses of the State? He concluded by expressing his earnest hope that by the final adoption of this system of Free Schools we should inaugurate a new era in the history of New York.

The President (Mr. MORGAN), on taking leave of the convention, took occasion to remark, in reply to the charge of despotism that had been preferred against the Free School system, that education would so elevate every mind that virtue, instead of vice, would abound; happiness, instead of misery, prevail; and independence, instead of despotism and servility, distinguish every individual. We impose taxes, as has been properly observed, for the support of the police, the prison, the poor-house, and the asylum. Is this despotism? He would tax the people for such an education as will do away with all these, and make true men and women of all our people. If this be despotism, God grant that such despotism may increase and flourish throughout the State and the world! "Let us declare," he said, "in thunder tones, that every child has a right to an education; that every child *shall be* educated; and that the law, by its strong hand, shall draw, if necessary, from the pockets of those who have the money, and not the heart to contribute of their abundance to such a glorious enterprise."

A letter was then read, from the venerable Dr. ELIPHALET NOTT, President of Union College, strongly recommending the adoption of the Free School system. The discussion was then resumed by Messrs. WALKER, of New York; RANDALL, of Albany; PIERCE, of Oneida, and others; after which the question on the adoption of the resolutions was unanimously carried.

The following address to the people of the State, prepared by a committee consisting of HORACE GREELEY and JAMES W. BEEKMAN, of New York; CHARLES B. SEDGWICK, of Onondaga; ALANSON HOLLY, of Wyoming; WILLIAM F. PHELPS, of Albany; SAMUEL B. WOOLWORTH, of Cortland; and O. G. STEELE, of Erie, was then reported, and read by Mr. GREELEY:

"FELLOW-CITIZENS: At the instance of your chosen law-makers, you voted last November on the question of opening your Common Schools, without charge or distinction, to all the children of fit age residing within your State, and your majority in favor of such opening was overwhelming. In this voting, you did not imply that the *details* of the Free School act of 1849 were perfect, nor were you understood as so deciding. You left the act open to amendment by each successive Legislature, whenever amendment not inconsistent with its vital principle should be deemed advisable. Your last Legislature, in full view of these facts, instead of correcting any errors which, in the first reduction of a great principle to practice, are well-nigh unavoidable, decided to re-submit the law, with all its alleged "imperfections on its head," for your approval or rejection this fall. In other words, the Legislature, while it left its own work undone, required you to do yours a second time. And now the enemies of Free Schools seek to profit by this neglect, coupled with the unfair manner in which the question is re-submitted, and to secure your suffrages in opposition to the free principle, by harping on and magnifying the defects and inequalities in the details of the law. They would have you believe that in voting with us you vote against any amendment of the present law.

"Against this statement we most emphatically protest. The issue ought to have been fairly and truly presented by the act of last session—"For Free Schools" or "Against" them; for that, and that only, is the question to be decided. A vote on our side simply affirms the principle that our Common Schools shall be free; a vote against us is, in effect, a vote to return to rate-bills and trustee exonerations—a vote to re-establish distinctions of caste in our Common Schools, and to subject a portion of our children to the bitter humiliation of being pointed out as district paupers. To revive these distinctions is to banish thousands of children from the schools altogether, and doom them to long-life ignorance, through the mistaken but natural pride of their poverty and kindred. A vote against us in the approaching election is a vote to recede from the educational platform of Massachusetts, in the direction of Virginia, Italy, Turkey. A vote against the law, as the question is now most unfairly presented, is a step toward popular ignorance, barbarism, and moral night.

"Whoever among you has had patience to follow an opponent of the law through his devious course of reasoning, well knows that his citadel is the assumption that "it is wrong to tax one man to educate another's children," unless it be the children of absolute paupers. This assumption, if conceded, is fatal, not to Free Schools merely, but to any Common Schools whatever. If elementary education be properly and only a parental duty, then the State should leave it wholly to the voluntary and unassisted efforts and combinations of parents. Then the taxation of a district to build a school-house is usurpation and extortion. Then all the laws which have been passed, making compulsory provision for Common Schools, or intended to increase their efficiency, are impertinent, agrarian, and confiscating. Yet few of our opponents will venture to take this or any other ground of radical hostility to the Free School principle. The difference between their position and ours is mainly one of degree. We abide consistently by the principles on which only can any public provision for education be justified; they stop half-way, and, in so doing, condemn their own course in coming so far.

"To the assertion that it is wrong to tax A to provide instruction for the children of B, we reply that we would tax both A and B for school purposes, each in proportion to his ability—not as parents, but as possessors of property, and because property is deeply interested in the education of all. There is no farm, no bank, no mill, no shop—unless it be a grog-shop—which is not more valuable and more profitable to its owner, if located among a well-educated, than if surrounded by an ignorant population. Simply as a matter of interest, we hold it to be a duty of property to itself to provide education for all. Not, therefore, as the children of A or of B, but as children of New York—her future cultivators, artisans, instructors, citizens, electors, and rulers—we plead for the education of all, at the cost and for the benefit of all. In a community where a single vote cast in ignorance may involve the country in war, in aggression, and untold calamities, property cannot *afford* that there be any considerable proportion of ignorant voters, nor ignorant mothers of voters. To whomsoever shall urge the duty of B to educate his own children, in spite of his relative poverty, we say, urge upon him that duty to the extent of your powers of persuasion, and we will second you as well as we may. After the State has done all in its power, there will be enough for every father to do in the way of educating and disciplining his children. But this rudimentary intellectual culture of the Common School is an undertaking, not of individual parents, but of the community—the State—and the State should provide therefor, as it provides for its other institutions. It has very wisely declined the care of Public Worship, which in other countries forms a very important portion of its duties and the public burthens, and has nobly assumed the charge of popular education, which other governments too generally repudiate. Having thus resolved that B's children shall be educated, not for his sake, but in furtherance of its own policy, and in deference to its own safety, the State would do wrong to tax his poverty to defray the cost of this safeguard to property. The Common Schools of New York are to her what their respective standing armies are to Russia and Austria, and it would be as fair to support the latter by a *per capita* tax as the former. The child of indigence who attends the district school is discharging a public duty, and should be as welcome there as the child of affluence and social distinction. He should be made to feel that his due training and development are the subject of general solicitude. *Property can better afford to educate four children in the school-house than one in the street.* The teacher when fairly remunerated, as he too often is not is a far less expensive functionary than the sheriff, the district attorney, or the judge. One burglar or thief costs more to the community than all the teachers of an average township. The statistics of our State prisons prove that at least three-fourths of our criminals are drawn from that one-fourth of our population which has enjoyed the least educational advantages—mainly, no such advantages at all. Let our Common Schools be abolished to-morrow, and property would soon be taxed many times their annual cost, in the shape of robberies, riots, and depredations. For every teacher dismissed, a new deputy sheriff, constable, or policeman, would be required. And the dismissal from our schools of those children of poor, but not abject, parents, whom the Free School law has called into them, would be identical in principle with the destruction of the schools altogether. A large portion of our children would be educated if there were no Common Schools, but these we know would not be.

"But we are asked why a citizen who has worked, and saved, and thrived should pay for schooling the children of his neighbor, who has drank, and frolicked, and squandered, till he has little or nothing left. We answer, he should do it in order that these needy and disgraced children may not become what their father is, and so, very probably, in time, a public burthen, as criminals or paupers. The children of the drunkard and reprobate have a hard enough lot, without being surrendered to his judgment and self-denial for the measure of their education. If they are to have no more instruction than *he* shall see fit, and feel able to pay for, a kind Heaven must regard them with a sad compassion, and man ought not utterly to leave them uncared for, and subjected to such moral and intellectual influences only as their desolate homes may afford. To stake the education of our State's future rulers and mothers on such parents' ideas of their own ability and their children's moral needs is madness—is treason to the common weal. They will be quite enough detained, even from Free Schools, by supposed inability to clothe or spare them; but to cast into the wrong scale a dead weight of paternal appetite and avarice, in the form of rate-bills, is to consign them heartlessly to intellectual darkness and moral perdition. And, in truth, the argument for taxing, in equal amounts, the improvidently destitute and the frugally affluent father of a family, for school purposes, is precisely as strong for taxing them in equal amounts to build court-houses, support paupers, dispense justice, or for any other purpose whatever. Nay, it is even stronger—for the drinking, thriftless, idle parent, is far more likely to bring expense on the community, in the shape of crime to be punished, or pauperism to be supported, than his thrifty and temperate neighbor; and, according to our adversaries' logic, he should pay more taxes on his log-cabin and patch of weedy garden than that neighbor on his spacious mansion and bounteous farm. The former will, probably, turn off two paupers to one of the latter, and should be assessed in a pauper rate-bill accordingly. And this argument from parental misconduct, against the justice of Free Schools, is of a piece with the rest.

"It is with unfeigned regret that we approach the argument against Free Schools, and, indeed, against Common Schools generally, which is based on religion. In the eyes of the true statesman, convictions of religious duty are of inestimable worth, and, even when mistaken, should be treated with all possible deference. Yet when we see the priesthoods by law established—and not these alone—in one country after another in Europe, resisting the establishment of any system of popular education which is not based on the recognition of their respective dogmas, as the undoubted truth of God, we are constrained to recognize and resist an assumption fatal to that universal diffusion of knowledge which is the chief pillar of republican freedom. Our State neither affirms nor condemns the dogmas of any church or sect, but commends each citizen, in matters of faith and worship, to the guidance of his own conscience and of such spiritual instructors as his parents in infancy and his own convictions in riper years shall designate. The Common School is not above nor adverse to this, but simply *aside from it*. It does not pretend to give religious (that is, dogmatic) instruction—far less to supersede it. It simply requires the attention of every child, for thirty hours per week, to intellectual culture, leaving the entire Sabbath, with Saturday, and the greater portion of the residue, for such purely religious nurture as parents may choose for their children. When the doors of the church and the Sabbath School are opened, the Common School is closed, and its inmates are clearly qualified by its teachings for profiting by the Sabbath's appropriate lessons. Why, then, should any church grudge the Common School those thirty hours for secular instruction? What is it to gain by dividing and subdividing school districts in such a manner as to render any system of universal education impossible? We entreat you, fellow-citizens, to resist the appeal which is made to some of you on religious grounds to vote against Free Schools. To vote us down will not really accomplish the ends of our dogmatic adversaries, for Common Schools will still remain. The religious objection, even if valid, is not relevant to the present issue, and ought not to be interposed to affect it.

"We will not, fellow-citizens, urge upon you the priceless worth of education as an individual possession. Our opponents complain that we harp on these blessings as if they had denied or belittled them. They, too, they assure us, prize knowledge as highly as we do, and feel affronted when we intimate the contrary. Let us, in closing, therefore, exhort you to remember that fortune is capricious, and riches have wings, so that no man now in active life can possibly secure his posterity against the chances and changes of this mutable world. The broad domain inherited but a few years since by the child of affluence, who little dreamed that poverty could ever sit by his hearth, has already, it may be, passed into the hands of strangers, and the late haughty possessor has hardly a shelter for his head. In the sight of the whole community, some are daily mounting from obscurity to the dizziest heights of wealth, while others are falling from a like altitude into the deepest gulf of penury and need. No man can ensure affluence or even competence to his descendants thirty years hence; but any one by his vote, or his neglect to vote, may say that those descendants, and those who follow them, shall, or shall not, enjoy that which no gold can purchase—no estimate can equal—the blessing of an adequate FREE EDUCATION. Let us entreat you to esteem this not only worth voting for, but working for—to hold it subordinate to no partisan, no personal, consideration—to work for such a vote and such a majority as shall put the question at rest forever. Do this, and the canvass of 1850 shall long be remembered as that in which New York proudly vindicated her pre-eminence as the Empire State, and relaid the foundations of her freedom and greatness in the intelligence, the virtue, the gratitude, and admiring affection of her children through all coming time!"

The campaign having thus been inaugurated, an animated and vigorous contest ensued; the opponents of the law insisting upon its unconditional repeal, and the friends of Free Schools, while conceding to the fullest extent the imperfections in the details of the existing law, insisting upon its retention upon the statute book for the preservation of the *principle* involved, at the same time pledging themselves to unite with its opponents in securing such amendments and modifications as public opinion should demand, and the best interests of education require. The preliminary contest was mainly confined to the rural districts of the State, most of the cities and large towns having already adopted the Free School system, through special legislative enactments. In the latter, however, and especially in the city of New York, the question of religious and sectarian education entered as an element into the canvass, as will be seen by the following appeal widely circulated by Mr. McMasters, the editor of the "Freeman's Journal," the leading Roman Catholic organ in the city:

"Hurrah for Repeal!—The Free School law, voted blindly at the general election last fall, has been submitted anew by the Legislature to the popular vote. Many thanks to the Legislature for this opportunity thus offered us for making our step backward from the downward course of State monopoly, State despotism, and State socialism into which recent legislative movements have been hurrying us. * * * * *

"The Free School law in question was intended to extend to the whole State of New York the system of Free Schools, as they exist, for instance, in this city. But it will, at least, give us hope that if the people of the State shall be delivered from this *odious act*, the people of this city will soon follow in demanding freedom *from schools that are a moral nuisance, and have no kind of claim* upon the confidence of the public. In other words, we hope that the attention awakened to the political juggling that has hoped to gain patronage *by spreading Free Schools through the State* will not be dulled till the *double-headed monster of the Public and Ward Schools* in this city shall be abolished, and either *the system of taxation for schools be abandoned*, or the money thus raised, and all other money appropriated to education, be equally and fairly distributed among all schools of reputable character.

"*This is our programme: To try and carry, at the election next fall, the repeal of the law establishing Free Schools throughout the State; and to follow this up, as quickly as possible, by repealing the Free School laws of this city.*

"To effect this good object, non-Catholics will adopt probably as many methods as they have different motives for desiring it. *We hope that most*

Catholics will be ready to act with these opponents of the State Free Schools fervently and effectively. Just now we wish to say a few words about the special method that we desire to see Catholics pursuing by themselves, and apart from other parties.

"Who does not know that the children of Catholics when they are mixed up with Protestant children, in school and elsewhere, become, in a majority of cases, worse and more thoroughly the children of hell than the others? Well, let Catholic schools be well and thoroughly organized in our villages and towns, and let these perishing Catholic children—who, when neglected, can only be designated as infant rowdies and premature ruffians—let these children be submitted, for simply three months, to the discipline of Catholic day-schools, *under the eye of the Catholic clergy*, and with their assiduous instruction, and an altered behavior, the moral reformation of these children will be the talk of the whole town! Instead of saying that the town is disorderly, because it is crowded with 'these wretched Catholic savages,' our very enemies will say, 'This Catholic religion is a strange thing; it really seems, when practiced, to transform men, women, and children!' They will draw comparisons between the meek and quiet behavior of Catholic children and the lawless freedom of those who frequent places of infidel education. And with such proofs before their eyes, the American people are too intelligent and candid—special bigots aside—to vote for the establishment of *godless Free Schools*, to the detriment of Christian education. This is one special way that Catholics might take to bring about the repeal of the Free School law. If our Catholic population can be brought to think, as their forefathers thought, that the great thing they have to do for their children is, not to leave them rich, nor powerful in the affairs of the world, but to make them good Catholics, honest, sober citizens, and faithful to their religion, they will bring about the thing that we desire. They will toil harder, if need be, or deny themselves of many innocent gratifications, or sacrifice their desire for accumulating money, in favor of the higher, more pressing duty—this nobler aim—this devoted act of love and desire for the future well-being of their children, and of the country where moral and social character is to depend on the right or wrong education of youth.

"*In no place, under no circumstances, is there any duty so urgently pressing on our Catholic people as that of having schools subject to the clergy, and where the earnest command of the* SOVEREIGN PONTIFF, OUR HOLY FATHER, PIUS IX., *may be carried out.*"

The views of the chief opponents of the law in the rural districts and counties may be gathered from the resolutions adopted at a convention of the citizens of Chemung, Tompkins, and Steuben, held at Jefferson, on the 24th of August, the Hon. H. D. BARTO, of Trumansburgh, in the chair, and J. L. DARLING, of Catharine secretary. After strongly censuring the Legislature of 1849 for originally passing and submitting an act to the people not demanded by a single petition, or in any way by public sentiment, and not even such a division of public opinion existed as to afford the shadow of a reason for such submission, and the Legislature of 1850 for its refusal to repeal the act when, in consequence of its defective provisions, it could not be put in successful operation, and they were specifically petitioned to do so, instead of attempting to amend or modify the law, they proceed:

"*Resolved*, That *it is not upon the details of the law that we base our opposition. We stand upon first principles.* We say that if the life of Free Schools depends upon the *taking of one man's property* for the purpose of *educating another man's children*, when that other person is abundantly able, and bound by reason and humanity, to educate his own children, that they *ought not to exist by such support.* * * * * * * *

"*Resolved*, That when the friends of this law themselves admit that, unamended, it is a bill of abominations, and when they call upon the people to *actually vote for the law*, but, *mentally*, for *some undefined abstraction*, which each one may conjure up for himself, according to his fancy, they are only practicing upon the credulity of the people, and deserve the merited rebuke which such conduct demands.

"*Resolved*, That a sound public sentiment upon the importance of education is far more desirable than any or all mere systems; and we look upon the present unfortunate discussions in regard to the school question as well calculated to disgust a large portion of the people with the whole subject of popular education.

"*Resolved*, That *we are in favor of a simple and plain system of popular education, without Normal Schools, teachers' institutes, district school journals, supported by the State, or hordes of school officers*—a system with full and ample provision for the education of the poor, and in which public and private zeal for education are in due proportions combined, but without presenting the *monstrous absurdity that the duty of education rests upon the property of the State* more than upon the parents and guardians of the children.

"*Resolved*, That all compulsory school establishments are as oppressive as church establishments, and no reasoning, no arguments, can be offered in support of the former which are not equally applicable to the latter."

So obnoxious, however, were the main features as well as the general principles of the law to the inhabitants of the rural sections of the State, that, at the general election in November, an aggregate majority of 40,874 was rolled up, in forty-two of the fifty-nine counties, in favor of its unconditional repeal. In the remaining seventeen counties, including the city and county of New York, Albany, Rensselaer, Onondaga, Erie, Dutchess, Schenectady, and Columbia, in which Free Schools had already been established, or were on the eve of establishment, and Montgomery, Seneca, Ulster, Rockland, Queens, Warren, and Westchester, where no such schools existed, the aggregate majority *against* repeal amounted to 71,912; leaving a clear majority in favor of the FREE SCHOOL SYSTEM of upward of TWENTY-FIVE THOUSAND. The majority against repeal in the city of New York, alone, was 37,827, and in Kings county, 10,000; only 987 votes having been cast in its favor in the former, and 1,000 in the latter, county.

Among those who, by their exertions and influence, contributed materially to the final establishment and recognition of the FREE SCHOOL PRINCIPLE, on this occasion, we may be permitted, without disparagement to others equally energetic and efficient, diffused throughout every section of the State, but less prominently identified with the movement, to enumerate, Governors WILLIAM H. SEWARD, HAMILTON FISH, and WASHINGTON HUNT; Superintendents YOUNG, BENTON, and MORGAN; JAMES W. BEEKMAN, HORACE GREELEY, HENRY J. RAYMOND, JOSIAH HOLBROOK, and HENRY NICOLL, of New York; THOMAS LEGGETT, JR., of Queens; FRANKLIN TUTHILL, of Suffolk; ANDREW W. LEGGETT, and CALEB ROSCOE, of Westchester; ALEXANDER G. JOHNSON, H. B. HASWELL, JOHN O. COLE, FRANKLIN TOWNSEND, BRADFORD R. WOOD, HENRY

MANDEVILLE, FRIEND HUMPHREY, J. W. BULKLEY, and WILLIAM F. PHELPS, of Albany; Maj.-Gen. JOHN E. WOOL, GEORGE M. TIBBITTS, and Prof. BAERMAN, of Rensselaer; JOHN BOWDISH, of Montgomery; HALSEY R. WING, of Warren; WILLIAM L. CRANDALL, editor of the *Free School Clarion;* HARVEY BALDWIN, CHARLES B. SEDGWICK, Hon. E. W. LEAVENWORTH, Rev. SAMUEL J. MAY, E. W. CURTISS, and BENJAMIN COWLES, of Onondaga; O. B. PIERCE, of Oneida; Dr. JOHN MILLER, S. B. WOOLWORTH, LEWIS KINGSLEY, and HENRY S. RANDALL, of Cortland; ALANSON HOLLY, of Wyoming; W. S. HUBBELL, and DAVID MCMASTER, of Steuben; CALEB LYON, of Lewis; Dr. H. D. DIDAMA, of Seneca; SALEM TOWN, of Cayuga; JABEZ D. HAMMOND, of Otsego; President ELIPHALET NOTT, of Schenectady; O. G. STEELE, VICTOR M. RICE, and Mr. STARR, of Erie; SILAS M. BURROUGHS, of Orleans; ORSON ARCHER, of Wayne; and CHARLES R. COBURN, of Tioga. The STATE TEACHERS' ASSOCIATION, the STATE MECHANICS' MUTUAL PROTECTION SOCIETY, the ONONDAGA COUNTY TEACHERS' INSTITUTE, and Conventions of TOWN SUPERINTENDENTS, and various other Local Associations and Institutes, contributed essentially to the success of the cause, and the final establishment of the PRINCIPLE OF FREE SCHOOLS.

The pledges given by the triumphant party in the contest, for the adoption of such amendments and modifications of the law as, while securing its fundamental principle, should render its details and practical administration more in accordance with the clearly manifested will of that large portion of the State which its provisions more directly affected, were promptly and faithfully redeemed. The Governor (WASHINGTON HUNT), in his first annual message to the Legislature, in January, 1851, thus adverted to the subject:

"The operations of the act of 1849, establishing Free Schools, have not produced all the beneficial effects, nor imparted the general satisfaction, anticipated by the friends of the measure. It has been the policy of our State, from an early period, to promote the cause of popular education by liberal and enlightened legislation. A munificent fund, created by a series of measures all aiming at the same great result, has been dedicated by the Constitution to the support of Common Schools, and the annual dividends from this source will gradually increase. The duty of the State to provide such means and facilities as will extend to all its children the blessings of education, and especially to confer upon the poor and unfortunate a participation in the benefits of our Common Schools, is a principle which has been fully recognized and long acted upon by the Legislature and the people.

"The vote of 1849, in favor of the Free School law, and the more recent vote, by a reduced majority, against its repeal, ought, doubtless, to be regarded as a reaffirmation of this important *principle*, but not of the *provisions of the bill*—leaving it incumbent upon the Legislature, in the exercise of a sound discretion, to make such enactments as will accomplish the general design, without injustice to any of our citizens. An essential change was made by the law under consideration, in imposing the entire burthen of the schools upon property, in the form of a tax, without reference to the direct benefits derived by the tax-payer. The provisions of the act for carrying this plan into effect have produced oppressive inequalities and loud complaints. In some districts, the discontent and strife attendant upon these evils have disturbed the harmony of society. An earnest effort should be made to reconcile differences of opinion, to remedy the grievances arising from the imperfect operation of the law, and to equalize the weight of taxation, on such principles of justice and equity as will ensure popular sanction. The success of our schools must depend, in a great degree, upon the united counsels and friendly co-operation of the people in each small community composing a district; and nothing can be more injurious to the system of Common School education than feuds and contentions among those who are responsible for its healthful action and preservation.

"It cannot be doubted that all property estates, whether large or small, will derive important advantages from the universal education of the people. A well-considered system, which shall ensure, to the children of all, the blessings of moral and intellectual culture, will plant foundations broad and deep for public and private virtue; and its effects will be seen in the diminution of vice and crime, the more general practice of industry, sobriety, and integrity, conservative and enlightened legislation, and universal obedience to the laws. In such a community, the rights of property are stable, and the contributions imposed on it are essentially lightened. But I entertain a firm conviction that *the present law requires a thorough revision*, and that an entire change in the mode of assessment is indispensable."

In the annual report of the Superintendent, transmitted to the Legislature on the 7th of January, Mr. MORGAN, in alluding to the Free School system, observes:

"The history of the past year, in reference to this great enterprise, has been one of mingled triumph and disaster. The principle incorporated in the act for the establishment of Free Schools has been again subjected to the test of public opinion. In their almost unanimous approval of that *principle* in the canvass of 1849, the electors very generally overlooked the *specific details* of the bill submitted to their sanction, confiding in the disposition of the Legislature to modify such of its features as might be practically objectionable. Serious obstacles to the successful operation of the law presented themselves, almost upon the threshold of its administration; and a spirit of opposition was manifested at the primary district meetings which too often resulted in the entire rejection of the estimates prepared by the trustees, and the limitation of the term of school to the lowest possible period authorized by law. Appeals were assiduously made to the cupidity of the heavy tax-payers—their interests sought to be arrayed against those of their less favored brethren and their children—and their passions, stimulated by the real inequalities as well as fancied injustice of the burdens imposed by the new law, were readily enlisted against every attempt to carry it into operation.

"By the re-submission of the law to the people, under the act of 1850, the friends of Free Schools found themselves in a very embarrassing position. They were compelled either to give their votes and influence in favor of the continuance of a law, some of the distinctive features of which were at variance both with their wishes and their judgment, or, by sanctioning its repeal, hazard the *principle* which had been deliberately adopted by the Legislature, and approved by the emphatic expression of the public will. The issue thus presented could not fail of being greatly misapprehended. While the electors secured the renewed triumph of the principle involved, *there can be no doubt that thousands of votes were cast for the repeal of the law by citizens who desired only its amendment*, and who would have recorded their suffrages in favor of a system of Free Schools, properly guarded, had the form of the ballot permitted them to do so. It remains, then, for the Legislature to give efficacy to this renewed expression of the popular will, by the enactment of a law *which shall definitely engraft the Free School principle upon our existing system of primary education, and at the same time remove all just cause of complaint as to the inequality of its burthens*. District taxation has been found to be unjust, unequal, and oppressive. It should, therefore, at once be abandoned, so far as the ordinary support of the schools is concerned. The funds necessary for the payment of teachers' wages, in addition to the amount received from the State Treasury, should be provided either by a *State tax*, equitably levied on real and personal property, according to a fixed and uniform valuation; by a *county and town tax*, levied and assessed in the same manner; or by such a *combination of these modes* as might be deemed most expedient and judicious.

"Should the Legislature deem it expedient to charge the annual support of the schools, over and above the revenue of the school fund, *upon the taxable property of the State*, and to retain the existing mode of distribution, the necessity of devising some method by which the standard of *valuation* should be, as nearly as practicable, uniform throughout the State, will be apparent. If this can be accomplished, or if the distribution of the funds raised were directed to be made upon the same basis with the apportionment of the tax, there can be no doubt, in the judgment of the Superintendent, that a STATE TAX for the support of our Common Schools will prove the simplest, most efficient, and beneficial mode of providing for the object in view—the establishment and maintenance of a system of Free School education, in accordance with the expressed wishes of the inhabitants of the State.

"If, however, this were found impracticable, the same result may be obtained by requiring the board of supervisors of each county of the State to raise *twice* the amount apportioned to each, as a *county tax*, and an equal amount to that apportioned to each town, as a *town tax*. This provision would simply increase the amount of school money, now by law required to be raised, one-third, while it would entirely dispense with district taxation for the current support of the schools. Inequalities in the standard of valuation adopted by the respective counties would, in this case, prove unjust and burdensome to none, as the existing law has made complete provision for the adjustment of such inequalities in the case of joint districts formed from parts of two or more counties or towns. The whole amount of taxable property of each county would contribute, in equal and fair proportions, to the support of the schools located in its territory; and the angry dissensions growing out of district taxation—the fruitful source of nearly all the opposition which has been made to the existing law—would be averted.

"Such an arrangement would, it is believed, prove almost universally acceptable to the people of the State. The principle involved has repeatedly received the sanction of public sentiment. It is in accordance with the enlightened spirit of the age. It is the only system compatible with the genius and spirit of our republican institutions. It is not a novelty now for the first time sought to be engrafted upon our legislation, but a principle recognized and carried into practical application in our sister State of Massachusetts from the earliest period of its colonial history—identified with her greatness and prosperity, her influence and her wealth—and transplanted from her soil to that of some of the younger States of the Union. In each of our own cities, and in many of our larger villages, it has been established and successfully sustained by the general approval of their citizens; *and, wherever it has obtained a foothold, it has never been abandoned*. It is only requisite to adjust the details of the system equitably and fairly to commend it to the approbation of every good citizen as the noblest palladium and most effectual support of our free institutions. The existing law has excited a degree of opposition which was not anticipated; but it is believed that it has grown out of the defects of the law, rather than from any prevailing hostility to the principle of Free Schools. No law can be successfully and prosperously administered under our government which does not receive the general approval of the people. *It is the earnest desire, therefore, of the Superintendent that the present law should be so amended as to produce greater equality, to remove all reasonable ground of complaint, and to render our great system of education more efficient and useful.*

"The idea of UNIVERSAL EDUCATION is the grand central idea of the age. Upon this broad and comprehensive basis, all the experience of the past, all the crowding phenomena of the present, and all our hopes and aspirations for the future must rest. Our forefathers have transmitted to us a noble inheritance of national intellectual, moral, and religious freedom. They have confided our destiny as a people to our own hands. Upon our individual and combined intelligence, virtue, and patriotism, rests the solution of the great problem of self-government. We should be untrue to ourselves, untrue to the cause of liberty, of civilization, and humanity, if we neglected the assiduous cultivation of those means by which, alone, we can secure the realization of the hopes we have excited. These means are *the universal education of our future citizens*, without discrimination or distinction. Wherever in our midst a human being exists with capacities and faculties to be developed, improved, cultivated, and directed, the avenues of knowledge should be freely opened, and every facility afforded to their unrestricted entrance. Ignorance should no more be countenanced than vice and crime. The one leads, almost inevitably, to the other. Banish ignorance, and in its stead introduce intelligence, science, knowledge, and increasing wisdom and enlightenment, and you remove, in most cases, all those incentives to idleness, vice, and crime, which now produce such a frightful harvest of retribution, misery, and wretchedness. Educate every child 'to the top of his faculties,' and you not only secure the community against the depredations of the ignorant and the criminal, but you bestow upon it, instead, productive artisans, good citizens, upright jurors and magistrates, enlightened statesmen, scientific discoverers and inventors, and the dispensers of a pervading influence in favor of honesty, virtue, and true goodness. Educate every child physically, morally, and intellectually, from the age of four to twenty-one, and your prisons, penitentiaries, and alms-houses will be converted into schools of industry and temples of science, and the immense amounts now contributed for their maintenance and support will be diverted into far more profitable channels.

"These are some of the results which must follow in the train of a wisely matured and judicious system of universal education. They are not imaginary; but sober deductions from well-established facts—deliberate conclusions from established principles—sanctioned by the concurrent testimony of experienced educators, and eminent statesmen and philanthropists. If facts are required to illustrate the connection between ignorance and crime, let the official return of convictions in the several criminal courts of the State for the last ten years be examined, and their instructive lesson heeded. *Out of nearly 28,000 persons convicted of crime, but 128 had enjoyed the benefits of a good Common School education; 414 only had what the returning officers characterise as a 'tolerable' education; and of the residue, about one-half only could either read or write.* Let similar statistics be gathered from the wretched inmates of our poor-house establishments, and similar results would, undoubtedly, be developed. Is it not, therefore, incomparably better, as a mere prudential question of political economy, to provide ample means for the education of the whole community, and to bring those means within the reach of every child, than to impose a much larger tax for the protection of that community against the depredations of the ignorant, the idle, and the vicious, and for the support of the imbecile, the thoughtless, and the intemperate!

"Every consideration connected with the present and future welfare of the community; every dictate of an enlightened humanity; every impulse of an enlarged and comprehensive spirit of philanthropy—combine in favor of this great principle. Public sentiment has declared in its favor. The new States which, within the past few years, have been added to the Union have adopted it as the basis of their system of public instruction: and the older States, as one by one they are reconstructing their fundamental laws and constitutions, are engrafting the same principle upon their institutions. Shall New York in this noble enterprise of education retrace her steps? Shall she disappoint the high hopes and expectations she has excited by receding from the advanced position she now occupies in the van of educational improvement? Her past career, in all those elements which go to make up the essential wealth and greatness of a people, has been one of progress and uninterrupted expansion. Her far-seeing legislators and statesmen, uninfluenced by the scepticism of the timid, the ignorant, and the faithless, and unawed by the denunciations of the hostile, prosecuted that great work of internal improvement which will forever illustrate the pride and glory of her political history. The rich results of the experiment thus boldly ventured upon have vindicated their wisdom. Is the development of the intellectual and moral resources of her millions of future citizens an object of less interest—demanding a less devoted consecration of the energies of her people—and worthy of a less firm and uncompromising perseverance? Disregarding the feelings of the present hour, and looking only to the future, will the consciousness of having laid the foundations of the universal education of our people be a less pleasing subject of contemplation than that of having aided in replenishing the coffers of her wealth?

"In conclusion, the Superintendent cannot feel that he has fully met the responsibility devolved upon him by his official relation to the schools of the State, were he to fail in again urging upon the Legislature the definite adoption of this beneficent measure. Let its details be so adjusted as to bear equally upon all—oppressively upon none. Let every discordant element of strife and passion be removed from the councils of the districts; let the necessary assessment for the great object in view be diffused over the vast aggregate of the wealth and property of the State. Then let teachers worthy of the name—teachers intellectually and morally qualified for the discharge of their high and responsible duties—dispense the benefits and blessings of education equally and impartially to the eight hundred thousand children who annually congregate within the district school-room. The children of the rich and the poor, the high and the low, the native and the foreigner, will then participate alike in the inexhaustible treasures of intellect—will commence their career upon a footing of equality, under the fostering guardianship of the State and gradually ripen into enlightened and useful citizens, prepared for all the varied duties of life, and the full enjoyment of all the blessings incident to humanity."

The number of children in attendance in the schools of the 11,397 districts of the State, during the year 1849, was 794,500; exceeding by 59,312 the number taught during the preceding year. The total expenditure for school purposes was $1,766,668.24; of which $839,845.98 was from public funds received from the State, and raised by tax on the several counties and towns, in accordance with law; $398,097.70 raised by district taxation, for the purchase of sites, building, renting, repairing, and insuring school-houses, providing the necessary fuel and apparatus, and exempting indigent children from the payment of teachers' wages; and $508,724.56 contributed on rate-bills. The number of volumes in the several district libraries had increased to 1,449,950, upward of forty thousand volumes having been added during the year. The Superintendent earnestly renewed his recommendation for the restoration of the office of County Superintendent, or the establishment of an assembly district system of local supervision.

On the 6th day of February, Mr. T. H. Benedict, of Westchester, from the majority of the Assembly Committee on Colleges, Academies, and Common Schools, to whom were referred the various petitions and memorials for amendments and modifications of the act of 1849, submitted an elaborate and able report, accompanied by a bill entitled "An Act to Establish FREE SCHOOLS throughout the State," declaring the Common Schools FREE to every child between the ages of five and twenty-one years; providing for the raising of an annual State tax of $800,000 for their support, in addition to the funds already provided by the Constitution; and directing the levy, by the trustees, of a *poll* or *capitation tax* on the inhabitants of each district for whatever balance might remain due for teachers' wages after the application of these funds. Mr. BURROUGHS, of Orleans, from the minority of the committee, reported a bill entitled "An Act in relation to Common Schools," also directing the sum of $800,000 to be annually levied by a State tax, but providing that *one-fourth* of its avails, together with *one-fourth of all other moneys* applicable to the support of Common Schools, should be *equally divided* among the several school districts, and the residue apportioned according to the number of children of suitable school age residing in each—any balance remaining due to be raised by rate-bill, in the manner heretofore provided by law, exempting from such rate-bills, and charging upon the district, the tuition of indigent children.

After an animated discussion, of great interest, during several weeks, the bill as reported by Mr. BURROUGHS, with its title changed to "AN ACT TO ESTABLISH FREE SCHOOLS THROUGHOUT THE STATE," and providing for an equal division of ONE-THIRD, instead of *one-fourth*, of the aggregate amount raised by taxation and accruing from the Common School funds among the several districts, passed the House by a vote of 72 to 21, and was concurred in by the Senate, on the 10th of April, by a vote of 22 to 4, receiving the signature of the Governor on the 12th of April, 1851.

Thus ended this protracted contest for the establishment of the FREE SCHOOL PRINCIPLE, leaving the palm of victory substantially with its advocates and champions, but retaining the *rate-bill system*, as the last vestige of its predecessor, fated in its turn, at no distant day, to disappear with the rapidly advancing progress of public sentiment.

Pending this controversy, in February, 1850, a communication was addressed to the Superintendent by the Rev. A. T. Young, of Warsaw, Wyoming county, requesting his interest in support of a petition forwarded to the Legislature, asking an exemption from taxation under the Free School Act of 1849, on the part of the supporters of Parochial Schools connected with the Presbyterian congregation of that town, or the grant of a specific portion of public money to such schools. This petition set forth that the congregation had established "a parochial school, to be instructed by such teachers only as profess religion, with the further regulation that the precepts and doctrines of religion should be incorporated into the system of daily instruction." To this communication MR. MORGAN replied as follows:

"No individual can be more deeply impressed with a conviction of the importance of a thorough Christian education than myself; and I have uniformly endeavored, in my official capacity as Superintendent of Common Schools, to inculcate a strict regard, on the part of officers and teachers, to this fundamental principle. No teacher, with my consent, either has been or can be permitted to remain in charge of any school whose influence is opposed to the Christian religion, or whose moral character and deportment are inconsistent with its requirements. Taken as a class, I know no body of our fellow-citizens, of equal numbers, more intelligent, virtuous, moral, and I may add Christian, than the teachers of our Common Schools.

"When, however, you ask that the State, in the dispensation of its funds, and requisition of its laws, shall discriminate between one religious denomination or class of Christians and others, and either exempt the former from their share of the general burden borne by the rest of the community, or bestow upon them special privileges not accorded to other denominations, you seek that which is utterly at variance with the whole tenor and spirit of our republican institutions, and which, in the case of any other religious denomination, you would, I am very sure, reprobate as unequal and unjust. Shall the great body of the Roman Catholics in the State be exempted from *their* general share of the tax for the support of public Free Schools, and the money raised upon the residue of the taxable property of the State be paid over to teachers employed by *their* respective churches, whose duty it shall be to incorporate into their system of daily instruction the peculiar tenets of *their* religious faith? Shall the same rule be applied to the numerous other Christian churches without the pale of what you and those you represent conceive to be evangelical religious truth? If not, what standard of Christianity shall the State, in its political capacity, recognize and adopt? Is it not perfectly manifest to every unprejudiced mind that the State, as such, can make no distinctions on the ground of religious belief—that its beneficence must be equal and impartial—and that while it may legitimately exclude from the institutions of learning under its control every species of immorality, licentiousness, profanity, or vice, it can neither require nor sanction—much less specially provide for and encourage—the inculcation of the peculiar tenets of any particular denomination of professing Christians?

"The great leading truths of Christianity—those which are common to all, and based upon the universal consent of the great and good in every age and every clime—those which may be deduced from the simple and faithful perusal of that inspired Volume which is the Great Charter of our faith, and should be the guide of our lives—these religious doctrines, and these alone, can be permitted to form a portion of the daily instruction of our Common Schools; and I trust that the time may never come when these elementary institutions shall be converted into seminaries for the inculcation and perpetuation of sectarian dogmas, of whatever church or creed.

"After this plain and free exposition of my views in regard to the subject-matter of your correspondence, it will be unnecessary for me to add that I cannot, consistently with my convictions of public duty, in any way co-operate in the views and efforts of the petitioners for special and exclusive legislation in their behalf. When a similar petition was prepared and strongly urged, some eight years since, in behalf of the Roman Catholic religious denomination of the city of New York, the Legislature, upon mature consideration, deemed it proper to deny the prayer of the petitioners, mainly upon the grounds I have herein taken; and I am unable to perceive any difference in principle in the petition then preferred and that in behalf of which you now invoke my interest and influence. I am convinced that you, and those you represent, fully concurred in the disposition of these petitions by the Legislature; and that both you and they are ready to recognize the binding efficacy of the Divine injunction, 'Whatsoever ye would that others should do to you, do ye even so to them.'"

Under special statutes, from time to time enacted during the preceding five years, Free Schools had been established and were in successful operation in Auburn, Brooklyn, Buffalo, Hudson, Lansingburgh, Lockport, Newtown, the city of New York, Poughkeepsie, Rochester, Salem, Syracuse, Troy, Utica, and Williamsburgh—usually under the charge of boards of education, elected by the people or appointed by the municipal authorities, with city or local superintendents. In all the cities and towns the schools were numerously attended, and in the most flourishing condition. In the city of Albany, the schools were also under the charge of a board of education, but the rate-bill system was still preserved; and in the town of Bushwick, Kings county; Cohoes, Albany county; Flushing, Queens county; Medina, Orleans county; Owego, Tioga county; and Galen, Wayne county—Union, or other incorporated schools, were maintained under flourishing auspices.

On the 10th of July, 1851, the Assembly passed a resolution authorizing the Governor to appoint a suitable person as a Commissioner, to embody in a single act, and report to the Legislature at its next session, a Common School Code for the State. Under this resolution, Gov. HUNT appointed SAMUEL S. RANDALL, of Albany, as such Commissioner, who immediately entered upon the execution of the duty, and on the 1st of January, 1852, transmitted his report to the Legislature. The prominent changes in the existing system recommended by the Commissioner were the following:

1. The *separation of the office of State Superintendent of Common Schools from that of Secretary of State, and its erection into a separate and distinct department;*

2. The *substitution of a permanent tax of one mill on every dollar of the real and personal property of the State, for the present State tax of $800,000*; and

3. The *restoration, in a modified form, of the office of County Superintendent of Common Schools.*

In reference to the second proposition, the Commissioner observes:

"1. The amount which each individual will be called upon to contribute for the support and maintenance of the Common Schools is *fixed and definite*, with reference to the valuation, by the town assessors, of his property. Under the existing provision, the tax-payer, when called upon for his share of the aggregate amount to be raised, has no means of knowing what proportion or percentage of the whole he contributes; and such payment, mingled as it is with other town, county, and State taxes, is incapable, without much difficulty, of being separated from them.

"2. Such amount is so trifling and inconsiderable, when compared with the importance of the object which it secures, that no individual will be likely to object to its payment. For every thousand dollars of taxable property which he possesses he will be called upon annually to contribute one dollar; and from this fund, in lieu of all other State, county, or town assessments, the schools of the twelve thousand districts of the State will be enabled to be kept open, without charge, during the entire year.

"3. The proposed provision will be *permanent and self-adjusting*. It will increase with the increasing aggregate valuation of the taxable property of the State, and be capable of meeting the increased educational demands of the several school districts without the necessity of any additional legislation.

"4. It will practically render our schools FREE, dispensing with the necessity of rate-bills, avoiding the odium of *exemptions* in the case of indigent persons, and placing our entire system of Common Schools upon that high and commanding basis which public sentiment has unequivocally indicated, and the nearly unanimous opinion of every enlightened friend of education long demanded and approved.

"That the property of the State should, under the legislative sanction and direction, provide for the education of all its future citizens—to that extent, at least, which shall prepare them, both intellectually and morally, for the proper discharge of all the duties and responsibilities devolved upon them as members of the commonwealth—is a proposition which, however it has been controverted by arguments addressed to the *selfish* propensities of our nature, every sound principle of legislation will be found to sustain.

* * * * * * * * *

"It is this principle which is sought to be fully and definitively engrafted upon our own Common School system by the provision under consideration—a principle which has received the sanction of the most eminent and revered of our statesmen; the practical operations of which have been thoroughly tested in our principal cities and villages; which has been repeatedly and deliberately approved by a large majority of the electors of the State; once and again recognized and sustained by the Legislature; and which now requires for its permanent and practical adoption, as a fundamental principle of our institutions, only such an appropriation as shall be fully adequate to the maintenance of Free Schools during the whole of the period for which they may be kept open in the various school districts of the State.

"By the existing provisions of law, Common Schools are declared free to every child between the ages of four and twenty one, for such a length of time in each of the districts as its distributive share of the eight hundred thousand dollar State tax and the annual income of the Common School fund will provide. When these funds are exhausted, the expenses of the schools are to be provided for by a rate-bill against the parents and guardians of the children, to be made out by the trustees, in proportion to the whole number of days and of children sent by each, exempting wholly or in part, as they may deem most expedient, indigent inhabitants; and also exempting from the operation of the warrant on such rate-bill such property as was, prior to the passage of the homestead exemption act, exempt from levy and sale on execution or civil process.

"The practical operation of these provisions will be comprehended by a glance at a few statistics embraced in the annual report of the State Superintendent for the year 1851. From that document it appears the whole amount *expended* in the several school districts of the State for the payment of *teachers' wages*, and the purchase of school apparatus and books for the school libraries, during the year embraced in the report, was $1,432,696.26; and that the schools during that year were taught for an average period of eight months in the respective districts by duly qualified teachers. One million and a half of dollars, in round numbers, may, therefore, be safely assumed as the *minimum* of the actual present cost of supporting schools throughout the State for an average period of eight months in each year. Less than this will not, it is presumed, at any future period, be required for this object; nor will any one, probably, be found desirous of restricting the average term of school to a less period than eight months. The whole amount now capable of being realized from the funds provided by the State, under the existing law for this purpose, is $1,100,000—a sum barely sufficient, under the most economical administration, to cover the expenses of the schools for an average period of six months—leaving the residue of the time during which they are kept in each year, to be provided for by the vexatious and annoying process of rate-bills. The aggregate valuation of the real and personal property of the State, as ascertained by the returns by the several assessors, under the new and improved system now in force, is about $1,100,000,000; and it is quite improbable that it will, at any future period, fall materially *below* this standard. A mill tax on this amount will yield the sum, in connection with the school fund, of $1,400,000—an amount amply adequate, but no more than adequate to the liberal support of the schools for an average period of ten months during each year—and if judiciously expended, capable, with the means already at the disposal of many of them under local laws, of meeting the entire wants of each separate school district throughout the State. As the aggregate valuation of the property of the State increases, it is fairly to be presumed the educational demands of the community will increase in an equal proportion, and the funds thus provided will keep pace with this increase without the necessity of additional legislation. Even should the number of districts remain substantially the same, there will be a steady augmentation of the number of children annually to be brought within the influence of the schools; and it may reasonably be expected that a higher standard of qualification on the part of teachers will be demanded, involving the necessity of a higher remuneration, and the permanent transference to this most laborious, honorable, and useful profession, of a higher grade of talent and ability.

"That a permanent provision of this kind would prove extensively beneficial in its effects upon the community at large, there can exist scarcely a doubt. Such an expenditure would return back upon every interest of society a vast and continually increasing amount of remuneration. It would constitute an investment infinitely more durable and profitable than any which the calculating wisdom of the mere financier, however able or skillful could command, and regarded in a mere pecuniary point of view, would amply vindicate the prescience and the foresight of the Legislature, which should authorize its adoption. In its political and moral effects, the wide and universal diffusion of knowledge, and the inculcation of virtuous principles and habits which it would inevitably secure, could not fail of reacting, with a most beneficent influence upon all our civil and social institutions."

The first of these propositions was carried into effect by the Legislature in 1854; the third (the restoration, in a modified form, of the office of County Superintendent) two years later, in 1856; and the second, or full recognition of the Free School principle, not until 1867.

The annual report of the Superintendent for the year ending on the 31st of December, 1850, was submitted to the Legislature on the 7th of January, 1852. The year embraced in the report covered nearly the entire period during which the Free School act of 1849 remained in operation—"a period characterized," says the Superintendent, "beyond any other in the history of our Common School system, by the agitation and excitement of the public mind consequent upon this measure; a period of transition between a system nearly unanimously adopted by the people, but which, in its practical operation, had proved in many respects eminently disastrous, and a system apparently more in accordance with the popular will. * * * The schools which had, for a period of more than thirty years, been kept open for an average term of eight months during each year, were reduced in many instances to four, and the provision for their support limited to the avails of the public funds. So strong and general was the current of opposition, especially in the rural districts, to the obnoxious details of the law, that the most powerful efforts were required, on the part of the friends of education generally, to prevent an entire abandonment of the great principle involved in its enactment, and which, wholly irrespective of the particular mode of its execution, had received the clear assent and full approbation of the people. Pending a conflict so embittered and extensive, embracing within its range nearly every district and neighborhood of the State, and affecting so many and such powerful interests, it could scarcely have been expected that the prosperity and welfare of the schools should not have been seriously and generally affected. A careful inspection of the returns will, however, show that while in some respects the statistical tables compare unfavorably with those of preceding years, their general results demonstrate a steady, reliable and gratifying improvement."

The number of children under instruction during the year reported, in the 11,000 districts from which returns were received—no reports having been made from 400 districts—was 800,430, of whom nearly 200,000 had been under instruction *for a less period than two months.* In 105 Colored Schools, 5,305 pupils had been taught. The number of volumes in the several district libraries was 1,507,077, showing an increase during the year reported of 57,127 volumes.

The whole amount of public money received and expended by the several districts, during the year embraced in the reports of the trustees, for the payment of teachers' wages, was	$782,469 29
Raised by district tax under the provisions of the act of 1849, for the same purpose	385,836 53
Raised by rate-bills voluntarily levied	136,949 54
Local funds applicable to the same purpose	20,117 66
	$1,325,373 03
In addition to this amount, the sum of	7,333 57
is reported as having been raised (voluntarily, it is presumed) to meet the expenses arising from the exemption of 1,254 children from rate-bills, and as raised by district tax to supply deficiencies in rate-bills made out previously to the act of 1849	15,915 08
There were also paid for teachers' wages in colored schools, over and above the public money applicable to said schools	1,925 23
Adding these two items, the total expenditure for teachers' wages during the year reported will amount to	$1,350,546 92
Amount of public money expended for district libraries	89,104 96
Total amount for teachers' wages and libraries	$1,439,653 88
The following additional sums were raised by district taxation for the purposes specified:	
For purchasing school-house sites	$58,855 91
For building school-houses	125,918 86
For hiring school-houses	8,439 00
For repairing school-houses	79,183 53
For insuring school-houses	5,152 29
For fuel	71,455 31
For book case, books and school apparatus	15,613 15
For other purposes	62,520 51
Aggregate amount of expenditure for school purposes during the year	$1,884,818 16

In reference to the proposed revision and codification of the School laws, the Superintendent says:

"By a resolution of the Assembly, of the 11th of July last, the Governor was authorized to appoint a commissioner whose duty it should be to prepare and report to the Legislature, at its ensuing session, an entire Common School code, in one act. Under this authority, the appointment of commissioner was conferred on SAMUEL S. RANDALL, late Deputy Superintendent of Common Schools, who proceeded at once to the discharge of the duty thus devolved upon him, and whose report will be forwarded to the Legislature at an early period of its session. Following, as this resolution of the Assembly did, immediately upon the completion of a full consolidation and arrangement of the existing provisions of law in relation to Common Schools, under the act of the last session, the commissioner deemed himself authorized to incorporate in the new revision such amendments and modifications of the system now in force as, in his best judgment, after full and free consultation with the most enlightened and experienced friends of education throughout the State, seemed desirable and necessary. The principal suggestions and recommendations made by him, in the discharge of this important and responsible duty, are fully in accordance with the views of the department; and their adoption will, it is confidently believed, place our Common School system upon a permanent and satisfactory basis. They are understood to embrace, as their leading and prominent objects, 1st. The separation of the office of Superintendent of Common Schools from that of Secretary of State, and its erection into a separate and distinct department; 2d. The substitution of a permanent annual State tax of one mill upon every dollar of the aggregate real and personal property of the State, for the support of Common Schools, in lieu of the present tax of eight hundred thousand dollars; and 3d. The restoration, in a modified form, and with suitable guards and restriction, of the system of county supervision.

"The proposed substitution of a permanent annual State tax of one mill upon every dollar of the real and personal property of the State, in lieu of the existing tax of eight hundred thousand dollars for the support of Common Schools, commends itself to the judgment of the undersigned as a measure fraught with incalculable blessings to the cause of universal education. If adopted and permanently engrafted upon our existing system of Common Schools, its effect will be to carry out, in the most simple, efficacious and perfect manner, the will of the people, repeatedly and distinctly expressed, that the property of the State shall provide for the elementary education of all its future citizens, and that all our Common Schools shall be entirely free to every child. This principle having been fully recognized and established, after mature consideration and discussion, it is unnecessary now to re-open the grounds upon which it was adopted, or to enter again upon the arguments which have so effectually demonstrated its soundness. The Legislature, at its last session, solemnly and definitely incorporated it as the basis of their enactment of a law, making a liberal appropriation from the aggregate property and funds of the State, for the maintenance and support of Common Schools. This appropriation, however, liberal and enlightened as it was, and worthy of the vast resources and immense wealth of the State, proves inadequate to the full accomplishment of the noble object in view—the education of all the children of the State, during the whole period ordinarily devoted in each year to Common School instruction. An inconsiderable fraction of a mill upon each dollar of the increased valuation of real and personal estate is all that is requisite, in addition to the provisions already made, to secure the inestimable benefit of Free Schools, in all coming time, to every child of the State. It would be utterly unworthy of the enlightened forecast of the great majority of our fellow-citizens to suppose that they are not prepared to make this slight additional sacrifice for the permanent accomplishment of an object of such great importance. The present State tax of $800,000, amounting as it did under the valuation in force at the period of its adoption to considerably more than a mill upon each dollar, is insufficient, with the aid of the annual revenue of the Common School Fund, to provide for the support of the schools of the State for an average period exceeding six months during each year. A permanent mill tax on the existing valuation, capable of adjusting itself from time to time to the fluctuating valuation of the property of the State, and to the increasing wants of the Schools, will, in conjunction with the public funds already applicable to that object, provide liberally for the support of every school in the State during the entire year.

"In opposition to these views it may probably be urged that the action of the Legislature, at its last session, providing for an annual State tax of $800,000 in addition to the annual revenue of the school fund for the support of Common Schools, and directing that any deficiency in this respect should be supplied by rate-bill, should, under the circumstances, be regarded as a final compromise between the views of the friends and opponents of an entirely Free School system; that it is inexpedient and injudicious again to throw open to legislative and popular discussion a subject upon which so considerable a diversity of feeling and of opinion is known to exist; that the very general acquiescence of the people in the present disposition of the matter is indicative of their satisfaction with the existing law, and that it is unwise, at this early period, to disturb these arrangements so recently, and with such great unanimity, adopted, especially in the absence of any experience of their practical workings, and of any general demand for their alteration or modification. These objections are, unquestionably, entitled to great weight; and unless they can be fairly overcome, the necessity or expediency of the proposed change must be regarded as doubtful.

"Under the peculiar circumstances attending its passage, the act of the last session was, unquestionably, the best that could be obtained by the friends of Free Schools. The only alternative presented was to return to the system in force prior to 1849, involving a virtual abandonment of the principle for which the friends of universal education had so long struggled and which had so repeatedly and signally triumphed. It will be recollected that although a popular majority of more than twenty thousand votes had been secured against the repeal of the act of 1849, forty seven of the fifty-nine counties in the State had cast their votes nominally in favor of such repeal. The representatives from those counties, constituting a large majority of both branches of the Legislature, while fully aware that the popular expression of their respective constituencies adverse to the continuance of the law in question, was not to be regarded as in opposition to the *principle* of Free Schools, felt themselves bound by that expression to pursue a *middle course*, between the entire rejection of that principle and its unlimited adoption.

Confident in the ultimate settlement of the question on a basis in accordance with the dictates of public sentiment, and relying on the intrinsic justice and soundness of the principle involved, the friends of Free Schools consented to the adoption of the compromise proposed, without the slightest understanding on their part, or as it is believed on the part of those who favored and brought forward the amendment, that it was to be a permanent disposition of the subject. It was, on the other hand, regarded certainly by the former as a temporary arrangement merely.

"If it be conceded that the public sentiment has unequivocally declared itself in favor of the adoption of the Free School principle—and on this point there cannot, in the judgment of the undersigned, be the slightest room to doubt—then any action of the Legislature, in contravention of or falling short of that principle, cannot justly be regarded as final or conclusive. However desirable it may be, under ordinary circumstances, to avoid a re-agitation of questions once fairly settled by legislative action, and especially where those questions affect an interest of such extent and importance as that under consideration, the will of the people, fairly and clearly expressed, is entitled to be carried into full effect; and if for any reason their representatives have failed to embody that will in their legislation, there can be no such binding efficacy in a *compromise* measure at variance in any essential respect with the declared verdict of the popular voice, as to preclude subsequent action at the earliest practicable period, in conformity with such verdict. The act of the last session was clearly in contravention of the popular will, repeatedly and distinctly expressed, so far as the provision for meeting any portion of the expense of instruction in our Common Schools, by rate-bill, was concerned; and although, after a long, animated and finally successful struggle at the ballot boxes for the complete recognition of the Free School system, the people were disposed, in view of the manifold difficulties attendant upon the full embodiment of that principle by the Legislature, to rest satisfied with the important step finally taken as the utmost that could, at that period, be accomplished, it is manifest that their compulsory acquiescence in this respect cannot preclude them from insisting, at any subsequent period, upon a complete and practical legislative recognition of the right of every child in the State to free admission to the Common Schools, during the period in which they may be open for instruction, untrammeled by any pecuniary restriction, however slight.

"There is another consideration connected with this subject, which cannot fail to address itself with great force to the statesmen and legislators of our State. Either the Free School system is in accordance with the popular will, or it is not. Either the principles upon which it is based are in conformity with the dictates of a sound and enlightened public policy, or they are at irreconcilable variance with it. In either case, there should be no medium course between the full recognition and adoption of the system and its practical incorporation as a portion of our institutions, and its rejection altogether and a return to the system as it previously existed. It is utterly incompatible with all sound principles of legislation to declare in one breath that 'Common Schools throughout the State shall be *free* to every child between the ages of five and twenty-one years,' and in another to provide for the compulsory imposition of a *rate-bill* for the expenses of a large portion of such tuition. It is eminently unworthy of the representatives of the Empire State thus to 'hold the word of promise to the ear, and break it to the hope.' Nearly two hundred and fifty thousand of the citizens and legal voters of the State, constituting a majority of one hundred and fifty thousand of all the votes cast, declared, in 1849, their desire that the Common Schools of the State should be entirely free; and notwithstanding the obvious and universally conceded defects of the law enacted to carry their wishes into effect, they refused, in 1850, by a majority of more than twenty thousand votes, to sanction its repeal, lest they should even seem to endanger the great principle they had so successfully vindicated and asserted. Having thus, repeatedly and deliberately, placed themselves upon the record in this respect, they confided in their representatives to remove all the objectionable features of the law, without affecting its vital principle. Had it been their desire to restore, either wholly or in part, the old rate-bill system, it is reasonable to suppose they would have proceeded directly to the accomplishment of their object by a decisive vote in favor of the repeal of the act of 1849. Their vote *against* such repeal, in the face of unanswerable objections to the details of that act, is beyond all question conclusive of their intention, at all hazards, to preserve, unimpaired, the Free School principle:

"The proposition, therefore, to authorize a permanent mill tax on the property of the State will, it is conceived, if adopted, effectually carry out the wishes of the people and their declared will. The amount is too trifling to be burdensome to any individual, while the object to be effected is one of the utmost magnitude and importance. Is there an individual in the State who would not cheerfully pay an annual assessment of one mill upon every dollar of his valuation, or one dollar upon every thousand, if thereby he could secure the blessings of education, not only for his own children, but for every child of suitable age in the State, for the entire term during which the schools are kept open in each year, in all coming time? Is it not far better that the entire expenses of tuition should be met in this manner by one simple, definite, self-adjusting process, adapting itself to the varying standard of property and valuation, and to the increasing wants of the schools, than that the trustees of each of the eleven thousand districts should be periodically burdened with the trouble and parents with the expense of a vexatious and harassing rate-bill? I cannot hesitate, therefore, cordially and earnestly to recommend the adoption of this measure as in my judgment best calculated to render our Common Schools in reality and permanently what they now are nominally, free; believing it to be due not only to the highest interests of education, but to a proper respect to the clearly expressed will of a majority of our fellow-citizens, that the noble enterprise, the foundations of which have been so strongly laid in an enlightened public sentiment, should, without unnecessary delay, be prosecuted to a completion."

In conclusion, the Superintendent observes:

"In bringing his official labors to a close, and surrendering the administration of the department to other hands, the undersigned can only indulge the hope that during the critical and stormy period in which the complicated interests of public instruction have been committed to his guidance, some advancement will be found to have been made in the right direction. On assuming the responsible charge entrusted to his hands, two objects presented themselves as, in his judgment, of sufficient importance to demand his individual attention and utmost efforts. The one was the preservation and perpetuation, in all its integrity, of our admirable system of district school libraries, seriously endangered by what he deemed and still deems a most injudicious provision of the existing law, authorizing, under certain conditions, an entire diversion of the munificent fund provided for the annual replenishment of these institutions; and the other was the enterprise of rendering every one of our eleven thousand schools free to every child of the State of a suitable age to participate in their benefits. In the accomplishment of the first of these objects entire success has been obtained, by an uncompromising refusal, in any case or under any circumstances, to give the requisite sanction of the department to the application of any portion of the library money to any other object than the purchase of books and scientific apparatus for the use of schools. Many and strong temptations have from time to time been presented for a departure from the strict and rigid rule thus prescribed; and doubtless frequent and serious offense has been given by the unyielding pertinacity with which it has been adhered to. The alternative, however, seemed to be presented, on the one hand, of a gradual and ultimately entire abandonment of that far-seeing and enlightened policy by which every school district and every neighborhood of the State was annually supplied with the means of intellectual and moral cultivation, and on the other, of a firm and decided refusal, in any case whatever, of that consent which the law required as a condition precedent to the diversion of the fund. The importance of the principle involved in this determination may have been over-rated, and if so, the remedy is at hand and may easily be applied.

"Our schools are not yet entirely free. Deeply as this is to be regretted, there are ample and abundant sources of consolation in a review of the contest which has been waged for the adoption of this great measure. So far as public opinion is concerned, the question may undoubtedly be regarded as definitely settled. Reforms of this nature, when based upon sound reason and enlightened policy, which underlie the principle of universal education in a country such as ours, never go backward. The indisputable right of every citizen of the American republic to such an education as shall enable him worthily and properly to discharge the varied and responsible duties incumbent upon him, as such, cannot long remain practically unrecognized in our republican institutions. It has already incorporated itself in the system of public instruction of several of our sister States; it has found its way into the municipal regulations of all our cities and many of the most important towns of our own State; and, above and beyond all, it has entwined itself into the deepest convictions and soundest regards of the great mass of the people. Its full assertion may be deferred, but cannot ultimately be repressed.

"In the vindication and maintenance of this principle, it has been my fortune, during the whole of the brief period of my connection with the department, to occupy a conspicuous position. As a necessary consequence of this position, voluntarily assumed and firmly maintained, I have been content to endure and to confront a more than ordinary share of obloquy; and, what was regarded by me as of infinitely greater consequence, to witness the inevitable reaction upon the schools of the State of a protracted and embittered controversy. That controversy is even yet undetermined, and it may require years to repair the breaches occasioned by its existence. But I have the consolation of knowing that the part which I have taken in this controversy was the result of a firm and abiding conviction of public and private duty—of duty to the State, whose confidence had been reposed in me as a public officer charged with the administration of a most responsible and important trust—of duty to my fellow-citizens deeply interested in the satisfactory adjustment of a question which came directly home to the business and the hearth of each one of them—and of duty to the eight hundred thousand children who annually throng the district school-houses of the State, to obtain that education without which their future prospects of usefulness or happiness were to be fatally blasted. Sustained and supported by these considerations, and by the active co-operation of many of the most enlightened friends of education in every section of the State, my course of action was plain; and, upon a careful and searching review of conduct and motive, I find nothing to retract or regret, but my own inability more effectually to realize the full convictions of my judgment and the most ardent wishes of my heart in this respect. If I have, though feebly and imperfectly, contributed in any essential degree to the ultimate triumph and full recognition of the noble principle of UNIVERSAL EDUCATION, THROUGH SCHOOLS FREE TO ALL—if, in part through my humble exertions, the future millions of children who shall hereafter congregate in our elementary institutions of learning shall be permitted freely to participate in the inestimable blessings of sound intellectual and moral instruction, without restriction or discrimination—my highest earthly ambition will have been amply realized."

SECTION III.—ADMINISTRATION OF SECRETARY HENRY S. RANDALL—1852 TO 1854.

Character of the Secretary.—Message of Gov. Hunt.—Embarrassments in the Collection of the State Tax.—Proposed Mill Tax.—Condition of the Schools.—Superintendent's Reports.—Academical Instruction.—New York Free Academy.—Character of Teachers.—Distribution of School Money.—Department of Public Instruction.—Compulsory Religious Observances in Common Schools.—The Quigley Case.—Decision of the Superintendent.—Election of Superintendent E. W. Leavenworth.—Separation of the Office of Superintendent from the Secretary's Department.—Schools in the Cities of New York, Brooklyn, Buffalo, Rochester, Utica, Poughkeepsie, Schenectady, Troy, Syracuse, Albany, Oswego and Auburn.

ON the first day of January, 1852, the Hon. HENRY S. RANDALL, of Cortland, who had been elected Secretary of State in November of the preceding year, entered upon the administration of the Common School department. He was a man of superior abilities fine literary acquirements, energetic character, and, in his official capacity as County Superintendent of Cortland, had rendered signal service as one of the ablest and most devoted and industrious of that class of officers. His experience in this position, and his thorough practical knowledge of the system, had eminently prepared him for the enlightened discharge of the responsible duties devolved upon him as the head of the department. In 1843, he had been, as we have seen, specially designated by Col. YOUNG to prepare an official report on the important subject of DISTRICT LIBRARIES; and so ably and satisfactorily was this duty performed that the principles and language of the report were adopted by the department as the basis upon which these libraries were to be formed. After the close of his official term he devoted himself to agricultural pursuits, of which he was very fond, and to literary authorship. As the well-known biographer of THOMAS JEFFERSON, the great author of the Declaration of Independence, and founder of the democratic party, his name has long been associated with those of standard authority in this department of our national literature. At the present time he occupies the position, and discharges the duties, of President of the Board of Trustees of the State Normal School at Cortland, and representative in the State Legislature from Cortland County.

HENRY W. JOHNSON, of New York, was appointed Deputy State Superintendent.

GOV. HUNT, in his message at the opening of the Legislature of 1852, stated the capital of the Common School fund at six and a half million of dollars, of the revenues of which nearly a million and a half had been expended during the preceding year in the payment of teachers' wages and the purchase of school libraries. The number of pupils in attendance upon the several Public Schools was 726,000. The Governor reviewed the action of the Legislature and the people of the State in reference to the effort to secure an entirely free system of Common Schools, and characterized the enactment of the preceding session as a temporary compromise between the advanced views of the advocates of Free Schools and the fears and prejudices of a majority of the tax-payers and inhabitants of the rural districts, long accustomed to the existing system and unwilling to sanction its entire abandonment. The progress of public opinion, in his judgment, might safely be relied upon to diffuse more liberal views of the relations of the State to its future citizens.

From the annual report of the Superintendent, Jan. 1, 1853, it appeared that the number of pupils in attendance in the several Common Schools of the State during the year 1851, was 8,765, and the amount of money expended in the support of schools, $2,249,814, of which about $1,000,000 was derived from the public money, and the residue collected by district tax and rate bills—the latter amounting to about $225,000. The sum of $477,918 was expended, during the year, in the purchase of sites and in building, hiring, repairing, insuring and furnishing school houses, supplying fuel, &c.

In reference to the State tax for the support of schools, the Superintendent says:

"In the school code reported to the Legislature during its last session by the Commissioner, Mr. S. S. Randall, and in the last annual report of the late Superintendent, it is proposed to substitute a *mill tax* for the present one. This is virtually, and indeed avowedly, a proposition to restore Free Schools.

"A per centum tax, beyond all question, is more defensible in theory than one of fixed amount; * * * and that a mill tax cannot fairly be considered an onerous burthen on property, for the great object of maintaining popular education—for that protection which property itself derives from the dissemination of intelligence through all classes of society—has been very distinctly admitted by the opponents of Free Schools themselves, by their assenting to the $800,000 tax. When imposed, it amounted to more than a tenth of one per cent. on the assessed value of the property of the State.

"Not doubting, however, that the wants of an advancing population will ultimately call for an increase of the State tax, and that when so increased it would be better on all accounts to make it a per centum, and therefore a self-adjusting one, the undersigned feels constrained to express the opinion, that the time has not arrived for such action. Nor is he disposed at present to recommend any action which will affect the interior policy of the schools.

"In the rapid transition from system to system—in the constant change of details made without the benefit of sufficient experience—which has marked the school legislation of the past four years, the natural result has followed. Grave errors have been committed. To retrieve them, new errors have been plunged into. * * * Melancholy as is the confession, and decided as are the exceptions to it, our schools, in the opinion of the undersigned, have deteriorated during the rapid changes of the last four years.

Whether we have reached a point in these mutations where it is best to pause and let existing regulations, where not obviously and seriously wrong, stand until a further developed experience and a more settled public sentiment shall call for well-considered changes, is the grave question now to be settled. On it the views of the undersigned are already expressed."

The Superintendent recommended a modification in the Academical system of the State by which each of these institutions should be required to receive annually from the Common Schools within its district, and gratuitously to educate, a specific number of pupils corresponding with its proportionate share of public money received from the State. He observes:

"The Free Academy in the city of New York presents a practical exemplification of the plan thus proposed for the whole State. The undersigned has, during the past season, visited this institution personally, examined its records, investigated its plan of action in detail, and witnessed its operations. To say that it is eminently successful in accomplishing the objects of its foundation, is but faint praise of the men whose philanthropy originated and whose energy secured that foundation, or of the able and efficient corps of teachers who manage its concerns. Within its halls the marks of caste and the distinction of wealth, elsewhere so pervading, are for once ignored. The sons of the rich and the poor—neither of them degraded beneficiaries, but the honored cadets of a parental government—meet on ground where neither has vantage. Sitting on the same benches; pursuing the same higher branches of science; drinking from the same rich fountain of classic literature; cultivating the same elegant tastes and personal accomplishments; the undersigned saw, with emotions he will not attempt to describe, the representatives of almost the extremes, and of every intermediate point, in social and pecuniary condition; the sons of the merchant whose vessels visit every ocean, and of the employees of his store-houses and his wharves; of fathers, whose names are historic in the professions, in literature, in arts and in arms, and of the obscure and toiling mass whose sinews support this social superstructure above them.

"The difference between such a foundation—where the best and brightest youths of the country, irrespective of all other distinctions, are brought together to be equally anointed and sandaled for the Olympic race of life and manhood, and renown—to be put in a position where high heart and bold endeavor will place the rewards of life equally within their reach—marks the development of a truly American idea, and is at once the symbol and the commencement of a new phase in educational and social progress. It is scarcely to be doubted that the great Metropolis, the pulsations of whose philanthropy are only equaled by those of her business enterprises—whose thoroughfares and suburbs are everywhere sprinkled with her magnificent charities—will add to this class of her institutions, *nor that she will ultimately perfect her system of free education by the establishment of a Free College on a scale proportioned to the wants of her population.*"

In reference to the position and prospects of the teachers of the State, the Superintendent says:

"Few estimate sufficiently the importance of teachers as a class or their influence on society. Nearly as much as parents, they mold the moral character of the young; and their influence is probably even more felt in developing the intellect and giving it direction throughout an extensive portion of society. Ridicule of teachers constitutes one of the stale jokes of literature; and its caricatures have not been without their influence on those whose dictums have weight in assigning both literary and social position. Prejudice against this occupation in our country is as unjust as it is impolitic. Where in the United States have teachers, as a class, been found behind the moral or intellectual cultivation of the body of the community in which they have been called upon to teach; nay, not in advance of it? How often has even the breath of suspicion fallen on the moral character of one of the twenty-five thousand Common School teachers of New York! Of their intellectual calibre, the bench, the bar, the sacred desk, the highest business and official positions of our country, bear emphatic testimony.* For unremitting industry in a laborious and physically-prostrating occupation, for a patient braving of inconveniences and annoyances, which those unfamiliar with the subject can hardly appreciate, for a zealous and high-toned devotion to the duties of their calling, ample opportunities of observation have satisfied the undersigned that no class of men excel the teachers of New York. And it is notorious that none, when the extent of their duties and responsibilities are taken into consideration, are so inadequately paid. Beyond a few cities and large villages, the wages paid to teachers do not equal those of any class of operatives whose occupations demand any previously acquired dexterity."

He also recommends the establishment of an additional Normal School in the western section of the State.

The report for the year 1854 shows that during the year 1852 the total amount of expenditure for teach-

* The author of this work was informed by Gen. Winfield Scott, in 1851, that every member of President Monroe's cabinet, with one exception, commenced life as a Common School teacher, including the names of John C. Calhoun, William H. Crawford, Smith Thompson, Benjamin W. Crowninshield, and William Wirt.

ers' wages was $1,931,870.16; of which $1,273,426.49 was from the avails of the State tax; $23,843.44 from local funds; $308,851.30 collected on rate-bills, and the residue raised by district taxation.

The library money expended during the year was $49,409.39; and the amount expended for school-houses, sites, furniture, &c., and raised by district tax, $487,876.05 —amounting in all to $2,409,248.52—showing an increase of over $20,000 from the expenditures of the preceding year.

The Superintendent, after recapitulating his views as expressed in his report of the preceding year as to the expediency of a change in the system of State taxation, by the substitution of a mill tax for the fixed sum now imposed, goes on to say:

"The question now arises, has the proper period yet arrived for any material revision of our school laws? Have existing defects proved so serious as to demand it? If so, has sufficient time been given for experience to add its suggestions to those of sound theory, in indicating the appropriate remedies? Have the fires of controversy so far died away as to permit that unanimity of purpose and effort which are indispensable to success?

"On the whole, the undersigned is disposed to answer these questions affirmatively; to assume that the time has arrived when sound conservatism lies in action. Existing defects, as will presently be shown, are deep-seated, and are exerting widely pernicious influences.

"A mill tax on the property of the State was recommended last year as the proper ultimate substitute for the present one. It was recommended by a previous Superintendent, and it seems to be the rate of taxation for school purposes generally fixed upon by the investigating friends of popular education as the one best calculated to do justice to all interests. *Its adoption would probably be accepted by all parties as a final disposition of the subject.*

"The distribution of the public school moneys in a manner to confer an equal share of their benefits on localities and individuals has been found attended with great difficulty. Prior to 1849, the proceeds of the school fund, and an equal sum raised by the towns, were ultimately divided among the towns on the basis of population, and among the school districts on the basis of the pupils returned as residing in them. Such a distribution would give to small districts in thinly populated regions, possessed of a limited amount of wealth, a comparatively small amount of money, and would consequently lead to the imposition of more onerous rate-bills, which would fall where there was the least ability to pay them. Yet this system was long acquiesced in. Both the law and public sentiment recognized the cost of education as mainly a personal burden which every man was required to incur for his own offspring. Following out the same idea, it was not felt that the Legislature had a right to attempt to equalize the burden of education, as between localities or individuals, by adopting any peculiar system of distributing the public moneys specifically designed to attain that end, but rather that it was bound to give every scholar his *pro rata* share of those moneys, and leave parents to provide what was further necessary as best they might.

"A different theory as to where rested the responsibility of educating the people began to prevail. As ignorance is the parent of crime and civil disorder, it was claimed that a free government was bound to provide for its own stability, and wealth to pay for its own security, by assuming the burden of popular education. It was insisted that after using the revenues set apart for that purpose, the Common Schools of the State ought to be supported by a direct tax on property. This principle, to its fullest extent, was engrafted into our laws in 1849. This wholly changed the theory on which a proper distribution of the school moneys rested. If the property of the State is required to support the education of the State, it follows that, the benefit received from it being everywhere the same, its burdens should in like manner be the same. And another important principle came into operation. When the State determined that education should be supported by public contribution, it gave to every citizen a common and equal right to the benefits accruing therefrom. The spirit and theory of the law was, not to aid parents in educating their offspring, by dividing a particular sum of money between them, *but that the State should assume the whole expense of such education, and raise whatever sum was necessary therefor.* Every child was equally entitled to an education, whether residing in the heart of the city of New York, or on the hills of Hamilton county. But, wholly overlooking these principles, the Free School Act of 1849 substantially retained the previously existing plan of distribution to counties and towns on the basis of population—to school districts on that of enumerated pupils. Not only was the cardinal theory of the law thus violated, but the unequal effects of such a distribution, when applied to such increased sums of money, became vastly more apparent than under the old law. In the densely populated districts of cities and villages, the schools received more than was sufficient for their support from the avails of the school fund and county and town taxes, while in the thinly inhabited country districts, it was necessary to resort to additional and onerous taxes to make up deficiencies.

"Results so flagrantly unjust could not long be tolerated. The rural regions, crushed by the operation of the law, through their representatives, repealed it. The agricultural population of the State have ever shown that they prize the blessings of universal education, and are willing to make as many sacrifices to secure it as the inhabitants of cities. They demonstrated this by patiently paying more in proportion to their property than the latter to educate their children, for a period of more than fifty years anterior to 1849. It was the *structure*, and not the *principle*, of the Free School law of 1849 which gave to the popular vote on it so well defined a local classification. The country cordially united with the cities in passing the school act of 1851, which was intended to recognize the same main principle, *that the property of the State shall educate the children of the State.*"

By the act of 1851, one-third of the public money (excepting for libraries) was directed to be *equally divided* among the several districts. "This," says the Superintendent, "effectually relieved the country districts. It is strenuously urged in many quarters that it has done more than this—that it has turned the scale in the opposite direction, and made the burden of supporting schools lighter, both to property and persons, in the country than in the cities and villages." Concurring in this view of the subject, he suggests the retention of the existing one-third equal quota distribution, but with the addition of another equal third on the basis of resident pupils of the several districts, substantially on the same principle as already recognized by the Legislature in the organization of Union School districts.

Mr. Randall concurred with his predecessor in strongly recommending the separation of the office of Superintendent of Common Schools from that of Secretary of State. "The dignity and importance of a school organization so extensive as ours," he remarked, "alike demand that its official head should be a separate and independent State officer, and the duties of the position demand all the time and the best talents that any one man can bring to them;" and he was of opinion that such an officer might be able to dispense with the necessity of a restoration of the system of County Superintendency, which, in the present state of public feeling toward that office, he deemed injudicious and unwise. He recommended, at least, a trial of the experiment before creating another class of local school officers.

In October, 1853, a complaint was made to the Superintendent by the Rev. Dr. QUIGLEY, a Roman Catholic clergyman of Schagticoke, in Rensselaer County, setting forth that, in many of the Common Schools of that and the adjoining county of Washington, the religion and faith of Catholic children were interfered with, by being compelled to join in prayers, and to read and commit to memory portions of a version of the Bible of which the Catholic Church disapproved; and stating specifically that on a certain day in August preceding, a Miss Gifford, a teacher in Washington County, ordered one of her pupils, twelve years of age, to study and read the Protestant Testament, and on his declining to do so, on the plea of his unwillingness to disobey the orders of his parents, and to violate the precepts of his religion, chastised him severely, and expelled him ignominiously from the school.

Mr. RANDALL, in his decision, a copy of which was communicated to the Legislature with his annual report, after citing the opinion of Superintendent DIX, concurred in by Superintendent SPENCER, that the teacher may open his school by prayer, "provided he does not encroach on the hours allotted to instruction, and *provided the attendance of the scholars is not exacted as a matter of school discipline*," goes on to say:

"No later or counter decisions are to be found on the records of this office, and the above therefore must be regarded as the hitherto well-settled rule in the premises, so far as the action of this department is concerned. Believing it founded on principles of equity, and in that spirit of entire religious toleration which characterizes our Constitution and laws, and which should characterize every institution, literary or other, founded by the State, I have no disposition to disturb it, and should have no hesitation in applying and enforcing it in the case presented by the complainant, or in any other brought before me on appeal.

"Beyond a mere *dictum* or opinion given by Superintendent Dix, in 1838, on the abstract propriety of making the Bible a reading-book in the Common Schools, in which he expressed himself convinced of such propriety, I find nothing bearing directly on this point in the orders and decisions of my predecessors. Opinions from some of them have been publicly referred to, but if given they were not made matters of record in this office.* Meanwhile the question has, at various periods, seriously agitated portions of the community, and even the aid of legislation has been invoked to settle it. The recent great increase and diffusion throughout the State of a Roman Catholic population who, while they profess to make the Bible the guide of life, wholly repudiate the common English version of it as unauthorized, and who, on conscientious grounds, refuse to read it or permit their children to read it, has thrown additional embarrassments in the way of any adjustment of the dispute which will be satisfactory to all. Notwithstanding these difficulties, I feel, on this first presentation of the matter before me, that I am bound to frankly and explicitly state my views, and the grounds on which I should base my official action, should appeals involving the question be brought before me.

"In theory, I have never been able to doubt that intellectual and religious instruction should go hand in hand. To divorce them entirely, and to only bestow attention on the former, is to draw forth and add to the powers of the mind, without giving it any moral helm to guide it; in other words, it is to increase the capacity without diminishing the propensity to do evil. To banish religious education from the schools is, in a multitude of instances, to consign it to the care of the vicious, the ignorant, the careless, or those who feel that they have not time to attend to it. The placing of it in its natural connection with intellectual education in the school-room has met, however, in our country with serious practical obstacles. The Government, not relying on the ability or willingness of every part of the State to maintain efficient schools for the education of the young by voluntary contributions, and recognizing the imperative necessity of universal education for the maintenance of our civil and political institutions, organized a general Common School system, and made provisions to aid those sending to school in sustaining it, by the payment of a large sum of money annually from the treasury. To prevent this money from being misapplied, it prescribed the conditions on which it shall be received and expended, the mode of appointing, and the duties of all school officers, and it created a special State officer, with administrative and judicial powers, to carry out and enforce the system. The Common Schools were thus clearly made a government institution. To introduce into them, or permit to be introduced into them, a course of religious instruction conformable to the views of any religious denomination, would be

* Similar opinions will be found, in a preceding page, to have been expressed by Superintendent Young.

tantamount to the adoption of a government religion—a step contrary to the Constitution, and equally at variance with the policy of a free government and the wishes of the people. To form for the schools a course of instruction which could bear the name of a religious one, and which would meet the views of all was manifestly impossible. To give to every sect a *pro rata* share of the school moneys, to enable it to support its own schools, and teach its own system of religious faith in them, would be, in the sparsely inhabited country districts, to divide the children within the territory convenient for attendance on a single school, and in which the support of all the inhabitants is frequently scarcely adequate, with the aid of the public moneys, to sustain a single efficient school, into a dozen or more schools. Indeed, under this arrangement a single indigent family would often be required to support its own school, to go without any, or to violate its conscience by joining with others in one in which a religious system was taught wholly at variance with its own. There are other reasons, not requiring enumeration, which have gone to convince the public mind of the impracticability of carrying out such a plan so as to attain the object sought, the education of all the people.

"In view of the above facts, the position was early, distinctly, and almost universally taken by our statesmen, legislators and prominent friends of education—men of the warmest religious zeal, and belonging to every sect—that religious education must be banished from the Common Schools and consigned to the family and the church. If felt that this was an evil, it was felt that it was the least one of which the circumstances admitted. Accordingly, the instruction in our schools has been limited to that ordinarily included under the head of intellectual culture, and to the propagation of those principles of morality in which all sects, and good men belonging to no sect, can equally agree. The tender consciences of all have been respected. We have seen that even prayer—that morning and evening duty which man owes to his Creator—which even the pagan and savage do not withhold from the gods of their blinded devotion—which, conducted in any proper spirit, is no more sectarian than that homage which constantly goes up from all nature, animate and inanimate, to the bountiful Giver of all things—has been decided by two of our most eminent superintendents as inadmissible, as a school exercise within school hours, and that no pupil's conscience or inclination shall be violated by being compelled to listen to it. This decision has been acquiesced in without a murmur by the whole religious public. The intelligent religious public have felt that there was no tenable middle ground between thorough religious instruction in our Common Schools and the broadest toleration. Driven by circumstances to adopt the latter position they have embraced it in its most comprehensive import, and have nerved themselves to the task of supplying a lamentable omission in the Public Schools, by increased assiduity to the spiritual wants of their offspring in the family circle, in the Sunday School, and in the church. In our crowded cities, where poverty sinks to its lowest ebb, and vice puts on its most unmitigated forms—where multitudes of children would receive no religious instruction from or through the instrumentality of their parents, voluntary church and individual organizations are putting forth their endeavors to supply such instruction. Many, doubtless, are not reached by these efforts; nor would they be reached if religion was taught in the Common Schools—for the children of the extremely poor and the vicious oftentimes could not or would not attend them.

"Not only has the principle of entire religious toleration in our schools been acquiesced in between the leading Protestant sects who regard each other as orthodox in the cardinal doctrines of Christianity, but between such and those pronounced by them to be utterly heretical. Not only have the Episcopalian, the Presbyterian, the Baptist and the Methodist met on common neutral ground in the school room, but with them the Unitarian, the Universalist, the Quaker, and even the denier of all creeds. No offensive school exercise or discipline has been made compulsory on any of these—no obnoxious tests forced upon them. Shall a solitary and invidious exception then be made against a church professing to be governed by the principles of Christianity, and which includes within its fold a large number of citizens whom our laws place on the same footing with all other citizens? I cannot subscribe to such doctrines.

"I believe that the Holy Scriptures, and especially the portion of them known as the New Testament, are proper to be read in schools by pupils who have attained sufficient literary and mental culture to understand their import. I believe they may, as a matter of right, be read as a class book by those whose parents desire it. But I am clearly of the opinion that the reading of no version of them can be forced on those whose consciences and religion object to such version."

The public confidence in the integrity and ability of the Superintendent was signally manifested, during his entire administration, by the omission of the Legislature to provide for the receipt and disbursement, through the usual channel of the State Treasury, of the avails of the State tax of $800,000, with the corresponding amounts required by the act of 1851 to be raised and paid over by the several counties. Although not required, in his official capacity, to execute any bonds for the safe keeping and proper expenditure of any portion of the public money, millions of dollars were thus paid over to and disbursed by him, and although repeatedly soliciting at the hands of the Legislature, and its financial and educational committees, the examination and revision of his accounts, no investigation was ever called for or made. In one instance, the quota of the largest and wealthiest county of the State —the city of New York—was neglected to be raised and forwarded in season for the annual apportionment and payment of the public money, rendering it indispensable for him to advance on his own personal responsibility the amount thus withheld. This anomalous state of things continued until after the expiration of the first year of his successor in office.

At the annual election in November, 1853, the Hon. ELIAS W. LEAVENWORTH of Onondaga, was elected Secretary of State, and *ex-officio* Superintendent of Common Schools. S. S. RANDALL was again appointed Deputy. Gov. SEYMOUR, in his message to the Legislature of 1854, strongly recommended the separate organization of a Department of Public Instruction. A bill for that purpose was accordingly introduced early in the session by the Hon. WILLIAM H. ROBERTSON of Westchester, Chairman of the Literature Committee of the Senate, and chiefly through his influence became a law in March ensuing. This important measure was warmly supported by Secretary LEAVENWORTH, chiefly upon the ground of the incompatibility of the duties pertaining to the office of Superintendent with those required of the Secretary of State, who, in addition to his strictly legitimate duties as such, had under various provisions of the law been made a member of the Canal Board, of the Board of Commissioners of the Canal Fund, and of the Land Office, a Trustee of the State Library, of the Capitol and of the State Hall, an *ex-officio* member of the Executive Committee of the State Normal School, and a Regent of the University, in addition to his burdensome duties as Superintendent of Common Schools. Public policy as well as public justice imperatively demanded the separation of these offices and the organization of an independent Department of Public Instruction, and this policy finally prevailed.

In the city of New York the Public School System had been entirely reorganized. The rapid progress of the Ward Schools, established under the act of 1842, the organization of the Free Academy in 1848, and the financial embarrassments of the Public School Society consequent upon their diminished resources, conduced in 1852 to the opening of negotiations between the representatives of the two rival systems for their consolidation. The terms finally agreed upon by the contracting parties were, 1st, the transfer by the Public School Society to the city of all their buildings and property, subject to all existing incumbrances thereon, and the discontinuance of its organization and schools; and, 2d, the appointment of fifteen of the trustees of the society, to be designated by themselves, as members of the Board of Education, and of three trustees in each ward, to serve for the term of three years, respectively. This arrangement was confirmed by the Legislature in an act passed on the 3d of June, 1853, and went into full operation during the ensuing year. Erastus C. Benedict was elected President of the new Board of Education; and S. S. Randall, City Superintendent, with Joseph McKean and Samuel W. Seton, Assistants. At the period of the consolidation there were eighteen schools of the Public School Society, with as many female and primary departments, while those of the ward schools numbered twenty-eight. When combined, under the new system, they consisted of the Free Academy, three Normal Schools, forty-six large schools, with each a male, female, and primary department, fifty-six separate primary schools, nine colored schools, and ten corporate schools—making in all 224 schools, under the jurisdiction of the Board of Education, with an aggregate annual attendance of nearly forty-four thousand pupils, educated, and supplied with all the necessary text-books, apparatus, and stationery, chiefly at the expense of the city. The property of the Public School Society, transferred to the city for educational purposes, was estimated at half a million of dollars over and above all incumbrances.

We cannot take leave of this Society, which had thus for nearly half a century assumed the charge of the free education of the children of the city, the members of which, consisting of men of the highest character and standing in the community, had for that long period gratuitously devoted their time and services to the promotion and advancement of popular education, without the tribute of our highest regard and esteem for their disinterested exertions, and the incalculable amount of good which their untiring zeal and devotion were enabled to accomplish in behalf of the rising generation. Millions of dollars of the public money had passed through their hands, not one dollar of which had, in any instance, been diverted from its legitimate object; and not less than 600,000 children had been instructed, and over one thousand teachers prepared for their responsible duties, under their kindly and genial supervision. Among the prominent members of this organization, "whose names posterity will not willingly let die," were De Witt Clinton, Leonard Bleecker, Lindley Murray, Henry Rutgers, Joseph Grinnell, Robert C. Cornell,

STEPHEN ALLEN, SAMUEL L. MITCHELL, GEORGE T. TRIMBLE, PETER COOPER, JAMES B. BRINSMADE, JAMES J. ROOSEVELT, JR., JOSEPH CURTIS, SAMUEL WOOD, SAMUEL W. SETON, JOHN MURRAY, JR., WILLIAM HIBBARD, JACOB LORILLARD, CHARLES E. PIERSON, JAMES F. DE PEYSTER, FREDERICK DE PEYSTER, BENJAMIN R. WINTHROP, JOHN DAVENPORT, WILLIAM H. NEILSON, THOMAS B. STILLMAN, ISAAC COLLINS, JOSEPH B. COLLINS, LINUS W. STEVENS, ISRAEL RUSSELL, HIRAM KETCHUM, PETER AUGUSTUS JAY, SAMUEL DEMILT, ROE LOCKWOOD, MAHLON DAY, JEREMIAH H. VAN RENSSELAER, MYNDERT VAN SCHAICK, MARINUS WILLETT, ABRAHAM V. WILLIAMS, JOHN DE LAMATER, THEODORE DWIGHT, JR., CALEB O. HALSTED, JOHN B. HALSTED, OLIVER HALSTED, WILLIS HALL, JOSEPH HOXIE, HENRY E. DAVIES, SHEPARD KNAPP, ABRAHAM R. LAWRENCE, ANSON G. PHELPS, PELATIAH PERIT, DANIEL F. TIEMAN, GULIAN C. VERPLANCK, and JOSEPH B. VARNUM. DE WITT CLINTON was the first President of the Society, and continued to occupy that position until his death, in 1828—a period of nearly a quarter of a century. He was succeeded by PETER AUGUSTUS JAY, who remained in office about ten years. ROBERT C. CORNELL was elected his successor, and, after his death, in 1845, GEORGE T. TRIMBLE filled the post, to the general acceptation of the public, until the dissolution of the Society, in 1853. Mr. TRIMBLE had, since 1820, been treasurer of the Board, and, in conjunction with SAMUEL W. SETON, who was appointed its agent in 1827, had exercised a constant and vigilant supervision over the Public Schools and the interests of the organization. Mr. SETON, after nearly fifty years' continued and efficient service as a school officer, died in November, 1869, at the advanced age of eighty-two years, occupying at the time of his death the position of Assistant Superintendent of Schools, which he had held since the organization of the Board of Education, in 1854. From 1844 to 1850, the venerable JOSIAH HOLBROOK, the founder of the lyceum system in Massachusetts, exerted a highly favorable influence over the schools by his lectures and practical instructions in map drawing, mineralogy, and elementary geology, and the promotion of a system of interchange of specimens of minerals, maps, drawings, penmanship, &c., between the schools of the city and those of the State, and other States and countries. This method of domestic and international exchange was encouraged and supported by the highest officers of the several States and the General Government, and by the principal representatives of foreign powers. Mr. HOLBROOK died in Virginia, in 1851, while engaged in the active prosecution of his benevolent labors.

In 1837, an act of the Legislature was passed creating the office of City Superintendent of Common Schools for the city of BUFFALO. Under this act, R. W. Haskins, Esq., temporarily occupied that position for a few months, and was succeeded, early in the ensuing year, by O. G. STEELE, Esq. To this public-spirited gentleman, more than to any other individual, were the citizens of Buffalo, at this early period, indebted for their excellent system of Public Schools, and for the first special city organization since that of the city of New York. In May, 1838, an act was passed dividing the city into fifteen permanent school districts, in all of which schools were established, and several spacious and convenient buildings, chiefly of brick, erected. These schools were placed in charge of the Common Council, who, under an amendatory act, passed in 1839, in accordance with the views of a public meeting of the citizens, presided over by the Hon. ALBERT H. TRACY, were empowered to purchase sites, and erect, improve, enlarge, and repair school-houses, and to furnish them with suitable apparatus, books, furniture, and appendages; to appoint a City Superintendent, employ teachers, and raise, by tax upon the real and personal property of the respective districts, the necessary sums for defraying all these expenditures, thereby rendering the system entirely free. The number of children taught in the several schools thus organized rapidly increased from 679 in 1837 to 4,450 in 1840, at an aggregate cost of $8,875.30, of which $1,585.18 only was contributed by the State, and the remaining $7,291.12 raised by city taxation. The schools were in session during the entire year, the prevailing method of instruction was monitorial, and the annual salaries of the male teachers ranged from $500 to $750. Mr. Steele was succeeded by S. CALDWELL, Esq., who, in 1843, reported the attendance upon the several schools at 5,573, and the expense of their maintenance at $20,437.16, with libraries numbering more than three thousand volumes. In 1845, Mr. STEELE was re-appointed; and in 1846 a third department was established for the advanced education of the pupils of the several public schools, which, in 1853, under the superintendency of VICTOR M. RICE, was converted into a Central High School. At the annual State election of 1849, when the question of Free Schools was submitted to the people, *three* votes only were cast in the city in the negative. In 1862, the number of Public Schools had increased to thirty-four, and 218 teachers, 190 of whom were females, with 15,830 pupils, and the cost of their maintenance to $88,598.67. The number of volumes in the several district libraries was 11,292.

The city of ROCHESTER was the next to establish a system of Free Public Schools. Under the provisions of an act passed in 1841, a Board of Education was organized, on the 15th of June of that year, consisting of two commissioners from each of the city wards, with power to appoint a City Superintendent, and provide all requisite facilities for school purposes, defraying the expense by city taxation. On the 5th of July, ISAAC F. MACK, Esq., was appointed Superintendent—"a man of graceful and winning manners, possessing much knowledge of men and things, varied accomplishments, and exceedingly popular withal, although he *really knew but little of schools or school systems*."* The number of pupils in attendance upon the several schools in 1842 was 3,454, increased in 1843 to 4,246, and in 1845 to 5,000; the number of volumes in the libraries, 5,000. In 1848, D. HOLBROOK, Esq., was appointed City Superintendent, who, whatever other qualifications he may have possessed, clearly was not destitute—judging from his report of 1862, referred to below—either of energy, executive ability, or *self-appreciation*. The amendatory act of 1850, still in force, was drawn up under his supervision. In 1857, a Central High School was established, which in 1862, under the direction of the Regents of the University, was converted into a Free Academy, and incorporated with the city system of public instruction, with about two hundred pupils. At this time, there were, in addition to this institution, ten grammar, sixteen intermediate, and sixteen primary schools in the city, with 107 teachers, 93 of whom

* Report of City Superintendent Holbrook to State Superintendent—Ninth Annual Report Sup't Pub. Instruction, 1863. Mr. Holbrook, however, confesses that on his retirement, after five years' service, "the endeavor to fill his place met with but indifferent success."

were females, and 8,552 children under instruction. The number of volumes in the several district libraries was 7,709.

As late as 1839, the Public Schools of the city of HUDSON were under the charge of the Lancaster School Society, to whom the public money, amounting in that year to $1,134.48, was paid over. Of the 1,192 children of suitable school age residing in the city, 590 only were taught in these schools. The act of 1841, as amended in 1843 and 1844, constituted the members of the Common Council of the city *ex-officio* Commissioners of Common Schools, with power to form school districts, purchase sites, build, repair, and furnish school-houses, and supply them with books and apparatus, and appoint three superintendents, who should constitute a board of general and special supervision, with power to contract for and superintend the erection, repair, and furnishing of school buildings; to employ, pay, and remove teachers, prescribe text-books, make out rate-bills, &c. Four times the amount of public money apportioned to the city from the State was directed to be annually raised and paid over to the Board of Superintendents, for the support of schools. In 1844, there were three schools, each containing from 150 to 200 pupils. In 1862, there were four schools, each with an average attendance of about 300 pupils, and an annual expenditure of $7,000, of which $3,000 was raised by tax. The number of volumes in the district libraries was 1,250.

In POUGHKEEPSIE also, as late as 1839, the whole amount of public money apportioned to the village, amounting to $1,313.23, was paid over to the trustees of the Lancaster School, for the instruction of 550, out of 1,778, children of suitable school age residing in the district. In 1843, an act was obtained for the organization of a Board of Education, and the establishment of a system of Free Schools. Three flourishing schools, properly graded, were opened, with about 600 pupils, at a cost of $4,400, $3,000 of which was raised by tax. In 1862, ten schools were in successful operation, with 4 male and 34 female teachers, and 2,500 pupils, at an aggregate cost of $10,916.63, of which one-half was raised by city taxation. The number of volumes in the district libraries was 11,292.

In the city of SCHENECTADY, the public money apportioned by the State, amounting in 1839 to $1,306.88, was also paid over to the Lancaster School Society, for the instruction of 360 pupils, out of over 1,000 residing in the city. This was subsequently converted into a Union School District, embracing, in 1862, eight public schools, with 4 male and 26 female teachers, and 1,932 pupils, sustained at an expenditure of $11,448.92, of which $6,789.44 was contributed by city taxation; and with libraries containing 3,000 volumes.

In the city of ALBANY, the Public Schools were in charge of a Board of nine Commissioners, appointed by the Mayor and Recorder of the city and the resident Regents of the University. There were, in 1862, 17 schools, with 100 teachers, 82 of whom were females, and 9,614 pupils. The sum of $71,439.07 was expended for the support of these schools, $34,000 of which was raised by city taxation. The number of volumes in the several district libraries was 5,750.

The Public Schools in the city of BROOKLYN were organized under an act passed in 1850, authorizing the Common Council of the city to appoint a Board of Education, consisting of thirty-three persons, one for each school district, holding office respectively for three years, and who were required annually to elect a City Superintendent, who is *ex-officio* Secretary of the Board. The first Superintendent was SAMUEL L. HOLMES, Esq., who was succeeded temporarily in 1853 by S. S. RANDALL, in 1854 by J. R. GIDDINGS, and in 1856 by the present incumbent, J. W. BULKLEY, Esq. In 1854, the cities of Brooklyn and Williamsburgh and the town of Bushwick were consolidated, increasing the Board of Education to forty-five members. At this time Brooklyn had sixteen large schools, with 174 teachers, and 11,500 pupils, besides two evening schools, with 17 teachers, and 1,000 pupils; Williamsburgh, with a Board of Education consisting of eighteen members, one-half of whom were trustees and one-half commissioners, had eleven schools, with 100 teachers, and 787 children; an evening school, with 700 pupils, taught by eight teachers; and a Saturday Normal School, of 113 teachers; and Bushwick, with three schools, had 16 teachers, and about a thousand pupils. The new organization, therefore, comprised 32 large schools, over 300 teachers, and 18,337 pupils, exclusive of about 2,000 in the evening schools.

In 1848, a City Superintendent of Common Schools was authorized to be elected for the City of OSWEGO, who should possess the powers and perform the duties imposed upon Town Superintendents. In 1853, a Board of Education, with the usual powers, was established.

In AUBURN, a similar Board was organized, under an act passed in 1850, and a City Superintendent appointed.

In SYRACUSE, previous to the year 1842, there was, with a population of 7,000 inhabitants and 1,600 children of suitable school age, but two school houses, one only of which was properly supplied with the conveniences and comforts which appertain to such buildings. The other was an elegant building of doric structure, one story only in height, with an accomplished teacher (Mr. SALISBURY). About a hundred pupils were, however, "huddled" together in another dilapidated building, erected in 1827, capable of comfortably accommodating only about seventy. "Finally," says a correspondent of the "District School Journal," "within the village proper there was a *school without a house;* and a strange story might be related by a fanciful historian of the wanderings of this migratory, mendicant school. At one time we find it located temporarily in a lower story of a public house, like the errant professors of the now declining art of mending broken spoons and crockery, and surrounded by the brawl and confusion of dram-drinking, and the arrival and departure of noisy travelers and their lumbering vehicles." At another period of its purgatorial wanderings, according to the relation of Mr. EDWARDS, County Superintendent, the school of fifty pupils was found cowering, like objects of persecution, in a crazy loft above a machine shop, containing a steam engine, several turning lathes, and other unquiet machinery, between which and the school was an apology for a floor of loose boards, which vibrated at every motion of the animate or inanimate machines. "There was, apparently," says the narrator, "a great emulation between the pupils, engines, and workmen, to produce the greatest confusion, and it required delicate perceptive faculties to decide which succeeded."

In 1843, however, five very handsome houses were erected at an aggregate cost of $10,000, containing ample accommodations for 2,000 pupils; and in 1850, an act was obtained authorizing the establishment of a Board of Education, consisting of two commissioners from each of the wards of the city, elected (after their first appointment by the Mayor and Common Council) by the people; and invested with all the necessary powers to make the schools free, and to provide them with suitable teachers, apparatus, text-books, and libraries. Under this organization the Public Schools rapidly reached a high degree of prosperity and efficiency.

A similar organization was effected in the cities of TROY and UTICA, and the Public Schools rendered free by the act of April 4, 1849, to amend the charter of the City of Troy, as amended by the acts of 1850 and 1851, and by the act in relation to Common Schools in the City of Utica, passed April 7, 1842, as amended by the acts of 1844, 1848, and 1850.

FIFTH PERIOD—1854 TO 1867.

STATE TAXATION AND RATE-BILLS.

SEC. I.—FIRST ADMINISTRATION OF SUPERINTENDENT VICTOR M. RICE—1854 TO 1857.

Recommendations of the Superintendent.—Messages of Gov. Clark. Modification of the System.—Election of School Commissioners. —Apportionment of Public Money.—Normal Schools.—Increase of State Tax.—Rate Bills.—District Libraries.—General Condition of the Schools.

EARLY in April, 1854, the Hon. VICTOR M. RICE, of Erie, was elected, on joint ballot of the Senate and Assembly, Superintendent of Public Instruction. Mr. RICE had previously, for several years, occupied the position of City Superintendent of the Buffalo Public Schools, and in that capacity had given evidence of an enlightened devotion to the interests of popular education. His social qualities were of a high order; and the attractiveness of his manners, and his familiar acquaintance with the officers and inhabitants of the rural as well as the city districts, rendered him an exceedingly popular and welcome visitant to all school gatherings and Teachers' Associations and Institutes. His extended personal intercourse with members of the Legislature throughout the State contributed essentially to his influence with that body in carrying into effect his various recommendations and suggestions. Probably no previous incumbent of the Department was more widely and generally known, more personally popular, or who rendered more efficient services in the improvement and perfection of the Common School system. His death occurred in December, 1860, one year after the expiration of his second official term.

His unsuccessful competitor in the election, Mr. S. S. RANDALL, was immediately on his accession reappointed Deputy Superintendent, which position he continued to occupy until his transfer to the supervision of the schools of the city of New York, in June of the same year, when J. J. CHAMBERS, Esq., of Westchester, was appointed in his place.

At the opening of the legislative session of 1855, the Governor (MYRON H. CLARK) in his message thus adverts to the system of Common School education:

"Among the subjects which will require your attention there is none of more importance than the system of public education of the State. The magnitude of this interest has always been felt and appreciated by the people, and the State has shown, from the earliest period of its existence, an earnest desire to provide the means for the adequate instruction of all the children within its limits. For a long time the system pursued was based on the assumption that education was mainly a matter of personal interest, and that the duty of providing it devolved exclusively upon parents, the instruction of the children of those whose property would not permit them to incur the expense of it themselves being made to depend upon public charity. The inefficiency of this policy—its failure to accomplish the object aimed at—and especially its direct tendency to create distinctions hostile to the spirit and character of our institutions—led to its abandonment; and a system based upon the principle that the State is even more deeply and permanently interested in the education of its children than their parents, and that the expense of providing it should be borne by the aggregate of the property within its limits, was adopted in its stead.

"The law is defective, however, in that it fails to carry out fully and completely the principle upon which it is based. Education in the district school is not yet entirely free. If the cost of the schools in any district exceeds the amount of money received from the State, the deficiency is made up by a rate-bill, assessed upon those who send their children to school; and those who are unable to pay this assessment are relieved at the public expense, and thus become the recipients of public charity. The worst element of the old system is thus preserved; and the fundamental principle of the new law fails of its application in its most essential point. Education is still regarded as a matter of charity, and not of right; and so long as this continues to be the case in *any* degree, or to *any* extent, it will detract from the full measure of usefulness which the system is designed to secure. *This evil in the system can be remedied only by* MAKING THE SCHOOLS ENTIRELY FREE.

"The attention of the Legislature should also be directed to measures for improving the character of the schools, for increasing their efficiency, and for elevating and extending the instruction which they impart. In a State where every citizen should take an active interest in the administration of public affairs, and may be called upon to perform the highest duties of public life, it is important that popular education should be carried to the highest point which the means of the State will allow. It has been objected to the system of Free Schools, that people do not prize that which costs them nothing, and that relieving individuals from the expense of educating their children will diminish their interest in the subject, and lead them to relax the vigilance which is essential to the highest excellence in the public schools. There is, undoubtedly, some force in the suggestion, though experience shows that it is much less than is sometimes supposed. But whether it be more or less, it is entitled to consideration, and provision should be made for obviating the objection in any system of education which the State may adopt. An obvious mode of doing this is by means of *an active and intelligent supervision*, by which the schools shall be regularly visited, and their discipline examined by competent officers selected for that purpose."

In his first annual report to the Legislature of 1855, Mr. RICE availed himself of the occasion to recommend, among other modifications of the school law then in force, all of which were subsequently adopted and incorporated with the existing system:

1. The election of School Commissioners for each county or assembly district, with sufficient compensation to secure the devotion, by capable and zealous men, of their whole energies to the work of local supervision.

2. The apportionment of the one-third of the public money, now distributed equally among the *districts*, upon the basis of the number of duly qualified *teachers* actually employed therein for a specific period.

3. That the inhabitants and legal voters of districts in which Union Free Schools were or should hereafter be established should be authorized to levy a tax on such districts for the payment of teachers' wages.

4. That the financial part of the school system should be separated from that of supervision, and that the supervisors of the several towns should be made the custodians of the school money apportioned by the State, giving the requisite bonds for its safe-keeping and proper disbursement in accordance with law.

5. That different grades of certificates of qualification to teachers, in accordance with their respective scholarship and executive capacity, should be prescribed by the examining officers.

6. That more ample provision should be made for a supply of competent teachers throughout the State, by the establishment of additional Normal Schools, and by a more liberal support to Teachers' Institutes.

7. While heartily concurring in the sentiments and reasonings of those who had urged upon the Legislature the propriety of establishing a mill tax, he was of opinion that the present period of gloom and depression in the industry and commerce of the country was unpropitious to its immediate adoption.

8. That the school laws should be revised, systematized, simplified, and re-enacted in one law, so as to form a complete Code of Public Instruction.

The number of school districts in the State was 11,799; and the number of children under instruction during the year 1858, 877,201. The amount of public money received and expended by the several districts, exclusive of library money, was

library money, was	$1,246,692 19
Local funds	21,647 57
Raised by district taxation under act of 1851	285,365 23
Paid on rate-bills for teachers' wages	830,190 93
Raised by district tax for exemptions of indigent persons	80,753 24
Raised by district tax for deficiencies on rate bills	13,874 93
" " " for colored schools	1,860 26
" " " for school-houses, sites, &c.	693,067 81
Amount of library money received	43,637 06
	$3,666,609 98

Exceeding by about $900,000 the amount so expended in 1852.

Notwithstanding the large amount thus received for libraries, there was a diminution in the number of volumes of nearly 32,000!

Several Union Schools had been organized in different sections of the State, under an act passed in June, 1853, and were exerting a highly beneficial influence on the interests of education.

Gov. CLARK, in his message to the Legislature of 1856, renewed his recommendation for the adoption of a mill tax, and for rendering the Common Schools entirely free, by the abolition of the rate-bill system.

The number of pupils in attendance upon the several Common Schools, during the year embraced in the second annual report of the Superintendent, was upward of nine hundred thousand, and the whole amount of money expended in their support upward of two millions of dollars. Of this amount, one million was contributed by the State from the avails of the Common School and United States Deposit funds and State taxation; $733,636 from district taxation, for the payment of teachers' wages and exemption of indigent persons; $382,359 on rate-bills from the parents of children sending to school; $2,293.25 for the support of colored schools; and, in addition, the sum of $783,000 was raised by district taxation for the purchase of sites and the erection, repairing, and furnishing of school-houses and their appendages, of which $136,219 were expended in enclosures and out-buildings.

In reference to the proposed modification of the system, by the substitution of a per centum tax of one mill or some lesser fraction of a dollar on the assessed real and personal property of the State, for the present fixed rate, the Superintendent observes:

"The undersigned feels it, as it has been felt by his predecessors, again his duty to urge the propriety of so graduating the school tax that it may bear some fixed proportion to the wealth upon which it is imposed. The policy of devoting a portion of the public means to secure the universal education of the people has long since ceased to be debatable in this State. Upon the lowest consideration of sheer economy, the State cannot afford to have its children grow up in ignorance. Their effectiveness as producers of wealth, as workers in any department of industry, depends principally upon their intelligence. The comparatively high degree of intelligence existing among our people is the circumstance which enables our artisans and manufacturers to maintain high wages, and yet produce at a cheaper cost than the laborers of Europe, whose remuneration only suffices for a pinched and scanty subsistence—the defect of special training being more than supplied by general education. It is very obvious that what is the private interest of each individual is also the general interest of the community. It is less obvious, but no less true, that no man can afford to have his neighbor ignorant and poor any more than he can afford to have him infectiously diseased, or criminally vicious. The increase of private wealth is only consistent with that of the general stock from which, through whatsoever transformation and exchanges, it must be derived. We are thus brought to the proposition recognized in our practice, that each individual is interested in the effectiveness of the industry of all his fellow citizens, and, consequently, in their education, in proportion to his stake in the aggregate wealth. It is unnecessary to resort to either political or moral considerations to sustain the policy and justice of taxation for the general education, though they are so much more apparent—as flowing from the sentiments as well as the reason—that they have too commonly been relied upon to the overshadowing of the economical argument. Their entire consistency with it follows from the truth taught by all history, that moral and political progress are inseparable from that advance in the power of man over the forces of nature which causes and constitutes wealth.

"It is not to be forgotten, however, that the State has duties as well as interests, and that children have rights as well as their parents. They are alike members and citizens of the State, which is but an association of all, for the protection and advantage of all, irrespective of the distinction of age, and whose very life, like that of the natural body, consists in its perpetual renewal and growth, by the accession of undeveloped elements. The central idea of republican government is that it subordinates property to mankind, protecting and administering material capital for the sake and in the interest of man—not managing men for the sake of capital. The State fails to fulfil its obligations to the child when it permits the parent, for any selfish or merely personal object, to rob him of the years which nature has appointed for bodily and spiritual development—for the gathering, and not for the expending, of mental and physical strength. It fails, equally, when it neglects to furnish the means and appliances without which the child's own property, in the time of his adolescence, would be rescued in vain from confiscation to the immediate profit of his parent, and lapse, unfruitful of any acquisition for future benefit to himself, to the State he is to serve in his maturity, and the children with whom he is, in his turn, to replenish its forces."

He therefore recommended, in addition to his suggestions of the preceding year, "*that the State tax for the support of schools be increased to three-quarters of a mill on each dollar of the assessed valuation of real and personal property, so that its proceeds should keep pace with the wealth of the State and the number of children to be educated.*"

This recommendation of a State tax, based upon a fixed percentage of the entire valuation of the property of the State, and capable of expansion with the wealth of the State and the educational requirements of its future citizens, made, in 1852, as heretofore stated, by the Commissioner appointed by Gov. HUNT, adopted in 1854 by Superintendent H. S. RANDALL, and now renewed by Mr. RICE, re-opened at once the warfare against the obnoxious *rate-bill system*, which had formed so conspicuous and powerful an element in the Free-School campaign. The $800,000 tax imposed by the Legislature of 1851, as a compromise between what were claimed as the extreme views of the friends and opponents of Free Schools, had not only failed to reduce, by any considerable amount, the burdens cast upon the several districts, in the support of their schools, but to meet the views and wishes of the liberal and most enlightened advocates of the existing system. The amount levied by rate-bill in the year 1851, the year previous to the actual operation of the law, was about $225,000; and the average annual amount so levied for a period of twenty years preceding, $450,000; while in 1855 it was $461,779.13. The law expressly required the trustees of each district in the State to exempt all indigent persons having children of a suitable age for school from all contribution toward the payment of teachers' wages, and to collect the amount of such exemptions from the taxable inhabitants of the district. The official returns made to the Superintendent's Department showed that *in a large majority of the eleven thousand districts of the State no exemptions whatever were made.* Between *forty and fifty thousand children* were officially ascertained to have been kept out of the schools from the inability of their parents or guardians to pay their proportion of the rate-bills; the refusal or omission of the trustees to exempt them from such payment, under the provisions of the law; or from unwillingness and repugnance on the part of such parents to avail themselves of their privileges to educate their children *in forma pauperis*, as a district charge. The friends of free and universal education insisted that in the election of 1849, when the question was submitted to the people, in a distinct and explicit form, whether the Common Schools of the State should be absolutely free to all, without discrimination or restriction, it was almost unanimously determined in the affirmative; that in the sharply contested election of 1850, although presented in an equivocal and embarrassing form, a decided majority had again, while condemning the special details of the act of 1849, re-affirmed the principle; that the Legislature of 1851, in retaining the obnoxious rate-bill feature, in direct contravention of the plain and repeatedly declared will of the people, had transcended their representative limits; and that while it was the province and the duty of that body, in accordance with the distinct and explicit verdict of their constituents, to remove every objectionable feature from the act, and to render its practical operation free from all burdensome inequality, it was most emphatically their duty to make the Common Schools *free* to every child, and to charge the expense of their maintenance and support upon the entire *property of the State*, equitably and fairly assessed. If three-quarters of a mill, as at first proposed, upon each dollar of such valuation, should fail to accomplish this result, then one mill, one and a quarter, or such other percentage should be adopted as would effect the object.

During this year (1856) the Legislature passed an act abolishing the offices of Town Superintendent and Inspector, authorizing and directing the election by the people of School Commissioners, in districts to be formed by the boards of supervisors of the respective counties, in conformity as nearly as practicable to the several Assembly districts of each, exclusive of cities and towns for which special laws had been or should be provided; such commissioners to hold their offices for the term of three years respectively, to have the general supervision of the Common Schools in their several districts, apportion the public money therein, advise and counsel with the school officers and inhabitants, look after the condition of the school-houses and condemn such as were unfit for use, recommend studies and text-books, examine and license teachers and annul their certificates for sufficient cause, and, when required by the State Superintendent, take testimony on appeals, and discharge such other duties as he may prescribe. Under the provisions of this act, 112 Commissioners were elected, and entered upon the discharge of their official duties. The share of public money belonging to each town was directed to be paid over by the several county treasurers to the supervisor, on his order, who was directed to pay it over, on the proper order of the trustees, to the teacher or other person entitled to receive it. A State tax of *three fourths of a mill*, on every dollar of the valuation of real and personal property in the State, was substituted for the $800,000 tax heretofore required to be annually raised for the Common Schools, one-third of the avails of which, deducting library money and other contingent expenses of the system, was directed to be equally divided among the several districts, and the remainder, including the library money, according to the population of each town. The share of each district, after setting apart its specific district quota, was directed to be divided by the commissioners into two equal parts, one of which, with the library money, to be distributed to their several districts in proportion to the number of children between five and twenty-one years residing in them, and the other according to the *average daily attendance* of pupils.

An act was also passed authorizing a loan of $6,000 to Genesee College and the Wesleyan Seminary connected therewith, conditioned that its board of trustees should establish, and place under the charge of the Superintendent of Public Instruction, twenty free and perpetual scholarships. The Superintendent was required to receive applications from any part of the State for the admission into these institutions of youths distinguished for ability and acquirements in any of the Common or Union Free Schools, and who might be recommended by the trustees or board of education thereof, and from such applicants to select, from time to time, so many as should equal the number of scholarships thus provided for.

From the annual report of the Superintendent for 1857, it appeared that the number of children in attendance upon the Common Schools during the year 1855, was 867,577, and that after deducting about 35,000 pupils in the several private schools, academies, and colleges from the whole number of resident children reported, there remained 200,000 children of suitable school age not in attendance upon any school whatever during the year. The whole amount of public money received during the year was $1,054,210.47 applicable to teachers' wages, and $50,806.50 to libraries. The amount raised by local taxes in city, village, and Union Free Schools where rate-bills were dispensed with was $720,774.28; that contributed on rate-bills in the country districts, $461,779.13; that raised by tax in those districts for exemption of indigent parents, and for deficiencies in the collection of rate-bills, $45,886.61; for the purchase of sites, $57,830.15; for building or purchasing school-houses, fences, &c., $384,101.88; for hiring school-houses, $17,568.09; for the repairing of school-houses, fences, and outbuildings, $100,553.98; for fuel and fires, $150,944.31; for the purchase of book-cases and school furniture, $50,761.97; for colored schools, $18,000; and for incidental expenses, school apparatus, &c., $341,000; making in all, $3,544,587. The number of volumes in the several district libraries was 1,418,100, being 87,270 less than in the preceding year, and 70,000 less than in 1853.

The Superintendent recommended an increase in the number of Normal Schools in the State, and that the services of eminent instructors should annually be engaged for lectures and practical teaching in the several Teachers' Institutes.

Section II.—Administration of Superintendent Henry H. Van Dyck—1857 to 1862.

Condition of the Common Schools.—Reports of the Superintendent.—State Association of Teachers.—Distribution of the School Fund.—District Libraries.—District Commissioners.—Teachers' Institutes.—Official Visitations.—Object Teaching.—Capital of the Common School Fund.—Controversy with the Comptroller.

On the second Tuesday of February, 1857, the Honorable Henry H. Van Dyck, of Albany, was elected, on joint ballot of the Senate and Assembly, Superintendent of Public Instruction. At the time of his election Mr. Van Dyck was one of the editors and proprietors of the "Atlas" newspaper published in Albany. He had previously, while a resident of Orange county, occupied the position of State Senator from the district of which that county formed a part. He was a man of superior abilities, inflexible integrity, unassuming manners, and fine social qualities. Honest himself, he had little toleration for dishonest practices on the part of any of the school officers placed under his supervision; and destitute himself of all pretension, he availed himself of every proper opportunity fearlessly to expose and rebuke *shams* of every description, whether in high or low places. After an administration of the Department for five years, he resigned his position for that of the head of the Banking Department, from which he was promoted by President Lincoln to the responsible post of Assistant Treasurer of the United States at New York, in which he remained until the past year.

From the annual report of the Superintendent for 1858, it appeared that the number of children in attendance upon the Common Schools in 1856 was 832,735; that 59 new school districts had been formed during the year; that the total expenditure for school purposes was $3,323,060; of which $1,100,432 were derived from the State apportionment; $1,752,377 raised by district tax, of which $1,216,710 was raised in the cities, and $536,607 in the country districts, in addition to the sum of $427,056 raised by rate-bills. For the payment of teachers' wages the sum of $716,685 was expended in the cities, and $1,308,081 in the country districts; for libraries, $6,306.68 in the former, and $25,857 in the latter; for school apparatus, $86,172 in the former, and $2,560 in the latter; for colored schools, $6,700.54 in the former, and $1,141 in the latter; for expenses of sites, school-houses, &c., $383,684 in the former, and $362,408 in the latter; and for incidental expenses, $206,975 in the former, and $102,666 in the latter. The number of volumes in the several school libraries was 1,377,933, being a decrease of 40,000 during the past year, and of 226,277 since 1853, notwithstanding the large sum—$55,000—annually appropriated for their increase. "A rational presumption would be," observes the Superintendent, "that the amount annually received from the State would, in most of the districts, be sufficient to guard against an actual diminution in the number of volumes possessed, but, so far from this being the case, there has been *an average decrease in the number of volumes during the last four years of* 56,569 *per annum*. Certain it is, that in many sections of the State, the interest heretofore felt in the preservation and increase of the district library has greatly diminished, if it has not entirely ceased."

The Superintendent, in view of the pecuniary exigencies of the State, and of individuals, and from an unwillingness unnecessarily to disturb the existing system of public instruction, felt himself bound to refrain from urging any increase in the rate of taxation over that already provided, with a view of rendering the schools entirely free—a consummation deemed by many highly desirable.

"To my mind," he observes, "it seems quite as important that means should be devised to render the money now contributed more diffusive in its benefits, and wider in its scope of application. If the State steps in, and by virtue of its sovereignty appropriates the property of the citizens to the education of all who choose to avail themselves of the benefit of the schools, the tax-payer has a right to demand that the sum thus contributed by him shall be made to confer the greatest amount of good of which its expenditure is capable. If the schools were full, and the means of instruction, as compared with those seeking to avail themselves thereof, deficient, a necessity would exist for extended accommodations and greater expenditure. But so far from this being the case, outside of the cities and villages, the almost universal concession is, that the schools are too small—the number in attendance being so limited as to render their support, beyond the time for which the State contribution would pay, burthensome. * * * It further appears that the contribution of more *money* than is now expended is not the only thing necessary to universal education. Indeed, the great obstacle to be contended against in reaching this desideratum is, not so much the want of facilities for imparting instruction, as the want of disposition on the part of a considerable portion of our population to avail themselves of those already furnished. The remedy for this evil of *non-attendance* is not so apparent. The liberty of the citizen in controlling the time and occupation of his children is not to be infringed for slight causes, or without great caution. Compulsory legislation, in this respect, could scarcely be enforced. But it is a question worthy of the consideration of the Legislature, whether the same end might not, to a considerable extent, be attained by the application of a discrimination in the distribution of the State funds founded on *the proportional number in actual attendance*. Such a provision would give to each tax-payer a direct pecuniary interest in securing the largest possible attendance in the schools, both as a means of securing a larger share of the State bounty, and as a defense against local taxation. If this or some other mode should be found operative in diminishing this great evil, it would, in the estimation of the undersigned, form the most palpable improvement of which the system is at present susceptible."

A change of the present school year, commencing on the 1st of January and ending on the 31st of December, to one commencing on the 1st of October and terminating on the 30th of September, was recommended, and promptly adopted by the Legislature.

In conclusion, the Superintendent observes:

"Though the Common Schools of the State are as yet far from exhibiting that perfection in character and extent of usefulness which is desirable, it is cause for congratulation that their progressive improvement is becoming each year more manifest. If the undersigned abstains from a lengthened disquisition upon the importance of general education, it is not attributable to an under-valuation of the benefits which knowledge in its most extended form is calculated to confer; but from a conviction that the representatives of the people must, from the distinguished post they occupy, be pre-supposed to hold in due estimation the advantages to be derived from a practical diffusion of its benefits."

The number of children attending the several Common Schools during the year 1857 was 842,137, of which 235,336 were in the city and 606,801 in the rural districts, showing an increase of over 9,000 from the preceding year. The amount of public money received from the State was $1,343,000, of which $371,000 were apportioned to the cities and $975,895.50 to the rural districts. The amount raised by district taxes was $1,846,542.71, of which $1,309,763.45 were raised in the city and only $536,777.26 in the rural districts. The additional sum of $390,315.50 was, however, paid on rate-bills in the latter, bringing its contribution to the general expenditure up to $927,292.76. The entire expenditure for school purposes in the State was $3,792,948.70, showing an increase over the preceding year of $380,600.47. Of this sum there were paid:

	Cities.	Rural Districts.
For teachers' wages	$926,768 49	$1,443,845 44
" libraries	6,706 69	83,838 97
" school apparatus	91,062 86	4,975 58
" colored schools	8,367 75	2,362 18
" school houses, sites, etc.	470,402 60	293,183 99
" incidental expenses	90,423 83	48,530 23
Total	$1,604,264 60	$1,966,664 90

The number of volumes in the several school district libraries was 1,402,253, being a decrease of nearly 48,000 volumes from those of the preceding year, and of upward of 200,000 since 1853.

"Concurrent testimony from various sections of the State," observes the Superintendent, "represents the district libraries as being little used, as rapidly deteriorating in condition and value, and as receiving little attention from the officers charged with their care or custody. I am not prepared to say that this indifference has as yet become universal; but that it is rapidly approximating this end cannot be doubted. Whether attributable to a bad selection of books, to the more general diffusion of periodical literature, to a want of means adequate to the addition of new works of interest, or all these causes combined, I am not able to determine. Whether the concentration of the district libraries into a town library, and the application of all the money apportioned to a town for library purposes to the purchase of works of enduring interest, under the direction of a board charged with the duty, would result in a practical benefit not attained under the present system, is a subject well worthy of the consideration of the Legislature. Certain it is, that the existing district libraries are rapidly depreciating both in numbers and in the value of the volumes on hand."

The system of supervision for the schools through the agency of District Commissioners, though attended with some inconveniences, and the subject of considerable complaint and local hostility, was found, upon the whole, productive of highly beneficial results, and its abrogation was decidedly deprecated by the Superintendent. He observes:

"Nothing can be more detrimental to the cause of Common School education than the constant vacillations by which the system has been attended—now under local inspectors and commissioners—anon under county superintendents—then back to town superintendents—now under district commissioners—each carrying out the peculiar views of the individual in charge, and none left in possession long enough to carry into effect any permanent system of measures. That now in operation has these merits at least: that under it something like uniformity in the qualifications of teachers may be attained; that, by bringing a greater extent of territory under one jurisdiction, a combined effort for improvement through the medium of Teachers' Institutes and Associations can be more readily carried into effect; that it brings the commissioner into more intimate acquaintance with the qualifications of teachers within his district, enabling him to select the competent and reject the time-serving; that the duration of his term, and the extent of his constituency, give him an independence of action that would not pertain to a more restricted locality and office; and that when its importance shall come to be duly estimated, and the value of the services rendered duly appreciated, men of higher qualification will be selected for the performance of its duties than could be expected in the case of an officer whose choice and jurisdiction should be limited to a single town. For these and many other reasons that might be adduced, I trust the Legislature will not deem it expedient to alter, in its essential features, the system of school supervision now in operation."

He also recommended that provision be made for the acquisition of title to sites for school-houses in the rural districts, by appraisement and appropriation, as in the case of highways, railroads, or other property for public use—great difficulty being frequently experienced in obtaining such sites near the center of districts. "In earlier days," he says, "when land was cheap, and when the spot covered by the house was all that was deemed requisite, such inconvenience was not often experienced. But the evil has now become one of serious magnitude, involving districts in quarrels, and tending to the serious injury of the schools."

In concluding his report for the year 1859, the Superintendent observes:

"The experience of another year, and a more extended observation of the practical condition of the schools, enables me to express a decided conviction as to their improvement in scope, efficiency, and usefulness. Though still falling below the standard of excellence that is desirable—though still far short of what we hope to make them, our Common Schools must, even in their imperfect condition, be regarded as the pride, the hope, the ornament of the State. No person can contrast their present character, and the studies pursued in them, with what they were when the present generation of adults were the recipients of their meager instruction, without a feeling of pride at the advancement accomplished. But it is my abiding conviction that no improvement really worthy of the term will be attained until those who preside in the schools shall become thoroughly qualified for the responsible station which they occupy. Says the philosophic GUIZOT, 'It can never be too often repeated that it is the *master* that makes the *school*.' What, then, are we to expect really great or good in the character of these institutions so long as they are left to the charge of persons whose superficial acquirements are but a mockery of true learning, and who have never spent an hour in cultivating a knowledge of that 'most difficult of all arts, the art of teaching?' Had that excellent litany which invokes deliverance 'from plague, pestilence, and famine—from battle, murder, and from sudden death'—also embodied a petition for exemption from incompetent school-teachers, it would not have trenched upon a subject in favor of which wise men and holy men might not properly raise their supplications. To remedy this great defect which now retards the progress of our schools, the commissioners in charge should be encouraged to discard the venal, the time-serving, the incompetent applicants for certificates, and thus create a demand for the services of those really fitted by nature and acquirement to discharge the responsible duty of instructing the youthful mind, and guiding it into proper channels. This is the dictate not less of duty than of true interest; for who can estimate the amount of injury resulting from the employment of incompetent teachers to the children placed under their care—whose time, once lost, can never be recalled; whose disgust for study, once engendered, may never be allayed; whose energies misdirected may never again move in the right channel; whose success in life may be wrecked upon the rock of the teacher's inefficiency or ignorance. Whatever measures may be devised by the Legislature to remedy this wide-spread evil, by advancing the character and qualifications of our teachers through facilities for instruction placed within their reach, and rendered indispensable to their employment, shall receive my earnest endeavors to carry them into effect. It is thus, by a course of gradual improvement, that our Common School system is to attain that expansion and perfection of which it is capable, and thus prepare its recipients to discharge the high duties pertaining to citizenship—to fit them for usefulness here and happiness hereafter."

On the second Tuesday in February, 1860, Mr. VAN DYCK was re-elected Superintendent of Public Instruction. Mr. E. W. KEYES was continued in the position of Deputy.

The annual report for the ensuing year (1860) shows an attendance of 851,533 pupils in the several Common Schools, during the preceding year, being an increase of over 9,000, and of 92,702 within the past ten years. The amount paid for teachers' wages, during the year, in the several cities, was $961,393.14, and the number of teachers 2,500, of whom 2,000 were females. In the rural districts the amount so paid was $1,461,980.66, and the number of teachers 12,132, more than one-half of whom were females. The amount of public money apportioned by the State was $4,156,744.08, which was about equally distributed between the city and country districts: the amount raised by district taxation, $2,000,000, of which $1,400,000 were raised in the cities; and $600,000, together with $414,000 contributed on rate-bill, in the country districts. During the past three years upward of $2,000,000 had been expended through taxes voluntarily imposed in the several districts for the purchase of sites, the building, hiring, purchasing, repairing, and insuring school-houses, and for fences, out-houses, furniture, &c., of which sum $1,263,363.76 were expended in the cities, and $750,000 in the rural districts. The whole amount expended during the year for school purposes was $3,664,617.57, about equally divided between the city and country districts.

Nearly three months had been spent by the Superintendent during the year in personally visiting and addressing Teachers' Institutes, and other educational assemblages, one of which was the State Convention of Commissioners and City Superintendents at Elmira, over whose deliberations he was called upon to preside. Several of the Institutes were also visited by Mr. E. W. Keyes, the Deputy Superintendent, to whose ability, industry, and zeal in this respect, as well as in regard to the general business of the Department, Mr. Van Dyck bears the highest testimony.

Twenty-three schools for Indian children were in operation in various sections of the State—several of them under the direction of native teachers, who discharged their duties with creditable fidelity and ability.

The Superintendent strongly recommended an alteration of the basis of distribution of the two-thirds of the public money now required to be apportioned according to the number of resident children of the proper school age, to an apportionment based upon the actual *average attendance* of such pupils during a period of not less than six months of each year. "The inevitable result of such a course," he says, "would be to make the inhabitants of each district directly interested in the largest practicable attendance upon the schools—to make such attendance more regular and persistent in its character—and to foster, at the same time, a spirit of interest and inquiry into the condition and progress of the schools, on the part of many who now regard them with comparative indifference." In conclusion he observes:

"Personal observation, and the concurrent testimony of all familiar with the subject, enable me to express a confident conviction that the past year has witnessed a decided improvement in the scope and efficiency of our Common Schools. This has chiefly resulted from the introduction of more competent teachers, joined to improved methods of instruction developed at the Teachers' Institutes, and through the medium of Teachers' Associations. That great defects still exist is not in the least problematical; and though deficiencies are easy of exposure, the application of a remedy is far more difficult. If, with our present experience, we could commence our school system *de novo*—if it had not grown with our growth, and entwined itself in its present form with all the partialities, prejudices, and aspirations of our people—a system could be doubtless devised more homogeneous in its character, and rising by regular gradation from mere elementary studies to the highest educational attainments. But this could only be done through governmental requisitions as to classification, attendance, and study, such as our citizens have not been accustomed to endure, and which, being incompatible with that volition of choice and freedom in action inseparable from free institutions, would not be tolerated by the community. In despite of glowing encomiums upon foreign systems, and even of attainable improvements in our own, our citizens will still claim the right of educating their children in their own way, and to an extent commensurate with the peculiar notions of propriety entertained by each individual. Impressed with this conviction, I would make our Common Schools—those neighborhood colleges from which the great mass of our thriving population must continue to graduate—as perfect in their details, as thorough in their mental discipline, as extensive in their scope of study, as the wants and wishes of the class for whom they are more immediately designed will allow. The greatest boon that can be bestowed upon them is to furnish them with accomplished teachers, who are familiar with the most approved methods of instruction, and who are capable of leading pupils from the simplest elements of knowledge through the branches pertaining to a sound English education. With all that we can do, we shall still find the inmates of our schools such as they have ever been, with various capacities for receiving knowledge—with minds immature and requiring careful training for their proper development—with no greater genius for the acquisition of knowledge than those who have preceded them. But we should open to them new studies, demanded by the present condition of society, of which they may avail themselves with advancing years; and furnish them with such facilities for the acquisition of rudimentary science as may be brought fairly within the scope of Common School instruction. Thus much at least is practicable; and though it may not embrace all that is either desirable or attainable, it will, in my estimation, be found preferable in practice to many of the sublimated theories to which the subject of Common School instruction has given birth.

"Popular education being in a great measure the offspring of the present century has not yielded its full fruits—but here, as elsewhere, 'as we sow, so also shall we reap.' The greatest amount of practicable *education* should be our aim—and in this term is included much more than instruction in those primary branches which constituted the meager fare imparted by the schools of other days, and still emulated in various localities. These form the tools by which education is achieved; and hold to it merely the relation which the chisel bears to the sculptor, or the brush to the painter. The material wealth of our citizens has increased beyond the conception of the most sanguine calculator in former days; and no limit to acquisition is yet discernible in the future. But there is reason to apprehend that general education is not advancing in the same ratio; in part from mistaken notions of economy, and partly from a self-satisfying view of the progress already attained. Surely whilst monarchical governments are seriously occupied in advancing the educational interests of their subjects, the citizens of a country whose institutions rest upon popular intelligence can ill afford to neglect any practicable improvement in that which involves the perpetuity of the government under which they live. The problem is still to be solved, whether the American of the succeeding generation shall hold the same pre-eminence in general intelligence which he has hitherto enjoyed, or whether he shall be excelled in this respect by the natives of other climes, whom inclination or ill-fortune may throw upon our shores. If we would maintain our national supremacy—if we would melt the mixed races with which our country is thronged into one homogeneous population—we must extend to all the benefits of thorough Common School education—we must indoctrinate our youth with the advantages of superior knowledge, and endow them with all the educational facilities requisite to a life of honor, usefulness, and virtue. You will, I doubt not, join in the aspiration that our educational system may eventuate in placing upon the stage of action a generation of intelligent citizens, who shall render our free institutions a blessing at home, as well as a beacon of hope to denizens of less favored lands."

On the 31st of January, 1861, Superintendent VAN DYCK transmitted to the Legislature his annual report for the year ending Sept. 30, 1860, from which it appeared that the number of districts in the State had increased to 11,382; the number of children under instruction during the year to 867,388, of whom nearly 600,000 were in the rural districts; the number of teachers to 15,021, of whom 12,290 were employed in the rural districts; and the number of school-houses to 11,650, of which 11,370 were in the rural districts, showing an excess over the previous year of 74, many of the old superstructures in these districts having been succeeded by new and more commodious buildings. The total expenditure during the year for this purpose was $642,290.63. The schools were in session for an average period of eight months.

"The returns clearly indicate," says the Superintendent, "that so far as our Common Schools are concerned, the business of teaching is rapidly passing into the hands of females. I have no lamentations to utter over this ostensible fact. Whilst there are circumstances under which the services of a male teacher may be indispensable, it is still my opinion that in most of our district schools the presence of a well qualified female teacher will eventuate in the moral and intellectual advantage of the pupils, beyond that which they would attain under the auspices of a majority of the teachers of the sterner sex."

The expenditures for school purposes during the year were as follows:

	Cities.	Rural Districts.
For teachers' wages	$1,118,078 14	$1,479,336 24
" libraries	6,816 04	27,169 83
" school apparatus	75,449 71	6,978 88
" colored schools	20,985 28	4,187 38
" school-houses, sites, &c.	361,821 60	280,968 83
" incidental expenses	208,433 63	153,856 04
	$1,791,164 60	$1,953,118 35
Being a total expenditure in all of		3,744,846 95

"Concurrent testimony from nearly every quarter of the State," says the Superintendent, "represents the *libraries in the rural districts as almost totally unused, and rapidly deteriorating in value.* The whole number of volumes reported during the past year is 1,286,536, which is 317,674 less than was reported in 1853, although $55,000 has been appropriated each year since that period for library purposes."

Referring to the various incongruities and deficiencies in the existing law for the establishment of Union Free School districts, for correcting which a bill had been prepared, and would be submitted by him to the Legislature for its approval, the Superintendent sarcastically adds:

"There are other incongruities in the act, not amongst the least of which is that which admits *of the imposition of a rate-bill upon the pupils. A Free School* supported by rate-bills *is such an anomaly as could be found sanctioned nowhere else save in the code of public instruction in the State of New York.*"

Twenty-four schools for the instruction of Indian children had been maintained during the year in the various reservations, at a cost of $4,396.

In conclusion the Superintendent observes:

"The material prosperity which marks our country—the happiness and intelligence which distinguishes its citizens—may be traced in no inconsiderable degree to the diffusion of education amongst all classes of our population. If that indomitable energy which characterizes our people was guided by knowledge more specific, the result of early study and thorough instruction, still more remarkable would be our progress in all the elements of national greatness. To contribute to this end by giving to the schools of New York a more elevated character and a wider range of usefulness is an object worthy of the combined wisdom of her legislators, which it shall be my earnest endeavor to carry into effect."

Mr. VAN DYCK having, in February succeeding, been elected by the Legislature to the position of Superintendent of the Banking Department, resigned his office as Superintendent of Public Instruction, the duties of which devolved upon the Deputy Superintendent, Mr. KEYES.

On the 8th of January, 1862, acting Superintendent EMERSON W. KEYES submitted the annual report of the Department, from which it appeared that in the 11,400 school districts of the State there were in attendance during the preceding year 872,854 pupils, being an increase of 5,000 over that of 1860; that the amount of public money apportioned by the State to the several districts was $1,331,901.71, of which $947,063 was apportioned to the rural districts; the amount raised by district taxes upward of $2,000,000, of which $1,500,000 was raised in the cities; and the amount contributed on rate-bills in the rural districts, nearly $400,000; the amount paid for teachers' wages, $2,655,451.70; for libraries, $8,144.47; for school apparatus, $88,600; for colored schools, $23,000; for the purchase of sites and buildings, repairing and furnishing school-houses, $656,000; and for other incidental expenses, $382,000—amounting in all to $3,841,270.81, about equally divided between the city and country districts, and exceeding by $97,000 the expenditure of the preceding year.

In reference to the district libraries, the acting Superintendent thus indignantly expresses himself:

"Section 4, chapter 237, Laws of 1838, appropriated the sum of $55,000 annually for three years, to be applied to the purchase of books for district libraries, and, by the operation of subsequent statutes, the same provision has been continued in force until the present time. The whole amount of these appropriations, including that for the current school year, is, therefore, $1,265,000.

"It has ever been our pride and boast that while the corruption and venality of reckless and unscrupulous men, both within and surrounding the high places of our national and State councils, have exposed the funds of almost every department of governmental administration to the illegal and sacrilegious invasion of peculating officials and rapacious jobbers of high and low degree, our School Fund stands forth as the sole bright and particular exception from this dark and degrading record; no appreciable portion of its revenues having ever been diverted to other than legitimate and worthy uses. But when I look for the *return* from this princely investment, and find it mainly represented by a motley collection of books, ranging in character from "Headley's Sacred Mountains" to the "Pirate's Own Book," numbering in the aggregate a million and a half of volumes, scattered among the various families of districts, constituting a part of the family library, or serving as toys for the children in the nursery; torn, worn, soiled, and dilapidated, saturated with grease, offering a temptation to ravenous rats; crowded into cupboards, thrown into cellars, stowed away in lofts, exposed to the action of water, of the sun, and of fire; or more frequently locked away into darkness unrelieved, and silence unbroken—I am constrained to believe that no plunder-hardened contractor or bribe-stained official ever yielded to the State so poor a return for his spoil as have the people of this State derived from this liberal and beneficent appropriation, through their own reckless and improvident use of it.

"The darkness of this picture is partially relieved by the fact that the cities and larger villages of the State, by whom no inconsiderable portion of this fund has been received, have been less negligent and wasteful in its expenditure, and that under the law of 1838, as also by the sanction of this Department under a previous statute, much of the appropriation has been applied to the payment of teachers' wages. Still, in the last five years, $189,798.10 have been expended in the rural districts for library purposes, while the number of volumes reported has diminished in the same period from 1,288,070 to 1,206,073, a loss of 81,996 volumes as a return for the expenditure named. I think this may safely be set down as among our permanent investments of the School Fund from which no revenue is derived!"

With regard to the supply of properly educated teachers, MR. KEYES says:

"A single Normal School, sending forth its one or two hundred students each year, is obviously inadequate to supply the needs of a State whose teachers are numbered by tens of thousands. The greater number of these thousands will not, and, under existing conditions, cannot, be made to engage in the business of teaching as a permanent pursuit; hence they are unwilling, even if the facilities were afforded, to devote the years for special preparation which the course of study in the Normal School requires.

"The practical question is therefore presented, how shall we reach this great body of transient teachers by whom most of the work of instruction in the schools of the State is to be performed? Common observation, the testimony of school commissioners, and the practical results of their labors, all establish most conclusively the disheartening fact, that left to themselves they will enter upon the business of teaching with the most limited knowledge of the subjects which they are to teach, with no just conception of the nature and office of true education, with no sense of moral obligation, and with no higher aims or nobler desire than to speed through the drudgery of their term, and grasp the wages that have been their sole stimulus to any exertion.

"To reach this mass and body of mind, to awaken it to some apprehension of the teacher's work, to stimulate desire, to arouse ambition, to quicken moral sensibility, to secure concert of action, and to impart some knowledge in those elementary branches in which they are most deficient, is found to be a work indispensable to the progress of our schools, and a work which can be done most effectively through the instrumentality known as TEACHERS' INSTITUTES.

"For many years after their introduction in our State, owing in part to a want of confidence in their utility, whereby legislative recognition and support were withheld, in part to a prevalent apathy among teachers, and in part to the want of efficient and thorough supervision, Teachers' Institutes led a fitful life, and finally languished and fell nearly or quite into disuse. But under the present system of supervision, a new impulse has been given to this system of efforts, and with such success that they may now be regarded as an established feature of our educational policy.

"The results of Teachers' Institutes the present year have been most gratifying. An apprehension was generally and most naturally entertained that owing to our national misfortunes, in the contemplation of which the whole mind of the people seemed to be absorbed, the attendance upon Teachers' Institutes would be greatly reduced, and the general interest and value of their instruction would be much less than in past and prosperous years. So far from realizing this apprehension, the attendance has been greater this year than ever before, as will be seen from the following comparison with 1859, the most prosperous year of which we have any previous record.

1859. Number of counties holding Institutes, 50.
No. of teachers in attendance, 6,766. Average per Co., 135 1-8.
1861. Number of counties holding Institutes, 47.
No. of teachers in attendance, 7,488. Average per Co., 159 1-8."

Of the success of the District Commissioners' system the acting Superintendent speaks in the highest terms:

"The present system of school supervision has demonstrated its vast superiority over that which it superseded, and is rapidly growing in popular favor and esteem. The objections to it are rapidly disappearing, as the disabilities that were incident to a change have been overcome, and experience has given opportunity for a better knowledge of its practical duties. It has been successfully established that the opposition to it arose less from defects in the system itself than from its defective administration.

"The steady progress and improvement of our educational effort, so clearly apparent upon a comprehensive survey of past and existing conditions, is a living testimony to the efficiency of the system when properly administered, and is a tribute to the general zeal and ability of those to whom the trust has been committed. I have already adverted to the salutary results of the system in reviving and establishing on a fixed basis the agency of Teachers' Institutes; and if this result were all that had been attained, it would more than repay for the introduction of the system as a part of our educational policy. But this is only a small part of the beneficent results derived from the system. An officer of extended jurisdiction has a higher and wider range of influence, is more generally consulted upon questions of school policy, and in matters of school controversy, and his opinions and advice have a consequence and weight that cannot attach to a local officer of limited jurisdiction."

During the year the acting Superintendent visited several of the schools in the cities of New York, Brooklyn, Syracuse, Buffalo, Oswego, Rochester, Auburn, and Utica, in addition to attending the sessions of forty Institutes; and, on these several occasions, addressed audiences amounting in the aggregate to twelve or fifteen thousand persons. In reference to these official visitations, he says:

"The Hon. Henry S. Randall, Superintendent of Schools, in his last report to the Legislature in 1853, urging the policy of a separate and distinct organization of this Department, enforces his recommendation in the following language:

"The Superintendent, if charged with no other duties, might attend occasional examinations of congregated or single schools, and occasional town or county inspections of teachers. He might be present at school celebrations, Teachers' Associations, Teachers' Institutes, and official meetings of town superintendents. He might constantly meet and mingle with the friends of education, and the practical workers in the business of education, conferring and receiving benefit by the interchange of views; weeding out the worthless teachers, rousing the inert, and giving just credit and prominence to the deserving. He might pass from county to county, drawing the school officers of each about him, addressing assemblages of the people, and calling parental and public attention to the improvement of the schools."

"In this view of the nature and scope of the duties of this Department I fully concur, although the unusual labor imposed upon me in the discharge of both its principal and subordinate duties have prevented me from carrying this policy into execution as fully as I had desired and hoped.

"I had planned a visitation of all the cities in the State, so many as practicable of the larger villages, and, in different counties, a fair representative number of the exclusively rural districts. These comprise three distinct grades or classes of schools, in respect to organization, administration, pecuniary resources, and other distinctive and essential elements of vigor and effectiveness. From careful observations, in a few only of each class, a fair idea may be formed of the general practical workings of our system in all. It was my purpose, in these visitations, to note the relative efficiency of these different classes of schools, as exhibited in their daily exercises, to observe and to record their characteristic features of excellence or of imperfectness, and to derive suggestions as to some possible and expedient means of incorporating in all the peculiar and distinguishing excellences of each. Partial as has been the execution of my plan, the results fully confirm my previous convictions of the utility of extended visitations by the Superintendent.

"Much practical and useful information which can be obtained from no reports, however voluminous or minute in statement, may be acquired; the public are stimulated, awakened, and encouraged to investigate concerning the importance of improving the condition of their schools; thoughts, views, and opinions are freely interchanged to mutual edification and profit, and the conclusions made a basis of suggestions as an example or a warning to others."

Upon the subject of "Object Teaching" the acting Superintendent makes the following pertinent suggestions:

"A growing conviction has taken possession of thinking and observing minds that what the great mass of our people acquire is less a knowledge of facts from books than *the power to use books intelligently in connection with all other means and sources of information.* Close confinement of pupils in schools five or six hours of the day, with the mind unoccupied and left to wander wearily in dreamy inaction, devoid of method or plan, catching its fancies and sporting them from the memory of out-door joys; or joining the class for a few minutes each day to confront the strange and mysterious symbols that puzzle and distract, rather than interest and inform—has long been felt to be a poor preparation for the duties of life, wherein the power to observe carefully, to think closely, to reason soundly, and to speak clearly is so indispensable to their competent discharge.

"And yet, with this conviction so generally entertained, our educational effort has been marked by comparatively little progress or improvement in methods of primary instruction. We have looked for educational improvement in the effort to get more studies into the schools, and to get the children over them more rapidly, rather than in any means for making a limited knowledge of books of higher service in the work of education, through the discipline wrought in the mind by its proper and thorough acquisition. Thus, more branches have been introduced, and an endless variety of books in the same branch has been manufactured, our whole practice being predicated, *logically enough*, upon the theory that true education is an extensive acquaintance with books; and hence, that educational improvement and progress are only secured by the continued manufacture of new books, each of which must be a little better or *simpler* than the last.

"The fallacy of this proceeding consists in the erroneous assumption that books are the sole or chief agency in the educational work, especially in its elementary stages. This has been the source of the errors and faults in our systems of primary instruction that have rendered the results so unsatisfactory to all intelligent observers, but without suggesting any adequate remedy for the evil.

"It was left for the distinguished educator and philosopher, Pestalozzi, to originate, and to develop to some extent, a system of primary instruction more in harmony with nature and the laws of mind. This system, now more commonly known as "Object Teaching," and for many years successfully practiced in the best schools of England and the Continent, proceeds upon the rational assumption that the senses, the observing powers, are those through which the child chiefly and naturally gains a notion of things; that is, obtains information, knowledge, *ideas*. The reasoning and reflective powers are latent in the mind of the young child, and are not brought into exercise until later in life, when its stock of ideas, its knowledge of things, and its powers of apprehension are so far complete as to require the use of these higher intellectual agencies in conducting the further investigations of the soul in the domain of ALL TRUTH. To address these faculties, therefore, at an early age of the pupil's progress, is productive of unfortunate results, chiefly in one of two ways: in a child of naturally quick apprehension, these powers become unduly excited and stimulated; one of slower apprehension becomes stolid and indifferent, discouraged by want of success and disheartened by the sense of disgrace to which his backwardness exposes him.

"Guided by these principles, the system of "Object Teaching" steadily addresses itself to the faculties of observation; presenting before the child familiar objects on which its attention is fixed—in the examination of which it becomes interested—in the study of which habits of order, accuracy, and thoroughness are formed, and the power of clear and correct expression of ideas is acquired."

The acting Superintendent called the attention of the Legislature to the appropriation by the Comptroller of the sum of $300,000, derived from the sale by the State of certain lands in the city of New York, owned by them, to the General instead of the Common School fund, in violation of the provisions of the Constitution. A spirited and able protest against this appropriation was addressed to the Comptroller by Mr. KEYES, but without avail.

The Comptroller appears to have held that the lands in question did not belong to the State on the first day of January, 1823, and hence that the proceeds from their sale were not subject to the provisions of the act of 1827, incorporating the provisions of the Constitution, which took effect on that day; and also that the class of lands under water, to which those in question belonged, had frequently been granted, without consideration, to riparian owners, which could not have been done had they been understood to form part of the capital of the Common School Fund.

To the first of these allegations Mr. KEYES replies:

"I regard your first proposition, that the proceeds of the sale of these lands are not a part of the Common School Fund, because they did not belong to the State on the first day of January, 1823, and hence were not subject to the provisions of the statute of 1827, as untenable for the following reasons:

"1. It recognizes the statute of 1827 as the only binding and conclusive authority concerning the proceeds of the lands belonging to the State; whereas, I rest my claim on behalf of the School Fund to the proceeds of those lands upon the provisions of the Constitution, independent of any legislative enactment.

"The Constitution of 1822 defines and makes perpetual the Common School Fund, and directs the application of its revenues. That fund is defined to embrace the accumulations of moneys for school purposes, under various legislative enactments up to that time (constituting what was then known as the Common School Fund), and the proceeds of all lands belonging to the State thereafter sold or disposed of. These two items, therefore, to wit, the old Common School Fund, embracing all the accumulations up to that time, and the proceeds of the sales of State lands, constituted the *new perpetual Common School Fund* of the Constitution of 1846.

"The Constitution of 1846 makes the capital of that fund, as above defined, *inviolate*. It need not, indeed it could not, well do more. What should constitute the capital of the Common School Fund had been defined, accepted, and acted upon, without question or dissent, by the Legislature and by the public at large, for nearly twenty-five years. In making inviolate the capital of the Common School Fund, therefore, the Constitution of 1846 made inviolate the accumulations up to that time, and the proceeds of all lands belonging to the State thereafter sold or disposed of, together with the increase of capital derived from the revenues of the United States Deposit Fund.

"It will be observed that in this constitutional provision there is no limitation to lands belonging to the State in 1823, but a broad, unrestricted declaration that the proceeds of *all lands* belonging to the State should, as a part of the capital of the School Fund, be preserved inviolate. This provision of the new Constitution acts upon conditions existing at the time of its adoption, and must be regarded as having its full force and effect as from that date; hence it follows that if any question could arise as to the application of that provision to the proceeds of lands to which the State should acquire title subsequently to the adoption of that Constitution, it could only arise as to the proceeds of lands of which the State has become owner since the first day of January, 1847. It will be conceded by you, I presume, that these lands have been the property of the State ever since they were formed. This was certainly anterior to 1847, at least with regard to most of them; and hence, even upon your assumption that the title of the State has vested since 1823, they are still subject to the constitutional requirements of 1846, which directs that the proceeds of all lands belonging to the State, as a part of the capital of the Common School Fund, shall be preserved inviolate.

"2. But further upon your first proposition. This embraces two assumptions. The first is, that the State had no title to these lands on the first day of January, 1828. The second is, that having no title at that time, the proceeds are not a part of the Common School Fund, because the statute of 1827 designates only such lands as were owned by the State in 1828. I have endeavored to expose the fallacy of the latter, by showing that the claim of the Common School Fund does not rest upon the statute of 1827, but upon the Constitution of 1846, re-adopting certain provisions in that of 1822; and hence, that title or ownership on the 1st of January, 1828, is not material.

"I now desire to establish the fact that the title of the State to these lands which have been sold is of much older date than 1828; and that hence, if the provisions of the statute of 1827 were the only ones under which the Common School Fund could claim these proceeds, the claim would still be valid and incontrovertible."

He then proceeds to show that the title to the property in question "vested when allegiance to the British government ceased and our own State sovereignty was declared and established through constitutional forms. The State succeeded the Crown, as sovereign proprietor of all the unappropriated lands within its borders; hence, the title of the State to those lands is as old as the sovereignty of the State itself."

In reference to the peculiar character of the lands originally lying under water, and forming a part of the bed of the Hudson and East rivers, the acting Superintendent contended that, inasmuch as the title of the State was perfect and undisputed previous to emergence, the fact of such subsequent emergence could in no manner have affected it, except by simply rendering the land marketable.

In concluding his report, Mr. KEYES observes:

"The necessity of ample provision for the education of the people, under institutions where the people are the government, was never so forcibly demonstrated as in the events of the last few months. * * * We have ever held it true that the education of our children is the hope of our land. In our State we have to no inconsiderable degree acted upon the conviction, and have liberally provided the means whereby the blessings of education should be universally diffused. And we have all along pointed to the results of this policy as demonstrating its wisdom. The enterprise of our people, their wonderful achievements, the expansion of trade, the astonishing accumulations of industrial force, the increase and diffusion of wealth and the comforts and luxuries it can purchase, the diffusion of general intelligence through the medium of books, magazines, and newspapers; and, more than these, the institutions of the church, the lyceum, and the social circle, the habits of honesty, industry, and peace, which make crime, idleness, and riot exceptional; our domestic character, our social order, our literary taste—all have been referred back to the school as their great patron, promoter, and source. So strong has been this conviction that upon the school—that is, upon the knowledge, the culture, and the discipline which it imparts—all our progress, our freedom, our prosperity, and our peace, have depended, that the sentiment in favor, not of education simply, but of the Common School, the school for the people, the national nursery of truth, intelligence, and loyalty—the sentiment in favor of this popular institution has become not only fixed but all-pervading.

"How humiliating would be the fact that, while in possession of all the elements of prosperity and power which are ours this day; while an expanding commerce still spreads her sails upon our waters or furls them in our ports; while our manufactories were never so prosperous, and our soil never teemed with more abundant harvests; while our public works yield a revenue unparalleled in the annals of the State; while the busy hum of industry, the cheer of festivity, and the merry laugh of joy still ring in our ears in notes scarcely broken by the discordant echoes from the seat of war—that, amid all these evidences of prosperity, the first sad and sickening confession of prostration and weakness should be found in the neglect to provide for the elevation and improvement of our educational system. Proud, as yet, and untarnished, is the escutcheon of the 'EMPIRE STATE!'"

"It is a most gratifying evidence of the soundness of our judgment and of the purity of our patriotism that nowhere has a desire for relaxation of vigor and energy in the support of popular education been suggested. The term of school has not been shortened because of the war, and it has nowhere been made a pretext for the employment of incompetent teachers. Educational gatherings have not been deferred, but have been well attended, and their deliberations have been marked by a spirit and earnestness unsurpassed in former years. As already seen, the attendance at Teachers' Institutes was greater than ever before, and the spirit of our people was never more thoroughly alive to the necessity of educational improvements."

SIXTH PERIOD—1862 TO 1871.

FREE SCHOOL TRIUMPH.

SECTION I.—SECOND ADMINISTRATION OF SUPERINTENDENT VICTOR M. RICE—1862 TO 1868.

Recapitulation.—District Libraries.—Condition of the Schools.—Teachers' Institutes.—Oswego Normal and Training School.—State Mill Tax.—Free School—Rate-Bills.—Application of Library Money to Teachers' Wages.—Code of Public Instruction.—Condition of School-Houses.—Apportionment of Public Money.—Female Teachers.—Teachers' Classes in Academies.—Normal Schools.—Appraisement of School-House Sites.—Irregular Attendance of Pupils.—Number of Uneducated Children.—Increase of State Tax.—Abolition of the Rate-Bill System.—Truant Children.—Free School Act of 1867.—Teachers' Associations.—Union Schools.—Cornell University.

WE approach now the final phase in the existing system of Common Schools. Step by step we have been led forward, under the guidance of mighty minds, from one advanced height to another, overcoming formidable obstacles, setting aside numerous impediments, surmounting all adverse influences, until we have finally reached the crowning table-land of our view, and can look forward, far in the distance, and around us on every side, over the magnificent prospect.

To GIDEON HAWLEY, the first Superintendent, is due the earliest *organization* of the system. Gen. DIX engrafted upon it the DISTRICT LIBRARY feature; but neither he nor his predecessors appear to have felt the want of a more complete and perfect SUPERVISION. The perspicuous mind of SPENCER seized upon this idea, and with characteristic energy reorganized the entire system upon this basis; but even he could not be induced to see the necessity or conceive the utility of NORMAL TEACHING; and Col. YOUNG, frankly accepting and adopting all the advanced ideas of his predecessor, superadded to the system this important feature, together with that of TEACHERS' INSTITUTES. Neither of these great men however, seem to have, at any time, entertained the conception of FREE SCHOOLS, the germ of which had been implanted by DE WITT CLINTON, in the foundation of the New York Public School Society, as early as 1805. Superintendent BENTON struck the key-note of this movement, and his successor, CHRISTOPHER MORGAN, promptly and enthusiastically adopted and carried it into immediate effect. In his intrepid and uncalculating haste, however, to realize at once the full benefit of this great principle, his "vaulting ambition o'erleaped itself," and a temporary reaction followed upon an apparently brilliantly successful campaign. Flaunting the popular banner of FREE SCHOOLS, and loudly asserting and proclaiming its "strange device," the odious RATE-BILL system, once expelled in the full flush of victory, like another Bourbon, resumed its unwelcome dynasty; and for a long interval excluded from the temples of popular instruction thousands upon thousands of the children of the poor, while taunting them with the promise of free and universal education. It was reserved for VICTOR M. RICE to touch as with the spear of Ithuriel this heartless monster of hypocrisy and oppression. After securing the restoration of the essential pillar of COUNTY SUPERVISION, which had been ruthlessly thrown down by unreflecting apathy, indifference, and prejudice; after displaying the official record that in nearly eight of the eleven thousand school districts in the State not a solitary instance of exemption of indigent parents from the merciless severity of the rate-bill could be traced, he unrolled the magic words of the law, which, like that of the Medes and Persians, had "altered not" in these long years of misrule: "THE COMMON SCHOOLS IN THE SEVERAL SCHOOL DISTRICTS OF THIS STATE SHALL BE FREE TO ALL PERSONS OVER FIVE AND UNDER TWENTY-ONE YEARS OF AGE RESIDING IN THE DISTRICT." "Free! Yes—free in the same sense that good dinners at our best hotels are free. *They are free to all who will pay a good price for them!*" And therewith this clear-headed, warm-hearted, and simple-minded man, boldly threw down his gage of mortal defiance, wrested from the oppressor his lying standard, flung to the breeze the true banner of freedom, and demanded at the hands of the Legislature the actual recognition of those substantial fruits of victory fairly won in the well-contested campaigns of 1849–50: "*That the general school laws be so amended that the odious rate-bill shall no longer prevent children from going to school;* THAT THE SCHOOLS SHALL BE AS FREE TO ALL OF PROPER AGE AND CONDITION AS THE AIR AND THE SUNLIGHT!" And he succeeded! The "air and the sunlight" now, alas! gently wave and sweetly sleep over his premature grave; but his imperishable record remains, and no time shall ever be able to obliterate its grand inscription!

It only remains for his successors faithfully to preserve the precious heritage which has thus been handed down by the great minds which have preceded them, to rescue from dilapidation and desecration each pillar of the stately fabric, which the crumbling touch of time, or the neglect or want of appreciation of its guardians, has suffered to decay, and to transmit to the latest posterity that bequest of FREE and UNI-

VERSAL EDUCATION which has been confided to their hands. The "mantle of the prophets" now rests on worthy and vigorous shoulders. May it never be otherwise!

Early in February, 1862, the Hon. VICTOR M. RICE was re-elected Superintendent of Public Instruction. SAMUEL D. BARR, Esq., of Westchester, was appointed Deputy.

From the annual report of the Superintendent for 1863, it appeared that the whole number of pupils under instruction in the Common Schools of the State, during the preceding year, was 892,550; the number of teachers employed 26,500, of whom 7,585 were males, and 18,915 females; the whole amount of public money expended in the payment of teachers' wages, $2,780,371.05, of which $1,220,497.26 had been expended in the cities and $1,559,873.79 in the rural districts; the whole amount raised by taxes $2,068,057.74, of which $1,560,456.40 was raised in the cities, and $507,601.35 in the rural districts, exclusive of $407,000 raised by rate-bill; and the whole amount of public money apportioned by the State $1,408,532.45. The actual expenditure for maintaining the schools, including the costs of sites, school houses, apparatus and incidental expenses, was $3,955,664.33, of which $1,969,806.35 was expended in the cities and $1,985,857.98 in the rural districts. The number of volumes in the several district libraries was 1,326,682.

The condition of these libraries appeared to have undergone an unfavorable change. The Commissioners in nearly every section of the State reported them as little used and steadily deteriorating in value. The small share of public money received in a great majority of the rural districts for library purposes, averaging only about $3.00 annually, was scarcely sufficient to replace the books worn out by use; while it was only in the large villages and more populous towns that the libraries were regularly replenished and properly appreciated. Ineffectual efforts had been made in the more sparsely settled towns to consolidate the several district libraries into one town library; and various suggestions for their improvement and increase had been, from time to time, made. In some of the cities legislative authority had been given to appropriate the library money, wholly or in part, to the payment of teachers' wages; and no sufficient reason appeared why the inhabitants of the rural districts might not be entrusted with this discretionary power. The Superintendent, however, declined making any specific recommendation on the subject at this time.

From the annual report of the Superintendent for 1864, it appeared that under the acts of 1862 and 1863, for the encouragement of Teachers' Institutes, fifty-five of these "temporary Normal Schools" had been held during the preceding year in forty-seven counties of the State, for periods of two weeks and upwards, in which over 9,000 teachers had received instruction, being 84 per cent. of the whole number of teachers employed in the several Commissioners' districts represented. An additional Normal or Training School had been established, under the authority of the Legislature, in the city of Oswego, for the preparation of primary Common School teachers.

In reference to the State tax of three-fourths of a mill for the support of schools, the Superintendent observes:

"The argument for a State tax is grounded upon the fraternal relation and obligations established by the Creator among men, and promulgated in that epitome of all wise conduct, the 'Golden Rule:' 'Whatsoever ye would

… annually, was scarcely suffi… … worn out by use; while it … villages and more populous towns … regularly replenished and pro… … actual efforts had been made … … towns to consolidate the … … into one town library; and … stions … ir improvement and increase … from … to time, made. In some of the … legislative … ority had been given to appr… the … … wholly or in part, to the … … ; and no sufficient reason … … of the rural districts … this discretionary power. … however, declined making any … on the subject at this time.

… report of the Superintendent for 18… … present … that under the acts of 1862 and 18… … encouragement of Teachers' Institutes, fifty- … of these "temporary Normal Schools" had been … during the preceding year in forty-seven counties … the State, for periods of two weeks and upwards, … over 9,… teachers had received instruction, … per cent. of the whole number of teachers … in the several Commissioners' districts repre… … National Normal or Training School … under the authority of the Legis- … of Oswego, for the preparation of … teachers.

… state tax of three fourths of a mill … for the … schools, the Superintendent observes:

* … tax is grounded upon the fraternal relation and obligation … … among men, and promote … that epitome of … the Golden Rule? 'Whatsoever ye would …

OSWEGO NORMAL SCHOOL.

that others should do unto you, do ye even so unto them.' To feed the hungry, to clothe the naked, and to alleviate human sufferings generally, is an acknowledged duty; and whoever possesses the power, and neglects or refuses to do it, disobeys the Divine injunction, and thus does violence to his own enlightened conscience. And if any man apprehends that his brother will be in distress to-morrow or next year, or years hence, and has the power to make provision against such distress, by aiding him in becoming more enlightened and better, or in any other way, and neglects or refuses to do so, he just as clearly sets at nought that abiding rule, and the generous promptings of his better nature, as if he were to deny to a thirsty person a cup of water, or a morsel of bread to the hungry. In the one case, it is true, the suffering is present, and in the other prospective; but both are within the compass of his understanding, and it is, therefore, equally his duty to alleviate the one, and provide against the occurrence of the other. Surely the rule of action which is binding upon one man in the case stated, is equally applicable to ten, to a hundred or a thousand men, and to the whole people as an organized State. Every intelligent man knows that ignorance is the mother of disobedience, whence follow the frailties and miseries of mankind; that proper culture begets understanding, whence follow the greatest development of the natural powers and the highest enjoyment. It is, therefore, the duty of every man, and no less the duty of the whole people, to use every available means to save the rising generations from ignorance and its attendant calamities, by making ample provision for their highest development and consequent extensive usefulness.

"A Christian State can not innocently disregard its obligations to protect the weak, to instruct the young, and to help the poor and dependent; nor can it innocently neglect to provide for its own safety, by providing for the safety and happiness of those composing it. The Legislature which provides for the definition, detection, and punishment of crimes, has done but half its duty; it is bound also to make provision against the commission of crime; and for this object, experience proves that the school and the school-master are more effective agencies than the detective police and the terrors of the law. Whilst it is not pretended that the best culture acquired in the schools is the sole means for the prevention of crime, yet it is abundantly proved by criminal statistics that the majority of those who suffer the penalty of violated law are ignorant, have not had the advantages of systematized instruction, have never been subjected to the smoothing and softening influence of obedience and discipline, and have never had their time or conduct regulated by wise authority; but, on the contrary, have grown up unlettered and in the unrestrained indulgence of their appetites and baser passions. It is also as clearly proved that crime, vice, and disloyalty are most prevalent in those countries, and those parts of a country, where there is the least general education; whilst in those communities which have more nearly complied with their obligations to make provision for the instruction of the young in useful knowledge, there has always been, as there doubtless will ever be, the greatest regard for law and order, the most rational liberty, and, as a sequence, the greatest individual and national prosperity and happiness. No State, which had provided common schools and higher institutions of learning for the education of her people, could have made war upon our Government, or attempted to tear down the good old flag, the emblem of liberty and union. No! Intelligence foresees the danger, and shuns it; while Ignorance leads her followers blind-fold into the very abyss of ruin.

"The general State tax produces a result which is sometimes overlooked. It compels those to perform their duty who would not, except upon legal compulsion. If the education of children were left entirely to the voluntary action of individuals, would not a great many, who now pay their just proportion for the support of schools, refuse or neglect to pay anything at all? Would not the whole burden then, if borne at all, fall upon the generous, the patriotic, the men of noble hearts? Surely such would be the result if, the principle were abandoned, that, 'the property of the State should educate the children of the State.' But experience has taught that the liberal and willing contributors to even so great a good, are not equal to the task which would be thus imposed upon them, and that tens of thousands would soon lack an opportunity of acquiring even the first rudiments of an education essential to the safe exercise of the right of franchise.

"This State tax, thanks to an enlightened public sentiment, lays hold of the property of the selfish and unwilling supporters of the public welfare, in whatever small corner they may have hoarded it: it extracts therefrom their equal share in the expense of educating all the children of the State.

"The law imposing this tax has also the distinguishing merit of recognizing and inculcating a common brotherhood; that it is the bounden duty of the people of any part of the State to have the same solicitude for the welfare of those in every other part thereof, however remote, as they have for themselves; and its instructions are given with the majesty of an irresistible authority. It teaches the unity of the State, and a mutual dependence and obligation, in proportion to ability, to provide for the common weal; that the richer localities, where capital has concentrated on account of natural or artificial advantages, shall contribute of their abundance to the poorer, to those counties less favored by location and special legislation for school and other purposes. No county, not even New York, which pays a large sum annually to such counties as Otsego, Delaware, Schoharie, Franklin, Clinton, and St. Lawrence, has a right to complain. For the rule that would set off New York by itself, and free it from this tax, would also free every ward in that city from the city tax for the same purpose, and an individual in any ward could claim, with equal propriety, exemption from taxation for the support of schools therein; and, following the same blind guide, he might claim exemption from every other tax imposed on account of the necessities and duties of an organized community. He could say to his neighbors and to the inhabitants of his ward, city, and State, 'I will take care of myself, and you may take care of yourselves;' and this rule having obtained, all organized action, regulated by law, would be at an end. I repeat, no part of the State has a right to complain of this tax. It is levied because it is the duty of the State to provide for the education of her children; and duty and right being correlative terms, her children have a right to demand that the doors of the school-houses shall be opened for their reception, and that competent teachers be employed to instruct them. The fact of their inability to enforce the observance of their rights in this respect, in the halls of legislation, has not heretofore failed, and, it is confidently believed, will never fail to bring to their aid the conscientious, patriotic, and intelligent representatives of the people.

"The amount appropriated by the State for the support of schools for last year, including the proceeds of this tax and the revenue derived from the Common School and U. S. Deposit Funds, was less than *one dollar and forty-three cents* per pupil in attendance *upon the schools*—a sum hardly within the bounds of liberality—and yet sufficiently large to aid materially the rural districts of the State. How general is the conviction that the common schools, in which more than ninety per cent. of our people obtain all their instruction, must be supported under the most depressing circumstances, is evinced by the liberal support extended to them during the past year, by the people themselves in their district school meetings, and through their local authorities. It will be observed that, during that time, there were raised by local taxation and by rate bill, in the rural districts, $866,922.83, and in the cities, $2,068,037.74, for their support. In no other way could the will of the people, in regard to the schools, have been more forcibly or fully manifested; and it is believed that the abandonment of a policy in furtherance of their will thus expressed—a policy to which they have been so long accustomed, and which has for its object the prosperity and independence of their children—could not meet with their approval.

"In conclusion, we would earnestly remind all those who take an interest in the public weal, that there is no doctrine of political ethics better established or more emphatically confirmed by the events of the present era than the one tritely expressed in the maxim that 'the salvation of a republican and democratic form of government depends upon the virtue and intelligence of the people to whom its administration is committed.' We would spare not in our efforts to warn legislators and every parent and guardian of the young, against the ever-impending peril of suffering the paramount duty of inculcating the proper education of the young to be in any degree neglected. Harmony, prosperity, and happiness will certainly attend upon the vigilant fulfillment of this duty; anarchy, poverty, and misery, will, as surely, be entailed by its neglect."

The Legislature of this year authorized the application of the library money, in all those districts receiving less than $3.00 a year for this purpose—eleven thousand in all—to the payment of teachers' wages, and in all other districts to the purchase of school apparatus, and this being supplied, to teachers' wages. So far as the rural districts were concerned, and most of the city schools, this enactment was virtually equivalent to an entire abandonment of the library system—manifestly and unquestionably a retrograde movement. It is earnestly to be hoped that before the million of volumes still remaining in the twelve thousand districts of the State shall have disappeared, this great and beneficent feature of our Common School system will be restored and placed upon a permanent and improved footing.

The consolidated "Code of Public Instruction," prepared and reported by the Superintendent, with the aid of the Hon. GEORGE W. CLINTON, of Buffalo, was this year passed into a law, and distributed, with the necessary forms and instructions, among the several districts of the State.

In February, 1865, Mr. RICE was again re-elected Superintendent of Public Instruction, and Mr. BARR remained in the position of Deputy. He was a most able, faithful, and efficient public officer, and possessed the entire confidence of the Superintendent. From the annual report of the Superintendent transmitted to the Legislature on the 7th of February, 1865, it appeared that the number of school districts was 11,717; the amount of money expended during the preceding year for building, purchasing, hiring, repairing, and insuring school-houses, for purchasing sites, and for fences, outhouses, &c., was $647,301.23, of which $370,815.34 was expended in the cities, and $276,485.89 in the rural districts. The provisions of the act of 1864 had contributed essentially to the improvement of the school-houses, and the sentiment of the inhabitants of the district in regard to them. "Those utterly unfit for the use of man or beast," observes the Superintendent, "have *in a few instances* been condemned by the united action of Commissioners and Supervisors, while a very large number have, by their direction, been repaired and provided, *as they never were before*, with proper fuel, pails, brooms, and other implements necessary to keep them clean and render them reasonably comfortable for use. It is gratifying to report these improvements, in view of their influence upon the comfort, morals, and memories of the pupils. I may be pardoned for cherishing the hopeful anticipation that within a few years, through the beneficent operations of that law, and a more enlightened public sentiment, 'the school-house spot,' in every neighborhood of this great State, will be made so attractive that the young will approach it with willing steps, and with the joyous assurance of a welcome from accomplished teachers, who will truly love and care for them."

The number of volumes in the district libraries was 1,125,438. The amount of public money expended for this purpose was $26,890.51, and for school apparatus $137,613.49, of which $128,447.79 was expended in the cities, and only $8,026.17 in the rural districts. The number of children in attendance upon the Common Schools during the year reported was 882,184. Adding to this number the pupils of the several colleges, academies, and private schools, there still remained 336,000 of suitable school age not in attendance upon any school, public or private, during the year.

The Legislature of 1864 had, on the recommendation of the Superintendent, provided by law that a specific portion of the public school money should thereafter be apportioned among the several districts, upon the basis of *average daily attendance*, thereby making it the pecuniary interest of every tax-payer to induce the regular attendance of his own and his neighbors' children. This provision had largely increased the number of pupils and the regularity of their attendance. The average time during which the schools were kept open was seven months in the rural districts, and ten months in the cities. Nearly eight-tenths of the whole number of teachers employed in the State were females.

"It is impossible," observes the Superintendent, "to over-estimate the value of the influence thus brought to bear upon the daily developing mind and character in our schools. To teach and train the young seems to be one of the chief missions of woman. Herself high-minded, the minds of those with whom she comes in daily contact unconsciously aspire. Gentle herself, she renders them gentle. Pure herself, she makes them pure. The fire which truly refines the ore of character can be kindled only by her hand. Woman is more deeply read than man in the mysteries of human nature—at least, in that of children. It might, perhaps, be nearer the truth to say that her superior knowledge in this respect is intuitive. Better her discipline of love than his reformatory theories, and austere rules, and stringent systems. Her touch conquers the rebelliousness which his but increases. Her persuasive reproofs far exceed his stern menaces and cold logic. Well may we be solicitous in regard to that pupil's course and destiny who does not pass from the scene of woman's ministrations with his moral sense so delicately attuned as to render the discords of a vicious life impossible; with his tastes vitalized, and his perceptions quickened; with his sensibilities and sympathies all ready for action; with his conscience trained to unremitting vigilance, and the best impulses of his heart in full play. I am sure that the future will be grateful for these labors of woman in our schools."

The amount expended for teachers' wages during the year was upwards of three millions of dollars, nearly equally divided between the city and country districts, and exceeding by $307,500, the amount so expended during the preceding year. The amount raised by taxes for school purposes, was $2,608,079.20, of which nearly $2,000,000 was raised in the cities; while on the other hand, $420,892.52 was raised on rate bills, in the rural districts, making their total contributions upwards of one million of dollars.

The sum of $1,445,749.70 was apportioned from the State among the several districts, of which $1,125,749.90 was from the avails of the State School tax, and the balance from the Common School and United States Deposit Funds. The entire receipts of the several districts from all sources during the year, including the balances remaining in the hands of their officers from the preceding year, were $5,060,250.20. Deducting similar balances for the year reported, the actual expenses of maintaining the schools during the year were, $4,549,870.66, of which $2,477,446.36 were expended in the cities and $2,072,324.30 in the rural districts, exceeding by about $800,000 the amount so expended during the preceding year.

Teachers' classes had been formed in eighty-four academies, designated by the Regents of the University for that purpose in accordance with the Act of 1856, in which 351 male and 1,292 female pupils had been instructed; and fifty-five Teachers' Institutes had been held in the several counties, in which 7,524 pupils had been nstructed during the usual period of two weeks.

"In conclusion," the Superintendent observes, "I am gratified to be able to report that the evidences of an increasing solicitude for the proper instruction of the young are accumulating in all parts of the State; and that even while making great and painful sacrifices, and herculean efforts to save the life of the Republic, our people, true to duty, and faithful to their posterity, have not remitted any of their interest in the schools."

The annual report of the Superintendent for 1866,

showed an increase in the number of districts to 11,780, and of the number of children instructed during the preceding year, to 881,184, or 35,443 over 1864. The amount of money expended for sites for building, purchasing, repairing, hiring, and insuring school-houses, and for fences, out-houses, &c., during the year reported, was $799,160.70, of which $516,902.04 was expended in the cities, and $282,258.66 in the rural districts.

"The necessity of well-built, commodious, clean and airy school-houses," observes the Superintendent, "has been so often urged upon public attention, that it would seem almost superfluous to mention it here; but so long as the evils arising from ill-constructed, uncomfortable, unwholesome and dilapidated houses exist, so long must the demand for improvement be reiterated till reform be consummated. Not only should the prime laws of health be regarded and obeyed in this matter, but the moral obligation to furnish all rational means to correct, purify, and cultivate the taste of the young should be recognized. The love of beauty in some of its myriad forms is inherent in every human breast not vitiated by corrupt surroundings; hence the philosophy no less than the propriety of making our school-houses temples of beauty, as they are temples of knowledge.

"There is a golden link between beauty and utility, and the expense of embellishing school-rooms and school-grounds is trifling, compared with the beneficial and refining influence of such care upon those plastic natures which must be molded into the men and women of future generations. Every 'live' teacher knows the pleasure with which even the smallest pupils greet a rich bouquet on the desk, or the joy with which a cherished bud is watched as it unfolds its hidden glories to the light, or their absorbing interest in the disposition of festooned evergreens for a holiday or a gala occasion, or the rapture which the inaugural of the new school piano awakens when it breathes a simple school ballad, or thrills all hearts with the inspiration of the Star-Spangled Banner. Who has not, in the most cherished dreams of childhood, the memory of some flower-laden, climbing vine, some favorite tree or shrub, on some green spot around which cluster the holiest associations? If such testimony be universal, and such influence potent for good, what so proper to decorate with trees and flowers as the school-house grounds, or where so appropriate to bestow works of art and taste as the school-room, or what more important to the happiness and improvement of the young, than the school-house built with a strict regard to beauty and utility, and made peculiarly attractive by such surroundings and embellishments?"

The amount expended for teachers' wages was $3,076,093.43, of which $1,932,438.26 was expended by the cities, and $2,043,635.17 in the rural districts, being an increase of $682,672.97 over the preceding year. The average annual salaries of the teachers employed were $563.70 in the cities and $169.34 in the rural districts. The amount raised by local taxation for school purposes, during the year was $3,501,070.20, of which $2,655,544.45 were raised in the cities and $845,525.75 in the rural districts. The sum of $655,158.78 was also contributed on rate-bills in the latter districts, making the entire amount raised in these, $1,500,684.53. The whole amount of public money received from the State was $1,446,000.00, of which $1,126,000.00 was derived from the State School Tax, and $320,000 from the Common School and United States Deposit Funds.

The total actual expense of maintaining the several Common Schools of the State for the year was $5,735,460.24, of which $3,084,357.69 was borne by the cities, and $2,651,102.55 by the rural districts.

In reference to sites for school-houses the Superintendent observes:

"It is both reason and law that the rights of individuals to private property must yield to public necessity. Therefore the sovereign people, through the action of the Legislature, may rightfully assume the control and ownership of private property for public use, providing therefor a just compensation to the owner.

"The State of New York *knows* that the education of her children is a matter of great public concern, and a sacred duty which she cannot innocently neglect. The children must, therefore, have school-houses, and the property of the people is taken to provide them; these school-houses must have sites—grounds whereon to stand—and the property of the people is taxed to pay for them. It is also a matter of public concern that the site of the school-house should be central, in a healthy location, and conveniently accessible for the attendance of the children; but in very many instances, as reported to this Department by those seeking relief, such desirable situation is owned by some gruff old bachelor who has spent his lonely years in inconsiderately repeating by word and deed, 'You take care of yourself, and I'll take care of myself;' or, by some unenlightened and parsimonious landlord, who, to avoid the payment of a few dollars towards building a new school-house, utterly refuses for any consideration, or at least for any reasonable consideration, to part with the spot of ground which would best accommodate his own and his neighbor's children.

"The old school-houses, rudely built forty or fifty years ago by our fathers and our grand-fathers, are now very generally unfit for any use; and owing to the changes which have taken place in the boundaries of districts, and in the number and location of residences, many of these sites, originally selected with little care as to their fitness, have ceased to be acceptable to the people; and others, which were well chosen, and which, with some additions from adjoining lands, might be made to accommodate the many, have as yet no play-grounds, and are of too small dimensions to admit even of the erection of the out-buildings demanded by propriety and decency. This last deficiency must greatly enhance the present urgent demand for the acquisition and appropriation of suitable sites for new school-houses, and for the enlargement of the grounds of old ones. The difficulty of getting possession of suitable grounds for these purposes will probably remain insurmountable, unless a law be passed by which, for a just compensation, such lands may be taken and appropriated to such public use.

"The sites of our school-houses should be chosen in places that are both convenient and pleasant; and where any land-owner plants himself in the way of obtaining such, the law should lay hands on him and remove him; thus enforcing the conviction that there is, for the children of this country, a grand highway to learning which no man may obstruct."

It appeared from the reports made to the Department, that there were 563,901 children residing in the State between the ages of six and seventeen years, not in attendance upon any school during the year! In his comments upon this startling fact, the Superintendent, after alluding to the loss in a pecuniary point of view from this neglect on the part of parents and guardians to avail themselves of the facilities afforded by the State for the education of their children, observes:

"Great as this loss appears, thus estimated, it is infinitely greater when regarded in a mental and moral point of view. What is lost is of too precious a nature to admit of measurement by any commercial standard of value. It is personal and direct to the children losing the instruction and its power for usefulness, and it subtracts just so much from the sum total of what should be the united power and wisdom of the future. The harvest time of youth is lost, and often times supplanted by damage and mischief. Human happiness, all the beneficial results which must surely flow from a knowledge of their political duties as citizens of a free country, from a proper appreciation of the principles of social ethics, and from a conscientious understanding of the obligations of obedience to the wholesome restrictions and directions of laws, both human and divine—all are jeopardized, or lost, or worse than lost.

"In whatever light presented, the fact of this non-attendance at the schools should command the serious attention of the Legislature. To the State and to the world this is of greater importance than all the canals, railroads and banks which deservedly occupy so much attention. 'Instruction is the good seed sown, which yieldeth some fifty and some an hundred fold.'

"But the question arises, What are the practical remedies? I answer that the time may come when the State will be obliged to make attendance obligatory for her own safety. She may be obliged to do so, compelled by her sense of duty to protect, in the enjoyment of their right in the schools, those who are too young and dependent to protect themselves. Surely, she can allow neither the minds nor the bodies of her children to starve, when herself blessed with abundance.

"Granting that every child has a right to only so much instruction as shall fit him for the most ordinary duties of the citizen and the man; then the school, and the use of the time of his life when his activities are in full play, are for him also; they are the means necessary to the end, and no parent or guardian can justly deprive him of either. No guardian is excusable for starving the mortal body of his ward; if he does so, the law steps in and deals with him, and no one complains of the humane interference, nor doubts the rightful authority of the law. How much more reprehensible is the wrong when, through thoughtlessness, parsimoniousness or malevolence, such starving process is inflicted upon the immortal mind! And if this starving system be persisted in after persuasive and all other corrective measures have been tried and failed, who will question the just expediency of a law to compel attendance upon school instruction?

"Such a law, however, should be the last resort. Invitation and persuasion are more in accordance with the genius of our institutions than the exercise of compulsory power; and it seems to me that the wisdom of the State should first undertake to make the schools so attractive, and mental application so pleasant and its results so desirable, that the multitudes of absentees and truants will voluntarily and cheerfully seek the school-room with punctuality. A resort to measures requisite for such purposes is so unquestionably within the jurisdiction of legislative power, that objection could not be raised.

"First, then, the State should make ample provision for the preparation of teachers, who will, by all their words and deeds, command the attention and gain the confidence and love of both parents and children. To secure such preparation, many more normal and training schools should be established and provided with a sufficient support; teachers' institutes and associations should be encouraged; and the appropriation for the former should be so increased, that two or more corps of skillful teachers can be constantly employed in the different counties in giving instruction to the local teachers. A comparatively small appropriation for this purpose would be of invaluable service. The salaries of the School Commissioners, also, should be so increased, as to enable them to devote their entire time to their noble work.

"Finally, the proposition that 'the property of the State should educate the children of the State,' should be carried out, by making the schools at once and for all FREE. From the inception of our school system, the support of schools by taxation of property has been sanctioned by successive legislative enactments. Since that early period, by authority of statute law, the property of school districts has been taxed for the purchase of sites, for erecting and furnishing school-houses, and for the payment of exemptions from and deficiencies in rate bills. The Constitution of 1821 dedicated to the Common School Fund all the proceeds of the lands belonging to the State, and the income therefrom, to the support of schools. The Constitution of 1846 confirms that dedication by declaring that the capital of that fund shall be preserved inviolate, and its revenues applied to the support of Common Schools, and the provision is included, that $25,000 from the revenue of the United States Deposit Fund shall be annually added to the Common School Fund. The Legislature of 1851, after the people had declared by an overwhelming vote in favor of taxation for the entire support of the schools, or, in other words, that the property of the State should educate the children of the State, authorized a State tax of $800,000 for this purpose; and the Legislature of 1856 increased this amount by making the tax three-fourths of a mill. Numerous special acts, based on the same just and wise policy, have been passed from time to time, by means of which the schools of our cities and of many of our villages, are supported wholly by taxation upon property. Under authority of law, the people of other villages and thickly populated districts have organized Union Free Schools; thus by voluntary action sanctioning this policy, and acknowledging its justice.

"If the hundreds of thousands intellectually starved by the operation of the *odious* rate-bill could rise up in contrast with those generously nourished by the free system, the revolution in favor of the latter would become an 'irrepressible conflict,' which would result in the total overthrow of that slavish love of gain, which denies the common brotherhood of man, and ignores the divine command, 'Love thy neighbor as thyself.' I can conceive no higher legislative obligation than that of making provisions by which the portals to the school shall be thrown more widely open; because I know of no other one mode by which attendance can be so generally encouraged in the rural districts.

"I may be allowed, in this connection, to manifest a special anxiety for the children of those soldiers and sailors who have died or been disabled while serving in the army or navy of the United States, by recommending that provision be made by which the Public Schools shall be required, and all other other institutions of learning that participate in the distribution of any of the public moneys be induced, to give them instruction free of tuition fees. It is believed that this boon should be generously and freely extended and made an *inheritance*, a *right*, recognized and secured by the majesty of law. Surely a manifestation of an *earnest gratitude* for the services and sacrifices of their fathers would be worthy of a grateful people. How so touchingly manifest that gratitude, as by such a provision for their children? If in other times the life of this nation shall be again imperiled, where so hopefully look for the loyal and the brave, as to these foster-children whose incentive shall be, not only to imitate the manly and patriotic deeds of their fathers, but to shield the Protectress, who, in their early years, folded them in her arms with a loving kindness second only to that of Him who gave to us the victory?"

In reference to the condition of the Common School Fund, the Superintendent calls the attention of the Legislature to the pending controversy between the Department and the Comptroller, originating during the temporary administration of Mr. KEYES, respecting the appropriation of $300,000, received by the State from the sale of public lands in the city of New York, to the General, instead of the Common School Fund, where it was claimed properly to belong, under the specific provisions of the Constitution. The Superintendent says:

"In the month of June, 1861, the State of New York, in consideration of the sum of $300,000, conveyed to the corporation of the city of New York certain lands owned by the State and situated in the city of New York, known as the 'West Washington Market,' the 'Watts-street Pier,' the 'Hubert-street Pier,' and a portion of the 'Lowber property.' The proceeds of this sale were, by the then Comptroller of the State of New York, Hon. Robert Denniston, acting by the advice of the Attorney General, passed to the credit of the *General Fund*. A protest against this proceeding was entered at the time by the then acting Superintendent of Public Instruction, Emerson W. Keyes, Esq.; which protest was in the shape of a memorial, addressed to the Comptroller.

"It is claimed that the *proceeds* of this sale should have been placed to the credit of the capital of the Common School Fund, under sec. 10, art. 7, Constitution of 1822, and art. 9 of the Constitution of 1846. Sec. 10, art. 7, Constitution of 1822, is as follows:

'The proceeds of all lands belonging to this State, except such parts thereof as may be reserved or appropriated to public use or ceded to the United States, which shall hereafter be sold or disposed of, together with the fund denominated the Common School Fund, shall be and remain a perpetual fund, the interest of which shall be inviolably appropriated and applied to the support of common schools throughout this State.

"This provision was embodied in the Revised Statutes of 1827, in almost the exact language above quoted.

"Article IX of the Constitution of 1846, reads as follows:

'The capital of the Common School Fund, the capital of the Literature Fund, and the capital of the United States Deposit Fund, shall be respectively preserved inviolate. The revenue of the said Common School Fund shall be applied to the support of common schools; the revenue of the said Literature Fund shall be applied to the support of academies; and the sum of twenty-five thousand dollars of the revenues of the United States Deposit Fund shall each year be appropriated to and made a part of the capital of the said Common School Fund.'

"The lands in question originally lay under water, forming a part of the bed of the Hudson and East Rivers, opposite the city of New York. The State assumed ownership of one of these tracts of land on the 24th of April, 1858.

"It was claimed by the Comptroller, at the time of the transfer of this property from the State to the city of New York, that the land in question was not owned by the State at the time of the adoption of the Constitution of 1823; and that, therefore, the act of the Legislature passed in 1827, embodying the constitutional provision, does not apply to this property; in other words, that the constitutional provision affected only such lands as were, at the time of the adoption of the Constitution, actually owned by the State.

"But there are no words of limitation in the constitutional provision, confining its operation to lands *then* owned by the State; nothing but the broad, all-embracing and positive declaration, that the proceeds of *all lands* belonging to the State should, as a part of the capital of the Common School Fund, be preserved inviolate. The provision being unlimited, and being a portion of the supreme law of the State, and having been substantially reproduced in the Constitution of 1846, it is difficult to see wherein it was less binding in the year 1861, when this transaction took place, than in 1823, when the old Constitution became the supreme law of the State. If the provision applied only to lands actually owned by the State at the time of the adoption of the Constitution, then it may be said, with equal force, that sec. 1, art. 1, of our present Constitution, which declares that 'No member of this State shall be disfranchised, or deprived of any of the rights or privileges secured to any citizen thereof, unless by the law of the land or the judgment of his peers,' applies to those persons only who were 'members of the State' at the adoption of the Constitution in 1846.

"But it is claimed that the title of the State to these lands extends far back beyond 1823.

"In 1777, the State of New York assumed and thereafter sustained independent sovereignty, and succeeded the British government as owner of all unoccupied lands within her boundaries. These lands were at that time unoccupied, and consequently they belonged to the State. It is true, they were under water; but that fact in no way affected the title of the State. Ownership is limited neither by height nor depth. By the common law rule, the owners of lands lying along and bounded by rivers not navigable, own to the center of the stream, including all islands and the bed of the stream. So, also, by the common law rule, which has been repeatedly declared adopted in this State, where lands adjoin *navigable rivers, the State owns the land from ordinary high water mark, including the bed of the stream.*

"I have called your attention to these transactions, fully impressed with the belief that the Common School Fund is smaller by more than $300,000, than it would have been, had the constitutional provision guaranteeing its inviolability been strictly adhered to. I respectfully and earnestly request a careful investigation of these matters at your hands."

In the same connection, the Superintendent adverted to a loss of about $4,000, alleged to have been sustained by the Fund, on a sale made by the Commissioners of the Land Office of property in Binghamton, bid off by the State on the foreclosure of a mortgage given on a loan made in 1858, in pursuance of law, from the Common School Fund to the Susquehanna Seminary in that village.

These transactions were subsequently adverted to in the reports of the Superintendent of the two ensuing years; but no adjustment of the controversy seems to have been effected.

The Superintendent concludes his report with the following recommendations:

1. "That the general State tax for the support of schools be increased by the addition of *one-fourth of a mill* on every dollar of valuation for the purpose of diminishing local or school district taxation for the same purpose.

2. "That the School law be so amended *that the odious rate-bill shall no longer prevent children from going to school*; that *the schools shall be as free to all of proper age and condition, as the air and sunlight*;

3. "That a commission be appointed to locate three or more normal and training schools, for the special preparation of teachers, in such eligible places as shall offer the greatest inducements, by way of buildings, school apparatus, etc.; and that an appropriation be made for their efficient support;

4. "That provision be made by which the public schools shall be required, and all other institutions of learning which participate in the distri-

bution of the public moneys shall be induced, to give free instruction to the children of soldiers and sailors who shall have died or been disabled, while in service in the army or navy of the United States; and

5. "That an act be passed for the appraisal of and acquiring title to lands designated for school-house sites."

Under a resolution of the Assembly, during the preceding session, directing the Superintendent to "collect all the information at his command respecting the methods by which other States of the Union and the Governments of Europe aim to secure the general education of their children; especially such laws and regulations having this object in view as are *compulsory* upon the natural and legal guardians of the children, and what amendments or additions, if any, may be made to our present school laws that will more effectually secure the education of every child in our State; and report the same to the Legislature," Mr. RICE, on the 15th of February, 1867, transmitted to that body a voluminous and very able report, prepared under his direction by A. G. JOHNSON, Esq., former Deputy Superintendent, comprising a full abstract of the laws of the several States relating to Common Schools, and the condition of educational matters in every country of the world where provision of any kind had been made by public authority.

In reference to the expediency of *compulsory* laws and regulations for enforcing the attendance of children upon public or private schools, the Superintendent, after premising that this species of legislation had never been adopted in the United States, beyond provision in Massachusetts and some of the larger cities in other States for the prevention of truancy, submitted the following remarks:

"The adversaries of compulsory attendance represent it as an arbitrary interference with parental authority. In well-organized society, the parental and filial relations are defined and regulated by law. The parent is clothed with certain powers, and charged with certain duties.

"The right of the parent to the guardianship of his children is founded on his desire and ability, natural or acquired, to supply their physical and mental wants. Society measures the solicitude and ability, on which the right of guardianship rests, by the extent of the parent's contributions to the healthful physical and mental development of his children. If they are insignificant—if natural affection and pecuniary ability, both or either, are wanting—then the right of guardianship fails likewise, and society properly takes the place of the parent, and itself assumes the control of them. Society provides for the orphan and destitute, and for those who are deserted or cruelly abused by unnatural parents. From the habitual drunkard and the insane it takes away both property and children.

"On what principle are such public laws founded? Because it is written, 'Thou shalt love thy neighbor as thyself;' and again, 'As ye would that others should do unto you, do ye even so to them;' and the controlling moral sense of society, educated and exalted by conforming to these injunctions of a Supreme Intelligence, accepts them as beneficent rules of action, and requires obedience to them as a public duty. Hence the annual appropriation to provide for the idiotic, the blind, the insane, the deaf and dumb, the orphan asylums, the Children's Aid Society, the dispensaries, and other public charities.

"In ancient Greece and Rome, the laws gave almost unlimited authority to the father over his children. He could destroy their lives in childhood, kill them at any age, and sell them into slavery. This absolute power was modified and softened by the family affections and by the manners and customs that among every people grow into a common law. In China, the father has the same power of life and death, and the national religion seems to be an exaggerated obedience to the command, 'Honor thy father and mother, that thy days may be long in the land.' In all Christian nations, however, at the present day, the laws have modified parental authority, and, among other things, prescribed that at a certain age—not the same everywhere—it shall be terminated.

"It is as completely within the scope of legislation to require a parent to educate his children as to clothe and feed them. Compulsory laws have not, in any country, assumed to do more. School teachers and school officers report absentees and truants. If the absentees are in private schools, or are receiving at home the same instruction that would be given in the public schools, the law is satisfied. Society, whether republican or monarchial, is but an extension of the family, and the family is no more the normal relation and condition of man than society or the aggregation of families. It has the right to enact laws for its regulation, and as it advances from the patriarchal state toward the highest degree of Christian civilization, its laws must be modified and adapted to its improved condition.

"To the inquiry why the monarchial governments of Europe have taken public education in charge, and why they insist upon making it general, the answer is, that they have had the sagacity to perceive that the new civilization, which an overruling Providence has decreed for mankind, is distinguished by the power and diffusion of knowledge, and they aim to shape and direct it to their own safety. If universal education is the means for an absolute monarchy to confirm its power, is it not still more necessary for a republic!

"*But it is believed that in this country education can be universal without being compulsory.* In Holland, every adult citizen can read and write. Attendance at school has never been enjoined by law, but supervision has been carried to an extent which would hardly be deemed legitimate in the State of New York. The same thing is true in the canton of Geneva, in Switzerland. In Iceland, where there is but one school, and no public primary school at all, every body can read and write, instruction being given by parents to their children at home in the long winter evenings. This has been the custom for a thousand years. In Norway, a cold and rugged country, with a sparse population, and where the schools are kept open in many parishes only one or two days in a week, and even sometimes only half a day, the teacher travelling from one school to another, it is still rare to meet with an adult who cannot read and write. In China, where there are no public primary schools, and where the only governmental incentive to study is the certainty of obtaining office as the reward of success at the competitive examinations, all the male population can read and write. In New England, where there have never been compulsory laws, except in Massachusetts, it is seldom that a native-born citizen is ignorant of the arts of reading, writing, and ciphering. Popular opinion is a law on this subject. It is a disgrace to be ignorant. The schools are open and free to all, and the child of the poorest parent has the same pains taken with his early instruction as the child of the richest citizen. They often read and study in the same books, and always sit on the same benches, and recite in the same classes. In our own State, those who cannot read, write, and cipher are comparatively few, and of these a very small proportion are native citizens. The children of the illiterate aliens very generally attend the public or church schools.

"*I doubt the expediency of laws compelling parents and guardians to send their children and wards of a proper school age to the public schools*, or to provide education for them at home or at private schools, until the persuasive power of good teachers, commodious and comfortable school-houses, and free schools shall have been tried, and tried in vain. In despotic and monarchial countries, the rulers say to the people, 'Go,' and fear or physical force compels obedience, but under a government established by the people, it is deemed wise to use the word of invitation, 'Come!'"

From the annual report of the Superintendent, on the 1st February, 1867, it appeared, from a careful and thorough investigation made by the Deputy Superintendent, Mr. Barr, that the actual number of school districts in the State, exclusive of those within the cities, was only 11,387, instead of 11,738 as reported—the error having arisen from reporting joint districts composed of adjoining territory in two, three or more separate towns in *each* of the towns from which they were composed. The sum expended during the year reported for the purchase of sites, building, repairing, and furnishing school-houses, &c., was $970,224.59, about equally distributed in the city and rural districts, and valued at $6,720,535 in the former, and $5,534,422 in the latter, averaging $22,346.47 each in the cities and about $500 in the country. The provision of law authorizing the school Commissioner and Supervisor to condemn dilapidated school-houses, and declare them unfit for use, had been executed by those officers with discretion, resulting not only in the replacement of these buildings by new and comfortable houses, but in keeping others in repair.

"The school-house," observes the Superintendent, "should be the handsomest and most pleasantly situated building in the district. It should be conveniently arranged and comfortably seated, ample in size, well ventilated and warmed. It should have, where possible, a good yard and play ground, not less than half an acre in extent, planted with shade trees, and surrounded with a substantial fence.

"The little commune of Winterthur, in the Swiss canton of Zurich, with only 5,000 inhabitants, has within the past three years built three school-houses, situated in the midst of gardens, and at a cost of $100,000. Such taste in the selection of sites and erection of buildings shows a just appreciation of the value of schools and knowledge. It would be a high privilege to be a citizen of Winterthur; we may be sure that a traveler visiting Winterthur would have nothing to say of beggars, paupers, and criminals. It is the abode of industry, plenty and intelligence.

"The contrast of what is, with what ought to be, in thousands of cases, is discreditable to the State. Our citizens should be awakened to their duty in this respect. If a regard for the comfort and health of the children is not motive sufficient to rouse them, there are economic considerations which ought to prevail. No really good teacher will engage to teach in a district with a wretched, uncomfortable shell of a house, and the employment of an incompetent teacher is a waste of the money of the State and of the parents, and of the precious time of the children. The cost of warming and repairing such a house is greater. An unsightly structure, unpainted, without blinds, with loose clapboards and doors without hinges, standing unfenced by the highway, is a fair mark for snow balls and stones from every idle and mischievous boy. Nobody cares enough about it to guard it from injury and demolition. A really beautiful house would be an object of interest and pride, would be attractive to teachers and pupils, and would enlist the care and protection of trustees and inhabitants."

The act of 1866, authorizing the appraisal of and acquisition of titles to sites, was found generally acceptable and useful in accelerating the erection of new and tasteful school edifices upon commodious and well chosen sites.

The number of volumes in the several district libraries was 1,181,811, and their estimated value $652,156. The sum of $27,500 had been expended in the purchase of suitable books during the year, and $186,693 for school apparatus, $173,870.48 of which had been expended in the city, and $8,617.69 only in the rural districts.

"It is believed," says the Superintendent, "that the district libraries in the rural districts have lived beyond the day of their highest usefulness. The history which the American people have been writing for themselves during the last six years, has almost entirely absorbed the public mind, and drawn the eyes of the young and the old to the daily and weekly newspaper, and other periodical literature of the day, so that the district libraries fail to receive their just share of attention. As an evidence of this it may be stated that about one-half of the sum annually apportioned to the rural districts for this purpose, is applied to the payment of teachers' wages.

"The amount expended for teachers' wages was:

Years.	Cities.	Rural Districts.	Total.
In 1866	$2,093,042 90	$2,463,847 76	$4,556,890 66
In 1865	1,932,438 26	2,043,655 17	3,976,093 43

"From this exhibit it appears that there has been an advance in the wages paid to teachers during the year, amounting in the aggregate to $580,797.23, being in the cities $160,604.64, and in the rural districts $420,192.59. The average, for the annual salaries of teachers, as shown by he above figures, is:

In the cities	$386 94
In the rural districts	208 76

"This gives for the average weekly wages of teachers:

In the cities	$13 64
In the rural districts	6 70

"The amount raised for school purposes by local taxation during the year was:

Years.	Cities.	Rural Districts.	Total.
In 1866....................	$2,945,186 39	$1,131,539 14	$4,076,725 53
In 1865....................	2,655,544 43	845,525 75	3,501,070 20

"The sum raised by rate-bill in the rural districts—$709,025.86—and also the estimated value of the board of teachers who 'boarded around'—$478,287.91—should be added to the amount raised by tax, to show the actual sum raised by local taxation and legal contribution, making $2,316,872.41."

The aggregate amount of public money apportioned during the year was $1,468,422.22, of which $1,148,422.22 was derived from the avails of the State tax, and the remaining $320,000 from the income of the Common School and U. S. Deposit Funds. Of this amount $1,406,336.22 were distributed among the several districts—about four millions of dollars raised by tax, $709,025 by rate bill, and the remaining sum necessary for the support of schools obtained from local funds. There were expended during the year, for the maintenance of the schools in the cities, $3,330,886.39, and in the rural districts $3,302,049.55—making in all $6,632,935.94: showing an increase of $897,475.70 over the expenditure of the preceding year. The number of children attending the schools during the year was 919,309, of which 326,798 were in the cities and 592,511 in the rural districts.

The number of districts in which indigent persons were exempted from the payment of rate bills was 2,327; the number in which no such exemptions were made, 7,764. "Thus," pertinently and forcibly observes the Superintendent, "it appears that in *over eighty districts in every hundred*, upon the confession of the trustees themselves, the law authorizing these officers to exempt the poor from this burden has proved of no effect. Section 39 of Title VII of the General School Law commences thus: "The Common Schools in the several school districts of this State SHALL BE

FREE to all persons over five and under twenty-one years of age, residing in the district." But, in fact, they are free only in the same sense that good dinners at our best hotels are free dinners. *They are free to all those who will pay a good price for them.*" In the 2,327 districts where, alone, exemptions were made, they were found to amount to $47,873.56, or an average of about $2,057.00 in each.

The number of districts in which the library money was used, for the payment of teachers' wages was 7,940; and the money so used amounted to $16,443,75, or nearly one-half the entire sum apportioned to the rural districts for that purpose.

In reference to Normal Schools, the Superintendent observes:

"The law of 1866 creating a Board of Commissioners to receive and act upon proposals for the establishment of four additional Normal Schools was progress in the right direction. The public spirit and liberality displayed in various parts of the State manifesting an interest in the education of teachers, so impressed the commissioners that they recommended by a unanimous vote, the establishment of six more such institutions.

"So far, it must be acknowledged that the State of New York, considering its population and material wealth, has done comparatively little for normal instruction. It has in operation at this time only two Normal and Training Schools. The aggregate value of the property offered by different localities for the location of the four Normal Schools authorized by the law of 1866, was $900,000, showing conclusively the general appreciation of the importance of these institutions. There is, indeed, a readiness on the part of the people in many of the villages and counties to unite with the State in the establishment and maintenance of as many of them as are wanted. We shall soon have six Normal Schools in operation. The number of pupils in each at one time will hardly exceed 250; of whom not more than one hundred can be expected to graduate. The average number of graduates may, therefore, be set down at 600 annually. The number of teachers required in the State is about 16,000. It would, therefore, take a period of twenty-six years for these schools to graduate so many. This statement would be discouraging, but for the fact that each thoroughly qualified teacher imparts his skill to many of his pupils, who themselves become teachers.

"But we cannot afford to wait during the school period of three generations. Our schools cannot be innocently neglected so long. Twenty Normal

CORTLAND NORMAL SCHOOL.

Schools, with the aid of academies and Teachers' Institutes, might be adequate. I therefore respectfully recommend the passage of an act continuing in existence the commission created by chapter 466 of the laws of 1866, with power to establish, pursuant to the terms and conditions therein prescribed, at least ten more Normal Schools. I am convinced of the vital importance of such action. If the Legislature in 1815, or even thirty years ago, had adopted this policy, it would have been an actual saving of money. The evidence of it would have been seen on every hand. We should have had a greater supply of trained teachers, devoted to their calling and successful; a higher grade of Common Schools, and a larger average attendance. The consequences of our past errors are now plainly seen. But our regret is lessened by the hope that wiser counsels are about to prevail, and that this glaring omission of our school system will be supplied."

In 81 academies of the State, 363 male and 1,122 female pupils had been instructed during the preceding year for a period of four months in the science of Common School teaching; and in fifty-two counties, 62 Teachers' Institutes, numbering 8,543 teachers, had been held.

In conclusion, the Superintendent observes:

"Though not yet perfect, the school system of this State is a most excellent one—simple, yet comprehensive; democratic in character, yet strong and efficient. All school officers, from the trustees of school districts up, are elected by, and are directly responsible to, the people for the manner in which the duties of their respective offices are performed, and, in addition to this responsibility, the law has provided appropriate penalties for neglect of duty, or malfeasance in office.

"The greatest defect in our school system is, as I have urged in previous reports, the continuance of the rate-bill system. Our Common Schools can never reach their highest degree of usefulness until they shall have been made entirely free. Although our Common Schools have made rapid progress in efficiency and usefulness during the past decade, I venture to prophesy that if the Legislature shall comply with the public demand, and throw open the doors of the Public School-houses, so that all the children of the State may receive the benefits of education 'without money and without price,' their progress in the coming decade will be even greater than it has been in the past.

"To meet this public demand, to confer upon the children of the State the blessings of free education, a bill has already been introduced into your honorable body entitled 'An act to amend an act, entitled an act to revise and consolidate the acts relating to public instruction,' which meets with my fullest approbation. Every amendment to the school law, proposed by that bill, ought, in my judgment, to become a part of the law. The main features of the bill are the provisions to raise, by State tax, a sum about equal to that raised in the districts by rate-bills, and to abolish the rate-bill system; to facilitate the erection and repair of school-houses, whose character I have hereinbefore reported, by giving to the School Commissioners and Supervisors additional discretionary power in regard to them.

"Some special act is needed by which idle, poor, and truant children in the cities may be provided for, not in jails or police stations, but at Reform Schools specially adapted to their condition and improvement.

"After having fully considered the duty of the State, the just claims of her children, the public sentiment and ability, I am, in conclusion, prepared to make the following specific recommendations, and to commend them hopefully to your consideration:

"1. That the general State tax for the support of schools be increased by the addition of *one-half of a mill* on every dollar of valuation, for the purpose of diminishing local or school district taxation.

"2. That the general laws be so amended that the odious rate-bill shall no longer prevent children from going to school; that the schools shall be as free to all of proper age and condition as the air and the sunlight.

"3. That the Commission created by the Act of 1866 be continued and authorized in their discretion to locate six additional Normal Schools, upon the terms and conditions prescribed in that act.

"4. That aid be rendered to the Children's Aid Society in the City of New York, and other societies doing the same beneficent and humane work in a prudent and economical manner.

"5. That an act be passed providing a mode of taking lands for or in addition to sites for public school-houses *in the cities and villages* of the State, and of acquiring title thereto, and determining the compensation to be paid therefor.

"6. That the General School law shall be so amended that School Commissioners shall have power to cause alterations and repairs to be made on district school-houses, at an expense not exceeding $200 in any one case; and that increased power be given to the School Commissioners and Supervisors, in the matter of condemning school-houses unfit for use, so that districts owning such condemned school-houses may be *compelled* to expend a moderate sum in building new ones.

"7. That instead of the Act of 1853, in relation to idle and truant children, an act be passed requiring cities to provide that suitable tenements be erected or leased for the education of small children, and that a distinction shall be made between the idle and truant who are usually running in the streets and alleys without employment, and the vagrant and vicious who are arrested for criminal offences; that those whose only fault is idleness and truancy, for want of parental care and watchfulness, may be gathered into city schools specially provided for them, and that those who are arrested and convicted of crimes, shall be committed, not to jails and penitentiaries, like common thieves, but sent to *Reform Schools*, and be taught some useful trade. This recommendation is made in the confident belief that it is not for the good of society that even the most degraded of such children be confined in prisons with hardened criminals, or that their services be sold to contractors, either for profit or emolument, or to make a house of refuge a self-sustaining institution; that, on the contrary, the real welfare of society demands their moral reformation by kindly treatment and culture, and their instruction in some gainful industry, so that when discharged, they may be both willing and able to earn an honest living."

During the session of the Legislature of 1867, in accordance with this recommendation, an act was passed abolishing the obnoxious rate-bill system—declaring the Common Schools of the State *absolutely free* to all children of the requisite school age—increasing the State tax, for their support, to one and one-quarter mill on each dollar of the assessed valuation of property, directing and defining the mode of its distribution, and making sundry other subordinate alterations and modifications in the existing law.

From the annual report of the Superintendent, on the 9th of March, 1868, it appeared that the amount expended during the preceding year for the purchase of sites, and the building, purchasing, hiring, repairing, and insuring school-houses, fences, and out-buildings, was $1,713,107, of which $1,012,483 were expended in the cities, and $700,624 in the rural districts, being an increase of $742,882, or upward of 76 per cent., over that of any preceding year, and more than 100 per cent. over the average annual expenditure for the same purpose during the past ten years. There still, however, remained upward of 1,000 districts without school-house sites, 9,502 whose sites were uninclosed, and 2,278 without privies. "That old and dilapidated school-houses," observes the Superintendent, "destitute of provision for the light, heat, and ventilation essential to the health and comfort of their occupants, and without the out-buildings demanded by a proper regard

25

for modesty and decency, ought not to be tolerated by a Christian people, is a proposition that needs only to be stated to produce conviction. This class of school-houses is generally found in the less populous and poorer districts; and the question suggests itself, how can the disgrace of their existence in any part of the State be removed? The answer is, by the proceeds of a general State tax to encourage and aid these districts in replacing them by new and convenient buildings. To the equity and propriety of such a tax for this purpose your attention is invited." He recommends the imposition of an eighth of one mill on the dollar, in addition to the present State tax, for the term of five years, for this specific purpose.

The number of volumes in the district libraries was 1,112,011, being a decrease of nearly 70,000 from that of the preceding year. In reference to this fact, the Superintendent says:

"There can, I think, be no question that the greater part of the district libraries have, as circulating mediums of instruction, passed the meridian of their usefulness. Thirty years have wrought a great change in this respect. Books, magazines, and newspapers now find their way to nearly every household in the land, and have almost superseded the use of the circulating library. But the necessity for the continuance of the district library, as a means of reference for the studious of both sexes, will always remain. This view of the subject calls for increased exertions in this department.

"The fact that more than half of the library money apportioned is expended for the payment of teachers' wages is evidence, if there were no other, that the libraries are no longer generally held in high estimation by the people. But there is other evidence. The law provides that 'the taxable inhabitants of each school district in the State shall have power, when lawfully assembled in any district meeting, to lay a tax on the district, not exceeding ten dollars in any one year, for the purchase of such books as they shall direct for the district library, and such further sum as they may deem necessary for the purchase of a book-case.' Yet the instances in which this tax is levied are rare. In the 12,000 school districts in the State, including those in cities, there are only 8,690 book-cases.

"It is notorious that in a very large number of districts the preservation of the books is not a matter of solicitude on the part of school-district officers. It has already been stated that the number of books reported in the libraries is

69,800 less than was reported for the previous year. This large discrepancy is attributable to the fact that some of the trustees report regularly by guess, without attempting to count the books, while others report in a similar manner, after vainly endeavoring to find volumes that are scattered among the inhabitants, and have grown old, dusty, and worm-eaten since they were laid by in garrets and dark corners. Nothing is expended for the care of the libraries, and the money appropriated for their support is not half enough to keep them in repair. The selection and purchase of books is left to the trustees, who have not the opportunity to make choice selections, but are compelled to make their purchases of retail dealers, at retail prices.

"These facts are adverse to any hope that the libraries, as at present managed, will grow in usefulness, and increase in favor with the people. A radical change is needed. Provision should be made for a much larger annual appropriation, for the selection of books upon a wiser and more economical plan, and for their better preservation. This appropriation ought to amount to at least ten dollars for each library. The books should be selected and purchased by a commission composed of gentlemen of unquestioned integrity and ability. Their distribution might be based upon the population of the districts, or the number of children of school age.

"It is confidently believed that if intelligent women were elected to the office of school district librarian, the books now missing would, within a single year, be collected from their hiding places. In the rural districts, the libraries are generally deposited in dwelling-houses, where woman presides, and their care would be in the line of her duties. Women are now the successful teachers of nearly all of the district schools, and no reason is apparent why they may not share those district offices for which, by nature and education, they are as admirably adapted as for the instruction of children."

The number of children in attendance upon the several schools during the year 1867 was 949,203, being an increase of upward of 30,000 over the preceding year. The amount expended for teachers' wages was $4,826,471.64, of which $2,217,028.94 were expended in the cities, and $2,609,442.70 in the rural districts, being an increase of $267,580 over the aggregate expenditure for this purpose of the preceding year.

The public money applicable to school purposes for the year reported was $2,400,134.65, of which $2,080,134.65 was derived from the State school tax, and the remainder from the Common School and deposit fund. Of this amount, $2,232,083.65 were apportioned among the several districts for the year 1868.

The total expenditures of the several districts for the year 1867 were as follows:

For teacher's wages	$4,826,471 64
For libraries	24,439 25
For apparatus	211,665 47
For colored schools	66,418 93
For school-houses, sites, &c.	1,718,107 01
For incidental expenses	830,706 83
For fixtures	887 80
	$7,685,201 93

Leaving a balance on hand, October 1, of $1,065,125.46.

Of the amounts thus expended, $3,092,893.20 were expended in the cities, and $3,090,308.02 in the rural districts, showing an increase of upward of $1,000,000 over the preceding year.

In 8,400 districts, the library money, to the amount of $17,587.47, was appropriated to the payment of teachers' wages.

The State Normal Schools at Albany, Oswego, Brockport, and Fredonia were in successful operation. Similar institutions were in progress, under authority of law, in Potsdam, St. Lawrence county, Cortland, Geneseo, and Buffalo.

"It is assumed," observes the Superintendent, "that the State has the ability to establish and maintain as many of these schools as are needed; and we have only to inquire, 'How many are necessary?' To this inquiry your attention is invited. There are in this State over 11,700 school districts. While the schools are in session, they employ constantly about 16,000 teachers; but the whole number annually employed, at different times, is over twenty-six thousand. This proves conclusively, that a large proportion of those who offer themselves as instructors make school teaching only a temporary business. Those who are most thoroughly qualified for the position, and who devote their whole time to it, are found, as a general rule, in the service of the cities and more populous villages, to which they are attracted by larger salaries. It is notorious that a large proportion of the rural districts are obliged to accept the services of persons who have had comparatively little special preparation for their work; and it is equally certain that this condition of things must continue so long as the State shall

BROCKPORT NORMAL SCHOOL.

be satisfied with the limited provision made for the special education of teachers.

"When the eight Normal Schools, for which provision has been made, shall have been in operation for several years, they will not maintain a constant supply of more than four thousand teachers, including both graduates and undergraduates. From the teachers' classes in the academies we may expect a thousand more; but these will be quite young persons—boys and girls, who will have spent but four months in special preparation. This is a short time, indeed, in which to compass the human understanding, and gain a clear conception of the laws of its healthful and vigorous growth. It can only be said, in favor of these classes, that they furnish teachers who are more useful than those of the same natural ability who have not received any special training.

"Teachers' Institutes are attended by all classes of teachers. It will have been observed that, during the past year, over nine thousand were thus assembled for a mutual interchange of views and experience. Thus the Institutes become the annual reviews of the State's armies of educators, which serve to remind them that by self-improvement they must keep step with the march of their profession, and that promotion awaits those only who press to the front. The Institutes will always be needed, no matter how many Normal Schools may be supported; but we cannot look to them for the thorough culture and discipline of mind acquired at these schools.

"When all the Normal Schools, now provided for, shall be in successful operation, they cannot, even with the aid of teachers' classes in the academies, and Teachers' Institutes, supply one-half of the Common Schools with qualified teachers. We need, certainly, as many more of those schools. The people have expressed a hearty willingness to aid the State in this matter. Already, in many eligible localities, they have offered to the State, as a gift, suitable, commodious, and well-furnished buildings. 'As is the teacher, so is the school,' is a precept that is rapidly gaining significance in the public mind. It must assume still greater importance, as a knowledge of the proper mode of conducting schools shall become more general and discriminating. In evidence of this fact, it may be stated that, during the past year, more applications were made to the Department for 'teachers of high character and qualifications' than for several preceding years. They were accompanied, for the most part, by the offer of liberal salaries; but no considerable number of such teachers could be found, who were unemployed; and, in too many instances, the applicants were obliged to accept of inferior services. At the best, the majority of the schools must meet with long and impatient delays in securing such teachers. It is to avoid these delays, and to secure the necessary and steady supply of competent instructors, that I recommend the passage of an act, which shall continue in existence the commission created by chapter 466 of the Laws of 1866, with power to locate, at any time within two years, at least four additional Normal and Training Schools upon the terms and conditions prescribed by that act."

In the teachers' classes in the several academies 1,400 pupils were instructed during the year, of whom 1,000 were females; and in the 66 Teachers' Institutes 9,676 teachers were in attendance, 7,000 of whom were females. The Superintendent says:

"Since 1854, these temporary Normal Schools have been growing in usefulness and in public favor, until they are justly regarded as an essential agency in the preparation of teachers.

"It is not claimed that these Institutes make superior scholars, but it is the unqualified testimony of those most competent to judge correctly that they impart more information in regard to the proper organization, government and instruction of schools than can be gained elsewhere in the same time, and at so little expense.

"It is a well-known fact, which may be stated without detracting from the merits of any one, that those who follow teaching for any considerable time are liable to become 'stereotyped and opinionated.' They are in daily contact with those who, by position, age, and acquirements, are their inferiors, and therefore do not presume to scrutinize or question how they teach or what they teach. No urgent necessity compels them to self-examination; to review the opinions and practices to which they have become accustomed and attached; hence they do not seek and examine for new sources of knowledge. They deem themselves equal to a task which does not enforce its demand for frequently renewed and varied effort. They are wedded to their theories and modes of instruction, and will so remain unless their errors are revealed to them by the light of discussion with their equals or superiors. These tendencies are counteracted at the Institutes. The more mature in years and experience are led, by a mutual interchange of opinions and sentiments, to abandon many false theories and practices, and to adopt others whose proper application in their schools awakens their ingenuity and enforces thought and research to which they have not before been accustomed; while the younger class of teachers acquire a certain amount of knowledge of their practical duties which they have no other opportunity to learn, and are also matured in their purpose to devote themselves zealously and cheerfully to their new vocation."

Respecting Teachers' Associations, he observes:

"Somewhat akin to the Institutes are the Teachers' Associations, which in some instances embrace the teachers of a town; in others the teachers of a Commissioner's district; and in others still the teachers of a county.

"They are in session one or two days, and are devoted chiefly to the interchange of friendly greetings, and to the illustration of methods in the practice of teaching. School officers and other citizens share with the teachers in the exercises. Their beneficient influence is not questioned, and their formation is encouraged by the School Commissioners and approved by this Department.

"The last session of the New York State Teachers' Association, held at Auburn, in the month of August last, was largely attended by the energetic, enthusiastic, and influential teachers from all parts of the State. Those who do most crowd the advance in the march of improvement were there; and it is encouraging that so respectable and influential a body of persons unanimously and heartily adopted resolutions approving of the establishment of more Normal Schools, and of making all the public schools free."

Of Union Free School Districts, he says:

"The Union Free School Act, which was passed in 1853 and amended in 1864, has contributed materially to the establishment and maintenance of a superior class of graded schools, and has diminished the number of applications for special laws to meet the increasing demand for such schools in districts thickly populated. In many cases there was a consolidation of two or more school districts for the purpose. Under the operation of this law enlarged powers are exercised, and sufficient property is associated to permit the incurring of heavier expenditure for school-houses and the employment of a proper number of competent teachers. Owing to the fact that in such districts the schools were free, the aggregate and regular attendance of pupils was largely increased. There being in many of them a gradation of departments from primary to academical, the labor of teachers was more effectively divided. It may be said in reference to their higher departments that in range and quality of instruction they have compared favorably with the best academies. They are generally provided with all necessary scientific apparatus, and are all under the immediate charge and supervision of boards of education, to whose zeal, fidelity, and intelligence as school officers, I have the utmost pleasure in bearing testimony."

In conclusion, the Superintendent thus alludes to the new Free School Act of 1867:

"The law passed at the last session of the Legislature, commonly known as the 'Free School Act,' is meeting the most sanguine hopes of its advocates. It took effect on the 1st day of October, 1867; and already the local school officers report an average daily attendance of pupils at the schools, twenty to thirty per cent. greater than it was during the same period of the year previous. In many districts, and particularly where there is a large proportion of foreign-born population, it has been found necessary to increase the accommodations, from this cause. They also report that the provisions of the act by which a general State tax is substituted for 'the odious rate-bill' is almost unanimously approved.

"The entire support of the schools by State taxation is not advocated. On the contrary, it is believed that any plan devised to make the burden of their support more nearly equal, should include district taxation to an amount sufficient to make the care of the school property, and economy of expenditure, matters of local interest. In my judgment, also, competition for the best school-houses, best teachers, and the best schools ought to be encouraged; and the expense of superior privileges thus gained ought to be paid by those who incur it and enjoy its immediate benefits. But the fact recurs that there is no just proportion between the State and local taxation; that the latter is now more than four times as great as the former. In evidence of this, let the fact be repeated that for the support of schools during the past school year, there was raised:

By local taxation	$5,101,754 59
By State tax	1,148,422 28

"This tax was increased one-half of a mill on each dollar of valuation, by chapter 406 of the laws of 1867, and the proceeds for the present and succeeding years will be about two millions of dollars. If you shall not deem it wise to increase this tax, the hope is cherished that you will have no occasion to diminish it.

"After having fully considered the duty of the State, the just claims of her children, the public interest in our schools, and the ability of the people to advance their welfare, I am prepared to make the following specific recommendation:

"The levying of a tax for five successive years of one eighth of a mill upon each dollar of taxable property in the State, for the purpose of aiding in the erection and improvement of school-houses and their appurtenances. The proceeds of this tax shall be apportioned among the cities and rural districts upon the same bases, except the basis of attendance, that the school moneys are now apportioned. The amount thus assigned to the several cities may be appropriated immediately, as their respective boards of education or other authorities shall determine, for the building or furnishing of school-houses, or the compensation of teachers. But the county treasurers shall not pay to any rural school district its share of such money, except upon a certificate by the School Commissioner and Supervisor of the town in which the district is situated, to the effect that their school-house is commodious, in good condition, and provided with all necessary conveniences. In cases where the money is withheld, it shall be retained by him, from year to year, till such certificate shall be presented. No district thus failing, for one or more years, to comply with this condition, shall forfeit the money withheld from it, provided that the omission shall not extend beyond the sixth year. At the end of this period, all such moneys remaining in the hands of any county treasurer shall be finally re-apportioned, in the same manner as other school moneys, to the several school districts in such county."

During this year the CORNELL UNIVERSITY was opened at Ithaca. A large number of people were in attendance during the inaugural ceremonies. The free scholarships provided by law in each of the assembly districts of the State, numbering 128, were filled by the proper appointments, and about 400 pupils admitted to the course of instruction. Of this institution the Governor, Lieutenant-Governor and Superintendent of Public Instruction, are *ex-officio* Trustees. Its funds consist of the avails of the College Land Scrip for 990,000 acres of public lands, donated as the share of the State of New York, by the Government of the United States, under the act of July 2, 1862, for the establishment of colleges in the several States for the benefit of agriculture and the mechanic arts and military science; and appropriated by the State in 1865, to the institution, of a munificent donation by EZRA CORNELL, the founder, of $500,000; together with a farm of two hundred acres, and a site for the University, valued at $500,000; and $10,000 for a cabinet of the Paleontology of New York. The selection of one pupil from each of the assembly districts of the State, for gratuitous instruction, is required to be made from those possessing the highest scholarship in the public schools and academies of the State, giving preference to the sons of those who have died in the military or naval service of the United States. "If this design," says Superintendent RICE, in his annual report for 1868, "be fully carried out, the Cornell University, *becomes the very cream of our Public School System.* Its students being selected because of superior mental and physical capacity, should be superior to those of any other University in the world. A wise provision at the outset forestalls all sectarian or religious preferences, as well as distinctions of rank or previous occupation, respecting eligibility to appointments or offices." The Hon. ANDREW D. WHITE, of Ithaca, is President of the institution, and GOLDWIN SMITH, of Oxford University, England, fills the chair of Political Economy.

SECTION II.—ADMINISTRATION OF SUPERINTENDENT ABRAM B. WEAVER—1868 TO 1871.

Annual Reports.—Condition of the Common Schools.—Prosperous Workings of the System.—District Libraries.—Perversion of the Fund for their Support.—Normal Schools.—Teachers' Departments in Academies.—Teachers' Institutes.—Union Free Schools.—Indian Schools.—Proposed Creation of a State Board of Education.—Condition of the Several City Public Schools.—General Statistical Summary.

ON the second Tuesday in February, 1868, ABRAM B. WEAVER of Oneida was appointed, on joint ballot of the Legislature, Superintendent of Public Instruction. Mr. WEAVER was a young man of promising abilities, great vigor of character, and considerable experience as a school officer. On entering upon the discharge of his new duties, he appears to have fully appreciated and adopted the advanced views and principles which had been incorporated into the system of Public Instruction by his predecessors, and immediately to have addressed himself to the reformation of all its faults and excrescences. EDWARD DANFORTH, Esq., for many years the able and efficient City Superintendent of Troy, was appointed Deputy State Superintendent.

The Superintendent, in his annual report of 1869, observes:

"The work of public instruction for the year ending Sept. 30, 1868, was prosecuted under new auspices. While the general structure of the school law was not disturbed, a material modification was made by the act of 1867, which took effect on the first day of October thereafter, and which, among other things, provided for the abolishment of rate-bills, and for increased local and State taxation for school purposes. This was, primarily, a change in the manner of raising the requisite funds; not an absolute increase of the aggregate amount to be raised. It involved and encouraged such increase, so far as the inhabitants in the several school districts should authorize it by substituting taxation exclusively on property, for a mixed assessment which, in part, was a tax on attendance.

"Thus relieved of an old impediment, and supplied with additional power and larger resources, the cause of public instruction, during the last fiscal year, has wrought results unequaled in all the past, and which, if they correctly denote a corresponding growth in the popular estimate of the value and advantages of our public schools, mark the beginning of a new and more auspicious era in the development of the educational system of the State. The effect of this amendment has not been confined to the financial policy thereby inaugurated. It is distinctly traceable in lengthened terms of school, in a larger and more uniform attendance, and in more liberal expenditures for school buildings and appliances. We are now enabled to study the influence of this measure for the first year of its operation, and to judge of its merits in the light of a limited experience. The liberal and progressive spirit that authorized it, will not fail to watch its workings with unabated interest.

"The State is fully committed to the policy of providing for all the children within its limits the opportunity to acquire at least a sound elementary education, sufficient for the duties of good citizenship and for personal usefulness. This comprehensive plan is not entirely new. It is the natural outgrowth and development of the original enterprise initiated by establishing Common Schools in 1812. With the exception of a brief period under the operation of the Free School law of 1849, which was declared unconstitutional by the courts on account of its conditional enactment, the system, as organized and conducted prior to the late change, though as efficient as could well be expected under conditions then existing, and entitled to lasting gratitude and respect for the good it has accomplished, never completely compassed the principles upon which it rested.

"The public considerations that induce the State to engage in this work distinctly recognize the proposition, that the education of all the children of all classes and conditions in society is essential to the highest welfare of the whole community, and that suitable provision for such education is a matter of common concern. But, as a large part of the expense was dependent upon attendance, and as the penalty of that attendance was the imposition of a rate-bill, it resulted that many children whose parents were unable or unwilling to incur that charge, and whose early associations were least calculated to direct them into the paths of learning, were deterred from attending the schools. This practice increased the expense for those who did attend, and that again reduced the number, while the two causes co-operating occasioned great waste of opportunity and effort, and speedily dispersed the schools after the public moneys were consumed. That chronic defect has, in a measure, been remedied by the recent reform. The State, having by its legislation, by its appropriations, by its supervision, by all its dealings with this question, pronounced in favor of popular education, and having labored for years to accomplish it, has at length adopted means more nearly commensurate with the work in hand. Our schools, heretofore common in theory and name, are now really so in practice; and since the first day of October, 1867, the inducement has been to enter them, and to enjoy unconditional advantages in the nature of compensation for attendance, instead of staying away to avoid contingent expenses."

The number of districts in the State now amounted to 11,736; and the number of children under instruction to 970,842, being an increase of upward of 21,000 over that of the preceding year. The whole number of children between the ages of five and twenty-one years, residing in the State, was reported at 1,464,669, although the accuracy of the enumeration was questioned by the Superintendent. The increased average attendance over the preceding year in the rural districts was 24,657, from which the Superintendent observes: "the conclusion is direct and inevitable, that by the abolition of the rate-bill the school-house doors have been opened to many against whom they were heretofore practically barred." The amount of public money received in the several districts during the year reported was $10,511,677.60, of which $2,302,515.70 were from the avails of the Common School and U. S. Deposit Funds and the State 1¼ mill tax, and $6,338,861.77 raised by local tax; and there were expended $9,040,942.02 for teachers' wages, libraries, school apparatus, sites, buildings, and other incidental expenses, being an INCREASE OF $1,357,740.80 over the preceding year. The sum expended for teachers' wages alone was $5,597,506.94—an increase of upward of $771,000! The total avails of the State tax were $2,207,611.42. The number of volumes in the several district libraries had diminished from 1,604,210 in 1853 to 1,064,830, verifying the prediction of Superintendent MORGAN in 1850, that if the precedent of a diversion of any part of this fund to any other purpose than the purchase of suitable books, "were once established, under whatever limitations or restrictions, and however warranted by the peculiar circumstances of particular cases, the inevitable result would be a more or less speedy absorption of the entire fund, and a virtual extinction of the whole library system." "The value of a good library," says Superintendent WEAVER, "as an instrumentality for disseminating useful knowledge, awakening a love for science and literature, and promoting general intelligence, when it is properly appreciated and used, is well understood, and doubtless accounts for the constancy with which the State has adhered to the system, even in its waning condition. It is equally clear that the liberality that has expended nearly two millions of dollars to convey these advantages to the people, in a practical form, has not been reciprocated by a judicious selection and proper care of the books. The annual reports from this department, since 1843, have, almost without exception, complained of delinquencies in these respects. Superintendent VAN DYCK, in his report for 1861, says, "Concurrent testimony from nearly every quarter of the State represents the libraries in the rural districts as almost totally unused, and rapidly deteriorating in value." These accounts are substantially corroborated in several reports by Superintendent RICE. It is quite manifest that the result to which these indications unmistakably point may be reached by a process more easy and economical than that now pursued. If the system is to be revived and preserved, it should receive prompt and thorough action to rescue it from utter failure."

The attendance upon the several Teachers' Institutes throughout the State was larger than ever before, amounting to 10,377, more than 82 per cent. of the whole number of teachers employed in all the district schools of the State.

In addition to the Normal Schools at Albany and Oswego, six new institutions of a similar kind had been established, in accordance with the acts of 1866, 1867, and 1868, at Brockport, Fredonia, Cortland, Potsdam, Genesco, and Buffalo. Classes for instruction in the "science of Common School teaching," had been maintained during the past year in eighty-nine academies of the State, in which 1,489 pupils were in attendance, 426 of whom were males, and 1,026 females.

In conclusion, the Superintendent observes:

"In response to the statutory requisition for 'plans and suggestions for the improvement of the schools and the advancement of public instruction in the State,' I have no radical theories to propose. In my judgment, real progress is not to be promoted by efforts of that kind, at this juncture. So far as the public schools are concerned, the State is in possession of educational machinery, the product of long time, earnest thought, and large experience, recently molded, and newly put into operation. To introduce abrupt changes now, would involve the abandonment of plans which, upon their first trial, have produced the best results ever attained, and promise, in their maturity, still more abundant success. The existing system, though by no means complete, is much more perfect in structure than in operation, and it seems to be the dictate of sound policy to labor for improvement by a strict and vigorous administration in all its parts. While the gratifying progress already achieved is no excuse for tolerating admitted defects, it is not to be forgotten that the best theories must bend in their application to unyielding circumstances. A systematic gradation of all our schools, in such a manner that scholars could advance from primary instruction through an orderly and progressive course of study, would be an unquestionable advantage. In the cities and villages, where the concentration of population affords facilities that do not exist in the rural districts, this plan has been adopted with the most satisfactory results. But it is a primary requirement that the public schools be accessibly located, to be generally useful, and this will perpetuate the problem of perfecting mixed schools, such as we now have, composed of scholars of diverse ages and degrees of advancement. This, in my estimation is not to be solved by an overstrained attempt to introduce a multiplicity of studies, many of them beyond the grasp and capacity of those to whom they may be assigned, but rather by the dissemination of such just views, through the agency of supervision, as shall beget a wholesome public sentiment, constraining attendance, and by thorough and rational instruction in the elementary branches. Unsound scholarship, decorated with the ornamental drapery of superficial learning, in mockery of education, is a sham that deserves to be disrobed. Advanced study is not to be despised, when well grounded. But the first and broad necessity is to furnish the best possible instruction in the Common Schools, where the masses of the people receive their only tuition, and in the common branches, which all men and women need to understand. To this end it will be my endeavor to use such authority and means as may be intrusted to me by the Legislature."

On the 3d of February, 1870, the Superintendent transmitted to the Legislature his second annual report.

"The people of this State," he observed, "evidently await the annual account of the operation and condition of their system of public instruction, with expectations corresponding to the magnitude, character, and cost of the work. There is no other department of their government for which they pay so much and so cheerfully; none so essential to their welfare; none so deeply imbedded in their affections. They regard it as the source of their social happiness; the conservator of public order; the foundation of their political privileges. It conveys to their homes the blessings of intelligence and refinement; it does more than any other agency to render theoretical equality actual; and affords the most certain assurance that our free institutions shall continue. Those who have such a great interest at stake are naturally solicitous concerning its management. They have a right to demand that the system shall be conscientiously administered; that the funds dedicated to the support of the schools shall be faithfully applied; and that the instruction given shall be pure and thorough." * *

"The effort to extend to all the youth in the State the advantages of education, during the year reported, closing Sept. 30, 1869, was more than ordinarily successful. Even the remarkable improvement that occurred during the first year of departure from rate-bills has been not only sustained, but surpassed; and the statistics, herewith submitted, show results for the second year of the operation of the FREE SCHOOL SYSTEM, which commend it to the confidence and support of all who believe that UNIVERSAL EDUCATION is the end to be attained."

The whole number of school districts in the State was 11,748, with 11,703 school-houses, the reported value of which, together with the sites, was $18,449,048, and their average value in the cities, $29,400.52, and in the rural districts, $678.17.

"These figures show," observes the Superintendent, "that the average value of school-houses in the rural districts is nearly *fifty-seven per cent.* greater than it was three years ago. This rapid increase in value proves that the people appreciate the importance of comfortable and commodious school-houses, and that, encouraged by a State system which promises stability, and which affords increased facilities each year for the acquirement of useful instruction, they are willing to tax themselves largely to assist in carrying out the plan." The amount expended during the year 1860 for school-houses, out-houses, sites, fences, furniture, and repairs was $2,455,453, of which $1,401,464 was expended in the cities, and $1,053,999 in the rural districts.

The whole number of children between the ages of five and twenty-one, residing in the several districts, was 1,463,299, of whom 607,583 were in the cities, and 855,716 in the rural districts. Of these, 998,664 attended the Common Schools during some portion of the year, being an increase of nearly 28,000 over the attendance of the preceding year. The average daily attendance was 468,421. Since the abolition of the rate-bill system both the aggregate and average attendance had largely increased, while the school term had been considerably lengthened, "thus justifying," says the Superintendent, "the prophecies of the friends of the plan of free education, and even exceeding their most sanguine expectations." The schools had been kept open, throughout the State, for an average period of thirty-five weeks, during the year.

The whole number of pupils instructed in the several Common Schools, Normal Schools, academies colleges, and private schools of the State, during the year 1860, was 1,161,155,—showing upwards of 300,000 children residing in the State, between the ages of five and twenty-one, not under instruction in any of these institutions, during any portion of the year. The number of teachers employed in the several Common Schools, during the year, was 28,310, of whom 6,230 were males, and 22,080, females, at an average annual salary of $642.87, in the cities, and $267.86, in the rural districts, or $15.16 per week in the former, and $7.86 in the latter. The amount expended for teachers' wages, during the year, was $6,029,180.59, of which $2,790,068.90 were expended in the cities, and $3,302,111.69 in the rural districts, showing an aggregate increase of nearly *half a million of dollars* over the preceding year. The number of volumes in the district libraries was 1,026,130: it appearing from previous reports of the Department that, in about 8,000 districts, the library money had been transferred, by a vote of the inhabitants, to the purchase of school apparatus and the payment of teachers' wages.

The avails of the State school tax of one and one-quarter mills upon each dollar of the assessed valuation of the State

for the first fiscal year reported were	$2,207,000 00
The receipts from the Common School fund	170,000 00
" " " U. S. Deposits fund	165,000 00
	$2,542,000 00

Of this amount, $2,425,822.36 were apportioned among the several counties, towns, and districts, for the support of schools. The sums raised by city and district tax for the same purpose, in accordance with the provisions of the Act of 1867, were, in the former, $4,243,631.02, and in the latter, $2,671,622.24,—amounting in all to $6,915,253.86. These funds, together with $30,478.12, derived from the proceeds of local school funds, $322,928.05, the estimated value of teachers' board in the rural districts, and $223,304.24, derived from other sources, together with the balance remaining on hand, unexpended from the preceding year, $1,394,538.63, amounting in all to $11,312,325.36, was expended in the following manner:

	Cities.	Rural districts.	Totals.
For teachers' wages........	$2,790,068 90	$3,302,111 69	$6,092,180 59
For libraries..............	11,703 62	15,194 03	26,897 65
For school apparatus......	177,741 71	23,741 77	201,483 48
For colored schools.........	58,863 82	6,006 18	64,870 00
For school-houses, sites, &c.,	1,401,464 03	1,053,993 98	2,455,458 01
For incidental expenses....	641,113 43	404,921 41	1,046,034 84
Forfeitures................		866 62	866 62
Balance on hand, Oct. 1....	1,206,575 32	218,963 75	1,425,539 07
	$6,287,031 03	$5,025,294 33	$11,312,325 36

Deducting from these totals the amount remaining on hand, the actual expense of maintaining the schools for the year 1869 was,

In the cities..................................	$5,080,455 71
In the rural districts..........................	4,806,330 58
Total..	$9,886,786 29

Showing an increase of $845,844.27 over the preceding year.

Under the provisions of the act of 1853, permitting the inhabitants of adjoining districts to resolve themselves into Union Free School districts, with boards of education possessing authority to grade and classify the several schools under their charge, and other special powers, about two hundred and fifty of these Union Schools had been organized, chiefly in villages and thickly populated towns.

"The condition of the school district libraries," says the Superintendent, "is notorious. To describe it, would be simply to rehearse, with little variation, the oft repeated story of neglect and waste that may be found in every annual report from this Department for the last fifteen years. Popular indifference is much to blame for this deplorable condition; but *the lax policy of the State, which has permitted the library money to be used for other purposes, is still more culpable.* Except in the comparatively few cases of cities and populous districts, where the amount of money received has been considerable, and has been faithfully applied, the system (if such it can properly be called, as now regulated by law), *is little better than a bungling device to fritter away $55,000 annually*, under the pretense of increasing, but with the practical effect, as the statistics show, of reducing the number of books from year to year. A plan originally framed to befriend libraries, has been vitiated by later enactments, so that it has operated to rob them, destroy respect for them, and well nigh ruin them. The management of the system is suicidal. With one hand, the State deals out money to the districts for the professed object of supporting the libraries, and at the same time, with the other hand, offers a permit to apply the funds to other uses, with a suggestion, if not an open recommendation, to do so. That practice, as was predicted years ago by Superintendent MORGAN, has proved demoralizing and ruinous. From 1838 till 1851, the towns were required to provide an amount equal to that furnished by the State. The people then understood that the enterprise was esteemed worthy the support derived from both these sources; and they correctly judged that books were worth caring for and using. During that period there was such a steady growth, that in 1853 the whole number of volumes amounted to 1,604,210. From that time the effect of *relinquishing the contribution from the towns* began to manifest itself, and the decline commenced. But in 1858 a more pernicious provision was adopted, allowing districts upon certain conditions, which have been sometimes complied with, but more frequently disregarded, to use the money for apparatus and teachers' wages. The decline was thereby accelerated, and has continued without interruption; so that in 1858, the whole number of volumes was 1,402,238; in 1863, 1,172,404; in 1868, 1,064,880, and in 1869, 1,026,130. Thus it appears that since 1853, there has been a decrease of more than half a million in the number of books reported, notwithstanding there has been apportioned to the districts $880,000 of library money!

"Such is the lamentable exhibition of the thriftless policy the State is pursuing, and of the disastrous end to which that course is rapidly tending. *The system should be promptly and thoroughly reformed, or speedily abolished. I recommend that it be reformed.* * * * * *

"The first thing to be done, is to change the too-well grounded popular impression, that the State is not in earnest in this matter. It is indispensable that the public mind be firmly impressed with the conviction *that the library money is to be sacredly applied to the purchase of books, and that on no pretext whatever shall one cent of it be used for any other object.* Entertaining this view, I have ceased to exercise the discretionary authority now vested in the Superintendent, to allow a diversion of the money; and have determined not to grant hereafter any permission of that kind. *The provision of law conferring that power should be repealed;* and each district, before it shall have the right to draw from the supervisor the money apportioned to it for a library, should be required to raise an equal sum for the same object."

Fifty-six Teachers' Institutes were held during the year reported, with an attendance during two weeks of 3,009 male and 6,466 female teachers.

The number of Indian schools in operation, in the several reservations, was twenty-six; the number of teachers employed 39, of whom 17 were Indians. Upwards of one thousand pupils were in attendance during portions of the year, with an average daily attendance of 482, during a period of thirty-three weeks.

Six Normal Schools were in successful operation in different sections of the State—at Albany, Oswego, Brockport, Cortland, Potsdam and Buffalo. An additional one at Geneseo was in process of erection. The whole number of pupils under instruction in these institutions, including those in the model and primary departments, was upwards of 4,000

Teachers' classes had also been maintained in ninety academies designated for that purpose by the Regents of the University, with an attendance of 540 male and 1,000 female pupils.

The annual convention of School Commissioners and City Superintendents, was held at Ithaca, in July, simultaneously with the meeting of the State Teachers' Association.

During the session of the Legislature of 1869, a bill was introduced in the Assembly "to abolish the Board of Regents of the University, and to establish a State Board of Education," charged with the general supervision of all the public schools, academies and colleges in the State, and with the administration of the laws relating to them. This bill was referred to the Committee on Public Education, who, without expressing any opinion upon its merits, reported it for the consideration of the House, together with a resolution, which was adopted, instructing the Superintendent of Public Instruction to report to the next Legislature what legislation, if any, in his judgment was necessary to place the colleges, academies, and free schools of the State, under a more efficient management.

In answer to this resolution, the Superintendent, after recapitulating the distinctive powers, duties, and functions of these several institutions, and of the officers delegated by the State with their general and special supervision, and discussing the practicability of placing the instruction furnished by the several academies on the same footing with those of the Common Schools—a measure which he deems inexpedient and unwise, except by the voluntary action of those immediately interested in such action—recommends the passage of an act containing the following leading proposition: "That the Board of Regents be made part of the Department of Education, as are commissioners and other school officers, having specific duties substantially the same as those now performed by them, and in addition that they be required to visit and inspect the several Normal Schools; that their report be made to the head of the Department; and that it be incorporated in his annual report to the Legislature, so that one document may present a complete view of the working of the entire system of education in the State."

With reference to the proposition for the establishment of a State Board of Education, the Superintendent conclusively demonstrates the comparative inefficiency of such a Board, however ably constituted, as a substitute for a single executive officer charged with the general supervision of the entire system; and in conclusion observes:

"The Public School system of this State is but an orderly plan of the people to educate themselves. For more than half a century they have been engaged in perfecting it, adopting every known improvement, with little regard to expense. From a partial and humble provision at the outset, they have built it up to the present comprehensive proportions, which embraces every locality and every class, and manage it with a liberality that offers to all a free and sufficient education. *They will permit alterations for the better, but they will not consent to its disintegration.* Experience has demonstrated to their satisfaction that the enterprise is profitable, and they desire to have it perpetuated. The popular intelligence in this State is worth more than it cost; and is priceless to those who would be without it but for the Public Schools. * * * * * * * *

"The simplest duty the State can exact of public officers is fidelity to the trust committed to their care. I RESPECTFULLY RECOMMEND THAT THE FREE SCHOOL SYSTEM BE GENEROUSLY SUPPORTED, AND THAT ITS INTEGRITY BE PRESERVED. THIS EXPRESSION OF MY OWN JUDGMENT, I BELIEVE, SPEAKS A PUBLIC SENTIMENT TOO EMPHATIC TO BE MISUNDERSTOOD, TOO JUST TO BE DISOBEYED, TOO STRONG TO BE RESISTED, AND, I TRUST, ACCORDS WITH THE DISPOSITION OF THE LEGISLATURE."

In the city of NEW YORK, the whole number of schools under the jurisdiction of the Board of Education, in 1853, the period when the consolidation of the Public and Ward Schools took effect, was 269, consisting of 52 Grammar Schools for boys, 52 for girls, 110 Primary Departments and Schools, 14 Colored Schools, 10 Corporate and Asylum Schools, 27 Evening Schools, 3 Saturday Normal Schools, and the Free Academy. The whole number of pupils taught during the year was 123,530, which in 1862 had increased to 192,684, and in 1870 to 239,612, with an average daily attendance of 103,708. The number of teachers employed in 1853 was 925, of whom 781 were females. In 1862, this number had increased to 1,896, of whom 1,700 were females, and in 1870, to 2,683, of whom 2,320 were females. The aggregate amount of expenditures for the support of the schools, during the year 1853, was $917,853.32, of which $785,141.64 were raised by city taxation. Of this aggregate amount about $400,000 were expended in the payment of teachers' wages, $40,000 in the support of the Free Academy, $6,000 for Normal Schools, $32,635 for Evening Schools, $19,548 for the Corporate Schools, $70,000 for the supply of text-books, stationery, &c., $9,760 for rent of school buildings, $16,000 for repairs, $200,000 for the purchase of sites and the building and furnishing of school-houses, and $100,000 for other incidental expenses of the Board of Education. In 1862, this aggregate had increased to $1,648,317.43, of which $1,143,540.85 had been raised by city taxation; $622,977 were paid for teachers' wages, $82,958 for school apparatus and supplies, $16,195 for Colored Schools, $285,000 for building, repairing, and furnishing school-houses, and the purchase of sites, and $177,000 for incidental expenses of the Board, salaries of officers, &c. In 1870, the aggregate amount expended was $2,817,000, of which $1,959,783 were raised by city taxation. The amount expended for teachers' wages was $1,809,243; for school apparatus and supplies, $136,970; for Colored Schools, $41,837; for building, repairing, and furnishing school-houses, and the purchase of sites, $398,86; and for incidental expenses of the Board, and salaries of its officers, $300,000. The estimated value of school-houses and sites was $6,020,000, of which $520,000 were invested in sites; and the number of volumes in the school libraries was 10,075, valued at $5,000.

On the 30th of April, 1869, an Act was passed changing the composition of the Board of Education from elective Commissioners, representing the seven districts into which the city had been formed by a previous act for this purpose, to twelve Commissioners, to be originally designated by the Mayor, and, after the year 1871, elected by the people on separate tickets, containing the names of seven only of the candidates, leaving the remaining five to be appointed by the Mayor from the candidates receiving the next highest votes—the Commissioners so elected and appointed to hold office for the term of three years.

The Board of Commissioners appointed by Mayor HALL, under the provisions of this act, and who are to serve during the present year, were RICHARD L. LARREMORE, TIMOTHY BRENNAN, SAMUEL A. LEWIS, WILLIAM E. DURYEA, WILLIAM WOOD, JOHN H. SHERWOOD, NATHANIEL SANDS, MAGNUS GROSS, BERNARD SMYTH, LORIN INGERSOLL, THOMAS MURPHY, and ISAAC BELL—the Mayor, as directed by the act, recognizing in such appointments the principle of minority representation. RICHARD L. LARREMORE was elected President, and WILLIAM HITCHMAN, Clerk of the new Board. The former, having been elected to a high judicial office in the city, resigned his position in April last, and was succeeded by BERNARD SMYTH, Esq., as President, and by NATHANIEL JARVIS, Jr., as a member of the Board. Mr. HITCHMAN was also succeeded as Clerk by LAWRENCE KIERNAN, Esq. S. S. RANDALL, having held the position of City Superintendent during a period of sixteen years, since 1854, declined a re-election, and was succeeded, on the 1st of June, 1870, by HENRY KIDDLE, Esq., who, together with S. W. SETON, THOMAS F. HARRISON, WILLIAM JONES, and NORMAN A. CALKINS, had occupied the position of Assistant Superintendents. THOMAS FANNING was appointed Assistant Superintendent in the place of Mr. KIDDLE.

The system of EVENING SCHOOLS for the instruction of those whose avocations or pursuits precluded attendance upon the day schools, had, at an early period, been inaugurated by the Board of Education; and thirty-one schools, including a High School for the instruction of advanced male pupils, had been organized, and were in successful operation from the 1st of October to the 15th of February (in the High school until the 1st of April), in each year, seventeen for male, eleven for female, and three for colored pupils of both sexes. A NORMAL SCHOOL for the benefit of the teachers of the several city schools, had also been opened on Saturday of each week, during the term of instruction, by the Public School Society, and adopted by the Board of Education, over which LEONARD HAZELTINE, Principal of School No. 13, presided, assisted by Miss SUSAN WRIGHT, also Principal of one of the Female Departments of the city schools, and a competent corps of instructors. This was succeeded in 1870, by the establishment of a daily NORMAL COLLEGE for the preparation of teachers, of which THOMAS HUNTER, Esq., Principal of Grammar School No. 35, was appointed President, ARTHUR HENRY DUNDEN, Esq., Vice President and Miss LYDIA F. WADLEIGH, Principal of the Senior Department of Grammar School 47, Lady Superintendent. An Experimental, or Model School, under the charge of Miss MARTHA A. DOAK, Vice Principal of the Primary Department of Grammar School No. 14, was also organized. These schools are now in successful operation, with upwards of 1,200 pupils. The Saturday Normal School was also retained as a part of the system for the instruction of teachers of the several city schools already employed. The title of the Free Academy was changed by the Legislature in 1868 to that of the "COLLEGE OF THE CITY OF NEW YORK," and on the resignation of Dr. WEBSTER, in the ensuing year, Major-General ALEXANDER S. WEBB was appointed President. This institution annually gratuitously educates about 600 pupils, graduates of the Public Schools, in all the studies of a college course, conferring the usual collegiate degrees. A HIGH SCHOOL, with a course of study intermediate between the Public Schools and the lowest collegiate class, has also been established by the Board of Education for male pupils of which DANIEL B. SCOTT is Head Master.

The general superiority and efficiency of the system of public instruction in the city of New York may be perceived through the following extracts from the report in April, 1866, of a Committee of the Common Council of the city of Boston, consisting of the Hon. F. W. LINCOLN, Mayor; three members of the Board of Aldermen; the Committee on Public Instruction of the Board of Councilmen; four members of the Board of School Commissioners, and John D. PHILBRICK, Esq., the City Superintendent. After a thorough inspection of the Public Schools of the city, they say:

"Under the administration of the system, as carried out by the Board of Education, a degree of order, precision, and energy of action has been attained, which has carried, and if persevered in must continue to carry forward the great work of popular education in the city of New York with a steady and strong progress, both in the broadness of its diffusion and the excellence of its character." * * "If the Board of Education retain their present powers, and act with the wisdom and energy they have heretofore manifested, there will, in a few years be a system of public education, and a condition of the public schools, altogether in advance, probably, of anything to be found in this country."

At about the same period, the Rev. JAMES FRASER, a member of the Board of Commissioners appointed by the English government to enquire into the Common School system of the United States and Canada, spent several weeks in the examination and investigation of the New York City schools. In his report laid before Parliament, he says:

"The field of administration of these New York school authorities is the most extensive in America—I suppose, in the mere article of education, and considering the details into which it descends, *the most extensive in the world*."

Similar high testimonials of the character of these

[illegible] n [illegible]
[illegible] arose
of the system
[illegible] New York [illegible]
[illegible] on the [illegible]
[illegible] Common
[illegible] the Hon.
the Board
[illegible] ration of
the Board
[illegible] Esq.
inspection

[illegible] Board of
[illegible] has been [illegible]
[illegible]
[illegible] York [illegible]
[illegible]
[illegible] their
[illegible]
[illegible] and a
[illegible] of any

[illegible] days' [illegible]
[illegible] appointed by
[illegible] the Common
[illegible] Council, spent
[illegible] investigation of
[illegible] report laid before

[illegible]stration of these New York
most extensive in America. I
[illegible] education, and consider-
[illegible] descends, *the most extensive*

of the character of these

POTSDAM NORMAL SCHOOL.

schools were given by a Legislative Committee appointed at the same time to inquire into their efficiency, and by a numerous delegation from the Boards of Education of the cities of Baltimore and Philadelphia.

The following extract from the annual report of the City Superintendent, for 1857, will afford a general description of the condition of the system of Public Schools in the city of New York, which, with very slight modifications, may be regarded as applicable to those of the other cities and large villages of the State, at this period:

"There can be little doubt that in respect to all the essential elements which go to make up a practical and efficient system of popular education and public instruction, the Grammar and Primary Schools and Departments of the city of New York, with their appendages—the Evening Schools, the Normal Schools, and the Free Academy, are fully equal, if not superior, to any in the world. For this excellence they are indebted, primarily, to the long continued and persevering exertions of those public-spirited and enlightened men who first conceived the idea of bringing home the blessings of education to the children of the poor and destitute, and then expanded that idea so as to embrace the children of all classes and conditions at the common expense of all who were capable of contributing in any degree to so noble an object; but secondarily and chiefly, to that constant and vigilant supervision, by the members of the Public School Society and Board of Education, their agents and officers, and the trustees and inspectors of the several Wards; to the permanent employment, at liberal salaries, of well qualified teachers; and to the adoption and maintenance in all the schools under their charge, of a uniform system of discipline, and of intellectual and moral instruction, admirably adapted to the judicious and harmonious development of the various faculties and capacities of the pupils. In all these respects, no other change seems desirable than such as the system itself is capable of evolving from its own materials—from the progress and advancement of educational science—from the improvements which experience, observation, and mutual interchange of views among teachers, School officers and friends of education are constantly suggesting—and from the pressure of a liberal and enlightened public sentiment, which cannot fail to appreciate the absolute necessity and paramount importance of a generous and universal education.

"One great and distinguishing excellence of our Public School system consists in the combination, which it unquestionably realizes, of a sound and thorough intellectual and moral culture, with the most agreeable and pleasant occupation of the time devoted to this object. Education, so far from assuming the form, too common in the history of the past, and still too prevalent in the experience of the present, of a stern and repulsive task, has with us been converted into a high and rational source of enjoyment and happiness. Our numerous school edifices are, both externally and internally, with few and rapidly decreasing exceptions, spacious, commodious, tasteful and pleasant—furnished with every convenience requisite to the comfortable accommodation of all—and presenting every inducement to the most careful and considerate parent to place his children within their walls. The order and discipline of the scholars, in all their departments and classes, are such as cannot but commend themselves to the admiration and approval of all. From two to four hundred children in each of the Grammar and Primary Schools, and from eight hundred to a thousand, and in some instances fifteen hundred children, in the Primary departments of the Grammar Schools, are each morning assembled quietly and systematically, without noise, confusion or disorder. Amid the profoundest stillness and attention, a select portion of the Christian Scriptures is read by the Principal or some officer of the Board or clergyman in attendance; the Lord's Prayer is then reverently repeated by the children, after the Principal, in concert; at the close of which, at the touch of the teacher's bell, their little voices, accompanied by the piano, break out into the beautiful music of their devotional and other songs—and then each class passes to its own rooms, under the charge of its instructor, to enter upon the various duties of the day. At the end of two or three hours they are again assembled for a temporary recess, made delightful by vocal and instrumental music, and alternated by relaxation and exercise in the ample play grounds; and, at the close of the school session, dismissed in perfect order. Thus pleasantly and happily the hours pass away in an atmosphere of love, kindness, and improvement; and the acquisition of knowledge is accompanied by the formation of habits of order, industry, punctuality, neatness, and mutual affection and regard. The school-room and its associations are rendered attractive and desirable to all—most attractive and desirable to those who stand most in need of their elevating and refining influences, and who, but for this beneficent agency, might never have known the blessings of a well-ordered and happy home, or participated in the inestimable advantages of a Christian education.

"At frequent intervals these schools are thrown open to the special visitation and inspection of the public,—to whom, indeed, they are at all times accessible—and on such occasions, the happy and animated countenances of the children, as their studies are reviewed, their compositions and declamations heard, their music and songs listened to, their needle-work, embroidery, penmanship, and drawing inspected by deeply interested and admiring crowds of visitors, and their premiums and rewards for scholarship, punctual attendance and good behavior awarded—sufficiently indicate the happiness which diffuses itself over this important portion of their young lives. Those only who have been familiar with the dreary and repulsive walls, the cheerless and desolate aspect, and the wearisome and monotonous routine of the schools of the olden time—who have witnessed and sympathized with the protracted sufferings of the hapless little ones, condemned to pass hours, days and months of ill-concealed torture on the miserable apologies for benches, without backs, and in rooms open to the rudest assaults of the wind and the tempest—who have listened to their shrieks as they were subjected to the brutal and unfeeling castigation of morose, ill-tempered and cruel pedagogues—and mourned over the time wasted and worse than wasted in these 'relics of barbarism' by ignorant, incompetent, and vicious teachers—can adequately realize the important change which has been effected in these respects, within the past few years, or fully appreciate the superiority of the present system of instruction."

The following table will show the aggregate and average attendance of the several public schools in the city of New York, at the present time:

		Whole number taught during the year.	Average Attendance.
47	Boys' Grammar Schools	33,500	16,158
42	Girls' " "	29,151	14,077
54	Primary Departments	88,391	37,352
40	Primary Schools	41,890	17,050
6	Schools for Colored Children	2,038	785
50	Corporate Schools	10,323	7,129
32	Evening Schools	24,084	10,407
1	Normal College	1,200	900
1	College of the City of New York	1,006	850
273	Total	259,673	104,708

No. of Teachers, 2,796; Males, 400; Females, 2,300; Special Teachers of French, German, Music, and Drawing, 53.

In the city of BROOKLYN, since the consolidation of that city with Williamsburgh and Bushwick, the number of school-houses has rapidly increased, and a greatly superior style of architecture was adopted. The present number is 47, with 42 Grammar and 29 Primary Departments, 13 Primary Schools, 4 Colored Schools 4 Asylum Schools, and 10 Evening Schools. In 1862, there were in these schools 28 male and 190 female teachers, in all, 218; in 1870, these numbers had increased to 60 male and 740 female teachers, in all, 800. In 1862, the total expenditures for school purposes was $314,927.96, of which $170,200 were raised by city taxation; while in 1870, the aggregate expenditure had risen to $947,411.99, of which $707,726 was raised by tax. Of this amount, $590,000 were expended in the payment of teachers' wages, $5,000 for school apparatus, $8,536 for colored schools, $9,317 in the purchase of sites, and about $4,000,000 in building, purchasing, hiring, repairing and insuring school-houses, and incidental expenses in warming, lighting, and cleaning the school-rooms, salaries of officers, &c. The number of volumes in the several school libraries is 37,000, valued at $50,000; and the estimated value of school-houses and sites is $2,241,784. The chief supervision of the schools remains in the hands of JOHN W. BULKLEY, Esq., who is assisted by JAMES CRUIKSHANK, LL. D. The Presidency of the Board of Education has been ably filled during the past twenty years by CYRUS P. SMITH, Esq., and Dr. JOHN S. THORNE.

Superintendent BULKLEY, in his annual report to the State Department for 1869, says: "If, in the review of our labor and its results, we find in our educational interest a stronger and more healthy pulse, a higher appreciation of the character and importance of our work, and a more liberal spirit, prompting to intelligent and self-sacrificing action, then we think we may say, without fear of contradiction, that substantial progress has been made. In evidence of this, we take pleasure in pointing to the new school-houses which have been built during the year, and to others now in process of building; to the modernizing, enlargement, and improvement of others, by which much additional room has been gained, and the facilities for instruction greatly increased; to a more intelligent appreciation of the duties of the school, by the teachers, and to the devotion, zeal, and perseverance apparent in the discharge of their daily duties; to a larger attendance and higher average of the pupils, than during any previous year; and to the results of study and instruction, in which we find that a higher standard has been attained, and more thorough work accomplished; and further, to an increased popular feeling in favor of the public schools generally. This is seen in the pressure upon the schools for admittance, in which multitudes fail, because there is no room to receive and accommodate them. In view of these and other considerations, we feel that we have good evidence of a healthy state, and the promise of future prosperity for the schools." * * * "By comparing the preceding, with corresponding statements of former years, it will be seen that the last year shows a large advance over any preceding one, in every particular. But notwithstanding all this, the rapid increase of our population is much in excess of the provision made for the accommodation and instruction of the children and youth of the city, who seek for admission into the public schools"

The number of pupils in attendance on the several schools of the city during the year 1867 was 54,844; in 1869 this number had increased to 85,705, with an average daily register of 35,000. In 1870, however, the aggregate attendance had fallen off to 72,286, and the average to 25,229.

In the city of BUFFALO, the number of public schools had increased from 34 in 1862, to 41 in 1869,—the number of teachers, from 218 to 365, of whom 311 were females; the number of pupils under instruction, from 15,386 to 21,180; and the annual expenditure for the support of the schools, from $88,508.67 to $250,883.01, of which $201,552.13 had been raised by city tax. The number of volumes in the several district libraries was 14,187; and the estimated value of the school-houses and sites, $508,477. The City Superintendents, during the interval, between 1862 and 1870, were, J. B. SACKETT, 1863; HENRY A. GARVIN, 1864–5; J. S. FOSDICK, 1867; SAMUEL SLADE, 1868–9; and THOMAS LOTHROP, 1870.

In the city of ROCHESTER, the number of public schools had increased from 17 in 1862 to 19 in 1869; the number of teachers, from 107 to 172, of whom 157 were females; the number of pupils under instruction, from 8,552 to 10,583; and the annual expenditure for the support of the schools, from $79,000 to $143,864.53, of which $80,000 was raised by city tax; the number of volumes in the several district libraries was 4,297; and the estimated value of the school-houses and sites, $157,000; City Superintendents—D. HOLBROOK, 1862–4; C. N. SIMMONS, 1865–9; S. A. ELLIS, 1870.

In the city of HUDSON, there are in the four public schools, 19 teachers, of whom 17 are females; the number of pupils has increased from 1,244 in 1862 to 1,772 in 1869; and the annual expenditure for the support of the schools, from $7,000 to $16,047, of which $7,000 was raised by city tax; the number of volumes in the several district libraries is 1,150; and the estimated value of the school-houses and sites, $34,000; City Superintendents—L. G. GUERNSEY, 1863; JAMES N. TOWNSEND, 1864–5–6; R. F. CLARK, 1867; J. N. TOWNSEND, 1869–70.

In the city of Oswego, there are in the fourteen districts, 6 male and 80 female teachers, with an increase in the number of pupils, from 4,000 in 1862 to 4,823 in 1869; and the annual expenditure, from $36,000 to $74,227, of which $49,497 was raised by city taxation; there are 4,000 volumes in the several district libraries; and the estimated value of the school-houses and sites was $124,180. E. A. SHELDON, Esq., occupied the position of City Superintendent until 1869, when he was succeeded by V. C. DOUGLASS, Esq.

In POUGHKEEPSIE, there are in the seven public schools 2 male and 50 female teachers, with an increase of the number of pupils, from 2,500 in 1866 to 2,865 in 1869, and of the annual expenditure, from $10,916.63 to $26,145.31, of which $13,000 was raised by tax; the number of volumes in the district library is 7,637; and the estimated value of the school-houses and sites, $54.500. The officers of the Board of Education, acting as City Superintendent, were, in 1863, E. J. BUCKINGHAM, President in 1864–5; G. C. BURNAP, President in 1867; R, BRITTAIN, Clerk in 1868; C. A. ANDRUS, Clerk in 1869–70; R. BRITTAIN, Clerk.

In SCHENECTADY, there are in the six public schools 2 male and 20 female teachers, with an attendance of 1,950 pupils against 1,932 in 1862. The annual expenditure has increased from $11,448.92 to $17,755.24, of which $10,320 was raised by tax. There are 3,000 volumes in the district libraries; and the estimated value of the school-houses and sites is $43,000. The City Superintendents were BENJAMIN STANTON, E. A. CHARLTON, and S. B. HOWE.

In the city of ALBANY, there are in the eighteen public schools 33 male and 106 female teachers, with an attendance of 9,713 pupils, against 9,614 in 1862. The annual expenditure for the support of the schools has increased from $71,429 in 1862 to $144,834, of which $103,624 was raised by city tax, The number of volumes in the district libraries is 5,268; and the estimated value of the school-houses and sites, $215,500. The Secretaries of the Board of Education and City Superintendents were HENRY B. HASWELL, JOHN HURDIS, JOHN MORGAN, Secretaries; H. B. HASWELL and JOHN O. COLE, City Superintendents.

In AUBURN, there are seven districts, with 7 male and 49 female teachers, and an attendance of about 3,000 pupils, against 2,420 in 1862. The annual expenditure for the support of schools has increased from $16,401 in 1862 to $27,070, of which $19,918 was raised by city tax. The number of volumes in the district libraries is 2,550; and the estimated value of school-houses and sites, $80,500. City Superintendents—C. P. WILLIAMS, WARREN HIGLEY, and E. A. CHARLTON.

In SYRACUSE, there are in the sixteen districts 10 male and 178 female teachers, with an increase in the number of children under instruction, from 5,822 in 1862 to 7,738 in 1869, and of the expenditure for the support of schools, from $34,212.61 to $191,244, of which $113,000 was raised by city taxation. The number of volumes in the libraries is only 600; and the estimated value of the school-houses and sites, $440,000. The City Superintendents were GEORGE L. FARNHAM; CHARLES E. STEVENS, and E. SMITH.

In TROY, there are in the eighteen districts 18 male and 130 female teachers, with an attendance of 10,420 pupils, against 8,045 in 1862, and an increase of expenditure, from $30,000 in that year to $104,677.85, of which $74,440 were raised by city taxation; number of volumes in the district libraries, 1,037; estimated value of school-houses and sites, $215,000; City Superintendents—E. DANFORTH and J. W. DUNHAM; President of Board of Education—WILLIAM KEMP.

The office of City Superintendent was created in October, 1862, and EDWARD DANFORTH, now State Deputy Superintendent, appointed as the first Superintendent, which position he continued to retain until 1868, when he was transferred to the State Department. Under his efficient administration, a complete classification and course of study was adopted in the several Public Schools of the city, upon one uniform basis, with annual promotions from one grade to another, and semi-annual public examinations of all the classes. Oral instruction was also introduced throughout the several grades, in the Primary, Intermediate and Grammar Schools. Systematic gymnastic exercises were carefully arranged and effectively carried out in all the departments. The High School, established in 1854, enlarged and improved in 1859, and incorporated by the Regents of the University in 1863, exerted from its origin a highly salutary influence upon the advancement and prosperity of the schools. It is open and free to all pupils over thirteen years of age possessing the requisite scholastic qualifications; and it possesses a valuable chemical and philosophical apparatus and a well selected library.

In the city of UTICA, there are sixteen districts, with 9 male and 54 female teachers, and an attendance of 4,190 pupils, against 3,552 in 1862, and an increase of annual expenditure for the support of the schools, from $36,216 to $65,515, of which $31,300 were raised by city taxation. The number of volumes in the several school libraries is 4,648; and the estimated value of school-houses and sites, $185,673. The City Superintendents were D. S. HEFFRON and A. McMILLAN.

In BINGHAMTON, there are nine districts, with 10 male and 37 female teachers, and an attendance of 2,094 pupils, with an expenditure in 1869 of $23,000, of which $17,552 were raised by city taxation; number of volumes in district libraries, 2,188; estimated value of school-houses and sites, $60,000; GEORGE S. FARNHAM, City Superintendent.

In ELMIRA, there are seven districts, with 6 male and 52 female teachers, and 3,492 pupils, and an expenditure, in 1869, of $75,623, of which $48,417 were raised by city taxation; number of volumes in district libraries, 1,103; estimated value of school-houses and sites, $112,000; O. ROBINSON and A. S. FITCH, Secretaries of the Board of Education.

Similar special organizations also exist in WATERTOWN, Jefferson county; LOCKPORT, Niagara county; NEWBURGH, Orange county; and OGDENSBURG, St. Lawrence county, all of which are in a flourishing and prosperous condition. The Union School district in WATERTOWN, organized in 1868, with a Union High School,—3 male and 30 female teachers, with 903 pupils, and an expenditure, for 1869, of $16,297, of which $11,500 are raised by tax; 3,555 volumes in the district libraries; $46,500 invested in school-houses and sites; WILLIAM G. WILLIAMS, Secretary of Board of Education.

The Union School at LOCKPORT has 3 male and 31 female teachers, with 3,080 pupils; expenditure in 1869, $64,000 for school purposes, of which $52,350 were raised by tax; has 3,500 volumes in district libraries, and an investment of $56,000 in school-houses and sites. JAMES FERGUSON, City Superintendent. NEWBURGH has seven districts, 8 male and 34 female teachers, 3,338 pupils under instruction, at a cost, in 1869, of $48,484, of which $34,710.50 were raised by tax; 7,750 volumes in the district libraries, and an investment of about $100,000 in school-houses and sites. H. A. JONES, City Superintendent. OGDENSBURGH has also seven districts, 11 male and 25 female teachers, 2,175 pupils, expends for school purposes $16,000, of which $7,253 are raised by tax; has about 3,000 volumes in the district libraries, and an investment of $66,500 in school-houses and sites. R. D. LOWRY, City Superintendent.

OSWEGO NORMAL AND TRAINING SCHOOL.

This institution was organized by State legislation, in 1867, by the adoption and enlargement of the Training School previously established in 1863, and is now one of the largest and most prosperous institutions of the kind in the country, having an attendance of about 500 pupils, and graduating annually between 80 and 100. EDWARD A. SHELDON, A. M., late City Superintendent, is the Principal and Professor of Mathematics, a position which he has occupied since the first organization of the institution; Joseph A. Prindle, A. M., Head Master and Professor of Natural Sciences and Ancient Languages; Isaac B. Poucher, A. M., Teacher of Arithmetic and Algebra; Herman Crusi, of Geometry, History, and Philosophy of Education, and of German and French; Mary Howe Smith, Geography and History; Matilda S. Cooper, Methods in Arithmetic, Grammar, and Object Lessons; Mrs. A. T. Randall, Reading and Elocution; Sarah J. Armstrong, Rhetoric, English Literature, and Composition; Mary E. Perkins, Drawing; Mary D. Sheldon, Gymnastics, Botany, and Latin; Martha McCumber, Principal Practicing Schools; and Kate Davis, of the Primary Department. Special attention is bestowed upon the preparation of Primary School teachers. The Practicing School is composed of about 400 children of primary and junior grades.

Brockport Training and Normal School.

Organized by act of the Legislature of April 7, 1866. The building is constructed of dark Medina sandstone, in the Norman style of architecture; is 300 feet long, and consists of a main or central building, 50 by 60 feet, and two wings, each 50 by 75 feet; together with two transverse wings, each 50 by 84 feet, running east and west, one at the northern and the other at the southern extremity. The central building is four stories in height, and the two wings three stories above the basement. The grounds comprise about six acres, at the head of College Street. Estimated value of building and grounds, $110,000; library and apparatus, $8,634.47; furniture, $4,300; in all, $122,934.47.

The Training School consists of a primary, an intermediate, and an academic department. Its object is to test the ability of pupil teachers—to reproduce the drill they have received in the Normal School—and to give them an opportunity of practising in their profession, both as to methods of teaching and governing. The academic department has courses of study corresponding to the courses in the Normal Department, called higher English and classical, and also a course preparatory for college, and a commercial course. The whole number of pupils taught during the year is about 650. The Hon. Jerome Fuller is President of the Board of Trustees, and Daniel Holmes, Esq., Secretary.

The Faculty is composed of the following:

C. D. McLean, A. M., LL. B., Principal.

Wm. J. Milne, A. M., Vice-Principal and Prof. Ancient Languages.

Francis B. Palmer, A. M., Principal Training School.
H. G. Burlingame, A. M., Teacher of Mathematics.
W. H. Lennon, A. M., " Nat. Sciences.
C. B. Fairchild, " Com'l Dep't.
Robert J. Gordon, " Penmanship.
Mrs. W. C. Sylla, Preceptress.
Miss Helen Roby, Teacher of Mathematics.
Miss Clara Roby, Head Teacher Intermediate Dep't.
Miss Sarah M. Efner, Teacher Mathematics & History.
Miss C. M. Chrisbwell, " English.
Mrs. Mary A. Cady, " Objects.
Mrs. M. J. Thompson, Head Teacher Primary Dep't.
Miss Elizabeth Richmond, Teacher of Reading and Vocal Music.
Miss Fanny Barnett, Teacher of Drawing.
Mrs. F. C. Alling, " Instrumental Music.

Cortland Normal and Training School.

Organized in 1868, under act of 1866.

The Normal School building is a spacious brick edifice, three stories in height above the basement. The first story contains two study rooms for pupils in the lower grades of the Training School, and, connected with each, four recitation rooms, three anterooms, and two cloak rooms. Upon this floor is also a central hallway, with two large cloak rooms, a dining room, parlor, library, and office, together with rooms for the accommodation of the steward and his family. The second story contains the chapel or study room for the Normal Department, the laboratory, two private rooms for teachers, two cloak rooms, six recitation rooms, and two halls leading from the chapel to recitation rooms. Upon the third floor are the gymnasium, well supplied with apparatus for calisthenic exercises, two bath rooms, and dormitory accommodations for lady boarders.

The grounds are commodiously located, near the center of the village, and are ample for walks and drives, pleasantly laid out, and remote from noise or disturbance.

The cost of the building and grounds, defrayed by the corporation of the village, was about $89,500; furniture, $6,500; and library and apparatus, $2,000; in all, about $98,000.

The Board of Trustees consists of the Hon. HENRY S. RANDALL, President; Hon. R. H. Duell, Secretary; Charles C. Taylor, Treasurer; Trustees, Hon. Horatio Ballard, Arnold Stafford, Henry Brewer, Norman Chamberlain, William Newkirk.

The school was opened March 3, 1869, under the charge of the following Board of Instructors:

JAMES H. HOOSE, Prin'l Dep't Metaphysics & Didactics.
Norman F. Wright, " Ancient Languages.
Frank S. Capen, " Mathematics.
Thomas B. Stowell, " Natural Sciences.
Martha Roe, Superintendent Intermediate & Primary Departments, Teacher of Methods and Objects.
Helen E. M. Babcock, Modern Languages and History.
Miss M. Marsh, Vocal Music.
Mary Morton, Drawing.
Helen K. Hubbard, Principal Intermediate Dep't.
Margaret Hunter, " Primary "
Miss M. F. Hendricks, Teacher of Reading, Elocution, and Gymnastics.
Miss Mary F. Hall, Critic in Primary Department.

The object of the Normal School is to qualify young men and women to serve as teachers in the Public Schools of the State; and of the Training School, to provide a practising school for the Normal students. The latter comprises a Primary, Intermediate, and Academic Department.

The whole number of pupils in attendance during the year was about 800.

POTSDAM NORMAL AND TRAINING SCHOOL.

Organized under act of 1867, on the 27th of April, 1869.

The attendance during the first year was as follows:

Normal School				134
Training School,	Academical	Department		89
"	"	Intermediate	"	125
"	"	Primary	"	119
				467

The school is located in the central part of the village, fronting the public park, which is free to the students. The building is constructed of Potsdam sandstone, and consists of a central building, 45 by 113 feet. From this, at a distance of 22 feet from the front, on each side, there are two wings, 30 feet deep by 40 front, and from the ends of each of these, at right angles, two others, 36 feet front by 72 deep. The entire building is 227 feet in length by 113 in depth, comprising a basement and three stories above. In the basement, are the dining room, kitchen, laundry, coal room, and cellar; on the first floor, the laboratory, Normal hall, Primary, and Intermediate Departments, library, Principal's room, and reception room; on the second, the Preceptress' and Matron's rooms, the academic study rooms, and recitation rooms for the Normal and Academic Departments; on the third, dormitories, recitation rooms, and gymnasium. On this floor is also the boarding hall, designed exclusively for lady pupils, affording excellent accommodations for fifty students, with bath rooms and a gymnasium. Each room is carpeted, and neatly furnished for the occupation of two ladies.

The Faculty is as follows:

MALCOLM MCVICAR, Principal and Prof. of Mental and Moral Philosophy and Didactics.

George H. Sweet, Vice-Principal and Prof. of English Literature and Ancient Languages.

Henry L. Harter, Prof. of Mathematics.

E. D. Blakeslee, Prof. of Natural Sciences.

Robert H. Dutton, Teacher of Vocal Music.

Miss Annie Allen, Preceptress and Teacher of Rhetoric and Composition.

Ellen J. Merritt, Teacher of Methods.

Lucy A. Leonard, " Mathematics.

Emma L. Qua, " English Grammar.

S. Julia Gilbert, " History, Geog. & Drawing.

Helen S. Wright, " Science of Government and English Language.

Sybil E. Russell, Teacher of Reading, Elocution, and Gymnastics.

Amelia Morey, Principal Intermediate Department.

Eleanor E. Jones, Principal Primary Department.

The course of instruction comprises an elementary English, and an advanced English and Classical course. The miscellaneous and reference libraries contain 1,164 volumes.

The Board of Trustees consists of HENRY S. WATKINS, President; Charles O. Tappan, Secretary; Jesse Reynolds, Treasurer; Aaron N. Dunning, George Ormiston, Hon. Noble L. Elderkin, Eben Fisher, John J. Gilbert, and Roswell Pettibone.

FREDONIA NORMAL AND TRAINING SCHOOL.

By an act of the Legislature passed February 16, 1869, the entire management of this school, originally organized in February, 1868, was, in consequence of some internal troubles, devolved upon the State Superintendent of Public Instruction, who appointed Dr. J. W. Armstrong, of the Oswego Normal School, Principal, with a competent body of professors and teachers, and the school was re-opened in September, 1869. The whole number of pupils in attendance in the Normal, Academic, Intermediate, and Junior Departments is about 600.

"The building," says the Superintendent, "is an elegant and substantial brick structure, conveniently located, three stories high, and affording accommodation for about 600 day scholars, and 125 boarders. Including the site, furniture, and other required provisions, it cost the village of Fredonia about $100,000." Its location is "in one of the pleasantest villages of the State, in the midst of a cultivated and appreciative community."

The Wadsworth Normal and Training School, at Geneseo, and the Buffalo Normal School, incorporated respectively in 1867 and 1866, are in process of erection.

GENERAL SUMMARY.

EXTERNAL AND INTERNAL ORGANIZATION OF THE SYSTEM.

THE entire territory of the State, comprising exclusively of the waters of the great lakes, an area of 45,658 square miles, has been subdivided into about 12,000 school districts, averaging about four square miles each, bringing ordinarily, in the rural districts, the remotest inhabitants within one mile from the centrally located school-house.

Common Schools in the several districts are free to all residents of the districts between the ages of four and twenty-one years, and residents of any district may be admitted, with the consent of the trustees, to the schools of any other district.

These districts are originally formed, or subsequently modified by the District Commissioners, with the exception of those organized under special laws in cities and villages. The inhabitants of the several districts who are legal voters, at their annual meetings, on the second Tuesday of October in each year, elect either one or three trustees, in their discretion, whose term of office is one year in the former and three in the latter case, a district clerk, a collector, and a librarian. They are also authorized to vote such taxes as may be necessary, for school apparatus, text-books, library, insurance, the payment of any balance that may be due the teacher, after the application of the public money provided by the State and other local funds, and for defraying the costs and expenses of the trustees in the prosecution or defense of suits brought by or against them.

The trustees are empowered to call district meetings, make out tax-lists and warrants, purchase sites and build or hire school-houses, insure the district property, contract with, employ, and pay teachers, and generally to manage the affairs of the district, and take care of its property, with corporate powers for this purpose. Between the first and fifteenth days of October in each year, they are required to make and transmit a report to the Commissioner, bearing date on the first of October, setting forth the time during which the school has been taught the preceding year by duly qualified teachers, the sum paid for the wages of such teachers, and for text-books and school apparatus, the number of children of the requisite school age residing in the district, the number taught during the year, the amount paid for teachers' wages, over and above the public State and local funds, the amount of taxes levied on the district for purchasing sites, building, hiring, purchasing, repairing, and insuring school-houses, for fuel, district libraries, or other legal objects of expenditure, and such other information as the State Superintendent may, from time to time, require. The duties of the district clerk, collector, and librarian may be inferred from their respective offices.

All teachers, in order to entitle themselves to any portion of the public money, must hold a diploma from one of the State Normal Schools, or a certificate of qualification from the State Superintendent, the School Commissioner of the district, or some other officer specially authorized by law to grant such certificate.

The Town Clerk of each town is required to keep in his office all books, maps, papers, and records concerning the several schools in his town; to keep a record of the apportionment of school money among the several districts, and to notify the trustees thereof; to receive and transmit to the Commissioner the annual report of the trustees; to file and preserve the boundaries of the several districts; record the accounts of the Supervisor, as hereinafter set forth; and act with the Commissioner, when required by him, in the formation and alteration of school-districts.

The school moneys, apportioned to the several counties by the State Superintendent, are paid over by the State Treasurer to the order of the several County Treasurers, and the share of each town by the County Treasurer to the order of the Supervisor of the town, by whom it is disbursed, on the order of the trustees of the several districts, to the teacher or other person entitled to receive the same. Bonds, with sufficient sureties, for the faithful application of the public moneys coming into their respective hands, are required of the State and County Treasurers and Supervisors of towns. The latter officers are also charged with the care and disposition of all local town school funds.

One hundred and twelve District Commissioners are elected once in every three years, by the legal voters of their respective districts, the boundaries of which were originally fixed by the Boards of Supervisors of the respective counties, under the authority of the act of 1856. They are authorized and empowered to visit and examine the several schools within their jurisdiction at least twice in each year, during the summer and winter terms, and as much oftener as practicable; to advise and counsel with the trustees; to examine into and report the condition of the school-houses; to recommend text-books and courses of study; examine and license teachers, and annul their certificates for sufficient cause; to ascertain, and if necessary correct, the description of district boundaries; to take and report testimony, whenever required by the State Superintendent, on appeals to that officer; and to apportion among the several districts, within their jurisdiction, the share of public money belonging to them respectively. In the several cities and large villages of the State, these various duties are devolved, under special laws, upon the respective Boards of Education, City Superintendents, and other local officers.

At the head of the whole system, controlling, regulating, and giving life and efficiency to all its parts, is the STATE SUPERINTENDENT OF PUBLIC INSTRUCTION, elected by joint ballot of the Senate and Assembly, for the term of three years. By virtue of his office, he has the general supervision of the several schools of the State, and the advisory control of their management, discipline, and course of instruction, and the final determination, on appeal, of all controversies arising under their local administration. He apportions and distributes the public money, examines its supplementary apportionment among the several districts by the Commissioners, and supervises its application, through the several officers charged with its disbursement, to its legitimate purposes; corresponds with, counsels, and advises the inhabitants, trustees, and other officers of the several districts, and establishes rules and regulations for the management of the district libraries. He is charged with the general control, visitation, and management of Teachers' Institutes in the several counties; the employment of teachers and lecturers therein, and the payment of the expenses incurred by the District Commissioners in conducting their exercises; with the appointment of State pupils in the institutions for the instruction of the deaf, dumb, and blind, upon the certificates of the proper local officers; with the apportionment and selection of pupils of the several State Normal Schools, and their general supervision, direction and management; with the charge and control of the several schools for the instruction of Indian children within the State; with the compilation of full abstracts of the reports of the Trustees and Commissioners of the several school districts; and with the preparation of an annual report to the Legislature of the condition of the several schools and institutions subject to his supervision, and the recommendation of such measures as, in his judgment, will contribute to their welfare and efficiency. He is, *ex officio*, chairman of the Executive Committee of the State Normal School at Albany, a Regent of the State University, and chairman of the committee of that body on teachers' classes in the academies of the State, a member of the Board of Trustees of the State Idiot Asylum at Syracuse, the People's College at Havana, and the Cornell University at Ithaca.

FUNDS FOR THE SUPPORT AND MAINTENANCE OF THE SYSTEM AND THE MANNER OF THEIR APPORTIONMENT.

The several sources from which the Common Schools of the State are supported are the following:

1. The income of the COMMON SCHOOL FUND. The productive capital of this fund, consisting of the proceeds of the sale of public lands, State loans, State and bank stocks, and money in the State Treasury, amounts at the present time to about $3,000,000, yielding an annual revenue of above $175,000, of which, however, $155,000 only is annually apportioned among the several school districts of the State.

2. The income of the *United States Deposit Fund*, amounting to $165,000, annually.

3. The general STATE TAX, which, being fixed by law at one and a quarter mills upon each dollar of the valuation of real and personal property in the State, yields at the present time somewhat over $2,000,000 per annum.

4. The income of local funds, chiefly the the proceeds of sales of what is known as "Gospel and School lots," set apart on the first establishment of the Common School System for the support of Schools, amounting to about $20,500, annually.

5. District, Village and City Taxation, voluntarily incurred in the purchase of sites, the building, purchasing, hiring, furnishing, repairing and insuring of school-houses, and the purchase of school apparatus, text-books, etc.

These various items may be stated as follows:

From the interest of the Common School Fund.........	$155,000
From the income of the United States Deposit Fund....	165,000
From the avails of Local Funds......................	20,500
From the avails of the State Tax....................	2,100,000
Total	$2,440,500

The avails of local taxation must, of course, counterbalance the expenditures calling for their appropriation, and need not be included in this statement. They will average generally not far from $6,500,000.

In the annual apportionment of these funds set apart for the support of Common Schools, the State Superintendent, after deducting from the income of the United States deposit fund, the amount necessary to pay the salaries of the several School Commissioners, the sum of five hundred dollars for each assembly district in every city, having a local Superintendent or other similar officer, under special laws, the library money appropriated by the Legislature, an equitable sum for the support of Indian schools, and the sum of $2,000 for contingencies, divides the remainder into two parts, equal to one-third and two-thirds of the amount, respectively. The one-third is apportioned, in accordance with the law, among the several school districts, according to the number of qualified teachers employed in each for a period not less than twenty eight weeks during the preceding year, one share being awarded to each district, for each qualified teacher so employed by them for that length of time in each year; and the remaining two-thirds, together with the library money, among the several counties, according to their population (excluding Indians), as shown by the last State or National census; separate apportionments being made to cities having special school acts. This apportionment, when completed, the Superintendent certifies to the several County Clerks, County Treasurers, District Commissioners and City Chamberlains or Treasurers; the amount so apportioned to each county or city, being payable on the order of such county or city Treasurer, on the first day of February, thereafter.

On the receipt of such certificate, the several District Commissioners of each county meet and proceed to apportion the money among the several districts of the county as follows: setting apart to each district its quota according to the number of qualified teachers employed during the preceding year, as above stated, and any sum assigned to such district as an equitable allowance, by the State Superintendent, and deducting these amounts from the aggregate sum apportioned for teachers' wages; they divide the remainder into two equal parts, one of which is apportioned to the districts in proportion to the number of children, between the ages of four and twenty-one residing in them, and the other according to the *average daily attendance* of resident pupils. The library money is then apportioned according to the number of resident children, between four and twenty-one years of age. A copy of this apportionment is transmitted to the County Treasurer and State Superintendent, respectively, and the Supervisor of each town officially informed of the aggregate amount of teachers, wages and library money apportioned to his town, and of the share of each, respectively, payable to the several districts.

GENERAL RESULTS.

The following is a summary of the statistical and financial reports of the Common Schools of the State for the year 1870:

RECEIPTS.

	Cities.	Rural Districts.	Total.
Amount on hand Oct. 1, 1869...	$1,133,804 48	$217,842 87	$1,351,646 65
Public money received.........	848,738 71	1,609,668 26	2,458,406 97
Proceeds of local funds........	717 54	21,632 91	22,350 45
Raised by local taxation........	3,762,861 18	2,799,788 81	6,562,649 99
Appropriation for teachers' board	....	294,291 05	294,291 05
From all other sources.........	58,121 76	157,500 08	215,621 84
Totals..................	$5,824,243 67	$5,100,628 48	$10,924,867 15

EXPENDITURES.

	Cities.	Rural Districts.	Total.
For teachers' wages	$3,036,439 98	$3,473,724 34	$6,510,164 82
For libraries	14,067 58	16,849 47	30,917 05
For school apparatus	155,275 16	23,781 77	179,056 93
For colored schools	60,790 75	6,791 81	67,582 56
For school-houses, sites, repairs, and furniture	1,079,160 61	903,386 68	1,982,547 29
All other incidental expenses	729,135 23	435,007 44	1,164,142 67
Forfeitures in Supervisors' hands	....	365 77	365 77
Amount on hand Oct. 1, 1870	749,874 36	240,216 20	990,090 56
Totals	$5,824,743 67	$5,100,123 48	$10,924,867 15

Deducting the amounts remaining on hand, the actual expense of maintaining the schools of the State, during the year ending October 1, 1870, was as follows:

In the several cities	$5,074,869 31
In the towns and rural districts	4,859,907 28
Total	$9,934,776 59

Showing an increase of about $48,000 over the expenditure of the preceding year.

In addition to the expenditures above enumerated for the support of Common Schools exclusively, the following, pertaining more especially to the higher institutions, departments, and agencies for the promotion of the system of Public Instruction, should be added:

State appropriation for support of Academies	$44,646 79
" " for teachers' classes in Academies	15,345 00
For the support of Teachers' Institutes	16,171 10
" " Normal Schools	128,723 59
" " Cornell University	25,000 00
" " Indian schools	6,837 98
For expenses of the Department of Public Instruction	19,127 09
" " Regents of the University	6,349 72
" " blank forms and registers for schools	13,000 00
	$275,201 27

Which, added to the total above given	9,934,776 89
Makes the entire amount expended during the year 1870, for the support of our educational system	$10,209,977 86

Or an increase, over the aggregate expenditure of the preceding year, of over $100,000.

The estimated value of the sites and school-houses owned by the several districts was as follows:

In the cities	$11,981,303 00
In the rural districts	8,467,110 00
Total	$20,448,413 00

The whole number of duly qualified teachers employed during an average period of 35 weeks in the year, was 28,239, of whom 21,688 were females, and 6,551 males. The number employed and on duty at the same time, during a period of 28 weeks (the legal school term, entitling the districts to their proportionate share of the public money), or upward, was 17,459, with an average annual salary, in the cities, of $680.30, and in the country districts, of $267.33.

The whole number of children between the ages of 5 and 21 residing in the several districts of the State, on the 30th of September, 1870, was reported at 1,488,440, of whom 623,2[illegible] were residing in the cities, and 865,229 in the rural districts. The whole number attending the public schools, for a longer or shorter period, during the year, was 1,029,852, of whom 409,477 resided in the cities, and 620,375 in the rural districts. The average attendance during the period the schools were kept open was 485,840; in the cities, 192,623. in the rural districts, 293,217.

The number reported as in attendance upon private schools, of every description, was 127,261; cities, 103,362; country, 23,899.

The whole number of volumes in the several district libraries of the State had diminished to 986,697, of which 130,980 were in the city, and 855,717 in the country districts. Total valuation, $509,394.

The whole number of school-houses in the State was 11,700, of which 11,333 were in the rural districts, and 367 in the cities. In the former, 468 were of stone, 858 of brick, 9,860 of framed wood, and 127 of logs; in the latter, 14 of stone, 308 brick, and 45 of wood.

The aggregate number of visitations and inspections made by the several District Commissioners, in the rural districts, during the year, was 10,680.

With respect to the existing organization of the Common School system, there seems to me one only radical defect, marring its symmetry, and seriously affecting its efficiency. The country districts of the State, comprising by far its largest portion, consist of contiguous territory, averaging an area of about four miles square, with generally a school population of about one hundred children, of all ages from four to twenty-one, taught for perhaps eight months of the year, in a single room of a cheaply constructed building. A female teacher, of average abilities and restricted scholarship, is usually engaged for the summer months, at a low rate, and a male teacher, of somewhat superior acquirements and skill, for the winter term. In the great majority of these districts, the teachers are changed every year, and not unfrequently the entire series of class-books and the entire course of instruction with them. Under these circumstances, it is obvious that comparatively little substantial progress can be made in the work of education. A systematic gradation of classes and studies is nearly impossible, and a very large portion of the work of one year is gone over, with different text-books and different methods of instruction and classification, during each succeeding year. And yet these are the only facilities which are available to nine-tenths of the children of the district for a Common School education—the only education, in all probability, which they are destined to receive—certainly the only education provided by the State! A re-organization of the system, in this important respect, seems imperatively to be called for. The million and a half of dollars, expended annually by the State for the education of at least half a million of this class of children might surely be made to realize more substantial advantages than these! And this might easily be accomplished by adopting for these country districts the system of graded schools, which gives such acknowledged efficiency to the city and village schools of the State. Let each of the present District Schools be fitted up and properly organized and graded as a Primary and Intermediate School, with a course of study ranging from the simple elementary branches, to and including those now ordinarily assigned to the lower classes of the city and village Grammar Departments, and furnishing all requisite facilities for the instruction of children of twelve years of age, and under. Then let two or more Grammar Schools, comprehending all the higher branches of study below those of the advanced classes of the Academy or High School, be provided in convenient locations in each town, at about equal distance from the District Schools, to which those in the several District or Primary Schools, who have completed the prescribed course of instruction, may graduate, and from whence they may pass in turn to the nearest Academical or High School. The several towns in the State rarely extend over an area of more than twenty square miles, and two Grammar Schools only in each, eligibly located, would be accessible, without great difficulty, to the more advanced pupils. In towns having a large population, three or four such schools could easily be sustained, and their number might in all cases be adjusted to the circumstances and educational wants of the town. The increased expense of such an arrangement would bear an inconsiderable proportion to the advantages and benefits certain to be derived from it. Under the existing system, the public funds are, to a very great extent, comparatively wasted; undue preference is given, in furnishing the means of a thorough and complete course of instruction, to the inhabitants of cities and villages; and hundreds of thousands of children living in remote and secluded districts are virtually deprived of privileges enjoyed by the more favored residents of towns, and which it is the duty of the State equally to dispense to them.

Such is a condensed view of our present system of COMMON SCHOOL EDUCATION—a system elaborated and matured by the exertions of the highest minds among us, during a period of sixty years—a system comprehending the best and dearest interests, present and prospective, of an enlightened and free people—full of promise for the future, and containing within itself the germs of individual, social, and national prosperity—a system identified with the highest hopes and interests of all classes of the community, and from which are destined to flow those streams of intelligence and of public and private virtue which alone can enable us worthily to fulfil the noble destinies involved in our free institutions.

But in this country, no system, however perfect—no enactments, however enlightened—and no authority however venerable, can attain to the full accomplishment of their object, however praiseworthy and laudable, without the hearty and efficient co-operation of public sentiment. The repeated and solemn recognition, by the representatives of the people, of the great interests of popular education and public instruction, and the nearly unanimous adoption, by the people themselves, of a system commended to the public favor as well by practical experience as by the concurring testimony of the most enlightened minds of our own and other countries, afford the most conclusive evidence not only of the importance which the great mass of our fellow-citizens attach to the promotion of sound intellectual and moral instruction, but of their fixed determination to place our Common Schools, where this instruction is chiefly dispensed to the children of the State, upon a footing which shall enable them most effectually to accomplish the great objects of their institution.

It is upon the extent and permanency of this feeling that the true friends of education most confidently rely, and this spirit, to which they appeal in looking forward to the just appreciation and judicious improvement of those means of moral and mental enlightenment which the beneficent policy of the State has placed at the disposal of its citizens. The renovation of our Common Schools, distributed as they are over every section of our entire territory, their elevation and expansion to meet the constantly increasing requirements of science and mental advancement, and their capability of laying broad and deep the foundations of character and usefulness, must depend upon the intelligent and fostering culture which they shall receive at the hands of those to whose immediate charge they are committed. There is no institution within the range of civilization upon which so much, for good or for evil, depends—upon which hang so many and such important issues to the future well-being of individuals and communities, as the COMMON DISTRICT SCHOOL. It is through that alembic that the lessons of the nursery and the family fireside, the earliest and most enduring instructions in pure morality, and the long-remembered precepts and examples of the social circle are distilled, and from it those lessons are destined to assume that tinge and hue which are permanently to be incorporated into the character and the life. Is it too much then to ask or to expect of parents, that, laying aside all minor considerations, abandoning all controversies and dissensions among themselves, in reference to local, partisan, and purely selfish objects—or, at the least, postponing them until the interests of their children are placed beyond the influence of these irritating topics—they will consecrate their undivided energies to the advancement and improvement of this beneficent institution? Resting, as it does, upon their support, indebted to them for all its means of usefulness, and dependent for its continued existence upon their discriminating favor and efficient sanction, the practical superiority of the existing system of public instruction; its comprehensiveness and simplicity; its abundant and ample resources, and its adaptation to the educational wants of every class of the community, will prove of little avail without the invigorating influences of that public sentiment which must emanate from the great mass of the reflecting and enlightened people of the State. The COMMON

SCHOOL must become the central interest of the citizen and the parent, the clergyman, the lawyer, the physician, the merchant, the manufacturer, the farmer, and the laborer. Each and all must realize that there, under more or less favoring auspices, as they themselves shall determine, developments are in progress which are destined, at no distant day, to exert a controlling influence over the institutions, habits, modes of thought, and action of society in all its complicated relations; and that the primary responsibility for the results which may thus be worked out, for weal or for woe, RESTS WITH THEM! By the removal of every obstacle to the progressive and harmonious action of the system of popular education, so carefully organized and amply endowed by the State; by a constant, methodical and intelligent co-operation with its constituted agents, in the elevation and advancement of that system in all its parts; and especially by an infusion into its entire course of discipline and instruction, of that high moral and Christian culture which can alone adequately realize the idea of a sound education, results of inconceivable magnitude and importance to individual, social and moral well being may confidently be anticipated. These results demand and will amply repay the consecration of the highest intellectual and moral energies, the most comprehensive benevolence, and the best affections of our common humanity!

CONCLUDING CHAPTER

GENERAL PRINCIPLES.—PHILOSOPHY OF EDUCATION.

Coleridge's Views.—Church and State.—Education Defined.—Physical, Intellectual, Moral, and Religious Education.

THE great system of Common School education and public instruction, the annals of which we have been thus far engaged in reviewing, rests for its foundation upon the principle that it is not only the inalienable right but the highest duty of the State, in the exercise of the powers conferred upon it by the popular will, to make ample and suitable provision for the education of all its future citizens. Governments were primarily instituted, undoubtedly, for the protection and defence of the lives, liberty and property of the governed; in return for which, obedience to the laws was to be rendered and order maintained. But the gradual advancement of civilization superadded to these primary and indispensable requisites, that most important of all, not only as a necessary means for their attainment, but as itself an end, for which only, governments themselves were most precious and valuable—the culture and discipline of the human mind. And this leads us to the important inquiry—important especially in reference to the present condition and future expansion of our systems of education—what are the essential constituents of that education which the State is bound to provide for its successive generations of citizens? and in what manner may they most effectually be provided?

That profound thinker, SAMUEL TAYLOR COLERIDGE,

in his admirable discourse on "Church and State," has thrown a flood of light on the relations which these two institutions were originally designed, in the structure of the British Constitution, to occupy towards each other. Starting from the proposition that "civilization itself is but a mixed good, if not far more, a corrupting influence—the hectic of disease, not the bloom of health—and a nation so distinguished more fitly to be called a varnished than a polished people, where this civilization is not grounded in cultivation, in the harmonious development of those qualities and faculties that characterize our humanity,"—he thus sketches the origin of what he terms "the nationality," or third estate, as contradistinguished from the first, or great landholders, by whom the *permanency* of the nation was provided for, and the second, or mercantile, manufacturing and laboring class, representing the elements of *progressiveness*:

"The nationality, therefore, was reserved for the support and maintenance of a permanent class or order with the following duties: A certain smaller number were to remain at the fountain heads of the humanities in cultivating and enlarging the knowledge already possessed, and in watching over the interests of physical and moral science, being likewise the instructors of such as constitute, or were to constitute, the remaining more numerous classes of the order. The members of this latter and more numerous body were to be distributed throughout the country, so as not to leave even the smallest and most integral part or division without a resident guide, guardian and instructor: the objects and final intention of the whole order being these—to preserve the stores and guard the treasures of past civilization, and thus to bind the present with the past: to perfect and add to the same, and thus to connect the present with the future; but especially to diffuse through the whole community, and to every native entitled to its laws and rights that quantity and quality of knowledge which was indispensable, both for the understanding of those rights and for the performance of the duties correspondent: finally, to secure for the nation, if not a superiority over the neighboring States, yet an equality at least in that character of general civilization which equally with, or rather more than fleets, armies and revenue, forms the ground of its offensive and defensive power. The object of the two former estates of the realm, which conjointly form the State, was to reconcile the interests of permanence with that of progression—law with liberty. The object of the National Church, the third remaining estate, was to secure and improve that civilization without which the nation could be neither permanent nor progressive.

"That in all ages, individuals who have directed their meditations and their studies to the noble character of our nature, to the cultivation of those powers and instincts which constitute the man—at least separate him from the animal, and distinguish the nobler from the animal part of his own being—will be led, by the supernatural in themselves, to the contemplation of a Power which is likewise supernatural: that science, and especially moral science, will lead to religion, and remain blended with it—this, I say, will, in all ages, be the course of things. * * * * The clerisy of the nation, or national church, in its primary acceptation and original intention, comprehended the learned of all denominations—the sages and professors of the law and jurisprudence, of medicine and physiology, of music, of military and civil architecture, of the physical and mathematical sciences—in short all the so-called liberal arts and sciences, the possession and application of which constitute the civilization of a country, as well as the theological. The last was, indeed, placed at the head of all: and of good right did it claim the precedency. But why? Because under the name of theology or divinity were contained the interpretation of languages, the conservation and tradition of past events, the momentous epochs and revolutions of the race and nation, the continuation of the records, logic, ethics, and the determination of ethical science in application to the rights and duties of men in all their various relations, social and civil; and lastly, the ground knowledge—the *prima scientia*, as it was named—philosophy, or the doctrine and discipline of ideas.

"Theology formed only a part of the objects, the theologians formed only a portion of the clerks or clergy of the national church. The theological order had precedency, indeed, and deservedly; but not because its members were priests. * * The theologians took the lead, because the science of theology was the root and the trunk of the knowledge that civilized man, because it gave unity and the circulating sap of life to all other sciences, by virtue of which alone they could be contemplated as forming collectively, the living tree of knowledge. It had the precedency, because under the name theology were comprised all the main aids, instruments and materials of national education, the *nisus formativus* of the body politic, the shaping and informing spirit, which educing or eliciting the latent man, in all the natives of the soil, trains them up to be citizens of the country, free subjects of the realm. And lastly, because to divinity belong those fundamental truths which are the common ground-work of our civil and our religious duties, not less indispensable to a right view of our temporal concerns, than to a rational faith respecting our immortal well being. NOT WITHOUT CELESTIAL OBSERVATIONS CAN EVEN TERRESTRIAL CHARTS BE ACCURATELY CONSTRUCTED."*

*Coleridge's works (Harper's Ed.), vol. vi, pp. 51-53.

I. Education, in its most universal acceptation, is understood to consist in the development, cultivation, expansion and discipline of the human mind, in all its faculties, to the utmost extent compatible with physical health and well-being, with the intellectual, moral, and religious capacity, and with the individual and social requirements, present and prospective, of those subjected to its processes. First in the order of time, and commensurate with the entire course, as the indispensable condition of all mental culture, the laws of *health* must be observed and taught—so thoroughly, if possible, as to preclude the necessity, at any future period, of painfully and laboriously, if not fruitlessly, exploring the profound mysteries of the laws of *disease*. The intellectual powers must then be enabled to comprehend and gradually to master the various discoveries of science, the principles, evolutions, and machinery of art, the lessons of history, and the great works of those master-spirits of literature, whose imagination and surpassing genius have enrolled their names among the list of those whom the latest posterity "will not willingly let die." Simultaneously with this process, the moral and spiritual faculties of the young immortal—the highest gift of God—must be assiduously cultivated. The great moral lessons of Christianity—unadulterated by sectarian teaching or denominational tenets, which may safely be left to the lessons of home and the church—should be communicated in all their purity, beauty, and sublimity; intimately associated with the happiest hours of youthful enjoyment—the happiest and most cherished memories of the glad spring time of life.

II. Regarding these, then, as the essential elements of education, I proceed to submit some remarks—not on the specific *manner* in which they may be communicated—for that must necessarily be infinitely diversified, and dependent to an incalculable extent upon individual faculty, temperament, condition and circumstances, as well of teachers as of pupils—but upon such general principles and methods, as experience, observation, study and much reflection have suggested.

1. There is great reason to believe that the fundamental laws of health are too generally neglected in our institutions for public instruction. The location and structure of school buildings—their surroundings—their facilities for ventilation and heating—their play-grounds and gymnastic apparatus—their out-buildings—and the distribution of the hours of study and of play—all require and deserve the most careful attention and intelligent supervision. Especial regard should be given to the frequent alternation of study and recreation—and to the thorough ventilation and equable temperature of the class-rooms. At least once in each hour these rooms should be vacated for at least five or ten minutes, and the pupils permitted to change their posture and occupation; and after the lapse of two hours, half or three-quarters of an hour given to recreation and exercise. Not more than five hours of instruction should be given in any one day to even the older and more advanced pupils—nor more than three to the younger. The instruction given to the latter should be chiefly oral and objective. The knowledge of *words* and of things, easily accessible or through well-executed drawings, should take precedence of books.

Nothing short of a miracle can present us with a sound mind unaccompanied by a sound body. We may develop to a preternatural activity the intellectual faculties of our children, and by a species of hot-house discipline be able to exhibit to the wondering gaze of our friends a youthful prodigy of genius and talent. But the bitter experience of many an agonized and bereaved parent has demonstrated that triumphs like these are brief and far too dearly bought. Exhausted nature soon asserts its supremacy and vindicates its violated laws. The overtasked brain gives way before the unnatural supply of nervous energy which has been forced to it, and a premature grave claims the victim of a misdirected education. Instead of encouraging, it is the part of true wisdom studiously to repress the undue manifestations of intellectual power, at an age when the physical organs have not attained that consistency, strength, durability and harmony which can alone fit them for co-operating with the mind in its onward and upward progress.

Sound education, as we have already seen, consists in a judicious, enlightened and systematic development of the *entire* constitution of our nature, physical, intellectual, moral and religious. It object is to fit us for the discharge of *all* the duties incumbent upon us as social, rational and accountable beings, for the enjoyment of happiness, and for the cultivation and advancement of all our faculties. It is therefore essentially requisite than an accurate knowledge of the human mind in all its relations, connections and dependences, so far as such knowledge is within our reach be attained. We are not called upon to speculate as to the abstract nature and source of mind, its materiality or immateriality, for these are questions incapable of solution by any powers conferred upon or known to us; nor are they in any manner essential to the right exercise of those which are conferred. So far as the present life is concerned, the Creator, in his wisdom, has seen fit indissolubly to connect the manifestations and operations of the mind with its material physical organs; and to make the former dependent for its vigor, strength and fitness to perform its various functions, upon the sound condition of the latter. To become acquainted with the *laws* by which the economy of our nature is adapted to the external circumstances which surround us, by virtue of which, health and consequent enjoyment result from an observance of the conditions affixed to our organic constitutions; and disease, debility, and consequent misery, from a violation or neglect of those conditions, we must at an early period familiarize ourselves with the instructive lessons of PHYSIOLOGY as expounded and explained, theoretically and practically, by those who possess the requisite capacity and experience in this important branch of knowledge. We may not, it is true, by the most strict conformity to the laws thus deduced, be able wholly to avert the ravages of disease, or to obtain an entire exemption from the physical ills incident to humanity. Were we even at liberty to conceive of such an advancement in science and knowledge, at any future period of the race, as should enable us to cope with pestilence in its desolating influences, or with the elements in their wildest fury or most eccentric evolutions, or to grapple with and overcome those innumerable agents of disease which now steal upon us when least expected and least prepared, and against which no known human skill or prescience avails; that period is, undoubtedly, far remote. There are disturbing influences in the air we breathe, in the earth upon which we tread, in all the elements, in short, which surround us; there are disturbing influences in the very blood which courses through our veins, and in the constitution, itself, of our physical and mental organs, which no human power known to us, can wholly neutralize or command. But it is much, very much, to know and to understand the fixed laws impressed upon our nature by the hand of Omnipotent wisdom and benevolence; to be able, so far as in us lies, to guard against their infringement, to carry out their design, and thus secure a comparative exemption from those debilitating influences which make up so great a portion of the cup of human wretchedness. It is much to understand and appreciate the intimate connection between bodily health and mental efficiency; a connection too long and too systematically ignored and disregarded. It is much to be able to dissipate the deplorable ignorance which has consigned to premature graves so many highly gifted minds, upon whom the fondest hopes of the domestic and social circle hung, and around whom clustered the most sanguine expectations for future usefulness, happiness and fame. It is much to substitute for the destructive system of precocious mental culture with which we have so generally heretofore been met at the very portals of knowledge and education, the pleasing and unconstrained exercise of those muscular functions, whose activity, in the spring-time of life, it has been found impossible wholly to repress, and the gratification of that insatiable thirst for instruction and information in the countless phenomena of nature, which is so apparent in the youthful mind.

No system of education can be regarded as perfect which is not based on an enlightened acquaintance with the fundamental principles of physiology; and no philanthropist, no teacher, no parent, who desires to ameliorate and elevate the physical as well as the mental and moral condition of those whom he has in charge, and in whose welfare he is interested, will withhold his influence and exertions in the dissemination of its instructive lessons, wherever the great work of education is in progress. Ignorance of those elementary principles which regulate and control the physical well-being of our common nature, is no longer excusable in those who undertake the task of instruction; and especially is it the duty and the interest of parents to familiarize themselves with a subject, a correct knowledge of which is of such surpassing importance to the happiness and welfare of those to whom, as they have given existence, so they are bound to render that existence, so far as rests with them, a source of enjoyment, advancement and mental purity.

2. Intellectual education may be defined as the cultivation of the science of sound logical thinking, or reasoning, based upon accurate and thorough observation of all the facts and circumstances pertaining to the subject matter of investigation, whatever that may be —mathematical, physical, moral, religious, metaphysical, historical, or ethical. Its object is the *ascertainment of truth*—truth of *facts*, whether in the world of matter or of mind—truth of inferences, conclusions, and principles, from those facts—unbiased by appearances, prejudices, partiality or preconception. "The main thing which we ought to teach our youth," says John Ruskin, "is to *see* something—all that the eyes which God hath given them are capable of seeing. The sum of what we *do* teach them, is to *say* something. As far as I have experience of instruction, no man ever dreams of teaching a boy to *get to the root of a matter*; to *think it out*; to get quit of passion or desire, in the process of thinking; or to fear no face of man in plainly asserting the ascertained result."* This can

* Modern Painters, vol. iv, p. 390, Appendix

only be accomplished in conjunction with the purest and most inflexible morality, honesty of heart, sincerity of aim, and ambition for the highest and noblest excellence. It can take root and flourish in no other soil. The ideas and conceptions of *duty*—those ideas and conceptions which form the basis of Christian morality—must first be developed and infused as a vital element of life and character. Without this, the fairest and most promising flowers of intellect will blossom but to fade—its richest soil will be overgrown with deadly tares—and all its manifestations, however apparently brilliant and hopeful, will prove delusive and unreal in the presence of those severe and uncompromising tests to which they must be subjected in the pursuit of truth. On this indispensable foundation the great aim of the teacher, in the cultivation of the reasoning and reflecting faculties, should be to secure a perfect understanding, and an accurate conception of the ideas unfolded—a habit of close discrimination, and clear deduction of facts and principles—and a rigid analysis of whatever is presented to the mind for its adoption or rejection. Innumerable sources of error will manifest themselves at every stage of this process; but it is often only by the examination and refutation of every possible form of error, that the mind can arrive at fundamental principles of truth; and the mental discipline which such an exercise, properly conducted, confers, is beyond all value.

In connection with these principles of life and methods of clear, logical, and fearless reasoning, there are few requisites of a sound mental and moral culture more important and desirable than that *comprehensiveness* which takes in not only all the relations which appertain to any given subject of study or thought, but its connection with and dependence upon other departments of knowledge and action. We frequently hear of men of "one idea;" and nothing is more common, in our intercourse with the world, and with the great minds of the past, than to observe the disproportionate importance which many seem to attach to the peculiar object of their labors and lives. The philosopher, the patriot, the statesman, the divine, the soldier, agriculturist, mechanic, discoverer or inventor —each strives to monopolize the attention and regards of the race for the subjects of his investigation and special research—while in reality, "all are but parts of one stupendous whole"—neither, of themselves, constituting the key stone of the arch which supports the stately structure of civilization—but all, in their combined action, each in its separate province, carrying forward, with an irresistible and constantly increasing impetus, the designs of creative beneficence and Omnipotent Wisdom. It is not to be denied that results of surpassing importance to the highest interests of humanity and to the progress of science, have been effected and are still being effected through the efforts of "men of one idea." We may be pointed to many of the great reformers in religion, in morals, in science, in legislation, in political and social economy, and in numerous other fields of intellectual labor, for striking and pertinent illustrations of this fact. These instances, however, may be regarded as constituting the *exceptions* rather than the rules of human conduct—as splendid interpositions of a necessary concentration of mental energy upon one central point for the accomplishment of a specific end which could in no other way be secured. Whenever the designs of Providence are destined or required to be furthered by the presence of those great and shining lights in the intellectual and moral world, whose beams are to irradiate the long succession of future ages, they may well deserve such an undivided devotion of thought and effort; but for the ordinary purposes, objects, aims, and ends of life, and even for the most assured success in the extraordinary and absorbing consecrations of human existence, a comprehensive mental discipline will be found the best preparative for practical and extended usefulness.

With respect to the much-vexed religious question which has so strongly agitated the public mind on three different occasions in the history of the system, and from the effects of which the community has scarcely recovered even yet, a few plain statements may, perhaps, suffice to place it on a proper footing, and to disentangle it from some of the sophistries with which it has been surrounded.

And, first, it must be borne in view that the religious or spiritual element forms a portion and a most important portion of the faculties of the universal human mind. With very rare exceptions, every human being in every civilized community recognizes the existence of a Supreme Being, the Creator and Governor of the universe, whom, under some form he worships and adores. Throughout the most enlightened countries of Europe and America that Being is the God of the Bible—the God of Christianity. By far the larger portion of the inhabitants of these great continents profess and believe the Christian religion. Independently, even, of its revelations, there is implanted deep in the human mind, a hope, a desire, a longing for immortality—aspirations for a future existence "far in the unapparent"—where the inequalities of this fleeting life shall be rectified—where pain and sorrow, sickness and death shall be no more known, and where the faculties and powers which here have been denied their legitimate expansion shall find full realization, free from all the clogs of matter and sense. Can any system of education venture to ignore these high faculties of the human mind?

In the BIBLE the Christian believer finds the full and assured realization of those his highest hopes—"life and immortality brought to light." For a period of more than eighteen centuries that religion has numbered its disciples by millions and tens of millions of enlightened worshippers, in each succeeding age; and now past the full meridian of the nineteenth century, they constitute in our own great Republic nearly the entire population of half the Western Continent. Divided as they are into two great, and numerous smaller sects—all concur in recognizing the Divine Authority of the BIBLE—differing only in its interpretation, and in the translation of a few sentences, paragraphs and words, the precise meaning of which cannot as yet be ascertained to the common satisfaction of all. The vast majority of our citizens worship the same Creator—adore the same Redeemer—believe the same Holy Record of his words, life, death, resurrection and ascension; and every right-minded, upright and virtuous individual, of whatever denomination, sect or belief—Christian, Jew or Mahometan—intuitively feels and acknowledges the purity, sublimity and truthfulness of the moral precepts, and allegorical illustrations which pervade the volume. While, therefore, as a distinctively Christian community we are imperatively called upon to recognize, in all our institutions, the inspired record of our faith, we are equally bound as educators, in the development and culture of the highest and noblest faculties of our common nature, to direct the earliest attention of our pupils to those great lessons of morality and virtue, those deep and clear fountains of ethical beauty, and those lofty speculations of duty, obligations, and humanity which are confessedly unfolded in these ancient writings, as in no other works of ancient or modern times.

In thus reverently and lovingly opening up to the expanding minds of the youth of each successive generation, the moral lessons of the Christianity we, as a people profess, it is, nevertheless, specially incumbent upon us, not only in view of the fact that the whole or portions of this Book and of the religion upon which it is founded, are discredited by large portions of our fellow-citizens, but of the still more important fact that among those by whom it is implicitly adopted and believed, an almost unlimited diversity of interpretation prevails—that no attempt should be made in any way, to bias the judgment or pre-occupy the mind of any pupil, in reference either to the truth, of any distinctive denominational doctrine, or the particular bearing of that truth, or the particular inferences to be drawn from it for or against any opposite or different interpretation. Like every other alleged truth of science, morality or history, so far as the legitimate purposes of public instruction are concerned, its evidence, its demonstration, its value, and the objects and purposes to which it is to be applied, as a mental possession or a practical instrument, should be left to be evolved by the mind and the heart of the student, with such collateral aid as may be procured from other and extraneous sources—in this instance from parents and from the lessons and inculcations of those to whom a special authority has been confided by those who alone have the right to direct. The work of education cannot be rightfully or properly performed—the imperative duty of the teacher cannot be fully and completely discharged,—without the prominent presentation of these great topics of human thought and interest. The history of the past three thousand years, cannot be understood, in all its leading and most important phases without the introduction of this essential element which, in its ceaseless flow down the centuries, has so deeply tinged and so powerfully affected its current. The present aspect of civilization can in nowise be adequately comprehended, or intelligently appreciated, in its absence. And divested of its high and holy influences, the human mind itself loses all its greatness, its grandeur, its hopes and visions of immortality, and finds itself dwarfed into insignificance or crushed under the inevitable weight of the calamities which everywhere surround it. But its heavenly lessons must be left by the public teacher to their own operation. No dogmatic inculcations of controverted tenets—no sectarian glosses of alleged doctrinal theology—no harsh discord of clashing interpretations or authoritative exposition—must be permitted to interfere either with the conscience of the pupil or the parent, or with the free and unbiased operation of his own judgment and will. Let the Holy Volume be reverently read "without note or comment" at the opening of each school, or at such other times as the teacher and officers may deem proper—followed, as in most of the public schools in the city of New York, by the repetition in concert of that beautiful and sublime prayer of our Lord, to which not even infidelity itself can take exception, and by some devotional hymn, free from all sectarian taint. If in any school there be any whose conscience or convictions of duty prevent from uniting in this simple act of worship to the Creator of the Universe, let their attendance be excused.

To this extent and only to this extent, the religious element should, in my judgment, enter into and form a portion of our system of public instruction. Whatever may be the peculiar religious faith or religious convictions of any portion of the community, and however desirous they may be of instilling into the minds of their children their own faith, convictions and doctrines, I fail to perceive anything in this course, which, if properly carried out in its spirit, can injuriously affect or contravene their wishes in this regard. No prejudices or prepossessions of whatever nature, for or against any distinctive view, or special interpretation of the Christian or Jewish Scriptures, will have been communicated: no verdict or allegation even of the absolute truth of either; or conceding its truth, no inferences of any kind drawn or attempted to be drawn from its statements or declarations. The *facts*, only of its existence—its antiquity—its pretensions—its history—its doctrines and lessons, unexplained and uninterpreted—are placed before the pupil, for his careful consideration, his reflection, his study, and his judgment, as facts pertaining to his faculties as a human being—facts of vast historical importance—an essential element of instruction, with which, constituted as his nature is, he could no more dispense than he could with any other, even the most important branches of his course of study. What credit shall be given to them—if any—what form they shall assume in their subsequent development—what inferences, conclusions, dogmas and doctrines they shall evolve in their future progress—all these results and consequences are left to the working of his own mind—the unbiased judgment of his own understanding—and to the operation of the various influences, domestic, social, theological or other which may be brought to bear upon him. Is there, then, in all this, any conceivable ground for the allegation or the pretence of unjust interference with the rights or the consciences of others?

A complete course of public instruction, including the higher branches at present pursued in our academic and collegiate institutions, might, very properly, comprehend in its *curriculum* a full scientific acquaintance with the history of theology in all its aspects, and a concise statement of the distinctive tenets of its various sects with the principal grounds upon which they were respectively based and the prominent arguments and objections by which they were sustained and opposed. Even to this extent no conceivable objection could reasonably be interposed, based upon conscientious grounds. But, in the existing condition of our system, only the elementary principles of the several sciences can be taught. The foundations of language and of the mathematics, the great leading events of history, the prominent outlines of geography, astronomy and natural, intellectual and moral philosophy and rhetoric, only can be communicated during the brief period allotted to common school instruction. As we cannot expect to send forth finished writers and orators, perfect engineers, philosophers, chemists, and astronomers, or great merchants, skillful lawyers, physicians and surgeons, manufacturers, legislators, commanders and statesmen, so neither can we thoroughly train clergymen, ministers and prelates for the complete discharge of their important functions, or instruct the members of their respective flocks in the knowledge of the dogmatic theology peculiar to each. In all these branches of learning we can only communicate elementary instruction, availing ourselves of the best and most authoritative text-books in each. This, and this only, with the BIBLE as our text-book, can we accomplish in the highest and noblest science of all—and this, surely, we may claim the right and assert the duty of doing.

"Strange indeed"—remarks the late Col. WILLIAM L. STONE, in his report as County Superintendent of New York, in 1844,—"at least, it appears so to me, that in this world of sin and crime, such grievous prejudices should exist against allowing our children to drink at the fountain of truth, whence are derived the loftiest notions of virtue, honor, justice, conscience, piety, and love of country—all just opinion of the Deity, of moral accountability, of a future state of happiness for those who do well, and of misery for the unrepenting wicked! Strange—at least, it appears so to me—regarding, as I have been taught to do, the BIBLE as the mainstay of every blessing with which our country has been favored—for it was the great chart of civil and religious liberty to the founders of this mighty Republic—should be deemed a dangerous book in the hands of the rising generation! Strange, that parents who wish their children to become acquainted with history, should shut from their eyes the only historical work in the world which is known, every word of it, to be true, and from the pages of which alone, can they become acquainted with the origin of our race, and the first three thousand years of the world's history! Strange, that those who would have their children trained in the paths of virtue, should hide from them the purest and most beautiful lessons of that attribute extant! Strange, that those who would have their children educated for the bar, should close against their inspection, the works of the greatest law-giver who has ever lived! Strange, that those who would have their offspring trained for the forum, should exclude from their studies the most glowing passages of eloquence to be found in any human language! Strange, that those who might fondly hope for a bard in their family, should inhibit the study of the loftiest strains of poetry ever written! Strange, that those who only aspire to a good, substantial English education for their children, should, nevertheless, debar them from the privilege of reading the book, which of all others contains the purest model of our language—a "well of English undefiled!" But stranger than all, that republicans, holding the belief of man's direct accountability to his Maker alone, on matters of religion—the enemies of Church and State

—should prohibit to their offspring the inspection of that Great Charter of civil and religious liberty, which has been conferred upon man directly by his Creator! But I forbear. In the beautiful language of an anonymous author before me, I regard the BIBLE 'as an invaluable treasure; a volume more precious than rubies; the repository of all that can enlighten the understanding, comfort the heart, and elevate the affections. It opens to us sources of pure and unalloyed felicity; it is the rich fountain of faith, of hope, of charity, of every holy principle and noble virtue. It gilds the dark vale of tears with beams of celestial peace and sacred joy. It infuses into the bitter cup of adversity, unutterable consolation, and presents to the enraptured vision of the poor and friendless sufferer, the radiant mansions of immortal fruition.' And such a Book must be banished from our schools!"

The appropriation of any portion of the public funds inviolably set apart by constitutional provision, for the support of Common Schools, to the maintenance of institutions not coming under this class, in which the peculiar doctrines and tenets of particular religious denominations and sects are taught, is clearly unwarranted either by law, or by any sound principles of justice or equity. Such institutions have the same right to a participation in the School fund that any other association of individuals established for the promotion of its own special objects and views, possesses, and no greater. So far as the Legislature, in its wisdom, may see fit, from funds at its own disposal, and not otherwise appropriated, to aid and encourage these or any other private, literary, scientific or charitable institutions, no one can doubt the right or propriety of its doing so, and no question save that of general policy or particular expediency can properly be raised. But it is obviously an utterly unjustifiable perversion of justice, as well as a palpable violation of the fundamental law of the State, to apply any portion of the funds specifically set apart and consecrated to the purposes of general and common instruction, or any funds contributed by the tax-payers generally, under the sanction and authority of law, for this specific purpose, to the support of institutions, established, maintained and devoted to another, religious, sectarian, philanthropic, or scientific. Such institutions are, undoubtedly, highly laudable and proper, and worthy of all suitable encouragement. The funds, however, for their support, should be drawn, not from the common fund, compulsorily levied from all of every sect, occupation or profession, but, with the exception of gratuitous contributions, from that of the particular denomination or society for whose benefit they are to be expended.

It is, undoubtedly, much and seriously, to be lamented that any portion of the children of the rising generation who would otherwise participate in the advantages of free common school education, should be withdrawn from the public schools, solely and exclusively that they may be educated in the peculiar tenets of any particular religious denomination. The perfect right of every parent to instill into the minds of his children, at the earliest period, those beliefs and religious convictions, usages and principles which he, himself, conscientiously deems essential to their temporal and eternal welfare, is neither controverted nor denied. But might not this paramount object be equally well accomplished, without depriving such children of the incalculable benefits of mingling with those of other sects, perhaps, but with whom they are necessarily to be associated in subsequent life,—whose society and intimacy in the school-room and its environs can, in no respect, interfere with or disturb their own religious views or destination,—and with whom they can explore the various fields of knowledge, untrammeled by any restrictions growing out of the adhesion of their parents to a particular form of faith? Is it desirable that separate schools shall exist for every separate religious or political sect or for every separate trade, calling, profession, nativity, or pursuit in life? Is it not wiser to promote and cherish a community and catholicity of feeling rather than the perpetuation of a sectarian spirit—to seek diligently for truth, through whatever channels it may be conveyed, rather than to erect formidable barriers of prejudice and preconception against its free admission—and assiduously to cultivate, enlarge and expand the mental, moral and religious faculties with which we are endowed, throughout all the fields which the highest and most varied science has thrown open to our exertions?

INDEX.

A.

ACADEMIES, 5, 58, 68, 426.

ACADEMICAL DEPARTMENTS for the education of teachers, 59, 60, 63, 65, 67, 80, 82, 83, 90, 105, 110, 111, 114, 117, 139, 163-4, 171, 172, 181, 182, 255, 303, 367, 388, 390, 398, 400, 409, 432-33, 486.

AFRICAN SCHOOLS in New York, 21. *See* COLORED SCHOOLS.

ALBANY, public schools in, 198, 267, 319, 412.

State Normal School at. *See* NORMAL SCHOOLS.

AMUSEMENTS, innocent, 127.

APPORTIONMENT of School money. *See* COMMON SCHOOL FUND, SCHOOL MONEYS.

AUBURN, city of, public schools in, 287, 330, 413.

B.

BARNARD, Hon. Daniel D., report of, 86.

BARNARD, Hon. Henry, 199, 208-9-10, 235.

BARNES, William, 215.

BARR, Samuel D., Dep. Supt. Pub. Instruction, 359, 364, 378.

BEARDSLEY, Hon. Levi, 85.

BEEKMAN, Hon. James W., 4, 101, 256, 368, 370.

BELL, Dr. Andrew, 28.

BENEDICT, Erastus C., 312.

BENEDICT, Hon. T. H., report and bill of, 283-84.

BENTON, Hon. N. S., Sec'y and Supt., character of, 198; at State Conventions, Syracuse and Albany, 190, 207, 215, 216; annual reports of, 213-14, 231-2, 241-3.

BETHEL BAPTIST CHURCH, New York, 43 to 47.

BETHUNE, Mrs. Joanna, 72.

BIBLE AND NEW TESTAMENT, use of, in schools, 23, 95, 188, 194-96, 200-207, 313, 307-10, 436-461.

BINGHAMTON, public schools in, 412.

BOUCK, Gov. William C., extracts from message of, 177.

BOWDISH, Hon. John, 228, 320, 277.

BROCKPORT Normal and Training School, 388, 422.

BROOKLYN, public schools of, 103, 118, 287, 319, 390, 413-15.
BROWN, Lysander H., 179, 234.
BUFFALO, public schools in, 103, 118, 287, 315-16, 413-16.
Normal and Training School, 388, 404, 427.
BULKLEY, John W., City Supt., Brooklyn, 212, 377, 390, 414-15.
BURROUGHS, Hon. Silas M., reports and bill of, 256, 277, 284.
BUSHWICK, schools in, 287.

C.

CALDWELL, S., 316.
CAMPBELL, Hon. Robert, 229.
CAMPBELL, Rev. William H., 187.
CHASE, Rev. Jonathan, 43, 46, 47.
CHRISTIAN EDUCATION, 444, 438-468.
See RELIGIOUS CONTROVERSIES.
SECTARIAN SCHOOLS.
CLARK, Gov. Myron H., extracts from message of, 334-5, 337.
CLARK, Prof. William W., 244.
CLINTON, Gov. George, extracts from messages of, 5, 6, 11, 12.
CLINTON, Gov. De Witt, 15, 28, 29, 61, 313, 314, 357; extracts from messages of, 27, 38, 39, 50, 51, 56, 61.
CLINTON, Hon. Geo. W., 384.
COBB, Lyman, 200, 201.
COCHRAN, David H., Principal Normal School, Albany, 245.
CODE of Public Instruction, 364.
COHOES, schools in, 287.
COLDEN, Cadwallader D., 47.
COLERIDGE, Samuel Taylor, views of, respecting education, 444-46.
COLE, John O., 276.
COLLEGES, 5.
COLLEGES, Academies, and Common Schools, reports, &c., of Committees of, 64, 90, 107, 141-44, 173, 182-86, 256, 277, 283-84.
COLLEGE of the City of New York, 402.
COLONIAL EDUCATION, 2-5.
COLORED CHILDREN, schools for, 41, 49, 248, 433, 436.
COMMISSIONERS of Common Schools, 8.
See DISTRICT COMMISSIONERS.
TOWN SUPERINTENDENTS.
for the establishment and organization of Common Schools, report of, 18 to 22.
COMMON COUNCIL of New York. See RELIGIOUS CONTROVERSIES.
COMMON SCHOOLS, 1, 2, 41, 78, 82, 146-50; foundation and establishment of, 6, 7; act for encouragement of, 7, 8; act of 1812 for establishment of, 33, 34, 116; present condition of, 433-34; number of pupils in, 433.
See SUPERINTENDENTS, annual reports of.

COMMON SCHOOL EDUCATION in England and America, special report of Supt. concerning, 376–77.

COMMON SCHOOL FUND. See SCHOOL MONEYS, 7, 8, 11, 14, 15, 18, 20, 21, 38, 40, 41, 58, 66, 79, 86, 87, 88, 103, 104, 117, 199, 231, 304, 306, 433–38.
- apportionment of, 304–8, 324, 332, 333, 342, 363–66, 429–30, 438–35.
- appropriation of to sectarian purposes, 462, 463.
- controversy with Comptroller respecting the appropriation of to General Fund, 351–54, 373–75.

COMMON SCHOOL LAWS, revision and codification of, 96, 116, 117, 287–290, 292–96, 301, 304–6, 354.

COMMON SCHOOL LIBRARIES. See DISTRICT LIBRARIES.

COMMON SCHOOL SYSTEM, general summary of, 432; suggestions for improvements in, 438–9; general principles of, 441–463.

COMPULSORY EDUCATION, special report of Supt. respecting expediency of, 376–78.

COMSTOCK, Adam, 7, 9, 11.

CONNECTICUT, Common School system of, 40, 67, 69, 102.

CONSTITUTIONAL CONVENTION of 1846, proceedings of, relating to Free Schools, 226–31.

CONSTITUTION, State, provision of, relating to Common School fund, 28 231.

COOPER, Edward, 216, 215.

CORNELL, Ezra, 393.

CORNELL UNIVERSITY, 392–3, 431, 436.

CORPORAL PUNISHMENT, 158–9.

CORTLAND Normal and Training School, 388, 404, 423.

COUNTY SUPERINTENDENTS of Common Schools, 106, 115–17, 165, 168–70, 172, 178–80, 190–91, 207, 210–11.
- petitions for repeal of office of, 141, 207.
- reports of committees on, 141–44.
- proceedings of State Conventions of, 144–162, 199–210, 215–228; abolition of office of, 232–40, 242–43; efforts for restoration of office of, 247, 250, 265, 287.

See DISTRICT COMMISSIONERS.

COUNTY TREASURERS, duties of, 420, 434–5.

CRANDALL, William L., 277.

D.

DANFORTH, Edward, City Supt. Troy and State Dep. Supt. Pub. Instruction, 394, 416–19.

DENMAN, J. S., 179, 199, 222.
DEPARTMENT of Public Instruction, 84, 312, 401.
DEPOSIT FUND. See U. S. DEPOSIT FUND.
DEPUTY SUPERINTENDENTS, 116, 231, 247, 254, 300, 311.
See COUNTY SUPERINTENDENTS.
DEWEY, Rev. Chester, 101, 212.
DISTRICT COMMISSIONERS, 325, 331, 338-9, 348-9, 404, 426, 430, 433-4-5, 438.
DISTRICT SCHOOL LIBRARIES, 64, 65, 81, 84, 85, 89, 90, 92, 96, 105, 107, 119, 110, 117, 139, 162-63, 172-77, 190, 214, 232, 248, 340, 288, 291, 304, 325-6, 327-31, 333, 335, 338, 346, 346-7, 357, 359-60, 363-4-5, 380, 382, 386-7-8, 396-7, 401-3, 428-9, 433-4, 436, 438.
DIX, Gen. John A., Sec'y and Supt., 78, 79, 350; annual reports of, 79, 82, 86, 88, 90-93, 94, 95; report of, as chairman of Committee of Regents of the University, 83, 84; character of, and results of his administration, 95, 96; letter of, 146.
DUTCH CHURCHES, 43, 45.
DUTCH COLONISTS, 2.
DWIGHT, Francis, editor Dist. School Journal, 101, 116, 144, 159, 160, 170, 187, 208, 236; death and character of, 212-13.

E.

EATON, Gov. Horace, 215, 218.
EATON, Prof. D. G., 244.
EDUCATION, advantages of, 41, 50, 85, 88, 101; general principles of, 444-463; philosophy of, 441-46; view of Coleridge respecting, 444-46; definition of, 447-49; physical, 447-51; intellectual, 452; moral, 453; religious, 453-463.
EMERSON, Frederick, 212.
EMERSON, George B., 144, 150-53, 156, 199, 208.
EUROPE, special report relative to education in, 376-77.
EVENING SCHOOLS, 408.

F.

FARNHAM, George L., City Supt. Syracuse and Binghamton, 320-22, 419.
FEMALE TEACHERS, 54, 160, 185, 186, 344, 366, 401, 433-4, 437-8.
Seminaries for instruction of, 84, 185.
FEMALE NORMAL COLLEGE, N. Y. City, 409.
FINANCIAL CONDITION of Common School system, 432-37.
FISH, Gov. Hamilton, extracts from message of, 247, 278.
FLAGG, Azariah C., Sec'y and Supt., character of, 64, 65, 70, 71; annual reports of, 53, 57, 59, 63, 66 to 70.
FLUSHING, public schools in, 287.
FOREIGNERS, education of children of, 102, 107-9.
FREDONIA Normal and Training School, 388, 427.

FREE ACADEMY and College, New York, 245, 408.
FREE SCHOLARSHIPS. *See* GENESEE COLLEGE—CORNELL UNIVERSITY.
FREE SCHOOL SOCIETY.
PUBLIC SCHOOL SOCIETY.
FREE SCHOOLS, 207, 208, 215–18, 219–231, 242, 250 283, 290–98, 324–5–7, 328–9, 330–1, 332, 337–8, 360–8, 375, 384, 385, 391–2, 395–6, 444.
State Convention at Syracuse, 257, 262–72, 302.
FREE SCHOOL SOCIETY in New York, 15, 48, 53; controversy with religious societies, 43–46.
See PUBLIC SCHOOL SOCIETY.
FURMAN, Richard, 7.

G.

GALEN, schools in, 287.
GALLAUDET, Rev. William, 144, 158–9, 160.
GENERAL PRINCIPLES of Common School education, 444–463.
GENERAL SUMMARY of the Common School system, 428.
GENESEE COLLEGE and Wesleyan Seminary, free scholarships in, 332.
GENESEO, Wadsworth Normal and Training School, 388, 427.
GOSPEL and SCHOOL LOTS, 6.
GOVERNORS' MESSAGES, extracts from, 5, 8, 11, 12, 15, 16, 27, 28, 29, 50, 51, 58, 61, 68, 78, 61, 85, 87, 89, 101, 102, 107–9, 135–6, 177, 189, 241, 247, 277, 278, 300, 311, 324–5–7.
GRAY, Daniel, 7.
GREELEY, Hon. Horace, addresses of, at State Free School Convention at Syracuse, 266–72, 278.
GRISCOM, Dr. John, 48, 145, 158, 160.

H.

HAMMOND, Hon. Jabez D., 10, 24, 34, 86, 87, 101, 144, 145, 160, 179, 227.
HARPER and Brothers, school libraries of, 112.
HASWELL, Henry B., 228.
HAVANA, Peoples' College at, 431.
HAVENS, Jonathan Nicoll, 7.
HAWLEY, Gideon, first Supt. Com. Schools, character of, 24, 83, 356; annual reports of, 25, 26, 27, 32, 84; removal of, 36, 37; member of Ex. Com. State Normal School, 187.
HENRY, James, Jr., 137, 138, 179, 201, 218, 227.
HIGH SCHOOLS, in New York, 48; memorial of citizens of Rochester respecting, 63; establishment of, in cities and villages, 118.
HOFFMAN, Hon. Michael, 186.
HOLBROOK, D., 217.
HOLBROOK, Rev. Josiah, 200, 276, 315.

HOLY SCRIPTURES. *See* BIBLE AND NEW TESTAMENT.
Statutory provision relative to use of, in N. Y. City, 138.
HOLMES, Samuel L., Gen. Dep. Supt., 231, 320.
HUDDLESTON, William, 4.
HUDSON, city of, public schools in, 118, 287, 318, 416.
HUGHES, Rt. Rev. John, 121.
HULBURD, Hon. C. T., chairman Com. on Colleges, &c., reports, &c., of, 172, 182 to 186, 234.
HUNT, Gov. Washington, extracts from messages of, 276, 277, 278, 300.
HUNTER, Thomas, President N. Y. Female Normal College, 408.

I.

INDIAN CHILDREN, schools for, 231, 249, 341, 345, 404, 433, 436.
INFANT SCHOOLS, 72, 73.
INHABITANTS and Voters of School Districts, 8, 9, 64, 428.
INTELLECTUAL EDUCATION, 432.

J.

JAY, Gov. John, 2.
JAY, Peter Augustus, 47, 314.
JOHNSON, Alexander G., Dep. Supt., 247, 277, 306.
JOHNSON, Henry W., Dep. Supt., 300.

K.

KETCHAM, Hiram, 131, 132.
KEYES, Emerson W., Dep. Supt., 340, 341; Acting Supt., 346.
Reports of, 340–335; controversy with Comptroller relative to appropriation of capital of School Fund, 331–54, 373–75.
KINGS COLLEGE, 5.
KINGS FARM SCHOOL, 4.
KING, Hon. John A., Ch'n Com. on Colleges, &c., report of, 107.
KING, Dr. Theodore F., 146, 147, 150, 160, 179, 215.
KING, Gen. Rufus, 218.
KINGSLEY, Hon. Lewis, report of, on Free Schools, 256–262, 277.

L

LANCASTER, Joseph, 28, 29, 80; visit to N. Y., and death, 82.
LANCASTERIAN SYSTEM of Instruction, 15, 21, 28–33, 39, 56–59, 61, 72, 73.
LANSINGBURGH, schools in, 287.
LEAVENWORTH, Hon. E. W., Sec'y and Supt., 277, 311.

LEGGETT, Thomas, Jr., 101, 276.
LEGGETT, Andrew W., 101, 276.
LEWIS, Gov. Morgan, extracts from Message of, 13, 18.
LIBRARIES. *See* DISTRICT LIBRARIES.
LIBRARY MONEY. *See* DISTRICT LIBRARIES,—232, 241, 249.
LITERATURE COMMITTEE, Senate, reports from, 51–54, 58, 61, 80.
LITERATURE LOTTERIES, 11.
LITTLE, D. H., 101.
LOCKPORT, Public Schools in, 287, 420.
LOOMIS, Arphaxed, 280, 281.
LYON, Hon. Caleb, 277.

M.

MACLAY, Hon. William B., Ch'n Com. on Colleges, &c., report of, on pet. for repeal of Co. Supt. law, 141–144.
MACOMB, Robert, 16.
MACK, Isaac F., 227, 317.
McKEEN, Joseph, Co. Supt., N. Y., 179, 312.
McMASTERS, James M., 204, 273.
MAINE, Common School System of, 67, 69.
MANDEVILLE, Rev. Henry, 264, 277.
MANN, Hon. Charles A., 258.
MANN, Horace, 144, 146, 148, 149, 150, 155–61, 215, 218–226.
MANUFACTURING ESTABLISHMENTS, education in, 63, 64, 70, 93.
MARCY, Gov. William L., 21; extracts from Messages of, 78, 81, 85, 87, 89.
MASSACHUSETTS, Common School System of, 67, 69, 186.
Normal Schools in, 181, 182.
MATHEWS, Rev. Dr. Cornelius, 47.
MAY, Rev. Samuel J., 200, 201, 206, 284.
MAYHEW, Hon. Ira, 178, 192.
MECHANICS' SOCIETY, N. Y., schools of, 48.
MECHANICS' MUTUAL PROTECTION SOCIETY, 277.
MEDINA, schools in, 287.
MERCHANTS' BANK, New York, 14.
METHODIST EPISCOPAL CHURCH, N. Y. City, 74, 76.
MILLER, Dr. John, 277.
MILNER, Rev. Dr., 47.
MISSING, John, 31.
MITCHELL, Dr. Samuel L., 18.
MORAL and Religious Instruction, 94, 453, 455–463. *See* BIBLE AND NEW TESTAMENT: RELIGIOUS CONTROVERSIES.
MORGAN, Hon. Christopher, Sec'y and Supt., 246–7, 317.
Annual Reports of, 247–58, 279–84–90–96.
Pres't Free School State Convention, 262, 267, 276.
Letter of, to Rev. A. T. Young, 283–6.
MUNRO, Hon. David, 228.
MURRAY, John, Jr., 18.

N.

NAY, David, 179, 203, 217-18.
NEWBURGH, Public Schools in, 420.
NEW TESTAMENT, use of in Common Schools, 194-6, 307-10. *See* BIBLE.
NEWTOWN, schools in, 287.
NEW YORK CITY, Trinity and other schools in, prior to the Revolution, 4.
Free School Society, 15, 43-8.
religious controversies and decisions of Common Council, 43-9, 74-7, 119-33.
Public School Society, 35, 74-7, 119-38, 312-13.
Commissioners of School Money in, report of, 183.
Ward Schools in, 137-8, 312.
Public Schools of, 15, 43, 35, 102, 287, 312-15, 406-13.
Free Academy and College, 243, 302-3, 409.
Female Normal College, 409.
NICOLL, Hon. Henry, 228, 229, 230, 276.
NORMAL SCHOOLS, 54, 58, 63, 65, 113, 150-59, 164, 171, 182-6-7, 210, 241, 243, 244, 303, 326, 373, 398, 403-4, 409, 360, 382-3-4, 386-9, 421-27, 432-3, 436.
Acts for establishment of, 187, 383, 404.
NORTH, Rev. Simeon, 212.
NOTT, Rev. Dr. Eliphalet, 268, 277.

O.

OBJECT TEACHING, 350-1.
OGDENSBURGH, Public Schools in, 420.
ONDERDONK, Rt. Rev. B. T., 47.
ONONDAGA COUNTY Teachers' Institute, 215, 277.
ORPHAN ASYLUM SCHOOLS, 47, 48, 74-7.
OSWEGO, Public Schools in, 390, 416.
Normal and Training School, 360, 388, 421.
OWEGO, Public Schools in, 287.

P.

PAGE, David P., Principal State Normal School, Albany, 187, 213, 218; death and character of, 243, 244.
PARENTS, duties and obligations of, 159, 453.
PATCHIN, Ira, 157, 159, 179.
PATTERSON, Hon. George W., 280.
PECK, Jedediah, 10, 11, 12, 16, 17-23.
PEOPLE'S COLLEGE at Havana, 431.
PERKINS, Prof. Geo. R., 187, 244.
PHELPS, Prof. Wm. F., 244, 266, 277.

PHILOSOPHY of Education, 444-6.
PHYSIOLOGY, study of, 430-31.
PHYSICAL EDUCATION, 448-51.
PIERCE, Prof. O. B., 216, 264, 268, 277.
POTSDAM Normal and Training School, 388, 404, 423.
POTTER, Rev. Dr. Alonzo, 101, 141, 146, 148, 152-5, 159, 160, 187, 199, 200, 201, 205-7, 208, 210-11, 238.
POTTER, Pierpont, 179.
POUGHKEEPSIE, schools in, 287, 318-19, 417.
POWELL, Rev. David, 188.
PROFANITY, habitual, disqualification of, as a teacher, 196, 197.
PUBLIC INSTRUCTION, Department of, 84, 311, 405, 436.
PUBLIC LANDS, 14, 20, 82. *See* COMMON SCHOOL FUND.
PUBLIC SCHOOL MONEY. *See* COMMON SCHOOL FUND.
PUBLIC SCHOOL SOCIETY of New York. *See* NEW YORK, 56, 71, 73, 77, 119-38, 312.
PUPILS, number of in common schools, 483, 437.
private schools, 483, 437.

Q.

QUIGLEY, Rev. Dr., decision on complaint of, 307-10.

R.

RANDALL, Hon. Henry S., Co. Supt., 179; special report of, on district libraries, 173-77, 277, 299; Sec'y and Supt., character of, 299, 300, 310; annual reports of, 301-6; decision of, relating to religious exercises in common schools, 307-10.
RANDALL, S. S., General Dep. Supt., 116, 233, 311, 324; acting Supt., 117; at State Free School Convention, 265, 268; report of, as Code Commissioner, 297-98, 301, 304-6; City Supt. Brooklyn, 390; City Supt. N. Y., 312.
RATE BILLS, 94, 102, 110, 251, 329-30, 331-2, 333-4, 335.
RAYMOND, Hon. Henry J., 276.
RECEIPTS and Expenditures for support of Common Schools, 432.
REESE, Dr. D. Meredith, Co. Supt. N. Y., 109, 201, 202-4.
REGENTS of the University, 5, 6, 11, 404-5, 436.
See ACADEMIES and ACADEMICAL DEPARTMENTS FOR TEACHERS.
RELIGIOUS CONTROVERSIES in New York, 43-9, 74-7, 119-38.
RELIGIOUS INSTRUCTION, 22, 94, 128, 129-31, 136, 307-10, 433-463.
RICE, Hon. Victor M., City Supt. Buffalo, 277, 316; Supt. Pub. Inst., character of, 322, 336-58; annual reports of, 323-6-7-31, 333-5, 339-63, 364-70, 378-91; special report of, respecting school systems of Europe and America, 376-8.
ROBERTSON, Hon. Wm. H., chairman Senate Lit. Com., report and bill of, creating Dept. Pub. Instr'n, 311.

ROCHESTER, City, Memorial from citizens of, 65; State Conventions of Co. Supts. at, 162; public schools of, 116, 287, 317, 416.
ROCHESTER, Henry E., Co. Supt. Monroe, 157, 158, 179, 249.
ROELANDSON, Adam, 3.
ROMAN CATHOLICS, memorials of. *See* RELIGIOUS CONTROVERSIES.
Schools of, 119.
Benevolent Society, 74.
ROSCOE, Caleb, 276.
RUTGERS, Col. Henry, 47.

S.

SALEM, schools in, 287.
SALISBURY, John H., 199, 321.
SCHENECTADY, schools in, 4, 319, 417.
SCHOOL APPARATUS, 433, 436.
SCHOOL BOOKS, uniformity in, 40, 64, 68, 69, 90, 106, 159.
SCHOOL CELEBRATIONS, 42.
SCHOOL COMMISSIONERS. *See* COMMISSIONERS — DISTRICT COMMISSIONERS.
SCHOOL DISCIPLINE, 158–9.
SCHOOL DISTRICTS, number of, 378–9, 432; organization of, 438.
SCHOOL-HOUSES and Sites, 94, 137–8, 213–14, 339, 364–5, 368, 369–70, 376, 379–80, 384, 385–6, 399, 400, 433–34, 436, 437, 438, 448.
SCHOOL LAWS, revision and codification of, 287–90, 292–8, 301, 304–6, 326.
SCHOOL LIBRARIES. *See* DISTRICT LIBRARIES.
SCHOOL MONEYS, apportionment and distribution of, 284, 304–6, 335, 332, 335, 342, 429–30, 438.
SCHOOL VISITORS, 57, 100, 101, 105, 106.
SECTARIAN SCHOOLS, 48–9, 74–7, 119–38, 285–6, 462, 463.
See RELIGIOUS CONTROVERSIES.
SEDGWICK, Charles B., 268.
SETON, Samuel W., 60, 312, 314.
SEWARD, Gov. William H., character of, 109, 377; extracts from messages of, 101, 103, 107, 108, 109, 135, 136.
SEYMOUR, Gov. Horatio, extracts from message of, 311.
SHUTE, John, 4.
SKINNER, Roger, 16.
SMITH, Goldwin, Prof. Political Economy, Cornell University, 398.
SMITH, William, 30.
SOLDIERS and Sailors, children of, 376.
SPENCER, Hon. John C., reports of, from Senate Literature Committee, 51–4, 58–61; Sec'y and Supt., character of, 97–100, 356; annual reports of, 102, 103–6, 109–16, 117, 118, 123; report of, on reference of memorials of Catholics in New York, 124–33; letters of, 146, 256–59.
STANTON, N. P., Jr., 215.
STATE BOARD OF EDUCATION, 405.

T.

TOWN CLERKS, duties of, 429–30.
TOWN, Salem, 101, 145, 156, 160, 183, 200, 277.
TOWN Superintendents, 172, 177, 176, 277, 381.
TOWN Supervisors, 331–2, 430.
TOWNSEND, Franklin. 276.
TOWNSEND, Hon. Robert, 230.
TRACY, Hon. Albert H., 316.
TRIMBLE, George T., 314.
TRINITY SCHOOL, New York, 4.
TROY, city of, Public Schools in, 118, 287, 322, 416–19.
TRUANT CHILDREN, provisions for, 384–5.
TRUSTEES of Common Schools, 8, 172, 429.
TUTHILL Hon. Franklin, 276.

U.

UNINSTRUCTED CHILDREN, number of, 370–78, 400, 401.
UNION FREE SCHOOLS, 118, 159, 323, 327, 391, 402.
UNITED STATES Deposit Fund, 67, 88, 89, 90. *See* COMMON SCHOOL FUND.
UNIVERSITY. *See* REGENTS OF THE UNIVERSITY.
UTICA, Public Schools in city of, 118, 287, 322, 419.

V.

VACCINATION of children attending Common Schools, 106.
VALENTINE, Thomas W., editor, N. Y. Teacher, 227.
VAN DYCK, Hon. Henry H., Sec'y and Supt., character of, 334.
Annual reports of, 334–343.
VIRGINIA, school system of, 57.
VISITORS of Common Schools, 57, 100, 101; reports of, 105, 106, 162.
VOCAL MUSIC in Schools, 106.

W.

WADSWORTH, James, 85, 101.
Normal and Training School, Geneseo, 427.
WAINWRIGHT, Rev. Dr., 42.
WATERTOWN, Public Schools in, 420.
WALKER, William, Co. Supt. N. Y., 264.
WEAVER, Hon. Abram B., Supt. Public Instruction,, 394.
Annual reports of, 394–408.
WEBB, Alexander S., President College of the City of New York, 402.
WEBSTER, Dr. Horace, 145, 159; Principal N. Y. Free Academy, 245.
WETMORE, Gen. Prosper M., Ch'n Com. on Colleges, &c., report of, in favor of Dept. Public Instruction, 84.

WHELP, John Nicholas, 4.
WHITE, Hon. Andrew D., Prest. Cornell University, 393.
WHITEHOUSE, Rev. Dr., 101.
WILLARD, Mrs. Emma, 200, 203.
WILLIAMSBURGH, Public Schools in, 287.
WING, Halsey R., Co. Supt. Warren, 157-9, 179, 277.
WOOD, Hon. Bradford R., 277.
WOODIN, David G., Co. Supt., Columbia, 179.
WOOLWORTH, Samuel B., Principal Normal School, Albany, 245, 266, 777.
WORDEN, Hon. Alva, 230.
WRIGHT, Albert, Co. Supt., Washington, 179, 201.
WRIGHT, William, " " 157, 179, 201, 228.
WRIGHT, Gov. Silas, extracts from Message of, 189.

Y.

YATES, John Van Ness, Sec'y and Supt., character of, 38, 48, 49; annual reports of, 39-41, 45; circular of, recommending school celebrations, 42.
YOUNG, Rev. A. T., 283.
YOUNG, Hon. A. W., 228.
YOUNG, Gov. John, extracts from Message of, 241.
YOUNG, Col. Samuel, Sec'y and Supt., 85; character of, 139-41, 357; annual reports of, 160, 162-72, 177-8, 187-9-93; letters of, 195-96; resolutions of State Convention of Co. Supts. in favor of, 208-10.

www.ingramcontent.com/pod-product-compliance
Lightning Source LLC
Chambersburg PA
CBHW051159300426
44116CB00006B/368
9783742807595